Collaborative Assessment

Collaborative Assessment

Working with Students Who
Are Blind or Visually Impaired,
Including Those with
Additional Disabilities

Edited by
Stephen A. Goodman
and Stuart H. Wittenstein

AFB

PRESS

NEW YORK

Library of Congress Cataloging-in-Publication Data

Collaborative assessment : working with students who are blind or visually impaired, including those with additional disabilities / edited by Stephen A. Goodman and Stuart H. Wittenstein.
    p. cm.
  Includes bibliographical references and index.
  ISBN 0-89128-869-4 (alk. paper)
    1. People with visual disabilities—Education. I. Goodman, Stephen A. II. Wittenstein, Stuart H.
  HV1626.C64 2003
  371.91′1—dc21   2003051855

The American Foundation for the Blind—the organization to which Helen Keller devoted more than 40 years of her life—is a national non-profit whose mission is to eliminate the inequities faced by the ten million Americans who are blind or visually impaired.

It is the policy of the American Foundation for the Blind to use in the first printing of its books acid-free paper that meet the ANSI Z39.48 Standard. The infinity symbol that appears above indicates that the paper in this printing meets that standard.

For Our Families

Contents

Foreword

Educating students who are visually impaired in the 21st century is a complex task. We are faced with a diverse population of students, educational reform that poses threats to high-quality service delivery, and a national perspective that places an increased emphasis on data-based outcomes and decision making. In an atmosphere in which specialized services may be minimized, assessment plays a critical and essential role in how we educate students who are visually impaired. In fact, assessment drives the implementation of curriculum and provides a blueprint for determining what should be taught and what methodologies should be initiated. *Collaborative Assessment* provides educators, families, administrators, and related service personnel with much-needed information about specialized assessment—assessment whose content, format, and presentation are appropriate for visually impaired students, including those with additional disabilities, and that is administered and interpreted by professionals trained to work with such students.

This comprehensive text is the first to present assessment in a way that can be understood by professionals and families alike. The authors have taken a complex art form and presented information about it in a user-friendly manner. This text is written by a team of individuals who view the assessment process as a collaborative endeavor. Each chapter focuses on a specific part of the comprehensive assessment. Specialized strategies and tests are described throughout the text, and in-depth case studies illustrate how the team of education professionals work together to present assessment results and to develop recommendations for school personnel and families.

The chapter authors, each an expert in his or her own right, demonstrate throughout the text their commitment to specialized assessment for students who are visually impaired. Not only do they address the assessment process for students currently in academic educational settings, they also describe the assessment needs of students who are visually impaired and have additional disabilities. The authors provide in-depth information on assessment techniques and resources for these students. In addition, the writing team presents effective ways to assess students in all areas of the expanded core curriculum. These essential elements have never been addressed in a comprehensive manner, and are critical components of specialized curriculum design and service delivery.

The California School for the Blind Assessment Program team and the editors, Stephen Goodman and Stuart Wittenstein, must be commended for this innovative and exciting addition to the literature. They have brought assessment to a new level of understanding by providing valuable information to our knowledge base and allowing us to view assessment as more than the administration of tests or the interpretation of findings. *Collaborative Assessment* allows us to focus on the needs of the student, thereby effecting educational change and making successful outcomes more likely.

Sharon Zell Sacks
Professor, Teacher Preparation Programs in Visual Impairment
California State University, Los Angeles

Editors' Preface

HOW TO GET THE MOST FROM THIS BOOK

This book was designed to provide information to a diverse readership who wish to understand the challenges, distinctions, and opportunities in assessing children who are blind, visually impaired, or deaf-blind, with and without additional disabilities. The editors and authors assume that these readers are likely to have varying levels of familiarity and expertise with the issues and concerns of such an assessment. Therefore, this book contains much information that is introductory about visual impairment and its effect on child development and learning, but also much information that is sophisticated and complex.

Thus, the answer to the question of how best to use this book is to chart your own path.

The editors expect that each person with a role in the assessment of students who are blind or visually impaired will discover an individual route through this material based on his or her needs. Although some may choose to read the book straight through, it is not necessary for professionals from each discipline to read the whole book to get all the information they need. For example, school psychologist might go straight to Chapter 6, "Psychological Assessment," and then to Chapters 10 and 11, "Report Writing" and "Collaboration in Action," coming back to Chapter 1, "Introduction to Visual Impairment" and Appendix A, "Common Causes of Vision Loss in Children and Implications for Assessment" as needed. A speech and language pathologist might follow a similar route, starting instead with Chapter 7, "Speech and Language Assessment."

Based on this concept of each reader finding his or her own path, some basic information is repeated in several chapters to ensure that all readers, no matter which path they chart for themselves, will be exposed to the essential concepts.

ACKNOWLEDGMENTS

The editors wish to thank the authors from the staff of the California School for the Blind Assessment Program for their dedication to and skill with the students they serve in this highly specialized area of our profession. We are quite simply awed by the skills of these assessment professionals and are fortunate to be able to share their expertise with the readers of this work.

The editors acknowledge the substantial influence and inspiration of Phil Hatlen's work to identify and disseminate the expanded core curriculum for children who are blind or visually impaired. Infused throughout this book is Hatlen's philosophical framework that informs us daily as to explicit areas which must be assessed in order to provide appropriate access and instruction.

Stephen A. Goodman
Stuart H. Wittenstein

Joanna Self

Authors' Acknowledgments

Many people fostered the creation of this book. The authors would like to thank those who read through various versions of the manuscript and offered suggestions to improve the accuracy, completeness of information, and writing style and to clarify the attitudes conveyed.

Several teachers of students who are visually impaired and orientation and mobility specialists provided their expertise: Kate Byrnes, Nita Crow, Amanda Lueck, Theresa Postello, Sandra Staples, and our former colleague at the California School for the Blind (CSB) Assessment Program, Barbara Maher. June Waugh, low vision specialist at CSB, provided constant encouragement and insightful feedback throughout the entire writing process.

Special thanks to Jerry Kuns, senior sales manager for the Access-Ability Division of Pulse Data HumanWare; and to Theresa Postello, teacher of students who are visually impaired, who both read the chapter on technology and provided wisdom and motivation.

Ellen Pritchard Dodge, speech and language pathologist, read the chapter on speech and language and inspired Marsha Silver.

Mike Cole, director of the Orientation Center for the Blind in Albany, California, provided not only a professional perspective but also personal insights from his experience growing up as a person who is blind. The tone of our writings was enriched by his candid comments.

Joanna Self, psychologist on the staff at the CSB Assessment Program, provided assistance in the writing of the chapter on psychological assessment, in addition to the support she gives us constantly as a colleague.

Jim Carreon, CSB technology teacher and specialist, gave us invaluable assistance with all the technical aspects of putting the book together, as well as being a source of support and inspiration for Joan Anderson.

Thanks to the professionals at the Meredith W. Morgan University of California Eye Center, who poured over the vision information to make sure it was correct: Angela Bau (now at the Berkeley Unified School District) and Helen Dornbush, educators at the center; and physicians Ian Bailey, Robert Greer, and Betsy Harvey. Thanks to Angela Bau also for tips on the use of English.

In addition thanks to all the students, families, and professionals who have worked with us on assessments of students who are blind or visually impaired through the years. Each assessment has informed this book and enriched our lives as professionals and as human beings.

About the Contributors

Stephen A. Goodman, M.A., M.S., is Director of Pupil Personnel Services at the California School for the Blind in Fremont; and an Instructor at California State College in Hayward and the University of Washington in Seattle. He has served as the School Psychologist for the Ithaca Public Schools, New York, and the Laguna Salada School District, Pacifica, California. His previous publications have been in the area of behavior management. He is Chair-Elect of Division 4 of the Association for Education and Rehabilitation of the Blind and Visually Impaired.

Stuart H. Wittenstein, Ed.D., is superintendent of the California School for the Blind in Fremont. An experienced teacher of braille reading and administrator of programs serving blind children, he has also been an adjunct professor in the programs to prepare teachers of visually impaired learners at Teachers College, Columbia University, and Hunter College, CUNY, in New York. He is the author of articles on braille literacy and specialized services in both the *Journal of Visual Impairment & Blindness* and *RE:view*. He is a past president of the Division on Visual Impairments of the Council for

Exceptional Children, and in 1994, received the division's Outstanding Dissertation of the Year Award.

Joan Anderson, M.S.Ed., is Technology Coordinator at the California School for the Blind in Fremont. She has presented at numerous conferences on the subject of computer access technology.

Lizbeth A. Barclay, M.A., is an Orientation & Mobility Specialist at the California School for the Blind in Fremont and a Lecturer at San Francisco State University. She has published previously in *Re:view* on the topic of academic success for braille readers.

Frances K. Liefert, M.A., is a member of the Association Program and an Orientation and Mobility Specialist and a Teacher of Visually Impaired Students at the California School for the Blind in Fremont. She is a frequent presenter at conferences on the subject of work with students with visual impairments.

J. Richard Russo, M.A., is Director/Psychologist of the Assessment Program at the California School for the Blind in Fremont. He was previously in private practice and was Chief Executive Officer of the California Association of School Psychologists. He is the co-author of a chapter on educational assessment in *Educating Students with Visual Impairments and Other Disabilities,* edited by Sharon Sacks and Rosanne Silberman.

Marsha A. Silver, M.S., is a Speech-Language Pathologist at the California School for the Blind in Fremont and a state consultant serving students with visual impairment.

INTRODUCTION

Frances K. Liefert
and Marsha A. Silver

WHY COLLABORATION?

Collaboration is good for everyone involved in an assessment because the whole is greater than the sum of the parts. No one discipline can possibly view a student as completely as can an alliance of family members and professionals who understand the student from various perspectives. Collaborative assessment brings us to the whole student at the beginning of our relationship with him or her and to each other. When professionals share their findings throughout the assessment process, not just at the end, this creates a completely different dynamic. Families feel that the invaluable information they have about their children is informing the process. Each professional has an opportunity to compare the findings of his or her discipline with those brought from other perspectives. As family members and professionals meet, all together or in different configurations, they build on each others' thought processes before answers are fully formulated. This creates an atmosphere for a more multidimensional, yet unified, view of the student. This comprehensive view, and the foundation for an intimate working relationship among all of those concerned with the student, will prove invaluable during the later goal-setting and instructional phases of each student's education. Data gathered through collaborative assessment allow professionals to set goals that will be more easily incorporated into everyday activities and will have a greater likelihood of being relevant to the student's life. The greater the collaboration between family and professionals, as well as among professionals, the greater the likelihood that the assessment will reflect the true needs of the student.

A comprehensive assessment for children who are blind or visually impaired requires a team of collaborators who represent several disciplines. Family members, a school psychologist, a speech and language pathologist, a classroom teacher from regular education or from a special day class, a resource specialist, a technology specialist, an occupational therapist, a physical therapist, a teacher of students who are visually impaired, an orientation and mobility (O&M) specialist, a teacher of adapted physical education, medical personnel, social workers, and an administrator may all be participants in the assessment of students who are visually impaired or blind, partly because many of these students also have additional disabilities. It is often up to the assessment team to determine whether or not a student who is visually impaired has additional disabilities.

As is the case with all children, some typical behaviors of children who are blind or visually impaired overlap several areas of child development. For example, self-stimulating behaviors, which are often seen in students who are blind or visually impaired, may look like autistic mannerisms. Many common characteristics of the communication of visually impaired students, such as a prolonged period of pronoun confusion and echolalia, may look like true expressive language deficits. Gaps in vocabulary development and concept acquisition may resemble cognitive delays or learning disabilities. Reading disabilities in a student with low vision may be masked by vision issues until later in the student's academic life; that is, teachers and parents may think that the student is having trouble learning to read in braille, print, and/or audiotape because of his or her vision and not discern a concurrent learning disability. To understand the basis of these commonly observed behaviors in students who are blind or visually impaired and who may have other disabilities, professionals from several fields must consult with the experts in vision.

WHO WILL BENEFIT FROM COLLABORATION?

For many members of the assessment team, the student being assessed may be the first person who is blind or visually impaired that they have met, let alone assessed. A speech and language pathologist without the ability to use pictures or a school psychologist without printed symbols may feel at a disadvantage when assessing a student who is blind or visually impaired. The psychologist, reading specialist, speech and language pathologist, and others must adapt their standard assessment battery right from the beginning. In addition to being full of visual prompts, the majority of nonverbal and verbal measures with which they are familiar have not been normed for students who are blind or visually impaired. Determining what is the norm for this group may be an uncharted endeavor. Teachers of students who are visually impaired and O&M specialists understand the common effects of vision loss on areas such as social development, communication, concept acquisition, and reading. They are able to help other team members choose from their tools those most likely to yield helpful assessment data. They may also be able to give advice about what kinds of adaptations would be helpful without changing the value or strength of the assessment tool. Likewise, vision specialists profit from the exchange with professionals of other disciplines to help discover the challenges to the student's learning that are not a direct result of the visual impairment, but that may be a result of the unique interaction of the student's strengths and weaknesses.

WHAT DOES COLLABORATION LOOK LIKE?

It may sound burdensome to add collaboration to a professional's already busy schedule that has just had a challenging assessment added to it. However, a collaborative assessment team can actually achieve its goal of a comprehensive picture of the student in less time than it would take for each professional alone to uncover all the information needed to develop an adequate plan for that student in his or her own discipline. Time to collaborate at key points along the assessment continuum is crucial and must be planned in advance. To find time in which to schedule meetings, assessors need to share modes of communication such as telephone numbers, e-mail addresses, and weekly schedules. They must find ways to assess efficiently as well as comprehensively.

The team must decide where an overlap in testing specific areas will occur and where it can be eliminated. The team can design formal and informal assessment opportunities in which multiple examiners can participate, either sequentially or simultaneously, as is illustrated by the detailed example of collaboration presented in the final chapter of this book.

Members of the team may pair up for assessment activities or videotape various parts of the assessment for the team to view later. They may take turns leading different steps of the process. Collaboration opportunities may include shadowing another assessor during a relevant lesson or assessment period, observing the student's social interaction with peers in an informal or unstructured activity, or observing the student in the community or in his or her home. For example, the speech and language pathologist might shadow the O&M specialist when a student goes out into the community. While the student's travel skills are being observed, the speech and language pathologist can also evaluate the student's ability to communicate with the public.

Diagnostic teaching is often an informative method of assessment and lends itself to teaming as well. Diagnostic teaching can be performed at many levels. For example, a student could be given the tasks of verbally describing an assessment activity he or she had done, of dictating that story to a teacher who brailled it, and of reading the finished braille story. Introducing a new routine that is within the student's developmental level and performing it together can give many answers to questions such as:

- How independent was the student?
- How dependent was he or she on the teacher's prompts?
- What kinds of prompts were beneficial?

- What kind of teaching modalities worked?
- What did not work?
- What helped the student to recognize and remember the routine over time?

The administration of formal tests, used by examiners who are knowledgeable about the effects of visual impairment on development, also has a place in the collaborative assessment procedure. This topic is discussed at length in various chapters.

Upon completing the assessment, it is important to compare and contrast overlapping areas with other assessors. Assessors need to look at the possible discrepancies in the findings and try to form from them a collective perspective of the student. Team members need to contact each other to make sure that assessment recommendations do not conflict with others and to support a unified approach to teaching that will lend itself to a strong individualized educational program (IEP) and the work of a collaborative teaching team.

Collaboration is the major theme of this book; the integration of assessment within the natural contexts and routines in which behavior would normally occur is the minor theme. Professionals who may be testing a student who has a disability with which they were previously unfamiliar may miss some of the student's most important strengths if they do not spend some time observing the student within his or her natural environments. It is important that each student be seen in several real contexts instead of only in the psychologist's office, the speech and language pathologist's cubicle, the desk at the back of the classroom, or the hallway right outside the classroom door. For example, when the most academically capable student who is blind or visually impaired is taken out into the community, it may become evident that he or she does not know how to make change, how to ask for help, or how to shop. On the other hand, a student with less advanced academic skills may function effortlessly in the community through his or her relative strengths in social interaction and spatial orientation. When working together, professionals of all fields, with help from students and their families, can adapt their methods of assessment and collaboratively meet the challenges of assessing all students who are blind or visually impaired.

USING THIS BOOK

For those experienced in assessment but unfamiliar with visual impairments, this work is meant to offer the information and outline competencies necessary to perform valid assessments for children who are blind or visually impaired. For those familiar with the education of students who are visually impaired, it will provide information about assessment and suggest ways in which professionals in a program for students who are visually impaired can foster collaboration among professionals responsible for assessment. It is hoped that this book will be shared among professionals assessing students who are blind or visually impaired to help form the kinds of teams described throughout the book. Lists of assessment targets and information about specific vision conditions can be distributed among assessment team members. A number of forms and checklists for assessing students have been included for readers' convenience. These can be duplicated or adapted for use elsewhere, as long as the source line and the words "reprinted from" or "adapted from" are included.

The authors are aware that most assessment teams will not have their headquarters in the same location, as does the California School for the Blind Assessment Program team. The contributors have drawn from their previous experience as school psychologists, itinerant teachers, and resource room teachers in local school districts to suggest how teams whose members must make time for travel and meetings can still collaborate effectively. We are hopeful that administrators reading this book will see the value of collaboration and facilitate schedules flexible enough to allow it.

Improving the assessment skills for and knowledge about blindness and visual impairment for professionals responsible for assessment will ensure that students who are blind or visually impaired receive appropriate and valid assessments. Such assessments are the foundation of the specialized programming critical to developing sound educational plans that meet the needs of each individual student.

Introduction to Visual Impairment

Frances K. Liefert

IN THIS CHAPTER:

- The impact of blindness on development
- Guidelines for eligibility for special education services
- How the eye functions
- Definitions of terms that describe vision loss

EXPERIENCING THE WORLD WITHOUT VISION

Imagine a child who is blind visiting the beach for the first time. He hears the lapping of waves on the shore, but may not identify it as water unless he is within touching distance. He feels the dry and wet sand, but has no way of perceiving the whole beach as it stretches along the shore. The sounds of others playing in the sun come to him, but he may not understand that Frisbees are flying or a volleyball is being hit, since he has never seen them. Perhaps his interest in listening to and imitating the family on the next blanket speaking in a language he does not understand goes unnoticed or is discouraged. He may be startled when someone slathers him with sunscreen, especially if it is cold and is applied suddenly, without warning or explanation. Someone may remove his shoes and set them aside without him being aware of where they are. The shoes will be lost to him until someone produces them at the end of the day. The boy may not initiate digging in the sand, not having seen others engaging in castle building. He may dislike the sensation of sand on his skin, particularly inside his sandals and swim trunks. If he is settled on a beach blanket and handed a sandwich and a cold juice box, it may feel like a magical event; cold food and drink appearing out of the warm air. The cawing of seagulls, the barking of a dog, and the buzzing of insects have no visual cues connected with them, making them mysterious, perhaps meaningless, or maybe anxiety-provoking. He may feel the vastness of the ocean, the expanse of the blue sky, and the openness of the beach through the wind, the sounds drifting in and out of hearing distance, and the warmth of the sun. Without visual images, however, his sense of what it is to be on a beach is very different from that of his sighted peers.

Imagine instead that a girl who is blind goes to the beach for the first time with someone who takes pleasure in introducing her to the joys of summer. She will have an entirely different experience. Her companion, who may be sighted or blind, has described where they are going so that she has some preparation for what awaits her as she first sets foot on the beach. She anticipates eating a picnic lunch on the beach, and she has helped to buy the food and pack it in the ice chest. The two beachgoers have loaded it into the car and carried it from the car to the beach. Together, they have paused to pick up some sand and feel it sift through their fingers before they venture to the shore. Her friend has pointed out how the sand becomes damper the closer they get to the water. She may have picked up some more sand on her own to examine the change in texture. She has helped spread the blanket on the sand, noticing how the wind makes it difficult to spread it flat. When she has listened to an explanation of why it is important to protect her skin from the sun, she is prepared to rub the parts she can reach with sunscreen and to ask for help with the parts she cannot reach. Her attention to the sounds, smells and tactile sensations at the beach is appreciated and forms an important part of the friends' conversation. With assistance, she has stashed her shoes in a bag on a particular corner of the blanket; her friend hopes she will remember where to retrieve them when it is time to put them on and go home.

The day has been rich in information and less scary than it might have been. Her friend has answered questions and shown her, in small, understandable, and pleasant steps, what is enjoyable and interesting at the beach. She may not comprehend how huge the ocean looks or how beautiful the sky is that day, but she has had a better chance of relaxing in the sun, enjoying a swim, and feeling like one of the magicians who produced the lovely picnic at the beach.

THE IMPACT OF VISUAL IMPAIRMENT ON CHILD DEVELOPMENT

This short and limited description of two different visits to a beach, have delineated clearly how blindness and visual impairment can have global effects on how a child perceives and interacts with the world. The following description of the impact of blindness and visual impairment on the key areas of child development—social skills and communication, language development, motor skills, sensory integration, and cognitive development—is most useful when considered in terms of which of them is affected and which educational discipline addresses each area.

When reviewing the impact of visual impairment on child development, it would be more appropriate, if more impractical, to discuss how visual impairment affects the development of each specific child because each child who is blind or visually impaired develops at his or her own pace, just as do children who are sighted. The child's gifts and impairments, as well as the child's environment, all contribute to his or her development. Given this caveat, the introductory description will present an overview of general information.

Most of the literature on the impact of visual impairment on child development compares the development of children who are blind or visually impaired to that of children who are sighted. David Warren (1984) has pointed out that although the general conclusions of most studies are that children who are blind or visually impaired have delayed development, there are examples throughout the literature of visually impaired children who are on a par with or exceed the norms for sighted children at each developmental milestone. Warren suggests that the provision of an appropriate environment as well as the extent of visual impairment and the presence of concomitant disabilities may make the difference in how children who are blind or visually impaired develop.

Even though children who are blind or visually impaired may be no different developmentally from their sighted peers by the time they reach young adulthood, the road through their early childhood may look very different from that taken by children who are sighted. The families of blind or visually impaired children may need to attend to different aspects of their environments than they would for sighted children. Thus a specialist in early childhood development who is familiar with visual impairment would be a helpful person to have on the team of assessment specialists, together with the parents.

Children who are blind or visually impaired lack the opportunity for what is termed "incidental learning," the ability to learn about the world simply by watching what goes on around them. Blindness or visual impairment may interfere with learning through the other senses as well, since sight is the sense that people who are sighted use most frequently to unify the experiences of their other senses. To compensate for the missing sources of information, caregivers must create an environment rich in other sensory experiences and that includes verbal descriptions early on. This kind of intervention can prevent the delays in language and social skills reported in the past for children who are blind or visually impaired (Warren, 1998). Therefore, a speech and language pathologist may be a helpful addition to the child's assessment team to help with the type of verbal input that would be meaningful.

Without the motivation of seeing things that attract a sighted child to venture out into the environment, movements—both gross motor and fine motor skills—may not develop at the same rate or in the same order that these skills develop in sighted children. Sensory interpretation is affected, since the visual synthesis of the "whole" is absent. Self-help skills, such as eating and dressing independently, may also be delayed or develop in a unique order. An occupational therapist, particularly one familiar with sensory integration

Elizabeth Hartmann

Students who are blind or visually impaired need experiences with real objects in order to understand basic concepts.

therapy, would be a welcome member of the child's assessment team. A physical therapist teamed with an orientation and mobility (O&M) specialist or a teacher of visually impaired students may be able to clarify which part of the motor delay is due to blindness and which may be a concomitant disability.

In children with disabilities in addition to visual impairment, the visual impairment will compound the effects of the other disabilities on the various areas of development. In her longitudinal study entitled Project PRISM, Ferrell (1998) observed children who were blind and visually impaired and receiving early intervention services. These services included teaching parents to interact with their infants and enrich their infants' environments by learning to read the various types of cues given by infants who are blind. The children in the study, who had no other disabilities besides visual impairment, showed little difference in development from their sighted peers, particularly in the area of communication. Those with additional disabilities had wider and more varied gaps in development. This finding is significant because it is estimated that among children who are considered to be blind and visually impaired, 50 to 60 percent have other disabilities (Chen, 1999; Holbrook, 1996; Ferrell et al., 1998).

Children who are blind or visually impaired count on adults around them to be like the companion on the beach in the second vignette described at the beginning of this chapter. Their development in all of the key areas noted previously depends on facilitated experiences with the world in the absence of incidental learning that occurs through watching others. A comprehensive assessment of the child's educational needs will therefore require collaboration from professionals in many disciplines in order to address each key area of development.

An overview of the development of a child who is blind or visually impaired is presented in the following sections, together with some information about the kinds of interventions that may prevent the developmental delays once thought to be inevitable for children who are blind or visually impaired. More specific information on each developmental area affected is provided in subsequent chapters.

Social Skills and Communication

From the very beginning of the child's life, eye contact, which may seem essential to the initial bonding between parent and infant, is often absent. This may leave the parent disappointed and wondering how to communicate with the newborn. Instead of becoming active in anticipation of the parent approaching, the infant may respond by lying very still in order to attend effectively to the sounds of voices and footsteps (Lueck et al., 1997). Infants who are visually impaired or blind may react to being picked up by stiffening rather than cuddling, perhaps because they have been unaware that someone was approaching and are startled by the sudden touch (Scott, 1977). In order to diminish this potentially negative experience, parents of infants who are blind or visually impaired should be encouraged to cuddle and handle their infants more and to accept feedback that is different from that of an infant who is sighted (Barraga, 1992). At this stage, educational assessment should include the family and a teacher of students who are visually impaired who understands early childhood development. By working closely together, they can establish an accurate picture of the infant's early development.

Learning to use social communication is a different experience for a child who is blind or visually impaired than it is for children who are sighted. The blind or visually impaired child may not have a chance to observe how other children enter social situations with each other and how they interact once engaged in an activity together. Children who are blind or visually impaired have facial

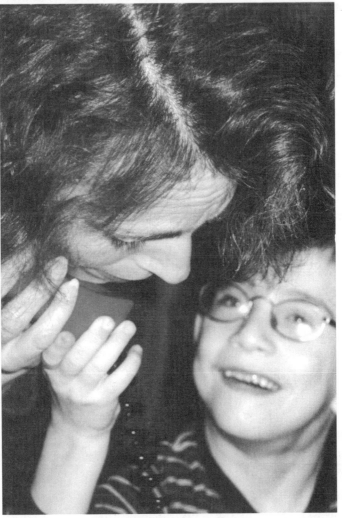

Frances K. Liefert

Students who are blind or visually impaired may need more modeling and prompting to make clear conversation, much as a student who is sighted needs prompts to talk to someone on the telephone.

expressions similar to those of sighted children when they are very young, but do not develop the use of those expressions as means of communication in the same way that sighted children do. A study by Fulcher (cited by Warren, 1984) found that older blind children showed less facial activity than younger blind children when asked to show emotions. In contrast, sighted children's repertoire of facial expressions increased with age. This difference, along with the blind or visually impaired child's inexperience with the many gestures sighted children use as communication devices, interferes with the ability of children who are blind or visually impaired to make themselves understood, particularly by sighted children.

Imagine a child who is blind trying to join sighted children on the beach who are building a sand castle. Her attempts to add sand to the castle may be resented by the sighted children, even if she avoids knocking down part of the creation. Never having seen pictures of a castle, she may not understand what the other children are trying to build. The other children may react to her as though she is younger than she is and, left to their own devices, may try to keep her from joining in their creative activities.

The child who is blind or visually impaired may need assistance at first to start his own sand project and to attract other children into following his lead in continuing it. This type of intervention is different from trying to force the children who are sighted to include the blind or visually impaired child, and ultimately more productive. Its goal is to teach the child who is blind or visually impaired how to be a leader and a team member on his or her own terms.

Language Development

Compounding the social difficulties described in the previous sections are the differences in language development among toddlers and young children who are blind or visually impaired. Children who are blind or visually impaired attain milestones such as uttering a first word at the same ages as their peers who are sighted (Lueck et al., 1997; Fraiberg, 1977). The difference may be that the exact meaning of language for children who are blind and visually impaired may differ from that intended and understood by people who are sighted. We have seen how the beach might appear to a child experiencing it for the first time without sight. The sensation of sand underfoot and in one's hands is very different from the view of sand stretching along the shore that sighted observers refer to as "beach." Many words and concepts that children who are sighted learn through visual observation may take on slightly different meaning to a child who experiences them through sensory channels other than vision.

As mentioned earlier, the incidental learning that may be taken for granted in children who are sighted does not occur for a child who is blind or visually impaired. The beach example shows that children who are blind or visually impaired need deliberate assistance in order to have experiences that will lead to meaningful language acquisition and use. Children who are sighted may have those experiences without such assistance. Even with help, blind or visually impaired children may attach slightly different meanings to the words they use and may acquire a different picture of the world although they use their residual vision in many ways. As can be seen in the descriptions of specific eye conditions in Appendix A, different causes of visual impairment can have different effects on children's learning styles. It is valuable to have a speech and language pathologist join the child's professional team as his or her language emerges. This specialist needs to address the social aspects of communication as well as the actual verbal language, and would benefit from collaboration with a teacher of visually impaired students.

Motor Skills

Although our imaginary beach visitor who is blind may one day become a champion swimmer, on his or her first trip to the beach he or she may not have had the motivation to run and jump into the waves that is typical of some sighted children. Vision seems to be a primary motivator for children to develop motor skills; in its absence, those skills may be delayed or develop in different sequences (Strickling, 1998; Warren, 1998).

For some infants who are blind or visually impaired, head and trunk control may develop later than in sighted infants, because the motivation for babies to lift their heads usually comes from visual stimulation. Babies who are blind or visually impaired may resist lying on their stomachs. If their caregivers always place them on their backs to avoid upsetting them, the infants have less incentive to learn to roll over. If they are not rolling over or lifting their upper body from lying on their stomachs, their shoulders, arms, wrists and hands do not develop at the same time and rate as those of sighted children (Strickling, 1998; Warren, 1998). On the other hand, sitting and standing typically occur at the same ages for infants who are blind or visually impaired as for infants who are sighted (Chen, 1999). Reaching for objects, crawling, and walking may be delayed in blind or visually impaired children because there is little or no visual incentive, and, if the baby has been left to lie on his or her back as he or she prefers, the motoric groundwork for such skills may not have been laid. It may frighten a baby who is blind or visually impaired to attempt walking because standing provides less contact between his or her body and the solid, comforting surface of the floor. Lifting a foot off the floor to move gives even less of a feeling of being supported and safe. In addition, just as the sounds of waves on the shore may be unidentifiable, and even scary, rather than attractive to the blind or visually impaired child, he or she may be hesitant to venture into open space where everything is unknown (Lueck et al., 1997).

The development of fine motor skills—the movement of small muscle groups farthest from the center of the body—is built on well-developed gross motor—or large muscle—skills as well as on visual observation (Korsten et al., 1993). Fine motor skills include the ability to use the hands effectively and to move parts of the mouth and face as required for eating and speaking clearly. Infants who are sighted seem to be entertained for long periods of time by watching their hands and experimenting with bringing them together. As they grow older, they have the chance to see people around them using their hands to do many kinds of tasks. The infant who is blind or visually impaired may not play with her hands unless someone initiates that play (Scott, 1977). Thus, without an appropriate environment, the delay in gross motor development, in the setting of visual impairment, may cause a delay in fine motor development.

Resistance to touching new things is not uncommon among children. Many children, both sighted and visually impaired, react strongly to the different textures of dry and wet sand on the beach and hate the sand, which sticks to the sunscreen on their skin or inside their wet bathing suit. Children who are sighted may hesitate to touch new things, or things that do not appeal to them visually. Children who are blind or visually impaired may hesitate to touch new things that have an unusual smell, make a strange noise, or are urged on them enthusiastically by people not sensitive to their possible reactions. Children with sensorineural differences in addition to visual impairment may be tactilely defensive—hypersensitive to touch, pressure, temperature, and pain. Whether the child is hypersensitive tactilely due to neurological disposition or just concerned about protecting his or her hands, a tendency to avoid touching makes it difficult for a child to learn to use his or her hands effectively (Holbrook, 1995). Many fine motor tasks, such as tying shoes or sorting coins, are more frustrating to learn without their visual component, and are even harder to learn with underdeveloped fine motor skills. Many areas of the child's life may be affected, from learning to wash and dress himself or herself to learning to read braille, which is a tactile reading medium.

A physical therapist and an adaptive physical education teacher can be consulted during assessment of the blind or visually impaired child's motor development. Their collaboration with the orientation and mobility (O&M) specialist and a teacher of students who are visually impaired will help to determine the information that will be most helpful to consider for the child's future program. The addition of an occupational therapist would be beneficial as well, particularly if there are concerns regarding the child's fine motor development.

Sensory Integration and Cognitive Development

The delayed development of locomotor skills and large muscle strength is both caused by and coupled with visual impairment and contributes to a delay in the blind or visually impaired baby's understanding of her position in space. The information used by infants and toddlers who are sighted to develop spatial awareness is not available to infants who are blind or visually impaired. Proprioceptive information which comes to the brain through movement—and vestibular information—which comes to the brain through changes in head position—usually work together with visual information to help sighted babies become aware of themselves in space. The missing visual component in babies who are blind or visually impaired not only keeps them from being motivated to move but may also interfere with their learning to use the information received from their proprioceptive and vestibular systems (Strickling, 1998). The understanding of spatial concepts, which is an important part of language and cognitive development, is therefore affected. Collaboration between the school psychologist and the O&M specialist is important to determine how developed the child's spatial understanding is and what activities could be recommended to ameliorate and compensate for any deficits in this area.

Children who were born prematurely or hospitalized as infants may have missed a good deal of movement. Unlike other infants, they were not carried, either in the womb or in their parents' arms, during the early part of their brain's development. As a result, their understanding of space and their position in it may be delayed or undeveloped (Ayers, 1979). The proprioceptive sense may be absent or underdeveloped. It is extremely difficult for a child to develop a concept of her position in space when both vision and the proprioceptive sense are compromised.

Understanding the relationship between information received by one sense and that received by another is harder to do without vision. A child who is sighted may quickly connect the sight of waves on the shore with experiences in the bathtub at home and put them together in the idea of "water." The child who is blind or visually impaired, who only hears the waves at first, may take longer to associate the cold, salty ocean with warm, soapy bath water. He or she may take even longer to develop a complete idea of what the ocean is like and of what else is correctly included in the category of "water." The teacher of visually impaired students can act as a consultant to all assessment team members to remind them of how the world may be perceived given the individual child's vision.

Additional Disabilities

As mentioned earlier in this chapter, it is estimated that 50 to 60 percent of children who are blind or visually impaired have additional disabilities (Chen, 1999; Holbrook, 1995; Ferrell et al., 1998). Retinopathy of prematurity, which is often accompanied by other disabilities, and cortical visual impairment (brain damage as the cause of visual impairment) are the primary causes of visual impairment in children in northern California today (Bernas-Pierce, 1998). This finding is probably consistent in most of the developed world. Many parents and caregivers of children who are blind or visually impaired therefore have the additional challenge of multiple physical and cognitive disabilities in their children. Infants who are born prematurely or who have disabilities identified at, or associated with, their birth are often separated from their parents for medical intervention. Rather than being cuddled and handled, they often lie attached to monitors in the neonatal intensive care unit of a hospital. Attachment between the children and their parents is delayed. Parents are often grieving for the loss of the nondisabled child they expected (Holbrook, 1996). As the children develop, their parents' experience of grief continues and evolves as the extent, and sometimes even the type, of delays and disabilities becomes evident. Some of this grief may be relieved by receiving services, both for the child directly and for the parents and siblings, from informed and caring professionals in the field of educating infants and children who are blind or visually impaired. These professionals, in turn, need support and information from school psychologists, speech and language pathologists, and occupational and physical therapists in order to put together a complete assessment of the child who is blind or visually impaired.

ELIGIBILITY FOR SERVICES

Assessment is the first step toward obtaining the special education services that are available for infants and children who are blind or visually impaired. The federal Individuals with Disabilities Education Act (IDEA), as amended in 1997, mandates that every child with a disability is eligible for service from public education providers from birth through their twenty-first year. Some states may provide additional service as well. Assessment is the basis for determining eligibility for services and educational placement, establishing long-term goals, and determining the benchmarks that will lead to achieving those goals. Assessment is also the basis for determining which specific services are needed and how they will be delivered, including their time and duration.

How does a child qualify for accommodations and services as a person with visual impairment or blindness? It is not hard to show that an infant, child, or young adult who is totally blind has educational needs that qualify for special education services under the law. But how is it determined whether children who are visually impaired but not blind qualify for service? IDEA states that children are eligible when "the child's disability affects involvement and progress in the general curriculum." For preschoolers, eligibility is determined by how the disability "affects participation in appropriate activities." IDEA goes on to state that "the term *child with a disability* means a child who has been evaluated . . . as having . . . a visual impairment including blindness" or other disabilities, "and who, by reason thereof, needs special education and related services." "Visual impairment including blindness means an impairment in vision that, even with correction, adversely affects a child's educational performance. The term includes both partial sight and blindness." (See 20 USC 1401(3)(A) and (B); 1401(26).)

Each subsequent chapter in this book reviews how an assessor can determine what specific services are needed for each child. Initial guidelines are presented here that can be used to determine whether visual impairment or blindness alone makes the child eligible for special education services.

Legal Blindness

Legal blindness is a clinical definition of visual ability that was created for purposes of assessing people's eligibility for services. Children who are legally blind are generally expected to have a clear basis for eligibility for special education services. Legal blindness is defined in the United States as having a "central visual acuity of 20/200 or less in the better eye after best correction with conventional spectacle lenses; or visual acuity better than 20/200 if there is a field defect in which the widest diameter of the visual field is no greater than 20 degrees" (Hazecamp, 1997).

Visual Acuity

Visual acuity, the first part of the definition of legal blindness, is the measurement of how well a person sees detail. An acuity of 20/200 means that the person can read symbols or letters on a chart in the doctor's office that are 20 feet away which most people could still see from 200 away. In the definition of legal blindness, the acuity is measured using both eyes with the best possible correction from eyeglasses or contact lenses. Acuity is generally measured for distance vision using 20/20 as the standard. Near vision is often described by what size print a person can read from a defined distance.

Sometimes optometrists and ophthalmologists have difficulty determining a child's acuity. They may describe the child's vision in terms of seeing hand motion or counting fingers at a certain distance, as being able to "fix and follow" a visual target, or simply whether the child perceives light or not. Children who have such annotations on their eye reports usually are defined as legally blind and are considered to be in need of services from a program for students who are visually impaired. The teacher of visually impaired students or the O&M specialist may be able to make a more informed assessment of the degree to which a child's visual requirements affect his or her functioning in the school setting by getting to know the child better than is possible in a one-time doctor's visit.

Field Loss

Visual *field loss*, the second part of the definition of legal blindness, is a loss in the size of the area that a person can see while looking in one direction. A field loss may be in the central vision, the peripheral vision, or a combination of the two.

The central vision is the vision used to see detail; it is used to see colors, to read, and to recognize faces. A loss of central vision makes reading print difficult or impossible and reduces or eliminates color perception.

Peripheral vision is the vision used to notice things "out of the corner of one's eye." It is the vision relied on in dimly lit areas and at night. Peripheral vision is not used to see color or detail. It is used to see movement and notice obstacles as one is moving. A large loss of the peripheral visual field makes it difficult or impossible to see at night and to avoid obstacles whose images fall in the area of the loss.

To be considered legally blind solely due to field loss, the loss must be considerable. A fully sighted person has visual fields of 90 degrees on the outside or temporal side of each eye, 60 degrees on the nasal side of each eye, 50 degrees above the eye, and 70 degrees below the eye. These fields are quite a bit larger than the 20 degrees used in the definition of legal blindness. A full field is 180 degrees from one side to the other. Therefore, even if a child is blind in one eye, if the other eye is still intact the child still has a large visual field (150 degrees) and may not need services from a program for students who are visually impaired. Usually when a child has a large field loss in both eyes, there is also a loss in visual acuity.

Low Vision

Children do not need to be legally blind to be eligible for services from an educational program for students who are visually impaired. Individuals with *low vision*, whose vision loss is severe enough to interfere with their everyday tasks, may also qualify for services. For example, field loss is not often just a restriction of the degrees of space around the eye in which the child can see. Many visual disabilities cause scattered field loss or blind spots. This type of field loss may not result in a neatly defined visual field of 20 degrees. However, the areas of loss may interfere with learning to the extent that intervention from a teacher of visually impaired students and an O&M specialist may be needed, particularly if the field loss is in the central vision.

Often visual disabilities cause a simultaneous change in acuity and a field loss that impair the child's vision to the extent that it is impossible to receive an adequate education without support from a program for visually impaired students. The measure of acuity loss or field loss alone may not meet the criteria of the definition of legal blindness, but their combination may make education impractical in a regular setting without support.

Some visual disabilities cause fluctuating vision. Children who see well in some situations and poorly in others or who cannot depend on their vision from day to day or moment to moment may also need the help of a program for visually impaired students. This is true of students who have conditions such as cortical visual impairment, optic nerve atrophy, or optic nerve hypoplasia. These and other common causes of vision loss are explained in Appendix A. Chapter 6 also presents a detailed examination of the assessment of students with cortical visual impairment and retinopathy of prematurity.

Frances K. Liefert

Students who are not legally blind but who have a significant visual impairment may need services from a teacher of students who are visually impaired if their visual impairment would affect their educational performance.

Other children are not legally blind but have a low enough acuity to warrant intervention from a teacher of visually impaired students. Often these children have visual conditions that may become more severe later in life, such as retinopathy of prematurity, cataracts, or retinitis pigmentosa. Even if further loss is not anticipated, generally children with a visual acuity of 20/70 or less will benefit from assessment to determine if they need services from a program for visually impaired students. If the loss in acuity is accompanied by field loss or fluctuating vision, it is even more important to assess the child and determine what services he or she needs.

HOW THE EYE FUNCTIONS

The definition of legal blindness does not take into account other factors that affect the ability to learn through vision. These include the ability of the eye to accommodate to varying distances from the object viewed, the ability to see objects with a low contrast with their background, and the ability of the eyes to move well together in all directions (Lueck et al., 1997). Appendix A lists specific eye conditions with descriptions of the ways in which they each may affect a child's ability to learn. To understand those descriptions, it is useful to understand how the eye and brain work together when the various components of the optical system are all functioning correctly. In order to see, three components must be intact: the eyes, the brain, and the stimulus in the form of light.

Light is reflected from an object to a person's eye. The light enters the eye through the cornea, which is the clear covering of the eye (see Figure 1.1). The cornea focuses the light, which is the first stage of clarifying the image.

The light travels through the aqueous humor, the clear fluid at the front of the eye, and passes through the pupil, which is opened and closed to varying degrees by the muscle called the iris, which is the colored part of the eye. The iris contracts or widens around the pupil depending on how much light there is. The healthy pupil becomes larger if there is less light and smaller if there is more light.

The light travels through the pupil onto the lens of the eye. The lens is responsible for further focusing of light onto the back of the

FIGURE 1.1

FIGURE 1.1
CROSS-SECTION OF THE EYE

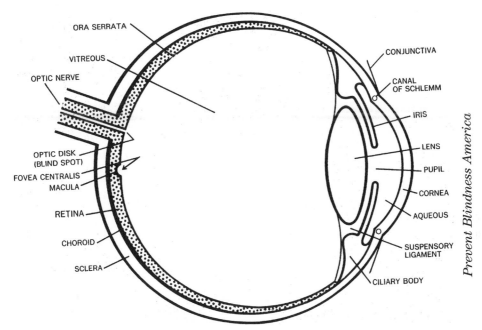

eye. It is especially flexible in children, unless they have an impairments that affects the lens. It changes shape to focus light from different distances. As people age, the lens becomes harder and is able to accommodate less, a condition called *presbyopia*.

From the lens the light travels into the vitreous humor, a gel-like substance that holds the shape of the eye. The vitreous humor behind the lens, as well as the aqueous humor in front of the lens, give some focus to the light entering the eye, although the cornea and the lens are primarily responsible for focus. The vitreous often has remnants of broken blood vessels floating in it, whose shadows are sometimes visible. These floaters remain in the eye for life and increase with age.

The light reaches the retina in the back of the eye, converging on a point of focus. The retina is made up of multiple layers full of light-sensitive cells. These cells connect with each other to form the optic nerve at the back of the eye. The cells responsible for central vision, which are used in well-lit conditions for seeing colors, identifying details, reading, and recognizing faces, for example, are called cones. They are mostly located in the center of the retina, especially in the macula. The peripheral cells that perceive movement and on which sighted people rely for vision in dim light are called rods.

Visual information that is collected on the retina is sent through the optic nerve to the brain. On its way, some of the information crosses sides at the visual chiasm. That is, some information from the right eye is tracked to the left side of the brain, and some information from the left eye is tracked to the right side. The visual cortex of the brain is located in a spot in the lower back of the skull. It interprets the visual stimulus and transmits the information to other parts of the brain to stimulate the appropriate reaction to what is seen.

Visual impairment is the result of injury, infection, or malformation of any of the components of the visual train. Parts of the eye itself can be damaged or can fail to develop, or the brain can be unable to receive and process the images transmitted to it.

THE IMPORTANCE OF A VISUAL DIAGNOSIS

Although certain generalities can be made about the effect of blindness and visual impairment on child development, it is important to recognize that all children who are blind or visually impaired are not affected in the same ways by their impairment. Development and performance in school are affected by the home and school environment and, perhaps, by concomitant disabilities. They are also affected differently depending on the cause of a particular visual impairment. Therefore, in assessing a child who is blind or visually impaired, it is important to take into account the underlying condition. Characteristics of each condition can help the assessor determine which findings derive from the visual impairment and which may have been caused by other factors in the child's constellation of disabilities and life experience or lack of experience.

By becoming familiar with the traits associated with the child's particular cause of visual impairment, the assessor may determine what to seek in assessing the child. An impairment such as cortical visual impairment has a global effect on a child's functioning, while a condition such as albinism may leave most of the child's abilities intact (see Appendix A). Varying degrees of visual impairment will, of course, have varying degrees of impact on the child's development and performance in school.

Familiarity with the eye condition affecting the child being assessed can help the assessor select such features as lighting conditions, print or symbol size, contrast of materials with their backgrounds, and distance between the child and the object he or she is being asked to view.

SUMMARY

This chapter has provided an overview of the impact of visual impairment and blindness on child development and education, a description of how the eye functions, and mention of common causes of visual impairment in children and their implications for assessment of the their educational needs. How much vision loss constitutes a need for special early intervention and educational assistance from a program for students who are blind or visually impaired has been reviewed.

The administrator is often the first person on the educational team to hear about a specific student and has a pivotal role in facilitating a comprehensive, collaborative assessment. The next chapter turns to the role of the school administrator in the assessment of a child who is blind or visually impaired.

REFERENCES

Ayers, A. J. (1979). *Sensory integration and the child*. Los Angeles: Western Psychological Services.

Barraga, N. (1992). *Visual handicaps and learning* (3rd ed.). Austin, TX: PRO-ED.

Bernas-Pierce, J. (1998). *Pediatric visual diagnosis fact sheets*. San Francisco, CA: Blind Babies Foundation.

Chen, D. (Ed.). (1999). *Essential elements in early intervention*. New York: AFB Press.

Ferrell, K. A. (with A. R. Shaw & S. J. Deitz). (1998). *Project PRISM: A longitudinal study of developmental patterns of children who are visually impaired. Final report* (Grant H023C10188, US Dept. of Education, Field-initiated research, CFDA 84.023). Greeley, CO: University of Northern Colorado. Available at http://vision.unco.edu/Faculty/Ferrell/PRISM/default.html

Fraiberg, S. (1977). *Insights from the blind.* New York: Basic Books.

Hazecamp, J. (1997). *Program guidelines for students who are visually impaired.* Sacramento: California Department of Education.

Holbrook, M. C. (Ed.). (1996). *Children with visual impairments: A parents' guide.* Bethesda, MD: Woodbine House.

Korsten, J. E., Dunn, D. K., Foss, T. V., & Francke, M. K. (1993). *Every move counts.* San Antonio, TX: Therapy Skill Builders.

Lueck, A. H., Chen, D., & Kekelis, L. S. (1997). *Developmental guidelines for infants with visual impairment.* Louisville, KY: American Printing House for the Blind.

Scott, E. P., Jan, J. E., & Freeman, R. D. (1977). *Can't your child see?* Baltimore, MD: University Park Press.

Strickling, C. (1998). *Impact of vision loss on motor development.* Austin: Texas School for the Blind and Visually Impaired.

Warren, D. H. (1984). *Blindness and early childhood development.* New York: American Foundation for the Blind.

Warren, D. H. (1998). *Blindness and children: An individual differences approach.* New York: Cambridge University Press.

2 The Role of the Administrator

Stephen A. Goodman

IN THIS CHAPTER:

- The role of the administrator as a collaborator in the assessment process
- Background on assessment of students who are blind or visually impaired
- The legal and educational bases for assessment of students who are blind or visually impaired
- Justification for forming a collaborative team
- The process of forming the team
- The support needed to maintain the team

This chapter is written for all administrators responsible for the assessment of students who are blind or visually impaired. Whether in a small agency with limited services or in a large school district with comprehensive assessment services available, collaboration by assessors from divergent fields will best serve these students. The administrator must demonstrate the commitment and ingenuity to assemble the needed assessors into a collaborative team.

For those in larger agencies, the administrator may simply arrange for the time for qualified examiners to meet. In smaller agencies, administrators may form cooperatives. Each participating member provides one or more of the team of assessors and assigns them to assess students in all agencies who are blind or visually impaired.

Administrators are very familiar with the requirement that a student designation as an individual who has exceptional needs must be based on assessment. However, few have had the opportunity to work with a student who is blind or visually impaired, especially young children. Because this assessment process may be different from that of other students needing special services, the administrator must organize a team of professionals with expertise in a variety of disciplines. Vision experts are essential members of this team.

The administrator is familiar with the great majority of steps involved in the evaluation process. Among the professionals needed will be the teacher of students who are visually impaired, the orientation and mobility (O&M) specialist, the school psychologist, and the speech and language pathologist. Assessors with other specialties may be included, depending on the needs of the particular student.

The ideal is to assemble a team of professionals who are trained to assess students who are blind or visually impaired. Because visual impairment is an infrequent disability, team members who do not routinely work with visually impaired students often do not have the opportunity to focus on this population. They may therefore be unaware of the specific accommodations needed to ensure valid assessments and reports and minimize any challenges to their findings.

BACKGROUND

There are similarities and differences between students who are sighted and those who are blind or visually impaired, which are discussed in other chapters, notably Chapter 1, "Introduction to Visual Impairment." The differences include those that are readily apparent and those that are not.

Readily apparent differences may be compensated for by making adaptations or accommodations. These include changes in materials and environments, such as preparing materials in braille or large print, and adjusting lighting conditions to meet the needs of the individual student. Differences that are less apparent to the assessor include those specific to the individual student. Development, both in rate and sequence, varies. Each of the wide variety of conditions requires specific adjustments to the assessment process and materials (see Appendix A for information on specific diagnoses and their general implications for assessment).

The approach to assessment also varies depending on the student's other handicapping conditions and how long he or she has experienced vision loss. These and other factors are not generally within the experience of most assessors but are critical for valid assessment.

BASIS FOR ASSESSMENT

The basis for assessing students who are blind or visually impaired comes from at least three sources, federal law, state law, and best practices. Each of these sources is discussed in turn in the following sections.

Federal Law and Regulations

Federal regulations since the Education of All Handicapped Children Act (P.L. 94-142), and most recently the Individuals with Disabilities Education Act (IDEA), have addressed assessment for special education generally and the assessment of students who are blind or visually impaired specifically. The regulations outline the responsibilities of the public agency conducting evaluations to determine an individual student's eligibility for special education and related services. They emphasize the need for standardized tests based on norms derived from blind or visually impaired individuals, in accessible media, and administered by trained professionals. Unfortunately, few such standardized tests exist and fewer are known by or available to assessors working with the general population. Few professionals beyond those with specific training to serve visually impaired students—teachers of visually impaired students and O&M instructors—have had any significant training in the assessment of these students. Many training programs for school psychologists, speech pathologists, and other specialists include one lecture on vision loss, often incorporated into the lecture on low-incidence disabilities. Therefore, the administrator's duty to fulfill the requirements to provide valid tests and knowledgeable personnel is challenging.

Standardized administration of tests is a basic element of providing valid information about students. Students who are blind or visually impaired usually require modifications in order to access test materials. Modifications and accommodations must be made by professionals who are aware of the student's functional vision and preferred learning media. Vision professionals are well versed in the necessary accommodations and when to provide them. Assessment professionals, usually psychologists, are knowledgeable about the effect that changes in standard procedures have on results and can assist in stating the results so as to describe the student's performance. (See Chapter 10 on "Report Writing.")

Various authors have recently noted that 50 to 60 percent of babies born blind today have additional disabilities (Hoyt, 1999; Chen, 1999; Holbrook, 1996; Ferrell, 1998). Assessors working with children who are blind or visually impaired must be aware that they are highly likely to have other disabling conditions. Reading that a baby was born prematurely, has syndrome "X," and has a vision loss should lead the assessor who frequently works with visually impaired students to explore many avenues and ask more questions. The assessor with little or no experience may overlook the other conditions in addition to visual impairment that affect the student's educational needs.

Perhaps more than is true for any other population, technological advances have expanded the equipment available to assist blind or visually impaired persons and have increased the ability of braille users and print users to exchange information (see Chapter 8). In the last few years, print users have been able to convert print into braille electronically and braille users have been able to convert braille into print. Equally impressive are the advances that have improved access links among audio production, print, and braille. The assessment of available and appropriate assistive technology required for a specific blind or visually impaired pupil has become an essential component of the overall assessment.

Law and State Regulations

State regulations must meet the minimum requirements as established in federal regulations; however, state regulations may exceed federal requirements. For example, California law addresses low incidence disabilities and services more directly than does federal law and is more explicit about steps that must be taken on behalf of individuals with educational needs. Specific recognition is given to the unique needs of persons who are blind or visually impaired. Areas to be assessed, techniques, and personnel are specifically listed in the California regulations.

The administrator can best serve students' needs by convening a team of knowledgeable professionals to implement such dictates. Two California studies have documented the historical status of the assessment of pupils who are blind or visually impaired. In 1988, "The Report of the Least Restrictive Environment Task Force," addressing the assessment of all students with low incidence disabilities, recommended that the California State Department of Education ensure the availability of "persons with expertise in these low incidence areas," because they would be needed as assessors. In 1992, the Task Force's report on regionalization of services noted that "Assessment personnel (who are predominantly teachers of the visually impaired) understand the variables that affect the unique educational needs of pupils with visual impairments." The studies summarize the current state of service provision to blind or visually impaired students. An inadequate supply of teachers of students who are visually impaired was responsible for delivering the majority of assessment services for pupils. Assessments by other professionals were rarely made.

Best Practices

Two major events significantly changed the direction of multidisciplinary assessment. *The National Agenda for the Education of Children and Youths with Visual Impairments, Including Those with Multiple Disabilities* (Corn et al., 1995) was the product of informal discussion among national leaders in the education of students who are blind or visually impaired. That discussion led to a concerted effort to identify and overcome the educational hurdles faced by students who are blind or visually impaired and their families. Eight goals were identified, the sixth of which reads:

> Assessment of students will be conducted, in collaboration with parents, by personnel having expertise in the education of students with visual impairments. Careful and comprehensive assessments of students with visual impairments are essential if instructional programs are to meet individual needs. Historically, school psychologists or educational diagnosticians were assigned the task of assessing all students with disabilities.
>
> This approach has often resulted in incomplete or inaccurate assessments. Of particular importance is that assessments be comprehensive. Because they have unique extra-academic needs to learn adaptive skills to compensate for their visual impairment, assessments that measure only academic skills are not appropriate for students with visual impairments. The assessment that consists of only academics and functional low vision is likewise unacceptable, because other factors, such as emotional readiness, independence, alternative communication modes, and adaptive skills, must also be considered. All areas of the core curriculum for students with visual impairments must be assessed. Only when all information concerning all areas of the core curriculum is available can responsible, knowledgeable decisions regarding a child's educational program take place. (Corn et al., 1995, p. 11)

At about the same time, Hatlen (1996) issued "The Core Curriculum for Blind and Visually Impaired Students, Including those with Additional Disabilities." (See Chapter 5 for a detailed discussion of the expanded core curriculum.) Hatlen eloquently stated that students who are blind or visually impaired, in order to participate equally in the core curriculum, must be provided the supports and accommodations necessary to ensure access. He called these supports and accommodations the expanded core curriculum and outlined eight areas that are crucial for success:

- Compensatory or functional academic skills, including communication modes
- O&M training
- Social interaction skills
- Independent living skills
- Recreation and leisure skills
- Career education
- Use of assistive technology
- Visual efficiency skills

In specifying these areas, Hatlen expands the area of assessment necessary to determine adequately the educational needs of a student who is blind or visually impaired. Best practice now dictates that these areas be added as areas of assessment for a visually impaired pupil. The assessment process outlined in this book benefits from and expands on these earlier efforts.

FORMING THE TEAM

Law, regulations, and best practice dictate that students who are blind or visually impaired be evaluated for the full range of services necessary for and available to them. Given this mandate, assessors must be available for any service that may be necessary. A standard group of professionals participate in most assessments because of their expertise in visual impairment. Every team must have a specialist in teaching the visually impaired (who also may serve as a technology specialist), an O&M instructor, and a low vision expert (a certified subspecialty educator). Based on his or her expertise in assessment, cognition, and social/emotional functioning, the psychologist is an essential member of the team. Because language development is an important issue for all pupils, but especially for visually impaired pupils, a speech/language/communication specialist is an important member of the team. Finally, parents have the most information to offer about the student being assessed and need to feel welcome to participate fully. Additional experts may be needed on a student-by-student basis and are included on the team as necessary.

Team members' personal characteristics are as important as their professional credentials. The demands of working as a member of a team are significantly different from those of an assessor who works in isolation. All participants must be open and willing to share their roles; be comfortable responding to the questions of other team members, including parents; be well versed in their individual discipline as well as knowledgeable regarding visual impairment; be excellent listeners; and must welcome challenge by colleagues regarding their assessment. Initiative, creativity, the skills of a detective, and a sense of humor are essential. It is unusual, but not unheard of, to find newly trained professionals with the knowledge and necessary skills to become fully contributing team members immediately. Even when experienced professionals are added, a well-planned period of education and team building is necessary for optimal results.

In the ideal situation, the team members work as highly compatible, if not interchangeable, assessors. Because of the their close working relationship, which can become increasingly personal, they must possess excellent interpersonal skills. The administrator creating the team must, more than in other hiring situations, ensure that the team's professional and personal characteristics are compatible. To this end, it is wise to have members of the existing team be involved in the recruiting, interviewing, and hiring when team members are added or replaced.

Professional training, experience, and skill should not be minimized. Outside of programs specifically training professionals to teach students who are blind or visually impaired, most professional training programs provide only a minimal introduction to vision. Among those who have been trained to teach blind or visually impaired pupils, few are equally knowledgeable about cognitive development, language development, psychological factors, and assessment as a process and tool. One must search diligently to find professionals who have the entire set of skills necessary. Those who gravitate toward the job are typically seekers of knowledge and lifelong learners. They are intrigued by the challenge of assessment and seek the self-satisfaction that derives from creating programs to enable students to maximize their achievement. They have had the opportunity to work with blind or visually impaired students, many of whom have additional disabilities, and seek the opportunity to provide more extensive assessment with the resulting improvement in program planning and administration.

Recruitment of other personnel requires concerted and directed efforts. One must go beyond the usual job announcement. It is worth the effort to describe the job fully and to detail the experience to be gained by working on the team. Emphasis should be placed on the opportunity to learn and to do research, since every new student presents new opportunities to learn. Successful recruiting efforts require finding the individual who wishes to be in a position that demands constant learning, extensive collaboration, and challenge from others; who enjoys the accomplishment found in identifying the learning styles of individual children; and who recognizes the reward of designing instructional programs through which every child may experience success.

PROVIDING SUPPORT FOR THE TEAM

Once the team is in place, the administrator's role is to provide the support necessary to enable the team to function. Elements of that support include team building and maintenance activities; provision of the team's materials, supplies, and a conducive work environment; and, most importantly, provision of the extra time necessary to conduct meaningful assessments of students who are blind or visually impaired.

Students who are blind or visually impaired create unique challenges for assessors. The physical environment and materials must be accessible. Creating the accessible environment and materials may require something different for each student. For example, large print requires a definition of how large; whereas modified lighting may mean reduction of glare, more intense lighting, or reduced lighting. To provide a valid assessment, each assessor requires a significant amount of time with the student in virtually every area being studied. Materials preparation and assessment may take more time than with sighted children because more areas must be assessed, including measurements of functional vision and determination of the learning media required for the presentation of materials and optimal learning. Time is also necessary for collaboration. Preparation of the team's report requires that the assessors provide extensive detail. Assessors must each be allotted several days to complete the report for each student, as detailed below.

Team Building

Members of the group all bring expertise to the team that may be disparate but warrants respect from every other team member. The administrator's role is to emphasize that the team is composed of equals, with team leadership held by the member whose particular professional expertise is relevant to the reason for the assessment. An exception is that each new member must be willing to defer to the experienced professional while learning the process used and while establishing himself or herself as a member of the team.

It takes time for team building to occur. Typically, it takes two or three months for the team's initial orientation and much more time to complete all of its work at the level of comfort desired. The team is certainly functional and productive during the process, but the quality and quantity of work will increase substantially over time and as team members' interdependence increases.

The administrator is responsible for fully informing all potential team members of the team's time line and work process. He or she should make every effort to communicate the work habits expected and the nature of collaboration that will be involved. The new team member's evaluation will be based on his or her ability to work collaboratively.

Team building is an extension of recruiting. It is part of the process of an administrator recruiting well, involving all members of the team in the recruiting process, listening to their input, and being cognizant of the professional and personal compatibilities of all staff.

Introducing new staff to colleagues and to their new job includes preparing existing team members for the new colleague and how he or she will be incorporated into the group. This change requires team members to redefine their roles and responsibilities. The competent administrator will ensure that new team members can expect to be questioned without their professional expertise being doubted. Every team member can learn from the variety of skills his or her colleagues contribute.

Two particular opportunities for team building arise as part of the process of assessment. During the case review before a student is scheduled for assessment, each member has the opportunity to demonstrate his or her skills. The administrator can take this opportunity to recognize each member's contributions and to use disagreements as a means to share information among professionals with different perspectives. The administrator can take the lead in setting a tone of collaboration and learning.

Considerable skill is required to facilitate the evolution of the team and strengthen the bonds between team members. Arguments occur, professional and personal feelings may be hurt. The administrator is responsible for assisting each person in developing the skills that allow them to understand professional differences and present them in a manner that will be constructive rather than hurtful. The administrator's job is to facilitate ground rules for the group's discussions and decisions, and to ensure that the team reaches consensus before any meeting is concluded.

A second opportunity for team building arises as a result of the intensity of the assessment process. Staff often need the time and opportunity during lunch breaks or before or after the work day to share the information they have gained with team members. This often leads to the sharing of personal information. The opportunity to develop a collaborative team through social activities must be built into the program. Because of the intensity of the experience and the proximity of staff, it is very helpful to have team members relate to each other personally as well as professionally.

Providing Time

The administrator must provide the tools with which the team needs to work, and the most important of these is time. Assessment of students who are blind or visually impaired takes far longer than that of many other groups of students. The rule of thumb for accommodating visually impaired students taking standardized achievement tests is to allow them 150 percent of the specified time if vision is their only disability. The presence of other disabilities further increases the time required for assessment, which is often difficult to predict. Many factors contribute the need for more time: establishing rapport does not happen quickly; selection and preparation of materials are each time-consuming processes; and it is optimal to conduct assessments in "real-life" situations. To observe a student plan, go shopping and pay for purchases, and prepare a meal and then eat it takes at least four hours. Asking questions about how each of these may be done takes only a few minutes, but the real-time assessment is far more reliable.

A valid, reliable assessment requires at least one day of planning, two days of assessment, one to one and one-half days of collaboration, two days of writing, and at least one-half day of reporting by each professional involved. At the end of this period, assessors always wish they had time for additional evaluation. The investment in time is large, although trade-offs such as having assessors work more independently or making recommendations based on less data, can be made that will result in the acquisition of some information in less time. This solution may be necessary in some situations. However, especially with students whose cases are complex, all the time necessary should be provided to prevent conflict, disagreement, and possible formal challenge such as Due Process Hearings.

Providing Supplies and Materials

Assessors often use real, everyday objects and experiences rather than models to simplify the assessment of concepts. Invariably assessors will investigate a student's use of adaptive technology, ranging from simplified keyboards to computerized notetakers and sophisticated software programs. Although standardized instruments are few and very specialized, a supply of them must be maintained, staff must be trained in their use, and new purchases need to be made frequently. A variety of optical and other devices need to be available, including closed-circuit television and magnifiers and low tech vision aids such as sunglasses (in a variety of colors), baseball caps with brims to reduce light, and portable lamps.

The amount of equipment to be used is so extensive that dedicated storage space is a requirement of the assessment effort. Assessment can begin almost anywhere, but it is necessary to consider how the designated room or office will be organized to accommodate the specific needs of students who are blind or visually impaired. Space requirements have always been an issue because braille materials and assistive equipment require more space than the materials used by the sighted pupil. Storage of braille materials requires at least six to eight times the space needed to store the equivalent print materials. The floor plan and room layout must also be organized to facilitate easy travel and use by students who are blind or visually impaired. It is highly recommended that staff familiar with the needs of blind or visually impaired students be involved in designing the environment from the earliest planning stages.

Having the appropriate environment makes staff more productive and efficient. Beyond the basic supplies, the team's working environment must be considered. Housing staff in the same office areas, or at least in close proximity, promotes interaction, collaborative work, and the exchange of ideas. Providing compatible word processing equipment does wonders to accelerate report writing. Procedural manuals can provide each team member with the guidance necessary to understand his or her role in the assessment. Carefully scheduling activities before the assessment begins helps to keep the process moving smoothly. Regularly scheduling collaboration during the assessment allows for midcourse corrections.

SUMMARY

The effort and commitment involved in collaborative assessment are extensive. The outcome results in the development of programs of excellence for students. The next chapter looks at what the assembled assessment team must do before beginning its actual assessment work with an individual student.

REFERENCES

Chen, D. (Ed.). (1999). *Essential elements in early intervention: Visual impairment and multiple disabilities.* New York: AFB Press.

Corn, A., Hatlen, P., Huebner, K. M., Ryan, F., & Siller, M.A. (1995). *The national agenda for the education of children and youths with visual impairments, including those with multiple disabilities.* New York: AFB Press.

Ferrell, K. A. (with A. R. Shaw & S. J. Deitz). (1998). *Project PRISM: A longitudinal study of developmental patterns of children who are visually impaired. Final report* (Grant H023C10188, US Dept. of Education, Field-initiated research, CFDA 84.023). Greeley, CO: University of Northern Colorado. Available at http://vision.unco.edu/Faculty/Ferrell/PRISM/default.html

Hatlen, P. (1996). *The core curriculum for blind and visually impaired students, including those with additional disabilities.* RE:view *28*(1), 25–32. Available: www.tsbvi.edu/agenda/corecurric.htm

Hoyt, C. (1999). Untitled presentation. Lowenfeld–Akison Early Childhood Symposium, The changing face of childhood eye disease, February 12, 2000, Fremont, CA.

Holbrook, M. C. (Ed.). (1996). *Children with visual impairments: A parents' guide.* Bethesda, MD: Woodbine House.

3 Preparation for Assessment

Lizbeth A. Barclay

IN THIS CHAPTER:

- Determining the scope of assessment
- Obtaining and analyzing information from a student's vision, medical, and educational history
- Determining the observational environments
- Collaborating with families, students, teachers, and assessment team members
- Preparing the assessment environment

CONTRIBUTION TO COLLABORATION

This chapter emphasizes the importance of collaboration among specialists to create the foundation that will enable a unified approach when assessing a student who is blind or visually impaired. By using a collaborative approach, assessors will all be working from the same frame of reference, speaking the same language, and therefore helping to create the best possible program for the students they serve.

In preparing to assess students who are blind or visually impaired, the team is often also considering the effects of additional disabilities. "Most [teachers of the visually impaired] report that almost 50 percent of their students exhibit additional disabilities with vision loss" (Sacks, 1998, p. 4). *Project PRISM* found that 59.9 percent of its participants were diagnosed with disabilities in addition to visual impairment (Ferrell, 1998). "The heterogeneity of this group of students makes it difficult for professionals, who traditionally are trained to work with students who exhibit only blindness or low vision as their primary disability, to serve such a diverse group; it requires specialized skills and training. For professionals whose expertise is not blindness or low vision, serving these students can be a challenge and a mystery" (Sacks, 1998, p. 4).

As specialists prepare to assess a student who is blind or visually impaired, thoughtful review of the student's records, communication with the student's parents and caregivers, and continuing dialogue and sharing of information with each other will help reduce the challenge that they all face.

While the teacher of students who are visually impaired, special day class teacher, or inclusion specialist may often be what is termed the case carrier or team leader in the group of teachers and specialists who educate the student, all educators and team members will share in this process and require preparation in order to proceed with their assessment. The case carrier will be in communication with the parents or caregivers throughout the process of preparation. The importance of their participation in the process is discussed later in this chapter.

DETERMINING THE SCOPE OF ASSESSMENT

The scope of each assessment will be determined by the reason for assessment. As presented in Chapter 1, the federal Individuals with Disabilities Education Act (IDEA) mandates that a student is eligible for special education services when his or her disability "adversely affects [his or her] educational performance." The evaluation to be conducted must be "full and individual" (see sec. 300.532 and 300.533). In addition, IDEA states that a child with a disability must be assessed "if conditions warrant a re-evaluation, or if the child's parent or teacher requests a re-evaluation, but at least once every three years" when they are receiving special educational services (see Sec. 300.536).

Legislation notwithstanding, appropriate and meaningful curricula can only be developed for students who are blind or visually impaired when their unique learning style and requirements are clearly understood. That understanding occurs through comprehensive assessment. The assessment may be an initial or triennial assessment, if the student has been previously receiving special educational services. Partial assessment may also occur as needed, whenever it is requested by a member of the individual education program (IEP) team.

Comprehensive Assessment

A comprehensive assessment will be conducted to help determine eligibility and educational requirements for a student who has been referred for educational services. It will also be conducted at least every 3 years for students who receive special educational services. When planning for a comprehensive assessment, the teacher of students who are visually impaired will focus on the functional vision evaluation, learning media assessment, and the areas of the expanded core curriculum for students who are blind or visually impaired (Hatlen, 1996). Assessment in these areas is discussed in Chapter 5, "Expanded Core Curriculum: Education." Chapter 8 and Chapter 9 explore in detail technology and orientation and mobility (O&M), respectively.

Cognitive development, psychosocial development, and adaptive behavior are assessed during a comprehensive assessment by a psychologist (see Chapter 6). Speech and language are often assessed in a comprehensive assessment, especially for children who are blind or visually impaired with additional disabilities. Aspects of speech and language assessment and collaboration from the perspective of the speech and language pathologist are explored in Chapter 7. Chapter 11 illustrates collaboration and the comprehensive assessment process through the use of a case study.

Partial Assessment

A partial assessment is sometimes necessary to understand more fully a child's learning requirements in a particular area. For the purposes of this definition, partial assessment is not the same as continuing diagnostic teaching, which combines ongoing assessment and instruction in order to guide a teacher's instructional practices (Koenig & Holbrook, 1993). Partial assessment has been formally determined to be necessary by the IEP team and will include only selected teachers or specialists. It might be conducted for the following reasons:

- to investigate one or more areas such as use of learning media or living skills
- to assess learning style and suspected learning disabilities
- to determine the need for additional special education services, such as speech and language or occupational therapy

This book primarily focuses on comprehensive assessment; however, the collaborative practices described can also apply to partial assessment.

VISION HISTORY

Finding Vision Information

When preparing for an assessment, whether initial or continuing, the first step is to obtain and analyze all information about the student's past and current vision. Current information about a student's vision can be found in an optometrist's report, an ophthalmologist's report, a low vision report, or a functional vision evaluation report. See Chapter 4 for more information on vision assessment. If the student is functionally blind (that is, a student whose primary channels for learning are tactile and auditory) (Hazecamp, 1997, p. 98), it will be important that all information from the ophthalmologist is up to date. If the student has had vision in the past, this will be important information to consider when preparing for assessment.

If the student has vision, information should be obtained from a current eye report prepared by the student's eye care specialist. The information is current if it has been obtained before the date that the specialist has recommended that a re-evaluation take place and if there has been no discernible fluctuation in vision. If a change in vision is suspected, a re-evaluation is recommended before assessment. It is always preferable to obtain new information just prior to assessment.

In reports from both optometrists and ophthalmologists, information can be obtained about the diagnosis of visual impairment, description of the various aspects of the visual impairment, and prescription of low vision devices, if they apply. The ophthalmologist's report will also contain any recommendations for surgery or medical treatment. The low vision evaluation will be conducted if it is thought that further optical or nonoptical low vision devices are necessary.

Vision reports vary from practitioner to practitioner in their usefulness and the amount and quality of information included. However, this information is essential to obtain when preparing for an assessment. Parents, caregivers, and teachers will succeed in maximizing the amount of information from their eye care specialist following an examination if they go to the examination prepared with questions about the information they wish to receive. Sidebar 3.1 lists the information found on a complete eye care report.

Analyzing the Vision History

Vision history plays an important role in concept development. A student who has had some or all of her vision for several years has a visual memory that assists her in comprehending certain concepts. Collaboration among the speech and language pathologist, orientation and mobility (O&M) specialist, teacher of students who are visually impaired, and classroom teacher will be especially fruitful when examining areas of concept development and language comprehension. The O&M specialist will assess concepts as they apply to the student's movement and travel. The speech and language

---

Sidebar 3.1   INFORMATION CONTAINED IN A THOROUGH VISION REPORT

- Cause of visual impairment
- Date of onset
- Distance acuity with and without correction
- Near vision acuity: recommended print size from specific distance, especially if a low vision specialist has been consulted
- Visual field assessment
- Binocular status (whether both eyes are used together), stereopsis (depth perception)
- Contrast sensitivity
- Prognosis
- Recommended eyeglasses prescription
- Recommended low vision devices, if a low vision examination has been done (magnifiers, CCTV, monocular, sunshades, etc.)
- Lighting recommendations (most often in a low vision examination report)
- Treatment needed: medical treatment is determined by an ophthalmologist
- Restrictions to activities
- Date for next visit to eye care specialist

---

pathologist will assess concepts as they apply to use of receptive and expressive language. Concept development plays an important role in skill development in all areas of the expanded core curriculum (Hatlen, 1996).

When reviewing the student's vision history, the following areas are useful to consider:

- If the student is blind, did he or she previously have vision ? How much?
- Compare new reports with old reports to assess any vision changes that have taken place over time.

- Is the eye condition stable or degenerative?
- Has the visual functioning increased or decreased?

When preparing for assessment, answers to the following questions are particularly important to the current and future choice of learning medium (that is, whether the student will read and write in print, braille, or a combination, or use any other methods):

- Is the visual impairment secondary to a neurological condition?
- Is the visual impairment due to a congenital condition, or did it occur as the result of an acute event such as an accident or severe illness?

Learning style and developmental level will be affected by these factors. When choosing assessment materials and observational domains, these factors must be considered. Refer to Appendix A, "Common Causes of Visual Impairment," for information about specific causes of visual impairment.

When planning an assessment for a student who has been in transition to a new learning mode because of vision loss, collaboration with the psychologist will be crucial. Social and emotional components of the assessment may be extremely important if the student is cognizant of that change. If the student has been a visual learner, any change in learning mode will be important to examine.

The Functional Vision Evaluation

The functional vision evaluation (see Chapter 4) is conducted by the teacher of students who are visually impaired or by the O&M specialist, or both. It differs from the optometrist or ophthalmologist's clinical evaluation because it assesses how the student uses vision in real-life situations. It combines all pertinent information obtained from the eye specialist and medical reports, the parents, and the student (if possible), and information obtained through teacher interviews and observations regarding the student's use of vision. Before an initial assessment, no functional vision evaluation will exist. Useful information can be gained by all members of the assessment team by observing the teacher of students who are visually impaired or O&M specialist as he or she conducts the functional vision evaluation. The teacher of students who are visually impaired and the O&M specialist can likewise gain useful information about the student's vision by observing his or her use of vision while other team members are assessing.

Through systematic observation of students in their natural environments, teachers can observe how students use their vision to perform routine tasks. This process and valuable resources for conducting a functional vision evaluation can be found in Chapter 4.

MEDICAL HISTORY

Medical conditions and acute events often affect the student's learning style and functioning level. The implications of these events and conditions are as varied as the individual personalities of students and so generalization should be avoided. However, in order to understand and analyze an assessment holistically, it is important to have a thorough understanding of a student's medical history.

Collaborating and sharing this information with all other specialists and teachers is extremely important because all members of the team require this information. Various members of the team may have different information about the student's medical history depending on their source of information and their relationship with the student's family.

When reviewing a student's medical history, team members should consider the following factors:

- Students who were born prematurely have often experienced many medical complications that not only affect their vision but also may have caused neurological impairment that itself greatly affects their overall development.
- Premature birth also means that students may have spent their first months of life in a hospital intensive care unit and will have a significantly delayed rate of development and experience difficulty integrating sensory information.
- Students with cortical vision impairment (CVI) may also have various learning disabilities that will affect their learning style

and approach to assessment. (More information regarding CVI can also be found in Chapter 6, "Psychological Assessment" and in Appendix A, "Common Causes of Visual Impairment.")

- If a student has missed a great deal of school because of hospitalization and rehabilitation, this will affect his or her rate of development.
- Children who have had shunts, and shunt revisions or failures, have often sustained neurological damage that will affect their learning style and rate of development. A shunt is a narrow tube placed in the ventricles of the brain to drain excess spinal fluid.

EDUCATIONAL HISTORY

The educational history is an important component of the preparation for assessment and can have a great impact on skill development. Information about the student's educational history can usually be obtained from the parents or other caregivers and his or her school records. Consider the following questions when reviewing the educational history:

Did the child receive early intervention, such as participation in an infant stimulation program? An early intervention program, for children two years of age or younger, is designed to provide therapy and/or instruction to help infants and toddlers with special needs improve their developmental skills.

Did the student attend preschool? Was the preschool program preacademic or experiential in nature? Programs that are experience-based and focus on concept development using functional and hands-on experiences while helping to develop the sensory system can have a profoundly positive effect on a child who is blind or visually impaired.

What schools has the student attended? It is more likely for a student's program to maintain continuity and stability when he or she can remain in the same school over time, rather than frequently moving and changing programs.

What is the student's current type of class placement (mainstream classroom, special day class, resource program, school for the blind, self-contained classroom) and what other types of placements has the student had? The types of classroom placements that have been tried and the current placement will affect the student's skill development and can chronicle his or her educational progress.

What is the student's current grade level? Because of their individual learning style and the extent of the expanded core curriculum, it is very common for children who are blind or visually impaired to be retained in the same grade for another year, especially during transitions such as entering elementary school from preschool, when going from elementary school to middle school, or during the high school years.

When did the student begin to receive services for visual impairment, what is the history of the service level for visual impairment, and what other services does the student receive? Services from specialists and the level of those services provide many clues about a student's developmental history and needs over time.

What are the findings from prior assessment(s)? It is important to examine prior test results carefully. Although results from standardized assessments of visually impaired students should be interpreted with caution (see Chapter 6, "Psychological Assessment"), they can be very informative when used to measure a student's progress over time. By examining prior assessment results, specialists can see what has been attempted in the past. This will give them an idea of what should be done again for comparison, and what has not been done and may be needed in the future.

FAMILY INVOLVEMENT

As the comments of one family member illustrate, the involvement of the family is crucial to achieving a complete picture of a student who is visually impaired:

> Observing Dan in his environment, where he is in so much more control, continues to be one of our best familiarization techniques. . . . When a child is unwilling or unable to show what he knows, or performs differently in various settings,

the educator simply must be made aware of his very best. The best educators we have encountered have always welcomed our input and allowed us to play a major role in the development and application of Dan's education. (Quinian, 1995, p. 127)

Although family involvement is mentioned as the third component in the assessment process, it is really the first priority. Whether or not the assessment is an initial one, meeting the family may take place before complete vision and medical information has been collected for a particular student. It is optimal that the family be involved in as many aspects of the assessment as possible. Partnership with parents and caregivers ensures a more holistic approach to a child's assessment and education.

From the first contact with the family and when permission to assess the student is obtained, continued discussion with families is crucial to ensure that all necessary areas of assessment are being addressed. Parents and caregivers can be involved through many aspects of the process including family interviews, preassessment conferences, and skills observation in the home. These are all opportunities for parents and caregivers to communicate their knowledge of the student as well as their hopes, questions, dreams, expectations, and goals for his or her education.

By involving parents and caregivers in the assessment process, educators validate the family as the most valuable source of information about the child. By inviting them into the partnership at the beginning of the process, they maximize the opportunity for sharing information and strategies between the home and school environments.

The Preassessment Meeting

Involving families in the assessment process means giving that process time. A preassessment meeting is effective in initiating the parent-teacher partnership for assessment. It is also an opportunity to obtain written permission for assessment. While one assessment team member may conduct this meeting and share the information

Frances K. Liefert

Partnership with parents and caregivers ensures a more holistic approach to a student's assessment and education.

with all other members of the team, it is also very effective when several teachers/specialists can participate. This builds a foundation for collaboration among all team members.

The preassessment meeting with parents and caregivers provides an opportunity to:

- Define the purpose of assessment
- Obtain written permission for assessment
- Identify parent concerns, questions, and goals regarding assessment and curricular outcomes
- Update vision and medical information
- Invite parent observation of the assessment process
- Describe the role of specialists during assessment
- Conduct a family history interview
- Schedule observation of the child at home

Family Interview

Family interviews are a good initial source of information. They serve to:

- Provide information about a child's behavior and functioning at home.
- Provide information about the student's family and home background that is relevant to their educational and social development.
- Help educators understand the family's concerns about the student's visual impairment and functional levels which will help the team to determine areas to assess.
- Provide insight about a student's learning style as observed by the parent.
- Provide clues about possible behavior modification strategies and rewards to use during assessment.

One way to create an interview questionnaire is to generate a list of questions while reviewing the student's prior vision, medical, and educational history. A tool for family interviews used by the California School for the Blind Assessment Program, the Parent Inventory and History Form, is included in Appendix B.

Observation in the Home

One of the most insightful ways for all specialists to gain information about a student's behavior and functioning within the home is to conduct a home-based activity observation. This is especially beneficial if parents and caregivers have particular concerns about a student's skill level in self-care activities such as dressing or eating. Examples of information that specific team members can obtain include the following:

- *Teacher of students who are visually impaired:* Functional vision and many areas of the expanded core curriculum for students who are visually impaired, such as daily living skills, social skills, and leisure and recreation skills.

- *Speech and language pathologist:* Most often a child's highest level of receptive and expressive language can be observed in his or her home.
- *O&M specialist:* A child's O&M behavior may be compared across environments.
- *Psychologist:* Behavior and adaptive behavior are often best observed at home.
- *Occupational therapist:* Motor skills during functional tasks can be observed in the child's most natural environment.

Observational checklists that can be used for home observation are included in the Resources of Chapter 4, "Vision Assessment," Chapter 5, "Expanded Core Curriculum: Education," Chapter 6, "Psychological Assessment," Chapter 7, "Speech and Language Assessment," and Chapter 9, "Expanded Core Curriculum: O&M."

The observation is part of the assessment, but when it is scheduled at the beginning of the assessment process it can also be viewed as a way to prepare for other parts of the assessment. Combining a home observation with subsequent discussion and a parent interview is a powerful way to obtain a wealth of preassessment and assessment information. By going to the student's home, a professional demonstrates an interest in understanding the family's concerns and perspectives. While observing a student perform a functional task performed daily, his or her actual skill level and need for assistance can be observed.

The assessment team can invite the parents and other caregivers to suggest a routine activity they would like to have observed. It could be the morning routine from the time the student wakes until he or she leaves for school. More simply, it could involve a meal at home or playtime after school with the student's siblings. An observational checklist helps to guide notetaking. It is often helpful to keep a written account of each aspect of the student's actions during the activity sequence, which can be used later when completing the assessment information.

As important as the observation itself is the opportunity afterwards to discuss what occurred with the family. When setting up the observation appointment, it is helpful to ask the parents or caregivers to set aside some uninterrupted time for discussion afterwards. The team members can take this opportunity to ask the caregivers questions about their techniques in working with the student and to determine their concerns and issues.

The Challenge of Family Involvement

"Special educators are sometimes frustrated by what they interpret to be resistance or apathy from family members with cultural perspectives that differ from their own. In fact, both educators and family members are faced with problematic and complex issues when they attempt to work together in the development and planning of meaningful educational programs" (Dennis & Giangreco, 1996). While involving the family in the assessment process is both essential and rewarding, it can be the most challenging aspect of the assessment process. Successful, productive involvement requires a high level of communication skills and cultural sensitivity.

Families may not be open to this process for a variety of reasons, which makes facilitating their involvement and partnership very challenging. However, most parents and caregivers want to be involved in planning a student's education. In their study, Dennis and Giangreco identified the following keys to conducting culturally sensitive interviews:

- Appreciate the uniqueness in each family.
- Be aware of the assessor's influence as a professional.
- Acknowledge each assessor's cultural biases.
- Seek new understandings and knowledge of cultures.
- Develop an awareness of cultural norms.
- Learn with families.

With these guiding principles in mind, all members of the assessment team can maximize their understanding of the student. The quality of the interaction between individuals and the conversations those interactions stimulate will yield the important information needed to assess the student holistically and create a meaningful program.

INVOLVING STUDENTS

Just as it is important to involve students in the decision-making and problem-solving aspects of their education, it is also important to involve them in the preparation process for assessment. The developmental level of each student will define the degree to which this is possible but, when appropriate, students should be involved. This involvement may be as basic as explaining to them the importance of the team gaining more knowledge about how they learn in order to help teach them better. As students mature in their self-knowledge and ability to communicate and advocate for themselves, their level of involvement should continue to increase.

A student can be involved in assessment preparation by:

- Providing information about what they perceive as their learning strengths and weaknesses
- Providing input about what they consider to be important to assess and learn
- Providing information about their preferences and necessities in materials and adaptations during testing

For more information about interacting with students who are blind or visually impaired, see Chapter 6.

DETERMINING OBSERVATIONAL ENVIRONMENTS

Important information about students can be observed in a variety of settings, depending on the scope of the assessment, the specialist, and the type of information being collected. Students' behavior and skills can vary tremendously in different environments depending on their comfort level and the expectations placed upon them. Examples of the types of skills that can be observed in different observational environments are detailed in the following sections:

- *Home:* For observation of living skills, which would be naturally taught in the home; social skills with family members; communication skills; and O&M skills in a familiar environment.

- *School:* For observation of academic, functional academic, O&M, social, and living skills that would naturally be taught at school, including the following subenvironments: classroom, cafeteria, restroom, playground, and getting to and from the school bus.
- *Day care:* If a student spends a large part of the day in a day care center or extended school day program, social skills and O&M are among the skills that might be observed.
- *Community:* If the student is in a community-based program, functional academics, communication skills, as well as O&M skills can be observed in various parts of the community such as at the supermarket, in a restaurant, or on the job.

CONSULTATION WITH THE CLASSROOM TEACHER

The observations, concerns and questions provided by the classroom teacher are key components in the formulation of an assessment plan. Continuing consultation between the classroom teacher and specialists is essential to successful implementation of educational goals and objectives. The process of learning about the student's program and curriculum requires time for observation and consultation. Observing the student in the classroom provides a forum for discussion and consultation with the classroom teacher.

While many specialists find it efficient to simply document their observations through notetaking, others may find it helpful to use an observational checklist to guide their observations. The *Assessment Kit*, compiled by Sewell (1997), includes several forms that can be used to help guide student classroom observation (this kit is discussed in more detail in The Resources for Chapters 5 and 8). In addition, two versions of a Checklist for Classroom Consultation, one for students in academic programs and one for students with additional disabilities, are included in Appendixes 3.1 and 3.2.

COLLABORATING WITH ALL TEAM MEMBERS

The teacher of students who are visually impaired is often the team leader for the assessment of students who are blind or visually impaired, since he or she is the first to receive pertinent medical and vision information. The team of special educators for a student may include an array of specialists in addition to their classroom teacher and the teacher of students who are visually impaired. Finding time for all team members to meet to share information, formulate questions, and discuss findings while preparing for or during assessment may seem impossible, given the intricacies of specialist schedules. As described in Chapter 2, "The Role of the Administrator," time can be saved, duplication of assessment can be avoided, and a more holistic assessment approach will be possible when team members make time to consult with each other.

In the preparation process it is essential for the teacher of students who are visually impaired to share information about the student's visual impairment, use of functional vision, and testing environment requirements. Teachers and specialists will benefit from consulting with the teacher of students who are visually impaired to make sure that their testing environments and materials are accessible and optimal.

Allowing sufficient time is very important when helping specialists prepare for assessment. It is imperative that students be given adequate time to respond to assessment questions and tasks. Students who are blind or visually impaired require more time than their sighted peers to respond to assessment and academic tasks. If a student has additional disabilities, he or she may require even more time to respond.

PREPARING THE ASSESSMENT ENVIRONMENT

There are many factors to consider in preparing the assessment environment. Collaboration with the teacher of students who are visually impaired is essential to ensure that the assessment environment and materials will be chosen and prepared keeping in mind components detailed in the following sections.

Learning Media

- Braille, large print, or tape-recorded materials: If assessment materials require reading, they must be provided in the student's preferred learning medium.
- Pictures: If pictures are necessary for assessment items, does the student have enough vision to interpret the pictures accurately?
- Format and layout: Some students will require a print format that is simplified or adapted so that there is plenty of space between testing items, and so that it is easy to visually follow.
- Contrast: Is there adequate high contrast, or is the printed material too light or broken? Print materials should be presented on a background of high contrast such as black on a white or yellow background. Print quality should be high and provide dark and unbroken lines.
- Detail: Can the student accurately interpret the detail visually within the pictures, diagrams, and objects? It is important to ensure that the student is not missing important details in the test illustrations.
- Visual field: Is the student's visual field sufficient to accurately see all necessary aspects of the test items?
- Positioning: It is important to place the test materials or present objects within the student's best visual field and range.

Low Vision Devices

Students must have access during assessment to any low vision devices, such as eyeglasses, magnifiers, or a closed-circuit television (CCTV) that they regularly use (see Chapter 4 for an explanation of these devices).

Mode of Student Output

The student must have access to the preferred mode of output, which could include braille, computer, or a braille notetaker if the student uses braille; or dark-lined paper, dark pen, or computer if the student uses large print. Sometimes students use a cassette recorder for a taped response if this has been determined as an appropriate accommodation by the IEP team.

Lighting

- Appropriate lighting is necessary during assessment. A student's individual comfort is important and will be determined by his or her visual impairment. Reduce glare by making sure that light is not reflecting off any shiny surfaces that the student must use, and by making sure that the student is not facing any windows or sources of light.
- An adjustable reading lamp can help to direct light onto the reading material.
- Incandescent lamps cause less glare than fluorescent lighting.

Use of Objects

- If objects are used to demonstrate certain concepts during assessment, real objects should be used, not miniature or representational objects (such as plastic fruit or toys).
- When using objects, students must be given adequate time to explore tactilely all test items before making a choice or response.

Ergonomically Correct Furniture

- The student is best served by using furniture that fits. The student ought to be seated so that his or her posture is well supported. If the student's feet do not touch the floor flat, use a small platform or step under them, so that they can touch with legs bent at the knees in a natural position when he or she is seated.
- Hands and arms are also most comfortable in a natural position when placed on the table, so that they can be used for support and optimal use during reading and writing tasks.
- A reading stand for print readers will help to lessen their back and neck fatigue.

Visual Fatigue

- Determine the student's optimal test time segments. Parents and the teacher of students who are visually impaired will have information about optimal testing periods if the student cannot give this information. Many students experience visual fatigue when engaging in close range visual tasks, such as reading, for extended periods. The assessment team should be aware of any signs of visual fatigue, such as increased reading errors, eye rubbing, decreased attention, headaches, and complaints.
- To help maximize a student's ability to use his or her vision during testing, alternate reading tasks with nonvisual—auditory or movement—activities.

Other Environmental Factors

- The testing environment is best when it is quiet and free from auditory distraction.
- The testing environment should be free from all other materials (papers, toys, objects) that might be distracting or cause clutter.

Suggestions for modifying assessment materials and making modifications specific to some common causes of visual impairment are included in Appendix A to this book.

SUMMARY

Once a solid foundation for assessment has been built through a collaborative process of preparation by all members of the assessment team, meaningful assessment can take place. Holistic assessment of students who are blind or visually impaired becomes possible through this process of ensuring family involvement, sharing information, observing students in natural contexts, and making time for meaningful discussion. What might be regarded as a challenge has now become a process that will lead to meaningful and student-centered program planning.

In the next chapter the initial area of assessment is described in detail. From deciphering the eye specialist's report to observing the student's use of vision in her daily life, Chapter 4, "Vision Assessment," includes the information all team members will want to know about the vision of the student being assessed.

REFERENCES

Dennis, R. E., & Giangreco, M. F. (1996). *Creating conversations: Reflections on cultural sensitivity in family interviewing. Exceptional Children, 63,* 103–116.

Ferrell, K. A. (with A. R. Shaw & S. J. Deitz). (1998). *Project PRISM: A longitudinal study of developmental patterns of children who are visually impaired. Final report* (Grant H023C10188, US Dept. of Education, Field-initiated research, CFDA 84.023). Greeley, CO: University of Northern Colorado. Available at http://vision.unco.edu/Faculty/Ferrell/PRISM/default.html

Hatlen, P. (1996). The core curriculum for blind and visually impaired students, including those with additional disabilities. *RE:view, 28*(1), 25–32. Available: www.tsbvi.edu/agenda/corecurric.htm

Hazecamp, J. (1997). *Program guidelines for students who are visually impaired.* Sacramento: California Department of Education, page 98.

Individuals with Disabilities Education Act, 20 U.S.C. ß1414(a) (1) & (2). (1997).

Koenig, A., & Holbrook, C. (1993). *Learning media assessment of students with visual impairments.* Austin: Texas School for the Blind and Visually Impaired.

Quinlan, B. (1955). *A family's perspective.* In Chen, D., & Dote-Kwan (Eds.). *Starting points: Instructional practices for young children whose multiple disabilities include visual impairment.* Los Angeles: Blind Childrens Center.

Sacks, S. (1998). Educating students who have visual impairments with other disabilities. In S. Sacks & R. Silberman (Eds.), *Educating children who have visual impairments with other disabilities* (pp. 3–38). Baltimore, MD: Paul H. Brookes Publishing.

Sewell, D. (1997). *The assessment kit: Kit of informed tools for academic students with visual impairment.* Austin: Texas School for the Blind and Visually Impaired.

CHECKLIST FOR CLASSROOM OBSERVATION
(For students in academic programs)

Student's name _____ Birthdate _____

Name of school _____

Name of classroom teacher _____

This observation/consultation was made by _____

Observation date _____

Cause of visual impairment _____

Visual acuity _____

Other disabilities _____

Type of class

Pre-school (regular) _____ Pre-school (visually impaired) _____

Kindergarten _____ Elementary: grade _____

Junior high: grade _____ High school: grade _____

Special day class _____

Resource room access: visually impaired _____ learning disabled _____

Student's daily schedule in detail:

_____

_____

_____

_____

_____

Other related services: _____

_____

How many people work with the student? _____

Does student have a one-to-one assistant? _____

Name _____

Assistant's duties _____

_____

Source: Lizbeth Barclay and Gaby Cohen, California School for the Blind Assessment Program, Fremont, CA, 2001. Reprinted with permission.

Number of other students in class _____

    Other disabilities served in class _____

    Adult-to-student ratio _____

Method for home-to-school communication _____

Communication:

Does student initiate greetings/conversation? _____

    w/peers _____ w/adults _____

Is student echolalic? _____

Does student answer questions asked by adults? _____

Does student answer questions asked by peers? _____

Does student ask for help? _____ By what methods (verbal, points,

    holds object out, adaptive device, etc.)? _____

Does the student follow directions given:

    One-to-one _____

    In small group _____

    To all class _____

If not, what level of prompt is needed? _____

Does student participate in class discussion? _____

Teacher concerns in this area: _____

_____

Academic:

Reading medium:

Braille

    Pre-braille skills _____

    Braille letter recognition _____ uncontracted (grade 1) _____
    contracted (grade 2) _____

Print

    Size _____ Distance _____

APPENDIX 3.1 (*continued*)

Source: Lizbeth Barclay and Gaby Cohen, California School for the Blind Assessment Program, Fremont, CA, 2001. Reprinted with permission.

Does student use:

    Glasses _____ Distance _____ Reading _____

    CCTV _____ Magnifier _____ Monocular _____

Describe: _____

Recorded material (audiotapes): _____

    School texts _____ Literature _____ Other _____

Does student read with comprehension? ____ At what grade level? ____

Does student listen with comprehension? ____ At what grade level? ____

In what format is math work provided? _____

Is student well organized? _____ Describe: _____

_____

Teacher concerns in this area: _____

_____

Access technology:

Does student use a computer? _____ Type _____

Adaptations _____

For what purposes? _____

_____

Additional access technology: _____

_____

Teacher concerns in this area: _____

_____

Learning environment and inclusion modifications:

Is student a full participant in large group activities? _____

    Small group activities _____ In a one-to-one activity _____

If not, describe behavior: _____

_____

APPENDIX 3.1 (*continued*)

Source: Lizbeth Barclay and Gaby Cohen, California School for the Blind Assessment Program, Fremont, CA, 2001. Reprinted with permission.

Seating location of student during large group activities: _____
   Small group activities _____

Are adaptations made for pictures or objects presented during large or
   small group activities? _____

Is modeling provided for student during action or motion activities
   during circle times? _____
   Describe type of modeling: _____
Are adults working from behind student when appropriate? _____
Type and amount of physical guidance given during various activities?

_____

Describe classroom lighting: _____
Are tactile, color, or braille markings used in room? _____

Is the student's posture well-supported during learning activities (correct
   size of furniture, etc.)? _____

Teacher concerns in this area: _____

_____

Adaptive skills at school:

Can student independently remove, hang up coat and other items
   (backpack, lunch, etc)? _____
Can student put coat back on independently? _____
Does student keep work area organized? _____
Does student realize if spills have occurred? _____ Does student
   clean up spills and messes? _____
Does student use toilet independently? _____
Does student wash hands independently? _____
   If with prompts, what type (verbal, physical)? _____
Does student independently eat snack and/or lunch? _____
Opens food containers _____ Finger feeds _____ Spoon _____
   Fork _____ Knife _____ Cleans up after eating _____

APPENDIX 3.1 (*continued*)
_____

Source: Lizbeth Barclay and Gaby Cohen, California School for the Blind Assessment
Program, Fremont, CA, 2001. Reprinted with permission.

Teacher concerns in this area: _____

_____

Mobility skills within classroom:

Does student follow voices or other people? _____

Does student trail to locate objective? _____

   With or without prompts? _____

Does student require constant prompts to move? _____

Does student seem well-oriented to room? _____

Does student locate specific classroom areas (bathroom, cubby, etc.)? _____

Does student locate specific outdoor areas (cafeteria, playground, etc.)? _____

Does student use sighted guide appropriately? _____

Does student use a cane? _____

Teacher concerns in this area: _____

_____

Social:

Does student have any special friends in class? _____

   In the school? _____ In the neighborhood? _____

Does the student participate in group activities in class? _____

Does student face speaker(s) during group activities? _____

Does the student participate in turn-taking activities with peers? _____

Does the student seek out other peers? _____ Adults? _____

Does the student play with peers? _____

Does the student offer to help others? _____

Describe student activities during recess: _____

_____

Teacher concerns in this area: _____

_____

APPENDIX 3.1 (*continued*)

Source: Lizbeth Barclay and Gaby Cohen, California School for the Blind Assessment Program, Fremont, CA, 2001. Reprinted with permission.

Behavior:

Does student exhibit any inappropriate behavior ? _____ If so,
  describe type, location, times of occurrence, etc.: _____

_____

_____

What type of intervention appears effective (when appropriate)? _____

Does student exhibit self-stimulating behaviors? _____

Describe: _____

Are transitions difficult for this student? _____

Describe: _____

Is there an optimal time of day for student attention and
  participation _____

Teacher concerns in this area: _____

_____

APPENDIX 3.1 (*continued*)
_____

Source: Lizbeth Barclay and Gaby Cohen, California School for the Blind Assessment
Program, Fremont, CA, 2001. Reprinted with permission.

CHECKLIST FOR CLASSROOM OBSERVATION
(For students who are visually impaired with additional disabilities)

Student's name _____ Birthdate _____

Name of school _____

Name of classroom teacher _____

This observation/consultation was made by _____

Observation date _____

Cause of visual impairment _____

Visual acuity _____

Other disabilities _____

Type of class

Pre-school (regular) _____ Pre-school (visually impaired) _____

Kindergarten _____ Elementary: grade _____

Junior high: grade _____ High school: grade _____

Special day class _____

If special day class, what type?

Visually impaired _____ Communication _____ Deaf-blind _____

Multihandicapped _____ Other _____

Class program (preacademic, academic, functional, daily living skills, communication emphasis, etc) _____

Student's daily schedule in detail:

Arrival _____ Lunch _____ Departure _____

Activities: _____

_____

_____

How many people work with the student? _____

Does student have a one-to-one assistant? _____

Name _____

Assistant's duties _____

_____

_____

Source: Lizbeth Barclay and Gaby Cohen, California School for the Blind Assessment Program, Fremont, CA, 2001. Reprinted with permission.

Number of other students in class _____

   Other disabilities served in class _____

   Adult-to-student ratio _____

Method for home-to-school communication _____

Sensory:

Is child visually attentive to people? _____

Does child make eye contact? _____

Is child visually attentive to surroundings? _____

Is child tactilely defensive? _____

   If so, to what substances? _____

Will child allow hands/arms to be touched? _____ Guided? _____

Is child sensitive to noise? _____ If so, what types? _____

Teacher concerns in this area: _____

_____

Communication:

What is communication system of child (verbal, signs, adaptive devices, tangible symbols, combination, other)? _____

Does child initiate greetings/conversation? _____

   w/peers _____ w/adults _____

Is child echolalic? _____

Does child answer questions asked by adults? _____ by peers _____

Does child accurately answer yes/no questions? _____

Does child ask for help? _____ By what methods (verbal, points, holds object out, adaptive device, etc.)? _____

Does the child follow oral or signed directions? _____

Does child follow picture directions or sequences? _____

Does child follow the following directions: Stand up _____

   Sit down _____ Come here _____ Go to . . . _____

   Face me _____ Turn around _____ Stop _____

Does child follow directions on a one-to-one basis? _____

Does child follow group directions? _____

APPENDIX 3.2 (*continued*)

Source: Lizbeth Barclay and Gaby Cohen, California School for the Blind Assessment Program, Fremont, CA, 2001. Reprinted with permission.

Teacher concerns in this area: _____

_____

Academic inclusion modifications:

Is child a full participant in large group activities? _____
    Small group activities _____ In a one-to-one activity _____
If not full participant, describe behavior: _____

_____

Seating location of student during large group activities: _____
    Small group activities _____
Are adaptations made for pictures or objects presented during large or
    small group activities? _____
Is modeling provided for student during action or motion activities at
    circle times? _____
    Describe type of modeling: _____
Are adults working from behind child? _____
Type and amount of physical guidance given during various activities?

_____

Teacher concerns in this area: _____

_____

Adaptations:

Describe classroom lighting: _____
Are tactile, color, or braille markings used in room? _____
Is the child's posture well-supported during learning activities (correct
    size of furniture, etc.)? _____

Adaptive skills at school:

Can child remove, hang up coat and other items (backpack, lunch, etc.)
    by self in correct area? _____
Can child put coat back on independently? _____
    Level of prompts: _____
Does child keep work area organized? _____

APPENDIX 3.2 (*continued*)

Source: Lizbeth Barclay and Gaby Cohen, California School for the Blind Assessment
Program, Fremont, CA, 2001. Reprinted with permission.

Does child realize if spills have occurred? _____ Does child clean up after self? _____

Does child use toilet independently? _____

Does child independently wash hands? _____
    If with prompts, what type (verbal, physical)? _____

Does child eat snack and/or lunch independently? _____
    If with prompts, what type? _____
    Opens food containers _____ Finger feeds _____ Spoon _____
    Fork _____ Knife _____ Cleans up after eating _____

Teacher concerns in this area: _____

_____

Mobility skills within classroom:

Does child follow voices or other people? _____

Does child trail to locate objective? _____
    With or without prompts? _____

Does child require constant prompts to move? _____

Does child seem well-oriented to room? _____

Does child locate specific classroom areas (bathroom, cubby, etc.)? _____

Does child locate specific outdoor areas (cafeteria, playground, etc.)? _____

Does child use sighted guide appropriately? _____

Does child use a cane? _____

Teacher concerns in this area: _____

_____

Social:

Does child have any special friends in class? _____
    In the school? _____ In the neighborhood? _____

Does the child participate in group activities in class? _____
    On the playground? _____

Does child face speaker(s) during group activities? _____

Does the child participate in turn-taking activities with peers? _____

APPENDIX 3.2 (*continued*)

Source: Lizbeth Barclay and Gaby Cohen, California School for the Blind Assessment Program, Fremont, CA, 2001. Reprinted with permission.

Does the child seek out other peers? _____ Adults? _____

Does the child play with peers? _____ Is there representative play? _____

Does the child offer to help others? _____

Teacher concerns in this area: _____

_____

Behavior:

Does child exhibit any inappropriate behavior? _____ If so, describe
   type, location, times of occurrence, etc.: _____

_____

Is the child on a "behavior plan"? Describe: _____

_____

What type of intervention appears effective? _____ Ineffective? _____

Does child exhibit self-stimulation behaviors? _____

Describe: _____

Are transitions difficult for this child? _____

Describe: _____

Is there an optimal time of day for student attention and
   participation? _____

Teacher concerns in this area: _____

_____

Academic/Preacademic:

*For children with additional disabilities who are learning academic
skills:*

Reading medium: _____

Does child read with comprehension? _____ At what grade level? _____

In what format is math work provided? _____

If braille:

Pre-braille skills (list) _____

Braille letter recognition _____

   Reads braille _____

APPENDIX 3.2 (*continued*)

_____

Source: Lizbeth Barclay and Gaby Cohen, California School for the Blind Assessment
Program, Fremont, CA, 2001. Reprinted with permission.

If reading braille, is material in uncontracted (grade 1) braille? _____
In contracted (grade 2) braille? _____

If print:

Print size: _____
From what distance? _____
List low vision aids and devices (glasses, magnifiers, monocular, book
stands, etc.): _____
Does child use CCTV? _____ Describe method of use: _____
_____

Listening:

Does child use recorded material (audiotapes)? _____
Recreational _____ School texts _____ Literature _____
Does child listen with comprehension? _____ At what grade
level? _____

Organization:

Does child locate her/his own curricular materials? _____
Does child put away her/his own curricular materials? _____
Does child utilize backpack? _____

Recess

Describe activities during recess: _____
_____

Teacher concerns in this area: _____
_____

APPENDIX 3.2 (*continued*)

Source: Lizbeth Barclay and Gaby Cohen, California School for the Blind Assessment
Program, Fremont, CA, 2001. Reprinted with permission.

Vision Assessment

Frances K. Liefert

IN THIS CHAPTER:

- Understanding eye care specialists' reports
- Overview of functional vision assessment

UNDERSTANDING EYE REPORTS

As described in Chapter 3, early in the assessment process it is important for all members of the assessment team to have a clear idea of what a student who is visually impaired but not blind can and cannot see. The report from the eye care specialist is the first place to look. All members of the team will benefit from access to the eye care specialist's report and from using the report to analyze the student's vision history as described in the previous chapter. Because eye reports may be difficult to understand for those who are not in the medical profession, a guide to reading eye reports is provided here.

A teacher of students who are visually impaired, an orientation and mobility (O&M) specialist, or a nurse who has experience reading such reports may be needed to interpret the report for the team. A teacher or O&M specialist from the program for students who are blind or visually impaired will also be the team member who conducts an assessment of the student's functional vision. As mentioned in the previous chapter, this assessment is different from the eye care specialist's examination because it is an observation of the student's use of vision in real life situations, such as reading various sizes of print, using different types of lighting, reading from a classroom board, and traveling in familiar and unfamiliar environments. A description of how a functional vision assessment is typically conducted and what elements are included in it follows the guide to reading eye reports.

Eye Care Specialists

When beginning an assessment, team members need to know about the eye condition affecting the student, and they must also find out information specific to the student with whom they will be working. Appendix A, "Common Causes of Visual Impairment," includes general descriptions of a number of eye conditions and their impact on an educational assessment. Other resources available to school professionals are the student's eye care specialist, his or her parents, the teacher of students who are blind or visually impaired, and the O&M specialist.

There are two types of eye care professionals whose reports are relevant to an educational assessment. The first are optometrists, who are eye care professionals who examine the eyes and detect eye disease. They measure students' visual acuity and the need for corrective lenses, as well as the size of the visual field in which the student sees. They also measure muscle balance of the eyes. Optometrists prescribe lenses and sometimes eye muscle exercises.

Some optometrists specialize in working with people who have what is termed low vision. A person is considered to have low vision when their vision loss affects their ability to use vision as a primary learning sense. Corn and Koenig have defined a person with low vision as "a person who has difficulty accomplishing visual tasks, even with prescribed corrective lenses, but who can enhance his or her ability to accomplish these tasks with the use of compensatory visual strategies, low vision and other devices, and environmental modifications" (Corn & Koenig, 1996, p. 4). People who have low vision may need to use low vision devices, described later in this chapter, in order to access books with frequently used print sizes.

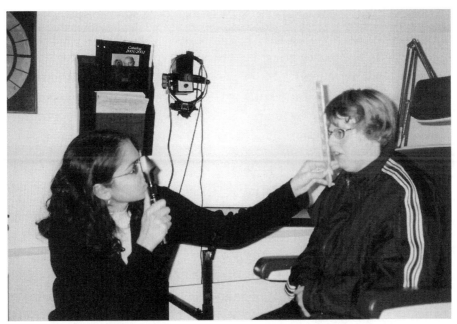

June Waugh

A low vision examination by an optometrist or ophthalmologist is the best way to determine whether a student would benefit from the use of low vision devices.

They may not be able to travel safely in the community without mobility devices, such as a long cane or a dog guide described in Chapter 9, "Expanded Core Curriculum: Orientation and Mobility."

Ophthalmologists are medical doctors who diagnose and treat diseases affecting vision. They care for the health of the eyes, including performing any surgery that is necessary. As do optometrists, they measure acuity and visual fields, and they prescribe corrective lenses when necessary.

Some students need time to learn about vision examinations before they visit the optometrist or ophthalmologist. It is sometimes helpful for teachers of students who are visually impaired to expose them to the printed charts designed for optometrists and ophthalmologists before students have an eye examination. The goal is not to teach the students to memorize eye charts, but to familiarize them with how eye examinations are performed. Students who can read can be taught to identify the letters on charts; children who cannot identify letters can be taught to recognize the pictures on charts.

This assists the eye care specialists determining whether the students are not identifying symbols because they cannot see them or because they do not know how to identify them. The eye care specialist can get a more accurate picture of the student's acuity and optimal print size if the student already knows how to respond to the testing equipment being used. There are many places to purchase such equipment. The two listed in the Resources section of this chapter under Sources of Equipment for Vision Assessment are especially helpful to educators.

Teachers of students who are visually impaired and O&M specialists assess the functional vision of the child. The assessment of functional vision is described more fully in the next section of this chapter.

Eye reports from ophthalmologists and optometrists vary greatly in the ease with which laypersons can understand them. Some eye care specialists report their findings in letters addressed to parents and school personnel. These reports are usually easy to understand. Others may report findings on a form, such as the one produced by the State of California included in Appendix D of this book. These reports may provide an outline of the information the assessor needs. Still other eye care specialists only write notes during the actual eye examination, which are copied and sent to the schools. Some are quite legible, and others are difficult to decode. Talking with the student's teacher of students who are visually impaired and referring to the functional vision report done by a teacher in that program will be especially helpful when the eye care specialist's report is hard to understand. Abbreviations commonly used by eye care specialists, especially in clinical notes, are listed and explained in Appendix C, "Abbreviations Used by Eye Care Specialists" at the end of this book.

If the guide offered here is not sufficient for a team member to decode an eye report, it may be necessary to call the eye care practitioner or to ask for assistance from the teacher of students who are visually impaired, the O&M specialist, or the school nurse, who may have experience deciphering such reports and may have already been in contact with the eye care professional. These teachers can also give information about the educational implications of the student's specific eye condition. (See also Appendix A, "Common Causes of Vision Loss in Children and Implications for Assessment.)

Eye Report Information

Some eye reports are more complete than others due to such factors as how responsive the student is to testing, how resourceful the eye care specialist is, and how well the student and eye care specialist know each other. A comprehensive eye report will provide the following kinds of information:

- Cause of visual impairment
- Date of onset
- Distance acuity with and without correction. (See Chapter 1, "Introduction to Visual Impairment," for a definition of acuity and a description of how it is measured.)
- Near vision acuity. This is the recommended print size from a specific distance, especially if a low vision specialist has been consulted.
- Visual field assessment
- Binocular status (whether both eyes are used together) and stereopsis (depth perception)
- Color vision
- Contrast sensitivity
- Prognosis
- Recommended eyeglasses prescription and uses for viewing at various distances
- Recommended low vision devices (such as magnifiers, closed-circuit television, monocular, and sunshades, described later in this chapter), if a low vision examination has been done
- Lighting recommendations (most often found in a low vision examination report)
- Treatment needed. (Medical treatment is determined by an ophthalmologist, whose role is defined more fully in Chapter 3.)
- Restrictions or adaptations to activities
- Date for next visit to eye care specialist

Prescriptions for Eyeglasses

The numbers on the prescription for the student's eyeglasses will give you some information about his or her vision, but they will not tell you how well the student can see when wearing the glasses. Eyeglasses do not always correct vision to 20/20, which is why doctors report what the student's vision is "with best correction." Looking through the eyeglasses will not tell you how the student sees without the glasses. In other words, the refractive correction of the prescriptive lenses (the amount the lenses change the focus of an image on the retina), will not produce the same effect as the refractive error in the child's eyes, which causes either too close a focus or too distant a focus. See Sidebar 4.1 for a description of the notations used on eyeglass prescriptions.

Low Vision Devices

Optometrists who specialize in low vision spend time determining what devices might be helpful to students for the activities in their daily lives that are affected by low vision. The low vision specialist interviews his or her patients to find out what sort of activities they enjoy and what visual activities they avoid or have difficulty with. He or she asks whether there are activities that patients would like to engage in but that are not accessible due to low vision. During a low vision examination, several activities that require vision might be tried. Various devices, described below, would be introduced to determine whether they might enable the student to perform certain tasks better or even to perform them at all without assistance.

Low vision devices are usually prescribed by optometrists rather than ophthalmologists, particularly if the person has been referred for a low vision examination. When a low vision device is being prescribed, it is important to remind the optometrist to take into account any concomitant disabilities the student being assessed may have. For example, a magnifier may benefit a student's vision if it is held at the proper focal distance from the object to be viewed. But if the student has an orthopedic disability affecting hand use, such

Prescriptions written for a plus number of diopters (the measure of the amount of curve in the lens) of correction are for eyes that are hyperopic (farsighted). The lenses will be convex and will magnify what the student is viewing. Lenses greater than +5 to +6 diopters may indicate that the student is extremely farsighted, but his or her acuity while wearing the glasses is not revealed by the prescription alone (Wilkinson, 2000). Lenses with a high plus number are prescribed for students whose own lenses have been removed through cataract surgery. "Lens power greater than +12D (diopters) may mean that the student has no crystalline lens inside his eye, because of cataract surgery resulting in *aphakia* (the absence of the lens), or it may mean that she is extremely farsighted" (Levack, 1991).

Prescriptive lenses may improve vision to 20/20 or may leave the student with an acuity somewhere between 20/20 and the uncorrected acuity. Sometimes students who are extremely farsighted may be given a mild positive prescription, such as +2.50, to make objects they view slightly sharper in focus, but the measurable acuity is not, and cannot be, improved. That is, the prescription may not improve the student's measurable acuity but will help his or her eyes not to have to work as hard.

Prescriptions with a negative number are for concave lenses that will improve vision for students who are myopic (nearsighted). Lenses of −6 to −8 diopters or higher indicate that the student has high myopia (extreme nearsightedness).

A correction for astigmatism, which involves an irregular curvature of the eye, may also be indicated on the prescription. Astigmatism is measured by comparing the refractive power of the greatest amount of curve in the cornea to the least amount. Eye care specialists imagine the surface of the eye with vertical and horizontal lines referred to as meridians. The meridian where the focusing power is either greatest or least is called the axis of the astigmatism for purposes of prescribing correction. The prescription is written with a plus or minus number, indicating the number of diopters of correction, and a number that indicates the horizontal or vertical meridian designated as the axis of the astigmatism. Prescriptions for astigmatism might look like this: −1.00 × 90 or −6.00 × 110. These numbers come after the prescription for correcting myopia or hyperopia. If the astigmatism is great enough, lenses may be prescribed that correct only the astigmatism (Jose, 1983).

Eye care specialists use "plano" to denote lenses with no prescription for myopia or hyperopia. A prescription for glasses that correct only for astigmatism may read: plano −6.00 × 180. Safety glasses may be prescribed without any correction, especially if a student has only one eye with vision, in order to protect him or her from accidental vision loss. Safety glasses are made from polycarbonate lenses, as are most glasses made for young people.

as cerebral palsy, a stand magnifier will be a much better choice than a handheld model.

If the student being assessed has just started using the low vision device, his or her use of it may not be reliable for consideration during assessment. Usually it is necessary to spend time teaching a student how to use a low vision device before it becomes a functional tool for him or her. A teacher of students who are visually impaired or an O&M specialist would be the best person to determine the student's proficiency with a low vision device. They will be assessing its use as part of this comprehensive assessment. If the student is adept at using the device, make sure it is available when appropriate during the assessment.

Low vision devices can be classified into two categories: optical and nonoptical. Optical devices include lenses that change the focus of the image on the user's retina. These include all kinds of magnifiers and telescopes. Nonoptical devices do not change the focus of the image on the retina, but enlarge the image, shade the eyes, or bring the image into a better position in relation to the viewer's eyes. These include sunglasses and closed-circuit televisions.

Optical Devices

Optical low vision devices include magnifiers and monoculars. Magnifiers are lenses that enlarge the image a person receives by changing the focus of the image on the user's retina. Magnifiers of various powers may be handheld or stand magnifiers. Handheld magnifiers are convenient for students who use their hands without difficulty. They are usually small enough to carry in a pocket or backpack. Stand magnifiers are positioned on reading materials and moved along the material as the student reads. They are available in many sizes and designs. Some magnifiers are designed to hang around the reader's neck and extend from the chest. Some have lights built into them that are helpful for students with certain eye conditions. It is best if the eye care specialist suggests specific magnifiers for the student. However, if this has not been part of the optometrist's examination, a teacher of students who are visually impaired may be able to recommend whether a magnifier would be useful, and which kind would be most useful, in the course of the functional vision assessment.

For distance viewing, other optical low vision devices are often useful, such as binoculars and monoculars. Monoculars, also referred to as handheld telescopes, are made up of lenses that magnify or reduce (depending on which end is next to the eye) features viewed in the distance. Binoculars, used by sports fans, opera buffs, and bird watchers, have two monoculars that are connected so that the user can see through one with each eye. Many people who are visually impaired prefer to use monoculars because they are primarily using their strongest eye. Monoculars are small and easy to handle. Others prefer binoculars because it is easier to stabilize them against a larger area of the face. Binoculars are in common use by people who are not visually impaired and therefore less conspicuous. Monoculars are available in many powers, so it is best to have the assistance of an eye care specialist in selecting the appropriate one. The higher the power of the monocular, the narrower the field of vision tends to be, and the more restricted the lighting. A student may use the monocular for such activities as viewing the board in the classroom, reading various signs in the community, viewing objects in a museum or animals at the zoo, and spotting traffic lights while waiting to cross the street. A monocular aids vision when the person using it is standing still or sitting. Due to the visual field restrictions imposed by monoculars, they are not used while moving.

Spectacle or head-mounted telescopes are available for use when both hands are needed for a task. Jewelers' loupes can be lifted or lowered to change the viewing distance from far to near. These are used by students who are visually impaired for tasks, such as science experiments, which require both hands to be available and require a view of the classroom board as well as of objects on the work table.

Nonoptical Devices

Nonoptical low vision devices are mentioned less frequently by eye care specialists, and the teacher of students who are visually impaired may be the one to recommend them. CCTVs are electronic devices commonly used to magnify reading material. These TVs have a camera built into their base that is focused on a movable tray on which the reading material is laid. The image from the camera is viewed on a TV screen or a monitor. The reader can enlarge the print to a much larger size than is practical using a copy machine. While reading with a CCTV, the viewer's posture is not compromised. He or she can sit straight and view the TV screen as closely as needed. The polarity of a CCTV can also be adjusted so that white symbols appear on a black background. This reversed polarity is preferred by many people who experience difficulty with glare or contrast sensitivity. Color CCTVs are available and they are especially useful for viewing pictures and charts that would not be completely legible when enlarged on a black and white copy machine or when viewed on a black and white CCTV.

The disadvantage of a CCTV is its size. Most are large, not portable, and take up a lot of table space. It is not practical to have

J. Richard Russo

A closed-circuit television and a measuring tape can be helpful to determine optimal print size and distance from the visual target.

them on a child's desk in a regular classroom, and children who are visually impaired sometimes resist using them because their use emphasizes the differences between them and their classmates. Recently, portable cameras have come onto the market, which have the advantage of being easy to carry and less conspicuous for students using them. Several models must be hooked up to a television screen or a head-mounted screen, and all require coordination on the part of the viewer to keep the camera focused on the appropriate place in the reading material.

A reading stand can help the reader maintain a healthy posture. Eye care specialists occasionally recommend that a student use a reading stand, but often it is left to the teacher to explore whether it would be helpful and to then help the student use one productively in the classroom. Many types of reading stands are available in many sizes. The reading material is held up on a slanted board so that the child who has low vision does not have to bend down to the desk top in order to read.

Computers offer a wide range of options for students who are blind or visually impaired. Software that enlarges images, provides auditory output, and allows small print to be scanned and other capabilities are discussed in Chapter 8, "Expanded Core Curriculum: Technology." Low tech products such as copy holders with adjustable arms also help people who are visually impaired to use computers. A copy holder is used to bring printed information a student is using close to his or her eyes and to the computer screen. The proximity makes it easier for the student to move his or her gaze between the paper and the computer screen than if the printed information lies flat on the desk.

The devices most commonly used by people with low vision are also used by people who are not visually impaired: tinted lenses (sunglasses), caps with visors, and adjustable lighting. With many eye conditions, such as albinism, cortical visual impairment, achromotopsia, optic nerve atrophy, and cataracts, excessive light reduces acuity and causes discomfort (see Appendix A). Visors and sunglasses also help reduce the adjustment time from bright to dimmer conditions. Finding the optimal tint for sunshades and encouraging the use of hats with dark brims is often the work of an eye care

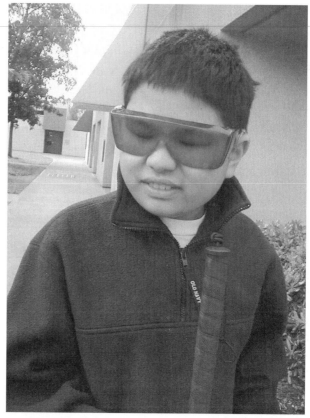

Frances K. Liefert

Tinted eyeglasses are an important low vision device for people who have a visual impairment that may cause great sensitivity to glare, such as rod-cone dystrophy, cortical visual impairment, cataracts, or glaucoma.

specialist who gives low vision examinations. Lights with rheostats to adjust brightness and with adjustable arms or goosenecks can be helpful to facilitate optimal lighting for specific tasks.

Follow-Up and Recommendations

The last component of an eye report from an eye care specialist is an indication of what kind of treatment the child requires. Here the eye care specialist states when the child should be seen again for an eye examination, whether or not medication has been prescribed, and whether there are any restrictions necessary on the child's activities.

FUNCTIONAL VISION ASSESSMENT

The student's functional vision is assessed by a teacher of students who are visually impaired or by an O&M specialist. The purpose of this assessment is to find out how the child uses the vision reported by the eye care specialist. As Anthony writes,

> While an optometric or ophthalmological exam in an eye doctor's office can yield vital information about the student's eye condition, the results may not be readily transferable to other settings. Unless care is taken to observe the student's visual performance in real-life environments, where lighting and contrast cannot always be controlled, a true picture of a student's functional vision cannot be obtained. (Anthony, 2000, p. 32)

During a functional vision assessment, the child is observed in his or her natural environments with the variety of visual challenges that he or she encounters in his or her daily routine. His or her successes and frustrations are observed in order to recommend ways in which his or her use of vision can be enhanced or, if it cannot be enhanced, to recommend task modifications that will help him or her to be successful. Lighting, types of print materials, and availability of low vision aids are all taken into consideration for the functional vision assessment.

Some gaps in the eye care specialist's report may be filled in during the functional vision assessment. However, a basic diagnosis, a standard measurement of acuity and visual fields, and recommendations about eyeglasses and/or possible surgery remain in the domain of the eye care specialist. For this reason, it is extremely important that a reliable eye care specialist see each child who is blind or visually impaired. Teachers who are trained to work with students who are blind or visually impaired are not trained to diagnose eye diseases. Even the most skilled teacher may misinterpret the behaviors he or she observes if an accurate diagnosis is not available.

Sidebar 4.2 INFORMATION IN A FUNCTIONAL VISION REPORT

The following information is ideally included in the eye care report but may not be. It should be ascertained if not already available and included in the functional vision report.

- Print/symbol size that allows the student to sustain reading or viewing for a certain period of time from a specific distance.
- Contrast sensitivity.
- Color vision.
- Estimated field loss.
    - Functional use of peripheral and central vision.
    - Observation of head tilt used as an adaptation to position the visual target in the visual field.
- Light sensitivity.
    - Preferred lighting for reading.
    - Reaction to glare.
    - Use of vision in dimly lit areas.
- Identification of "crowded" symbols: how the student reads symbols of different sizes next to each other, such as letters in a word.
- Tracking ability: reading print on a line.
- Practical use of low vision devices such as magnifiers and monoculars in the student's natural environments.

The following information is usually not included in the eye care report but should be included in the functional visual assessment.

- Vision use in a variety of lighting situations, both indoors and out, including different lighting sources, different times of day, and different weather conditions.
- Reaction to changes in lighting, such as going from a dimly lit room to a bright playground or vice versa.
- Ability to identify colors in the student's natural environments, including identifying landmarks by color while walking; use of colors to identify objects.
- Vision use compared to use of other senses when exploring real objects, pictures or symbols, both near and distant.

(continued)

Sidebar 4.2   INFORMATION IN A FUNCTIONAL VISION REPORT *(continued)*

- Figure/ground discrimination.
- Fluctuation in vision and any patterns in the fluctuation.
- Usefulness of nonoptical low vision devices such as CCTV, computer modifications, reading stands.
- Postural concerns: types of furniture and aids that provide comfortable, supported posture while using vision for learning.
- Most beneficial type of learning media (print, braille and other tactile, auditory, or a combination).

The eye care specialist's report may not include the amount of detail the assessment team needs in order to make appropriate accommodations during the assessment. Sidebar 4.2 lists information that an eye care specialist may include in a report but which may need to be determined by a teacher of visually impaired students if it is not available in the eye care specialist's report. The teacher of visually impaired students assesses an individual student's functioning across environments.

The teacher of students who are visually impaired who is doing the functional vision assessment may benefit from some equipment designed for use by eye care specialists. Cards with continuous text in different sizes and in different fonts are helpful for determining which print size is optimal for sustained reading (several sizes larger than the smallest size visible to the student). Students can also use them to demonstrate the preferred distance at which they like to read material of various sizes. Different types of lighting, monoculars, and magnifiers may also be helpful for use during functional vision assessments. This equipment is available from the sources listed in the Resources for this chapter.

Sidebar 4.2 also lists information that eye care specialists typically do not include in their reports and that a teacher of students who are visually impaired or an O&M specialist will want to include

Elizabeth Hartmann

It is important to observe the student's vision use in a variety of settings.

in the functional vision assessment report. This information is offered to inform professionals who do not work with students who are blind or visually impaired on a regular basis about what information should be available from the professionals who do work in such programs. This description may also be helpful for teachers of students who are visually impaired and O&M specialists to keep in mind when they are doing a functional vision assessment.

Functional vision is most often assessed through observation rather than formal testing. Many checklists and kits are available that are helpful to remind the assessor of the information that needs to be included in the functional vision report. These often appear as part of guides to vision assessment. Some commonly used checklists and functional vision assessment kits, most of which include detailed information for their use, are listed in the Resources for this chapter.

SUMMARY

As seen in Chapter 3, "Preparation for Assessment," researching and observing visual functioning are only the starting points for assessment. Next, we will take a look at the whole child who is being assessed. The child is certainly more than his or her visual impairment, however intriguing it has been to determine his or her functional vision. The next element of assessment is an investigation of his or her educational needs, not only in the standard academic areas, but also in all areas in which a child who is blind or visually impaired might need teacher-guided experiences in order to succeed in becoming a responsible, independent adult.

REFERENCES

Corn, A. L., & Koenig, A. J. (1996). Perspectives on low vision. In Corn & Koenig (Eds.), *Foundations of low vision: Clinical and functional perspectives* (pp. 3–25). New York: AFB Press.

Anthony, T. L. (2000). Performing a functional low vision assessment. In F. M. D'Andrea & C. Farrenkopf (Eds.), *Looking to learn: Promoting literacy for students with low vision* (pp. 32–83). New York: AFB Press.

Jose, R. (1983). *Understanding low vision.* New York: American Foundation for the Blind.

Levack, N. (1991). *Low vision: A resource guide with adaptations for students with visual impairments.* Austin: Texas School for the Blind and Visually Impaired.

RESOURCES FOR VISION ASSESSMENT

In addition to the vision assessment tools listed here, many assessment tools for assessing orientation and mobility (O&M) skills have sections for assessing the use of vision for O&M. See Chapter 9, "Expanded Core Curriculum: Orientation and Mobility," for an annotated list of O&M assessment tools.

Assessment Tools for Infants, Toddlers, and Preschoolers

Children's Vision Concerns: Look Beyond the Eyes: "Functional Vision Assessment Checklist for Pre-verbal and Non-verbal Children"
Author: Harrell, L.
Ages: Infants and preschoolers
Publisher: L. Harrell Productions
      P.O. Box 2385
      Placerville, CA 95667
Date: 1993
Type of instrument: Checklist

Comments: Lois Harrell, a longtime counselor for parents with the Blind Babies Foundation in San Francisco, California, has compiled a checklist that is compact and includes the basic information teachers and parents want to know about how infants and toddlers function visually. Harrell describes how to conduct a functional vision assessment in order to complete the checklist. Her emphasis is on making the experience enjoyable.

First Look: Vision Evaluation and Assessment for Infants, Toddlers, and Preschoolers, Birth Through Five Years of Age

Ages: Birth through 5 years
Publisher: Early Education Unit
      Special Education Division
      California Department of
      Education Publications
      Division
      P.O. Box 271
      Sacramento, CA 95812
Date: 1988
Type of instrument: Checklist

Comments: Includes clear instructions about optimal conditions for assessing an infant's functional vision, good developmental guidelines, and well-structured questionnaires to be filled out by the assessor and the parents.

ISAVE: Individualized Systematic Assessment of Visual Efficiency
Author: Langley, B.
Ages: Infants, children, and young adults
Publisher: American Printing House
      for the Blind
      P.O. Box 6085
      Louisville, KY 40206
Date: 1998
Type of instrument: Checklist

Comments: *ISAVE* was developed to assess the functional vision of all infants and toddlers who are blind or visually impaired as well as the functional vision of children and young adults who have significant disabilities in addition to visual impairment. The kit includes materials for assessing functional vision and booklets of information about various aspects of functional vision, as well as protocols on which to record the findings. Acuity, visual discrimination, visual fields, and perceptual skills can all be assessed using *ISAVE*.

Oregon Project for Visually Impaired and Blind Preschool Children
Authors: Anderson, S., Boigon, S., and Davis, K.
Ages: Birth to 6 years
Publisher: Jackson County Education
Service District
101 North Grape Street
Medford, OR 97501
Date: 1991
Type of instrument: Checklist

Comments: A comprehensive assessment of the development of young children who are blind or visually impaired. It includes a section on functional vision assessment, and is designed to be used over a period of several years to note a child's development.

PAVII: Parents and Visually Impaired Infants—Identifying Vision Impairments in Infants: "Functional Vision Screening Checklist"
Authors: Chen, D., Friedman, C. T., and Calvello, G.
Ages: Birth to 3 years
Publisher: American Printing House
for the Blind
P.O. Box 6085
Louisville, KY 40206
Date: 1990
Type of instrument: Checklist

Comments: This screening tool for the functional vision of infants not only gives specific functional vision skills to watch for but also supplies the schedule on which these skills are typically achieved. The descriptions of visual

milestones are particularly helpful in understanding how an infant's vision develops.

Assessment Tools for School-Age Children and Young Adults

Diagnostic Assessment Procedure
Volume I of *Program to Develop Efficiency in Visual Functioning*
Author: Barraga, N.
Ages: 3 years to adult
Publisher: American Printing House
for the Blind
P.O. Box 6085
Louisville, KY 40206
Date: 1978
Type of instrument: Checklist with kit of assessment materials

Comments: Assesses functional vision and visual perception for students who are visually impaired. The six-page checklist of observations of children with low vision can be used to record observations of general visual behavior in natural settings for preschoolers, school age children, and young adults.

Functional Vision Assessment Form in Low Vision: A Resource Guide with Adaptations for Students with Visual Impairments
Author: Levack, N., Stone, G., & Bishop, V.
Ages: All
Publisher: Texas School for the Blind
and Visually Impaired
1100 West 45th St.
Austin, TX 78756
www.tsbvi.edu
Date: 1991
Type of instrument: Checklist

Comments: This tool includes space to record observations of the student engaged in any tasks using near, intermediate, and distance vision that the assessor considers relevant to the functional vision assessment. A series of questions follows the record sheets focused on behaviors showing the sensations, visual cognition/perception, and visual motor skills used by the student. Academic considerations and the ability to adjust to different environments visually are also included. Using this tool usually requires a longer period of time than a single assessment visit, but it can be effectively used as an initial functional vision assessment.

Functional Vision Assessment Instruments
Authors: Teachers in the Visually Impaired Division of Special Education
Grades: Preschool/kindergarten, elementary, secondary
Publisher: Los Angeles Unified School District
        Frances Blend School
        5210 W. Clinton St.
        Los Angeles, CA 90004
Date: 1988
Type of instruments: Checklists

Comments: A series of assessment instruments for preschool/kindergarten, elementary, secondary, and multiply disabled students. These instruments include space to report on information from eye care specialists as well as on observations in situations typical for students in the various categories. Areas observed include near vision, distance vision, and visual behaviors. The instruments are each approximately four pages long and can usually be completed

in one visit by an assessor. Accompanying the assessment instruments are report forms that can be filled out and presented to other teachers and to families.

ISAVE: Individualized Systematic Assessment of Visual Efficiency
Author: Langley, B.
Grades: All
Publisher: American Printing House
        for the Blind
        P.O. Box 6085
        Louisville, KY 40206
Date: 1998
Type of instrument: Checklists

Comments: *ISAVE* is described in the section on Assessment Tools for Infants, Toddlers, and Preschoolers.

Visual Functioning Assessment Tool
Authors: Byrnes, K., Pinkney, P., and Scheffers, W.
Grades: All
Publisher: Stoelting Company
        620 Wheat Lane
        Wood Dale, IL 60191.
Date: 1982
Type of instrument: Checklist

Comments: A thorough listing of possible situations in which a student would use vision. It begins with questions about the appearance of the eyes and continues through eye movements, depth perception, eye-hand coordination, eye-foot coordination, visual imitation and memory, concepts of self and objects in space, ability to interpret pictures, and various aspects of vision use for mobility. It includes methods for assessing visual perception as well. It is a lengthy checklist and is most practical as a continuing assessment tool.

Assessment Tools for Students who are Multiply Disabled

Children's Vision Concerns: Look Beyond the Eyes: "Functional Vision Assessment Checklist for Pre-verbal and Non-verbal Children"
Author: Harrell, L.
Ages: Birth to 3 years old
Publisher: L. Harrell Productions
        P.O. Box 2385
        Placerville, CA 95667
Date: 1993
Type of instrument: Checklist

Comments: This is a comprehensive and efficient checklist for recording observations of vision in children who do not give verbal responses. Harrell describes how to conduct a functional vision assessment in order to complete the checklist. Her emphasis is on making the experience enjoyable.

Functional and Instructional Scheme
Author: Nielsen, L.
Ages: Children functioning at 3 years or younger
Publisher: Available in the US from
        Vision Associates
        2109 US Hwy 90 West,
        Ste. 170 #312
        Lake City, FL 32055
        (407) 352-1200
        (386) 752-7839
        www.visionkits.com
Date: 1990
Type of instrument: Checklist

Comments: Nielsen, a Danish educator, has developed the "active learning"

tools for working with children with cortical visual impairment. This comprehensive tool can be used for continuing assessment.

Functional Vision Assessment Instruments
Authors: Teachers from The Visually Impaired Division of Special Education
Ages: 3 to young adult
Publisher: Los Angeles Unified School
        District
        5210 W. Clinton St.
        Los Angeles, CA 90004
Date: 1988, revised 2002
Type of instrument: Checklists

Comments: *Functional Vision Assessment Instruments* are described in the section on Assessment Tools for School Age Children and Young Adults.

Visual Functioning Assessment Tool
Authors: Byrnes, K., Pinkney, P., and Scheffers, W.
Ages: 3 to adult
Publisher: Stoelting Company
        620 Wheat Lane
        Wood Dale, IL 60191
Date: 1982
Type of Instrument: Checklist

Comments: *Visual Functioning Assessment Tool* is described in the section on Assessment Tools for School Age Children and Young Adults.

Assessment Tools of Visual Perception Skills

Tests of visual perception skills are included in this section even though they are not all designed specifically for use with children who are visually impaired. These tests reflect brain function more than functional vision, but they can also reveal how the student being assessed uses vision. It is important to discuss the results with the entire assessment team, making sure to include the school psychologist, the teacher of students who are visually impaired and the O&M specialist.

Developmental Test of Visual-Motor Integration, Fourth Edition
Authors: Beery, K. E., and Buktenica, N. A.
Ages: 3 to adult
Publisher: Modern Curriculum Press
P.O. Box 480
Parsippany, NJ 07054
Date: 1997
Type of instrument: Normative referenced

Comments: Children from ages 3 to 18 are asked to copy geometric figures of increasing difficulty. A short form is available to be used with children from 3 to 7 (18 items), and a complete version for use with ages 3 to adult (27 items). This test has the reputation of being well researched and culturally unbiased.

Developmental Test of Visual Perception, Second Edition (DTVP-2)
Authors: Hammill, D. D., Pearson, N. A., and Voress, J. K.
Ages: 4 to 10 years
Publisher: ProEd
8700 Shoal Creek Blvd.
Austin, TX 78757
Date: 1993
Type of instrument: Normative referenced

Comments: A revision of Frostig's original test of the same name, which has been widely used. It tests eye-hand coordination, copying, spatial relations, position in space, figure-ground differentiation, visual closure, visual-motor speed, and form constancy.

Diagnostic Assessment Procedure, Vol. I of *Program to Develop Efficiency in Visual Functioning*
Author: Barraga, N.
Ages: 3 years to adult
Publisher: American Printing House for the Blind
P.O. Box 6085
Louisville, KY 40206
Date: 1978
Type of instrument: Checklist with kit of materials for assessment

Comments: See description under Assessment Tools for School-Age Children and Young Adults. The full kit includes materials for assessing the use of vision by children under 6 years of age and a booklet of visual challenges to assess older children's use of vision. It also includes Low Vision Observation Checklist, which is useful for recording visual behavior and the attitude toward visual impairment of the child being assessed.

Test of Visual-Perceptual Skills (non-motor) (TVPS) and TVPS, Upper Level
Author: Gardner, M. F.
Ages: 4 to 13 years (TVPS) and 13 to 17 years (TVPS, Upper Level)
Publisher: Psychological and Educational Publications, Inc.
P.O. Box 520
Hydesville, CA 95547
Date: 1996

Type of instrument: Normative referrenced

Comments: These tests present a series of visual stimuli on printed pages of booklets that make their own book stands. They reveal information about students' strengths and weaknesses in the use of vision and require only that a student point to the appropriate answer. Areas tested are visual discrimination, visual memory, visual-spatial relationships, visual form constancy, visual sequential memory, visual figure-ground differentiation, and visual closure.

Visual Functioning Assessment Tool
Authors: Bynes, K., Pinkney, P., and Scheffers, W.
Ages: 3 to adult
Publisher: Stoelting Company
        620 Wheat Lane
        Wood Dale, IL 60191.
Date: 1982
Type of instrument: Checklist

Comments: *Visual Functioning Assessment Tool* has sections for assessing visual perception, as well as visual functioning. As mentioned earlier, it is best used as an on-going assessment tool.

Sources of Equipment for Vision Assessment

Vision Associates
2109 US Hwy 90 West, Ste. 70 #312
Lake City, FL 32055

Comments: Vision Associates sells kits of equipment for vision assessments as well as individual pieces of equipment. The kits include tips on how best to use the various types of equipment. Vision Associates recommends that some of the equipment it sells be used by eye care professionals rather than teachers.

Lighthouse International
111 E. 59th St.
New York, NY 10022
Phone: (212) 821-9200
        (800) 829-0500
TTY: (212) 821-9713
www.lighthouse.org
E-mail: info@lighthouse.org

Comments: The Lighthouse International Professional Products Catalog includes many types of low vision aids as well as testing materials such as eye charts, color vision tests, and continuous text reading cards.

Expanded Core Curriculum: Education

Lizbeth A. Barclay

IN THIS CHAPTER:

- The origin and importance of the expanded core curriculum

- Assessment and the expanded core curriculum

- The expanded core curriculum and sensory motor skills

- Assessment and the core curriculum

- Modes of assessment

- Learning media assessment and collaboration

- Students with severe multiple impairments and the expanded core curriculum

It is only through collaboration that teachers and specialists can skillfully and efficiently assess all areas of the expanded core curriculum that are appropriate for their student. This chapter discusses educational assessment, using the expanded core curriculum as its foundation. The areas of technology and orientation and mobility (O&M), which are within the expanded core curriculum, will be discussed in greater detail in Chapters 8 and 9.

THE ORIGIN AND IMPORTANCE OF THE EXPANDED CORE CURRICULUM

In a 1955 letter to Kathern Gruber, Helen Keller wrote, "True teaching cannot be learned from text-books any more than a surgeon can acquire his skill by reading about surgery" (Keller, 2000, p. 44). Most educators in the field of visual impairment today would strongly agree with Helen Keller. While many of the students whom they teach are indeed in academic programs where they are spending a great deal of time with their textbooks in hand, these same students require hands-on experience and active participation in the activities of living to reinforce and solidify their understanding. Many students who are blind or visually impaired and have additional disabilities require an experienced-based program even more, in order to facilitate their concept development and skill development in the critical skills that will lead to independence (Chen & Dote-Kwan, 1995).

As Hatlen (1996) wrote, "There are experiences and concepts casually and incidentally learned by sighted students that must be systematically and sequentially taught to the visually impaired student. The core curriculum for visually impaired students is not the same as for sighted students. Indeed, it is much larger and more complex." Consequently, the area of educational assessment for students who are blind or visually impaired is broad and far-reaching.

What is the appropriate curriculum for students who are blind or visually impaired? In the field of education of students who are visually impaired, a strongly held conviction is that their course of study must include much more than what is considered the core curriculum for sighted students in public schools. The core curriculum consists of the knowledge and skills expected to be learned by a student by the time he or she graduates from high school. Educators generally agree that the core curriculum, or general course of study, for children in public schools includes English language arts, other languages to the extent possible, mathematics, health, social studies, economics, fine arts, science, physical education, history, business education, and vocational education. However, awareness that a curriculum for students who are visually impaired must be much broader than the standard core curriculum was formalized only fairly recently.

In 1993, at an annual meeting at the American Printing House for the Blind, educators began discussing the formulation of priorities for improving educational programming for children with visual impairment. As noted in Chapter 2, this discussion eventually led to what was to become the *National Agenda for the Education of Children and Youths with Visual Impairments, Including Those with Multiple Disabilities* (1995). From that movement, came "The Core Curriculum for Blind and Visually Impaired Students, Including those with Additional Disabilities," which was described by Phil Hatlen (1996), and was then later referred to as simply the expanded core curriculum. The U.S. Department of Education, Office of Special Education and Rehabilitative Services (OSERS, 2000) provided policy guidance for educators in implementing the Individuals with Disabilities Education Act (IDEA). The guidelines specifically address the importance of meeting the unique needs of students who are visually impaired, especially in such areas as braille instruction, O&M, and assistive technology, and include the following language supporting the inclusion of the concept of an expanded core curriculum:

Additional Factors in IEP Development
The following needs also may need to be considered and appropriately addressed by the child's IEP team to ensure a child's appropriate access to the general curriculum:

- Compensatory skills, such as communication and listening modalities;
- Extended school year services, if determined necessary to provide FAPE (free appropriate public education) to the student; social interaction skills; recreation and leisure skills; career education; and for students with low vision, visual efficiency skills. (OSERS, 2000)

Children in academic programs who are blind or visually impaired receive assessment and instruction in all areas of the core curriculum along with their sighted peers. The expanded core curriculum, or the curriculum accepted by educators in the field of visual impairment, is optimal and necessary. The areas of the expanded core curriculum cover the unique disability-specific skills that students who are visually impaired need to live independently and productively. The skill areas include compensatory or functional academic skills and communication modes, O&M skills, social interaction skills, recreation and leisure skills, career education, technology, and visual efficiency skills (Hatlen, 1996).

ASSESSMENT AND THE EXPANDED CORE CURRICULUM

The questions posed at the beginning of an assessment often have to do primarily with a student's academic performance. Caregivers and teachers are concerned about their students' ability to progress with their sighted peers in school and ask questions such as, "How can Sarah reach her full academic potential?" and "What is Michael's learning style?" While these questions seemingly refer to progress within the core curriculum, it is through the expanded core curriculum that these questions can be most successfully approached and answered. For a student who is blind or visually impaired, the expanded core curriculum will bridge the gap to allow him or her full access to the core curriculum if that is appropriate. The expanded core curriculum will provide the necessary skills for a student's eventual independence and quality of life.

Although the questions referring to academic success are important, those regarding the unique educational needs of students who are blind or visually impaired must also be answered. A student may be successful in the core curriculum areas of reading and math but not possess the social skills necessary to make and maintain friendships in school, or succeed socially in the workplace. If that same student has not, for instance, learned basic hygiene skills, he or she will not be able to maintain a job. The ability to travel independently to the grocery store, to work, or to visit a friend will have a long-term effect on a person's quality of life. These are just a few examples that illustrate the eventual impact and importance of the expanded core curriculum. Sidebar 5.1 lists examples of specific

Compensatory or Functional Academic Skills, Including Communication Modes

- Concept development
- Listening and speaking skills
- Study and organizational skills
- Adaptations for gaining access to areas of the core curriculum
- Braille reading and writing
- Use of large print
- Use of print with optical devices
- Communication modes for students with additional disabilities (such as tactile symbols, a calendar system, sign language, and recorded materials)

Social Interaction Skills

- Socialization
- Affective education
- Knowledge of human sexuality
- Knowledge of visual impairment

O&M Skills

- Understanding physical environment and space
- Orientation to different environments
- Ability to travel in school and community environments
- Opportunities for unrestricted independent movement and play

Daily Living Skills

- Personal hygiene
- Dressing
- Housekeeping
- Food preparation
- Eating
- Money management

(continued on next page)

- Telephone
- Time
- Personal organization

Recreation and Leisure Skills

- Competitive sports (e.g., bowling; goalball, an adapted soccer-like game using a ball with auditory signal; marathon running)
- Noncompetitive sports (e.g., swimming, jogging)
- Hobbies
- Choosing recreational activities

Career/Vocational Skills

- Awareness
- Exploration
- Preparation
- Participation
- Prevocational skills (work habits, attitudes, motivation)
- Vocational interests

Technology

- Keyboarding skills
- Braille access devices
- Visual assistive software and devices
- Auditory assistive software and devices
- Choosing appropriate options
- Device maintenance and troubleshooting

Visual Efficiency Skills

- Use of nonoptical low vision devices
- Use of optical low vision devices
- Use of a combination of senses
- Use of environmental cues and modifications
- Recognizing when not to use vision

Source: Adapted from J. Hazekamp, *Program Guidelines for Students Who Are Visually Impaired* (Sacramento: California Department of Education, 1997).

Frances K. Liefert

The expanded core curriculum provides for practice in the skills necessary for the students' ultimate independence and quality of life.

skill areas within the general domains of the expanded core curriculum to be considered for assessment.

When viewed in detail, many aspects of the expanded core curriculum may seem developmentally inappropriate for some students who have additional disabilities. But when approached by looking at the general skill domains, the areas lend themselves easily to areas of assessment for students of all development levels.

SENSORY MOTOR SKILLS AND THE EXPANDED CORE CURRICULUM

Growing up without vision, or with incomplete or confusing visual information and perception, puts a child at risk for delays in his or her meaningful organization of environmental information (Strickling, 1998). The delay in this organization can affect the acquisition of motor skills. In the *Program Guidelines for Students Who Are Visually Impaired*, Hazekamp (1997) states, "A visual impairment may affect one's gross and fine motor skills; alternative sensory discrimination and sensory integration skills; and abilities to develop appropriate posture, balance, strength, and movement."

Although the area of sensory motor skills is not included in the expanded core curriculum, it should be kept in mind when assessing all areas of the curriculum because of its impact on the ability to develop all other skills. If it is suspected that a student has sensory motor delays, assessment of sensory motor skills by an occupational or physical therapist is recommended.

Delays or disturbances in sensory motor skills can have a profound impact on skill development in all areas of the expanded core curriculum. Examples of that impact are listed in Sidebar 5.2.

Students who have other disabilities in addition to visual impairment are at even greater risk for delays in the area of sensory motor skills. Neurological impairment and cerebral palsy (CP) that can result from the effects of extreme prematurity are frequent among students who are visually impaired (Rosen, 1998). Children with CP have motor impairment that affects many possible areas of motor development. When working with a child who has motor impairment due to neurologic damage, it is imperative that his or her sensory motor skills be specifically assessed by an occupational therapist or a physical therapist. Chapter 9 provides detailed information on sensory-motor integration.

ASSESSMENT AND THE CORE CURRICULUM: BUILDING THE BRIDGE

With an increasing emphasis on implementing standards and accountability in schools, children who are blind or visually impaired and are in mainstream programs usually undergo standardized testing along with their sighted peers. While this type of testing within the core curriculum yields a certain type of information—the student's level of academic achievement—it does not provide other

Sidebar 5.2   EFFECTS OF DELAYS IN SENSORY MOTOR SKILLS ON AREAS OF THE EXPANDED CORE CURRICULUM

The following are some examples of how delays in sensory motor skill development affect the various compensatory academic skills, including communication modes, included in the expanded core curriculum:

- Delays in motor skills and/or sensory integration will affect a student's progress in concept development. In addition, tactile and fine motor abilities play a very important role in braille reading.

- Social interaction skills: A student's ability to interact socially is affected by his or her ability to independently move and organize sensory information.

- Recreation and leisure skills: The development of many skills of recreation and leisure is dependent on the ability to tolerate activities and the development of fine and gross motor skills.

- Use of assistive technology: A student's ability to access assistive technology relies on the development of a certain level of fine motor skills and the ability to organize sensory information.

- O&M: Gross motor skills and sensory integration play a crucial role in the student's ultimate success in purposeful and knowledgeable movement through space.

- Independent living skills: The ability to perform independently acts of personal hygiene, dressing, eating, and food preparation all depend on fine and gross motor abilities, as well as the ability to tolerate and discriminate tactilely.

- Career education: Success in vocational and career choices is contingent on all the previously mentioned areas of the expanded core curriculum, which depend on development of sensory motor skills.

- Visual efficiency skills: Use of low vision aids requires a certain level of fine motor skills, as well as the organization of sensory information.

essential information: What type of learner is this student? What is his or her level of academic independence? What adaptations are necessary to help him or her increase achievement? To obtain this information, teachers and specialists must often further assess areas of the core curriculum, while gathering information about skills in the expanded core curriculum. For instance, a student's style or ability in braille reading (included among the compensatory or functional academic skills, including communication modes) is optimally assessed during reading assessment. Reading is part of the core curriculum, and it is impossible to assess braille reading thoroughly without assessing reading fluency and comprehension, which are considered to be within the core curriculum, in addition to knowledge of the code.

As mentioned in Chapter 1, for students who are blind or visually impaired and may have a learning disability, this is particularly important. Teachers and specialists will look carefully at the core curriculum areas of reading, writing, and mathematics in conjunction with assessment of the expanded core curriculum in order to understand better the student's learning style, level of independence, and adaptive skills when learning in those academic areas. Sidebar 5.3 lists factors to consider when assessing areas of the core curriculum.

Tools for assessing the core curriculum areas of literacy skills and mathematics can be found in the Resources section for this chapter.

ASSESSMENT METHODS

IDEA states, "A variety of assessment tools and strategies are used to gather relevant functional and developmental information about the child, including information provided by the parent, and information related to enabling the child to be involved in and progress in the general curriculum (or for a preschool child, to participate in appropriate activities)" (Sec. 614). The ways in which assessment information is gathered can be as varied as the students being evaluated. Various assessment techniques have been thoroughly described by Bradley-Johnson (1994), Lewis and Russo (1998), and Brown and Silberman (1998). This chapter highlights and discusses three of the most common modes of assessment—formal testing, performance assessment, observation—and how they can be used collaboratively. Chapter 11 illustrates their combined use within a case study. An example of a student's educational assessment—that of a young girl named Rosy—is presented in Appendix 5.1.

- Can the information required for a complete assessment be obtained from the standard school assessments?

For instance, in the area of literacy skills, a typical standardized reading assessment that is administered in elementary school, will yield valuable information about a student's reading skills in comparison to his or her classmates, but it will not reveal specific strengths and weaknesses with regard to a student's compensatory skills while reading braille or large print, nor will it provide an assessor with all the necesssary information if that student is suspected of having a learning disability. Further testing in the core curriculum area of reading will be necessary.

Conversely, it is important to carefully review a student's academic records to ensure that they are not over-tested. If adequate information about a student's progress in the core curriculum *can* be obtained from the standardized testing results, it is not necessary to test in those areas.

- Does the assessment reveal information about a student's learning style?

Students who have been given standardized academic assessments with their classmates will have the scores from those assessments in their records. However, administering a comprehensive academic assessment such as *KeyMath Revised: A Diagnostic Inventory of Essential Mathematics*, will allow an assessor to gain information about the student's learning style. For instance, the assessor will learn about the student's approach to using tactile graphics if he or she is a braille user, or ability to interpret a variety of print formats and graphics if he or she uses print. He or she will also observe the student's abilities in problem solving, or in tasks involving spatial abilities, utilizing rote memory skills, and many other aspects of learning style.

- If a standardized instrument is used, when adapted, the test should be used cautiously.

Caveats regarding the test's lack of true validity should be included in any report. The standardized assessment tool can be repeated in the future to document growth of skills over time.

- Test results should be interpreted together with the results of a variety of other assessment modes.

Formal Testing

Norm-Referenced Tests

Standardized tests or norm-referenced assessments are formal tests. Standardized tests must be administered and scored in a precise manner that is described by each test publisher. As defined and described by Lewis and Russo (1998), they are formal testing instruments that have been field-tested so that standards of performance are statistically established. The standards are established during test development when the test is administered to a large group of individuals, known as the normative group. The normative group is selected because of their similarity to the group of students for whom the test is designed. Normative groups rarely include students with disabilities and, consequently, norm-referenced tests should be used and interpreted with great caution when used to assess students who are visually impaired. The use of norm-referenced tests with students who are visually impaired is also discussed in Chapter 6. When used and interpreted carefully and when the same assessment instruments are used and the information is compared, norm-referenced testing can be particularly helpful for gathering information about a student's level of functioning and his or her progress in development over time. Therefore, collaboration among teachers and specialists becomes crucial when using standardized instruments.

An example of a norm-referenced test commonly administered to students with and without disabilities during educational assessment is the *KeyMath Revised, A Diagnostic Inventory of Essential Mathematics* (see the Resources section of this chapter for more information). The students in the normative sample for *KeyMath Revised* were chosen to represent a cross-section of variables that included gender, race/ethnicity, geographic region, parental education, and educational placement. "The demographic information was based upon the 1994 Current Population Survey distributed in raw-data form by the Bureau of the Census and targets for educational placement were set according to the Seventeenth Annual Report to Congress on the Implementation of the Individuals with Disabilities Education Act" (Connolly, 1998). While this implies that students with disabilities were included in the norm sample, it can be assumed that this assessment was designed for a broad range of students within the general elementary school population. Yet, when administered with care to some students who are visually impaired in academic programs, not only will information be gleaned about the students' skill levels in a variety of areas of mathematics, but the assessment may also give many clues to how a student learns. During the process of administering the *KeyMath Revised*, an assessor can gain information about a student's reasoning skills, tactile skills when using tactile graphics (if the student's primary learning medium is braille), ability to interpret graphics (either visually or tactilely), ability to apply functional math concepts, spatial abilities in math, and interpretation of word problems (language comprehension). When the *KeyMath Revised* is used during the next educational assessment, a student's progress and skill development over time can be measured.

Psychologists and speech and language pathologists commonly use standardized tests during assessment. Because each student who is blind or visually impaired is unique in his or her visual and learning requirements, collaboration between the teacher of visually impaired students and other specialists is crucial, both prior to and during assessment. This will ensure that the assessment tool being considered is appropriate for the student, and will allow input about environmental modifications that will ensure complete access to the assessment information. Information about specific tests commonly used by these specialists and specific considerations when using standardized testing can be found in Chapters 6 and 7. Sidebar 5.4 lists a series of questions that the collaborating members of the assessment team will want to consider when using standardized instruments.

Criterion-Referenced Testing

Criterion-referenced tests are commonly used with students who are blind or visually impaired to assess what they can do in both academic and functional skills areas. For that reason they are a valuable way for parents, teachers, and specialists to examine a child's skill levels and progress over time. Like norm-referenced tests,

---

Sidebar 5.4   QUESTIONS TO CONSIDER WHEN USING STANDARDIZED INSTRUMENTS

Prior to the Assessment

- Is the instrument accessible to the student?
- Is the testing environment modified specifically to meet the needs of the student?

When Analyzing Results

- What information does this test give about the student's learning style?
- What information provided by this test reflects the student's aptitude and not his or her disability?
- How has the student's understanding of concepts, which may be inaccurate because of visual impairment, interfered with his or her performance on certain test items?
- What developmental growth has the test documented as having taken place over time?
- How does the information about a student's developmental level obtained from a standardized assessment compare with that obtained from assessments by other specialists and to the student's performance in nonstandardized forms of assessment?

---

they are standardized, but rather than based upon the performance of a normative group, criteria for passing is based upon performance of a curricular goal which is considered a benchmark. Unlike norm-referenced tests they can be adapted so that the reading medium, pictures and objects can be altered to meet the individual needs of the student.

An example of a criterion-referenced test is a reading inventory. Use of a reading inventory allows the skills a child has mastered—such as reading fluency, speed, and comprehension—to be assessed, while the assessor observes such areas as the student's tactile approach if he or she is a braille reader, or the student's level of visual skills and stamina if he or she reads print.

Another example of a criterion referenced test is the *Oregon Project* (described more fully in the Resources section of this

---

Sidebar 5.5   QUESTIONS TO CONSIDER WHEN USING CRITERION-REFERENCED TESTS

- What adaptations to materials made it possible for the student to perform the skill?
- How does time influence the student's ability to perform the skill?
- How does the information from the criterion-referenced test compare with the information gathered through standardized testing and performance assessment?

---

chapter). The *Oregon Project* is an assessment and curriculum designed for use with students who are visually impaired. Its skills inventory contains eight developmental areas including skills that have been developmentally sequenced and arranged in age-related categories. By using this type of assessment over time, parents or other caretakers and educators can track a student's progress in development and use the curriculum as a resource for instruction. A list of questions the assessment team members may wish to consider when using criterion-referenced tests is found in Sidebar 5.5.

Performance Assessment

Most special education teachers routinely use performance assessment in the individualized education program (IEP) planning process as they document, through description, the students' progress in many skills and tasks. In this process, also referred to as authentic assessment, the student is required to demonstrate a specified skill within a routine environment, such as demonstrating O&M skills while shopping for groceries at his or her neighborhood store.

Portfolio assessment is another type of performance assessment by which students' work samples are collected and progress of their work executed over time is evaluated. Such concrete examples of a student's work are valuable artifacts that can lead to meaningful and appropriate curriculum planning.

Elizabeth Hartmann

As this student performs her job, all aspects of her skill development are noted in a performance-based assessment.

Performance assessment is very closely linked to diagnostic teaching. Diagnostic teaching combines assessment and instruction, and is guided by the following principles (Koenig and Holbrook, 1989, p. 15):

- Instruction and assessment cannot be separated in effective teaching.
- Students learn and develop as individuals, not as a group.
- Information gathered from assessment should be used immediately to change instruction in order to make learning more efficient.
- Systematic problem-solving techniques can be used to explore areas in a student's development that are unknown.

By engaging in the process of diagnostic teaching while using performance-based assessment, the assessment team gains information that can be immediately utilized to develop appropriate teaching

---

Sidebar 5.6   QUESTIONS TO CONSIDER WHEN USING PERFORMANCE ASSESSMENT

- How do the student's performance work samples vary within the different domains of home, school, and community?
- Do the performance work samples demonstrate progress in skill development?
- What adaptations can be made to increase the student's skill development?
- What common language and routine components should be utilized by everyone who will assess and later teach this skill?
- Is it necessary for everyone to use the same language and routine components in order for the skill to be performed successfully or can it be performed under any circumstances?

---

strategies and adaptations. Through this partnership, assessment and teaching are effectively linked. Sidebar 5.6 lists some questions that assessment team members will want to consider when using performance-based assessment.

Observation

As mentioned in previous chapters, observation is a powerful way to obtain assessment information. Observation can take place at the student's home, school, or in the community. It can take place during ordinary routines that occur throughout the student's day or within functional routines that can be orchestrated by teachers or specialists for the purpose of diagnostic teaching.

By observing a student during a functional activity that he or she performs daily, with or without assistance—such as dressing, eating, or preparing breakfast—information can be obtained about:

- Level of independence in the skills observed
- Level of communication during the activity (often a student's highest level of communication)
- Adaptations that will be helpful

- Motor skills that affect the performance of tasks
- Environmental factors that affect the performance of a task

When observing a student, it is helpful to take notes about each aspect of what is occurring, noting the child's verbal response, level of necessary assistance, adaptations, environmental factors (such as whether the television is on while student is dressing), motor issues, and any other pertinent factors. It is sometimes helpful to use a checklist during observation of a student such as those found in the curriculum *Independent Living* from the Texas School for the Blind and Visually Impaired (see the Resources section of this chapter for more information on these and other assessment tools).

When observing in the student's classroom, information will be gathered to use both in preparation for the assessment (see Chapter 3) and as part of the assessment process. Time spent simply observing a student in his or her classroom can reveal the following information that can be valuable to all assessors:

- How all materials and information can be adapted and made accessible
- The student's level of reading fluency within mainstream activities
- The level of the student's independence and proficiency while handling curriculum materials
- The level of the student's personal academic organization
- The student's posture: balance and physical support during learning activities
- The level of the student's participation in his or her class
- The level of the student's independence and proficiency while performing personal tasks such as going to the restroom or putting on a jacket
- The quality of the student's social interactions
- How the student participates and interacts during small and large group activities
- The student's level of assertiveness or passivity within the class
- How the student handles transition times

- The student's level of independent travel within the classroom and school building or campus
- The student's skill level in utilizing technology

Observation of a student in community-based activities can also provide rich information. A student who has difficulties in academic subjects may possess skills of social competence while in the community that enables him or her to excel while negotiating a familiar environment. The O&M specialist may observe this regularly during lessons in a variety of community environments. Observation of students in the community may also be pertinent when they participate in community-based or vocational programs. Examples of skills that may be observed in the community include:

- The quality of social interaction between the student and members of the community
- The level of independence during travel within the community
- Evidence of the understanding of safe conduct within the community
- Evidence of an understanding of different occupations within the community

LEARNING MEDIA ASSESSMENT AND COLLABORATION

Helen Keller wrote in her 1929 autobiography *Midstream*, "More than any other time, when I hold a beloved book in my hand my limitations fall from me, my spirit is free" (Keller, 2000, p. 47). Her words resonate with a heartfelt passion that characterizes the spirit of educators, parents and other caregivers as they strive to ensure that their students learn to read and write. Students who are visually impaired range widely in ability and so their level and style of learning will likewise be extremely diverse and individual. Although reading and writing are usually included in learning media assessment, considering this diversity of students, other ways of learning and taking in information should also be included. Learning media assessment not only means determining if a student will learn to read via instruction in braille, print or large print, it also includes the exploration of learning media for students who will primarily use objects or pictures for their communication and calendar systems.

Koenig and Holbrook (1993) define learning media assessment as "an objective process of systematically selecting learning and literacy media for students with visual impairments. This assessment process guides the educational team in making deliberate and informed decisions on the total range of instructional media needed to facilitate learning for students with visual impairments." The key words in Koenig and Holbrook's definition are "total range of instructional media."

When examining a student's learning style through assessment, it is usually found that although a student has a primary or preferred sensory channel, the student uses more than one sensory channel during learning and may change his primary learning media over time, or, use different types of learning media from task to task, depending on the type of task. This means that learning media assessment is a long-term and continuous process. While many of the components of learning media assessment can take place during a comprehensive educational assessment, observational information about a child's use of sensory channels and how they use various types of learning media must be gathered over time and through diagnostic teaching. Students who rely primarily on touch and listening to gather information will be candidates for a braille reading program that provides primarily tactile and auditory modes of learning. Students who use their vision efficiently while completing tasks at near distances will probably be candidates for a program that utilizes print, either with or without enlargement, and/or pictures. Assessment tools that are helpful in gathering information about learning media assessment are found in the Resources section of this chapter.

Learning media assessment is included within the expanded core curriculum's area of compensatory or functional academic skills, including communication modes. Learning media assessment includes not only the use of vision- and reading-specific assessments

Frances K. Liefert

Ongoing learning media assessment ensures that students will have access to their optimal learning tools, using appropriate types of learning media for particular tasks.

and checklists, but also continuing diagnostic teaching, observation of the student at home and in the classroom, and discussion among parents, teachers, and specialists. All of these yield important information that contributes to understanding a specific student's learning media requirements and learning style. It is usually considered one of the specialized areas of assessment carried out by the teacher of students who are visually impaired. However, collaboration with all members of the assessment team allows for a holistic learning media assessment. The following sections detail how specific members of the assessment team contribute to a complete learning media assessment.

Parents and Caregivers

At home, parents and caregivers are the best observers of a student's use of sensory modalities. Their perspective about a student's tactile, visual, or auditory approach to a variety of tasks, both academic and functional, can give many clues about the student's primary learning medium.

Classroom Teacher

The classroom teacher can provide information about the student's approach to the wide array of learning tasks that take place daily within the classroom. This might include information on the choices of reading medium a student makes for different types of assignments, his or her level of participation during group reading, or the sensory modality a student appears to use predominantly while engaged in a cooking activity.

Orientation & Mobility (O&M) Specialist

The O&M specialist can provide information about the student's use of functional vision, concept development, motor skills, and general knowledge, all of which play important roles in learning media selection.

Psychologist

Information about the student's cognitive skills, especially comparative strength in sensory perception and learning style, can be provided by the psychologist.

Speech and Language Pathologist

Receptive and expressive language and concept development are all key components in a student's choice of learning media. The speech and language pathologist will be a rich source of information in these areas.

Occupational Therapist

The occupational therapist will provide information about a child's motor development that is pertinent to his or her selection of learning media. For instance, if braille reading is being considered for a child with cerebral palsy, fine motor abilities and tone will be important areas for assessment by the occupational therapist.

STUDENTS WITH SEVERE MULTIPLE IMPAIRMENTS AND THE EXPANDED CORE CURRICULUM

Assessment of the student who has severe multiple impairments raises many questions for the assessment team. Individual team members may face the following questions: How can I assess a student who does not indicate any awareness that I am there? How can the team assess a nonambulatory student who has no expressive communication skills? How can I assess a student who is asleep most of the time? What and how will I teach this student? Sometimes in light of issues of quality of life for these students, the expanded core curriculum may seem irrelevant, and yet, when used as a framework for collaborative assessment, it addresses those issues.

The students who have severe multiple impairments are diverse, but for the purposes of clarification here, they are students whose neurological development includes severe cognitive delay and sensory impairment. They also may have difficulty obtaining information from visual and auditory modes. They are students who may have severe motor impairment and who often have significant impairment in their ability to organize all sensory information. While some students who have multiple impairments may be learning a vast array of daily living, functional academic and community skills, others whose multiple impairments are more severe will be learning how to respond to the environment, people and objects. While assessment of these students is challenging, much information can be obtained through careful evaluation. Through close collaboration, teachers and specialists can work together to design an assessment plan to address the following concerns (Mar, 1996):

- What procedures best support this student's learning?
- What strategies or materials promote the student's attention or motivation?
- How can the student use multisensory information to approach new tasks?
- How is information best communicated to this student?
- What factors contribute to the student's problem behaviors?
- What assistive devices would enhance his or her classroom performance?
- Is the student able to associate specific meaning with communication?
- To what degree does the student understand and take part in various work and self-care routines?
- What adaptations will enhance social interests and interactions?

When assessing a student whose multiple disabilities are profound, emphasis will be focused upon discerning the optimal conditions under which that student can learn. Learning can only take place when a student's biobehavioral states are understood. According to Levack and Smith (1996), biobehavioral state refers to a student's state of arousal or readiness to receive information, which is dependent upon biological and behavioral influences. Biological influences include hunger, tiredness, comfort, and health; behavioral influences include emotions, interest, and environmental events.

In light of these factors, how do educators incorporate the areas of the expanded core curriculum into the assessment plan? While no individual teacher or specialist will assess all areas of the expanded core curriculum, collectively the assessment team will probably assess all areas. The following examples of how different areas of the expanded core curriculum might be assessed illustrate the absolute necessity of the team approach.

Compensatory Academic Skills, Including Communication Modes

With input from the parent, classroom teacher, and other specialists, the speech and language pathologist may assess communication and communication strategies and systems. Close collaboration with the family will facilitate understanding of the discrete behaviors that may constitute a student's communication.

The parent, teachers, and specialists will assess a student's understanding of concepts within natural contexts. Observing students during functional activities, such as dressing or eating, will yield information about any level of understanding of concepts as they are used within the natural context.

Social Interaction Skills

The classroom teacher and teacher of students who are visually impaired may assess the student's level of response to different people in the school setting. They may work together with parents and caregivers to ensure that the student's social and emotional needs are being met.

Recreation and Leisure Skills

Parents, teachers, and specialists will report on movement, touch, or sound that the student finds pleasurable. Such information as whether the student responds positively to music, water play, or motion will have significance when choosing recreational activities for him or her.

Use of Assistive Technology

The technology specialist will work closely with the parents, speech and language pathologist, and other teachers and specialists to assess the student's ability to use assistive technology for communication or inclusion in activities. The team will work with the technology specialist by providing data on choice options and the subtle means that the student may currently use to indicate preference.

Orientation and Mobility

Together with the occupational therapist and/or physical therapist, the O&M specialist will assess the student's sensory motor skills and purposeful movement.

Independent Living Skills

Parents, teachers, and specialists will assess and report on all levels of participation and/or independence in activities of daily living. The speech and language specialist and O&M specialist may lead the team in a consistent approach of pairing language with movement to teach and reinforce specified concepts during acts of hygiene, dressing, eating, and food preparation. The technology specialist will help determine how assistive technology can be incorporated into daily living skills, such as food preparation.

Visual Efficiency Skills

Functional vision assessment will involve collaboration among the parents, teacher of students who are visually impaired, O&M specialist, classroom teachers, and the occupational therapist. The focus will be on understanding the conditions that create an optimal visual environment for the student, while assessing his or her biobehavioral state. The occupational and/or physical therapist may be especially helpful in assessing the best possible positioning strategies that will provide balance to facilitate the student's maximum use of vision.

Career Education

While this is sometimes an area not considered for students with severe multiple impairments, the transition issues associated with determining future environments certainly are. Questions regarding future environments should be considered by parents and caregivers, as the needs, preferences, and abilities of their students change over time. It is through the team approach that the future environment options will be thoroughly explored.

The Resources section of this chapter provides further information and tools for assessing children with severe multiple disabilities.

SUMMARY

The expanded core curriculum, which was designed to meet the basic educational needs of students who are blind or visually impaired, is the menu for educators to use when planning an assessment. It not only provides students who are visually impaired with access to the core curriculum but it also builds the skills necessary for eventual independence and increased quality of life. A variety of assessment modes and tools can be used when assessing the areas of the expanded core curriculum. All members of the assessment team will gain essential information about the student when the expanded core curriculum is used as the guide for assessment.

The next chapter considers the school psychologist's role in the assessment team. As mentioned in this chapter, the school psychologist plays an essential role in the assessment of children who are blind or visually impaired. His or her expertise is invaluable and may need to be coupled with the expertise of professionals who routinely work with students who are blind and visually impaired in order to maximize the value of assessment with respect to the expanded core curriculum.

REFERENCES

Bradley-Johnson, S. (1994). *Psychoeducational assessment of students who are visually impaired or blind.* Austin, TX: Pro-ed.

Brown, F., & Silberman, R. K. (1998). Alternative approaches to assessing students who have visual impairments with severe disabilities. In S. Z. Sacks & R. K. Silberman (Eds.), *Educating students who have visual impairment with other disabilities.* (pp. 73–100). Baltimore, MD: Paul H. Brookes.

Chen, D. & Dote-Kwan, J. (1995). *Starting points, instructional practices for young children whose multiple disabilities include visual impairment.* Santa Ana, CA: Blind Children's Learning Center.

Connolly, A. J. (1998). *KeyMath revised, A diagnostic inventory of essential mathematics.* Circle Pines, MN: American Guidance Services.

Corn, A. L., Hatlen, P. Huebner, K., Ryan, F., & Siller, M. A. (1995). *The national agenda for the education of children and youths with visual impairments, including those with multiple disabilities.* New York: AFB Press.

Hatlen, P. (1996). The core curriculum for blind and visually impaired students, including those with additional disabilities. *RE*:view, 28,(1), 25–32.

Hazekamp, J. (1997). *Program guidelines for students who are visually impaired.* Sacramento, CA: Department of Education.

Holbrook, C. M. & Koenig, A. J. (2000). Planning Instruction in Unique Skills. In Koeing, A. J. & Holbrook, C. M (Eds.), *Foundations of Education, Second Edition, Vol. II Instructional Strategies for Teaching Children and Youth with Visual Impairments.* (pp. 206–207). New York: AFB Press.

Keller, H. (2000). *To love this life: Quotations by Helen Keller.* New York: AFB Press.

Koenig, A. J., & Holbrook, M. C. (1989). Determining the reading medium for students with visual impairments: A diagnostic teaching approach. *Journal of Visual Impairment & Blindness, 83,* 61–68.

Koenig, A. J., & Holbrook, M. C. (1993). *Learning media assessment of students with visual impairments.* Austin: Texas School for the Blind and Visually Impaired.

Lewis, S., & Russo, R. (1998). Educational assessment for students who have visual impairments with other disabilities. In S. Z. Sacks & R. K. Silberman (Eds.), *Educating students who have visual impairment with other disabilities.* (pp. 39–72). Baltimore, MD: Paul H. Brookes.

Levack, N., & Smith, N. (1996). *Teaching students with visual and multiple impairments, a resource guide.* Austin: Texas School for the Blind and Visually Impaired.

Mar, H. (1996). Psychological evaluation of children who are deaf-blind: An overview with recommendations for practice. In *DB—Link* (p. 2). Helen Keller National Center for Deaf-Blind Youths and Adults, New England Region.

Office of Special Education and Rehabilitative Services. (2000). Educating blind and visually impaired students: Policy guidance. *Federal Register, 65*(111), 36585–36594.

Rosen, S. (1998). Educating students who have visual impairments with neurological disabilities. In S. Z. Sacks and R. K. Silberman (Eds.), *Educating students who have visual impairment with other disabilities.* (pp. 221–262). Baltimore, MD: Paul H. Brookes.

APPENDIX 5.1

CASE STUDY: ROSY'S EDUCATIONAL ASSESSMENT
Lizbeth A. Barclay

The story of Rosy's educational assessment is told from the viewpoint of the teacher of students who are visually impaired. It illustrates the use of the expanded core curriculum as the foundation for assessment by demonstrating how information was obtained in the following ways:

- Information gained through assessment by the teacher of visually impaired students
- Information gained through observation
- Information gained/shared through collaboration with parents, teachers, and specialists

While this case study specifically describes the assessment used by the teacher of students who are visually impaired, it will illustrate the collaborative process by which all specialists can share information gained during assessment using the expanded core curriculum as a guide.

Meet Rosy

Rosy, a delightful 7-year-old, was born extremely prematurely. She was the surviving twin, born at 26 weeks gestation, weighing one pound, six ounces. At the time of her assessment, Rosy was shy and delicate, but she demonstrated a wonderful sense of humor and whimsy. She enjoyed an active imaginary life, often bringing her stuffed puppy Genevieve along with her during assessment.

Rosy was very cooperative during her assessment sessions, and although she seemed easily distracted, it was easy to redirect her to academic tasks. Using print as her primary reading medium, Rosy was beginning to gain aptitude in some early literacy skills. She demonstrated an interest in learning to read, and at the time of the assessment was using picture clues and initial consonants to "read" some words.

Her mother reported that Rosy had some friends at school, but that she was very shy and made friends rather slowly.

Questions Asked Prior to Assessment

Rosy's parents asked:

"Can you tell us more about the possibility of Rosy learning braille?"
"How can we teach Rosy to express her fears and to answer more genuinely when asked a question, instead of attempting simply to be compliant?"

Rosy's teachers and specialists asked:

"What reading medium should Rosy use?"
"What can we do so that Rosy's school environment best meets her needs?"
"What kind of adaptive equipment should Rosy use?"

These primary questions focused on academic and social/emotional areas of the expanded core curriculum. After the team had further conversations with her mother and teachers, many additional concerns and issues regarding Rosy's progress and her curriculum emerged. In addition, it was time for her triennial assessment, and so Rosy's assessment was comprehensive in nature, covering all areas of the expanded core curriculum.

Preparation for Assessment

MEDICAL INFORMATION

Rosy's medical difficulties after birth included retinopathy of prematurity (ROP; see Appendix A), and heart and respiratory problems (bronchopulmonary dysplasia). As Rosy matured, her developmental milestones were delayed. She began to speak her first words at around the age of three and a half and walked when she was two years old.

At the age of three, Rosy began experiencing grand mal seizures, for which she was hospitalized after she stopped breathing and turned blue. Her mother reported that after this series of seizures Rosy had lost significant motor and communication skills. She was then diagnosed as having mild cerebral palsy. At the time of the assessment, Rosy was taking an antiseizure medication and had been seizure free for several years.

VISION INFORMATION

Prior to the assessment, Rosy was examined at a low vision clinic that specializes in examining the vision of children with multiple disabilities. According to the report by the clinic's doctors, Rosy's ROP more severely affected her right eye, which now had an opacified cornea and no light perception. Her left eye was myopic (nearsighted), with some astigmatism. Rosy's pupil in that eye was chronically dilated, causing light sensitivity. Rosy wore glasses to correct her nearsightedness and to protect the vision in her left eye.

In her left eye, Rosy's contrast sensitivity and color vision were found to be normal. Her visual acuity was measured from a distance of 15 inches to be about 20/200. From a distance of about 30 inches, Rosy's acuity dropped to 20/300. It was also found that Rosy experienced significant reduction in visual acuity when symbols are crowded together (as in words), called the crowding effect.

Rosy's functional vision was observed during the assessment. She was observed to use her vision quite well for examining objects and while traveling. She was motivated to use her vision and enjoyed looking at books and pictures, and exploring the environment.

Rosy's use of vision was at times deceptive because upon close examination it was observed that she used context to interpret visual information. She was very interested in, and had a great deal of exposure to, books and photographs. When items or details in pictures were small, Rosy used previously obtained information to guess what they were. Sometimes this was successful, but at other times she was inaccurate. She often made gross generalizations, such as that everything round and red was an apple.

EDUCATIONAL HISTORY

At 10 months of age Rosy attended an infant program with her mother, and between three and five years of age she attended a private preschool program that included a high level of parent participation. From the age of five through seven, Rosy attended a special education preschool program in her neighborhood. During her years in preschool, she was served by a teacher of students who are visually impaired.

At the time of Rosy's assessment, she attended kindergarten in her neighborhood school. She received services from an itinerant teacher of visually impaired students, an orientation and mobility (O&M) specialist, a speech and language pathologist, as well as an adapted physical education specialist. She also had an instructional assistant part of the time in class.

SHARING INFORMATION

The teacher of students who are visually impaired was the team leader for this assessment. She had gathered the majority of initial information and maintained close collaboration with Rosy's classroom teacher and mother. Consequently, she was responsible for relating pertinent information to other assessment team members. All of Rosy's medical, vision, and educational background was shared. In a team meeting, this information was reviewed and assessment approaches and opportunities for collaboration were discussed.

Collaboration with Rosy's family was key to the success of her assessment. Many discussions with Rosy's mother took place prior to and throughout the assessment to help clarify questions and elucidate Rosy's behavior during assessment. After initial phone conversations, as background information was being gathered and studied, a visit to Rosy's home was scheduled. During the visit, the Assessment Program's Parent Inventory and History Form was used to obtain additional information about Rosy's family and her academic history (see Appendix B).

Once an assessment approach was decided upon by the team, the information was shared with Rosy's mother. She was invited to observe (unseen and unheard by Rosy) any part of the assessment, and cautioned to save her questions and comments for the breaks between assessment sessions. This way, she could be a part of the assessment process by providing insight along the way without distracting Rosy. She watched portions of the assessment and was particularly helpful to various members of the team by making suggestions about modifying Rosy's behavior. She also shared many of Rosy's work samples to help demonstrate her daughter's learning style. Her insight about Rosy throughout the assessment process was invaluable. Through this type of collaboration with Rosy's family and all team members, all areas of the expanded core curriculum could be addressed through the assessment process. Assessment information would be obtained in the following ways:

- Review of records
- Formal assessment
- Criterion-referenced checklists
- Parent interview
- Observation of Rosy in familiar and unfamiliar settings

Educational Assessment and the Expanded Core Curriculum

The following summary illustrates the collaborative approach used by Rosy's educational team during her assessment. The modes of assessment used in each area of the expanded core curriculum are described. The areas of reading, math, and writing in the core curriculum were addressed within Rosy's assessment as they pertained to compensatory or functional academic skills. The review of each area includes sections devoted to information gained through assessment, observation, and/or collaboration.

COMPENSATORY OR FUNCTIONAL ACADEMIC SKILLS, INCLUDING COMMUNICATION MODES

Concept Development

These include spatial, temporal, quantitative, positional, directional, and sequential concepts.

OBSERVATION
Rosy's understanding of concepts within natural contexts was observed in her home as she carried out functional tasks such as dressing and eating; and at school, as she participated in academic and nonacademic tasks.

COLLABORATION
Assessment information about Rosy's understanding of concepts was also shared by the O&M specialist, who used the *The Hill Performance Test of Selected Positional Concepts* (Hill, 1981); and the speech and language pathologist, who used the *Boehm Test of Basic Concepts* (Boehm, 2000).

Core Curriculm: Reading

ASSESSMENT
Rosy's use of learning media was an important question during this assessment and so a variety of assessment tools were used. The *Learning Media Assessment's* (Koenig & Holbrook, 1993) Use of Sensory Channels checklist was used to gain

more information about Rosy's sensory preferences. The *Brigance Reading Readiness & Basic Reading Skills* instrument (Brigance, 1999) was used as a guide to explore Rosy's reading readiness skills in print. The *The Braille Requisite Skills Inventory* (Labossiere, 1995) was a helpful tool to assess Rosy's fine motor and cognitive skills with regard to readiness for braille reading. *The Test of Visual Perception, non-motor* (Gardner, 1996) was attempted with Rosy to understand better how she interpreted her vision, but it was abandoned when her responses indicated that she did not completely understand the concepts of "same" and "different" in this academic context.

OBSERVATION

Rosy was observed as she read words from her kindergarten reading series. It was generally thought by Rosy's teachers that she was reading the sentences that were placed by picture cues in her text. During this observation it was noted that she was only recognizing the initial consonants of each word and had memorized the general shape of the words. When asked to name each letter within words, she could not. The classroom teacher was not using the letter size prescribed by the low vision clinic (44 point). When the prescribed letter size was used, Rosy had greater success in identifying each letter of each word, providing a better chance to learn decoding skills rather than to rely only on memory, word shape, and context.

Because of Rosy's difficulties with the crowding effect, it was found that the only way that she could read each letter of a word was to isolate each letter by covering the others around it. This crowding effect, in combination with Rosy's current need for a 44 point print size, presented a significant challenge to Rosy's progress in print reading.

COLLABORATION

Because of Rosy's extreme prematurity and subsequent disabilities, it was especially important and very enlightening to examine information gathered by all other specialists in order to understand better her readiness for reading.

The psychologist administered the *Slosson Intelligence Test—Revised* (Slosson et al., 1991) and used projective drawings to obtain more information about Rosy's cognitive processing. The speech and language pathologist used the *Language Processing Test* (Hanner & Richard, 1995) and *The Phonological Awareness Test* (Robertson & Salter, 1997).

Rosy's mother noted, and the team observed, that Rosy had been immersed in and tremendously enjoyed a rich exposure to literature. Rosy loved books and everything about them.

The question, "Should braille be taught in addition to print?" seemed to be a simple one given an initial look at Rosy's challenges with regard to print. However, given Rosy's overall developmental level, her mild cerebral palsy, and her patterns in language processing and understanding of concepts, the answer to this question became much more complicated. This information was obtained through collaboration with Rosy's mother, the psychologist, speech and language pathologist, the O&M specialist, and from prior information from occupational therapy reports. The team had many discussions about the complicated aspects of this issue. Rosy's mother believed that Rosy should be provided with instruction in emergent braille literacy skills in addition to print, and she was an important member of the team.

Core Curriculm: Writing

OBSERVATION
Rosy wrote an approximation of her own name as a writing sample. Her delay in fine motor skills was evident in this area.

Core Curriculm: Mathematics

ASSESSMENT
Checklists from Texas School for the Blind and Visually Impaired (TSBVI) Functional Academics: A Curriculum for Students with Visual Impairments (Hauser, Levack, & Newton, 1999) were used to examine Rosy's beginning math skills. The lists used were Basic Math Assessment, Money Assessment and Time Assessment. Due to Rosy's age and developmental level, only portions of these checklists were used.

Listening Skills:

ASSESSMENT
Passages of the *Diagnostic Reading Scales* (Spache, 1981) were read to Rosy and the comprehension questions were asked to determine her approximate grade level when listening to grade-level passages.

OBSERVATION
When observed in her classroom, Rosy's listening to classroom instruction varied according to the activity and her comprehension of it, how accessible it was, and her energy level.

COLLABORATION
The speech and language pathologist and the psychologist were particularly interested in the contrast between Rosy's grade level in listening comprehension and her level in early reading skills. Information about Rosy's classroom behavior in terms of listening was also very important to them.

Study Skills:

OBSERVATION
Rosy's attention to task, ability to follow directions, and level of participation in one-to-one, small group, and large group activities were observed during assessment and in her classroom setting.

COLLABORATION

The psychologist asked Rosy's mother and her classroom teacher to complete *The Disruptive Behavior Rating Scale* (Erford, 1993) and their responses were compared to Rosy's ability to maintain attention at home and in school. Information obtained from observation and from these checklists was shared to give the team more insight about Rosy's behavior in academic settings.

USE OF ASSISTIVE TECHNOLOGY

Observation

Rosy was observed as she played early education video games at home. Her ability to use the mouse was impressive. Use of an adapted keyboard with large, high-contrast letters in alphabetical order was demonstrated to Rosy and her mother, in addition to software that provides speech. Rosy used a hunt and peck approach to demonstrate that she could easily locate letters dictated to her. She responded well to the combination of speech and large print on the computer screen.

SOCIAL EMOTIONAL SKILLS

Social Interaction

OBSERVATION
Rosy's social interaction was observed at school, both during classroom activities and on the playground at recess.

ASSESSMENT
The *Social Skills Assessment Tool for Children with Visual Impairments* (McCallum & Sacks, 1994) was used to guide the observation.

When at school, Rosy seemed shy and somewhat isolated from her peers, preferring solitary play. She interacted easily with the adults who worked with her. Rosy's mother reported that at school there were children who sometimes enjoyed doing things with Rosy.

Knowledge of Human Sexuality and Knowledge of Visual Impairment:

These are two very important areas within social/emotional skills. Rosy did not have the level of receptive or expressive language to answer questions regarding her knowledge of either visual impairment or human sexuality. However, Rosy's mother was given checklists in those areas from *Functional Academic Assessments* (Hauser et al., 1999) for future use and guidance.

RECREATION AND LEISURE

Assessment

The *Functional Academics Assessments*, Recreation and Leisure Skills checklist (Hauser et al., 1999) was given in interview form to Rosy and her mother together.

Collaboration

The information gained through observation and informal assessment was shared with all team members. The speech and language pathologist related information that she collected as she took a language sample during a play session with Rosy. Rosy's wonderful imagination and playful nature were evident during the session.

SENSORIMOTOR SKILLS: TACTILE, FINE MOTOR, AND GROSS MOTOR

Observation

Rosy's tactile preferences and fine and gross motor skills were observed in many academic, play, and daily living skills activities at home and school. Rosy's fastidious practices while eating gave big clues to her tactile defensiveness. Watching Rosy handle her clothing as she dressed gave an abundance of information about her fine motor, motor planning, and balance skills. During play on the playground Rosy ran confidently and climbed equipment with determination and also caution.

Collaboration

Rosy's mother shared many examples of Rosy's history of tactile defensiveness. Like many other children born prematurely, Rosy remained hospitalized in the neonatal unit for three months. She endured many interventions necessary to her health. As a result, she was extremely orally and tactilely defensive as an infant and toddler. This tactual defensiveness had gradually decreased over time, yet remnants of it still remained.

Rosy had received service from an occupational therapist for several years and although the occupational therapist was currently not a part of the assessment team, information from Rosy's files had been studied prior to the assessment.

All members of the team shared information regarding Rosy's sensorimotor skills. The O&M specialist observed her gross motor skills during play activities and during cane travel. Information about Rosy's motor skills, especially with regard to balance and motor planning, was shared. Rosy's tactile approach and skill level during curricular tasks were discussed throughout her assessment. Questions about how well Rosy processed sensory information were pondered, given her medical history and the implications of neurological damage. These motor skill areas will have an impact on Rosy's future acquisition of curricular skills, as well as her skills of independence, such as O&M and daily living skills.

ORIENTATION AND MOBILITY SKILLS

Collaboration

The O&M specialist utilized portions of the *Peabody Mobility Programs* (Harley et al., 1989), *Teaching Age-Appropriate Purposeful Skills* (Pogrund et al., 1993), and the *Dodson-Burk and Hill Preschool O&M Screening—Form B* (for older, ambulatory children) (Dodson-Burk & Hill, 1989) while assessing Rosy.

The O&M specialist shared information regarding Rosy's level of concept development, motor skills, spatial abilities, sequential memory, and general understanding of environment and space. This information was invaluable in helping all of the specialists better understand Rosy's learning style. Of particular importance to the area of reading were the areas of concept development and sequential memory.

Further questions for team discussion resulted from this collaboration, such as:

- What concepts will Rosy need to learn in order to become a proficient reader in either print or braille? and,
- What impact will Rosy's difficulties in sequential memory have on her abilities in reading and writing?

The difficulties noted by the O&M specialist were also found in testing results obtained by the speech and language pathologist and the psychologist, as well as in observations by Rosy's classroom teacher and teacher of visually impaired students. The sharing of this important information helped the team better understand Rosy's requirements for intervention.

DAILY LIVING SKILLS

Observation

In order to obtain more information about Rosy's level of independence and need for adaptation in activities of personal hygiene and dressing, Rosy was observed at home as she dressed and got ready for school. During breakfast, her eating skills were observed, as well as at lunch in a restaurant during a community outing.

Collaboration

These observational opportunities in functional contexts were rich in information shared by all specialists. The psychologist also obtained information about Rosy's daily living skills by interviewing Rosy's mother, using the *Vineland Adaptive Behavior Scales* (Spanow et al., 1985). The speech and language pathologist was especially interested in Rosy's oral motor abilities and her level of social language when eating at the restaurant. The O&M specialist obtained information regarding Rosy's knowledge and skill level while traveling with an adult in the community.

CAREER AND VOCATIONAL SKILLS

Observation

Both at home and at school, Rosy's level of independence and attention to task were noted.

Collaboration

Rosy's receptive and expressive language skills were not yet at a level at which she could participate in answering questions about career readiness. Her awareness of work and the community were discussed with her mother, who had many questions about how to help prepare Rosy for the eventuality of work. Many resources for career readiness were shared with her.

VISUAL EFFICIENCY SKILLS

Collaboration

Prior to the assessment, Rosy's examination at the low vision clinic was observed by the O&M specialist and information about Rosy's vision was shared with all team members. Throughout the assessment, the O&M specialist and the teacher of students who are visually impaired observed Rosy's functional vision, sharing pertinent information through e-mail and discussion with other team members as needed.

Highlights of the Findings

Although the preceding sections on Rosy's assessment are presented from the point of view of the teacher of students who are visually impaired, it is clear to see the importance and necessity of close collaboration with other specialists during the assessment process. Each assessor who worked with Rosy wrote a report and recommendations that supported Rosy's acquisition of skills within the expanded core curriculum.

THE PSYCHOLOGIST'S FINDINGS

In a summary of findings about Rosy, the psychologist wrote:

> Rosy is delayed in many areas of functioning but appears to be making progress. Many students whose vision loss is due to extreme prematurity show characteristics and learning patterns that are associated with neurological impairment and learning disabilities. These include high levels of distractibility, difficulty in retrieving information, and difficulties with internalizing and generalizing newly acquired skills. It should be understood that although Rosy may show many of these characteristics, she has made improvement in the recent past and this is very positive.

THE SPEECH AND LANGUAGE PATHOLOGIST'S FINDINGS

The speech and language pathologist found the following:

> Rosy's social language was a relative strength. During free play, she used simple yet well-formed sentences to express comments, questions, take

turns, initiate new ideas, and express feelings of the play characters. Rosy and her mother had a good balance of turn-taking in their conversation.

Rosy also displayed a relative strength in verbal imitation. She listened to what others said and mimicked this in appropriate contexts. During a community outing to a fast food restaurant, Rosy was able to order her food and converse appropriately with the examiners.

Brief sampling of formal testing as well as informal assessment revealed Rosy to have a very poor system for retrieval of information. She was usually unable to verbalize what she knew upon request. For example, when asked to name some colors or to name some body parts, Rosy was largely unable to do so. Occasionally, extra time helped her, but only when accompanied by a verbal prompt such as, "Yellow is a color, name another one."

Rosy also demonstrated significant difficulty going from one type of task to another. She frequently failed to understand that there was a different response or task being presented. For example, the *Language Processing Test* (Hanner & Richard, 1995) was used informally to look at Rosy's verbal processing. She was first asked to label pictures and then to state their functions, which she did reasonably well. She was then asked to make associations with the same words, for example, "What goes with a shoe?" Rosy continued to state functions and had significant difficulty shifting into another frame of mind when the task appeared similar.

FINDINGS FROM THE TEACHER OF STUDENTS WHO ARE VISUALLY IMPAIRED

Highlights of the findings of the teacher of students who are visually impaired included the following:

> Rosy approached most tasks visually. She was observed to use color and object cues to help her interpret visual information. Sometimes she was accurate in interpreting visual information, but at other times she missed the visual detail that was necessary for accuracy.
>
> At times, Rosy was observed to have difficulty with sequencing, but repetition of tasks and modeling were found to be effective learning techniques for her.
>
> Rosy's fine motor strength, dexterity, and motor planning affected her academic and functional skill acquisition. Rosy required modeling and much practice in order to learn each new motor skill.

With regard to print reading, the teacher of students who are visually impaired noted:

Rosy's enjoyment of literature, language, and printed words was very apparent throughout the assessment as she traveled with her books and looked at them during rest periods often each day. Rosy's love of stories and make-believe was evident as she played with dolls and characters from her stories.

Rosy demonstrated the sounds of most consonants. The reading curriculum being used in Rosy's school program pairs pictures with sentences and children begin to associate the pictures with the visual configuration of the words. Rosy read the sentences that were on the reading worksheets but she was unable to read the individual letters within the words. At this point it is believed that Rosy was looking primarily at the initial consonants of words and remembering the shape and length of the word, because she had difficulty reading all of the letters within words in order to sound them out phonetically. Rosy frequently confused the letters "I" and "l" as well as "s" and "c."

With regard to braille readiness skills, the teacher of students who are visually impaired noted:

Rosy demonstrated many of the braille reading readiness skills that are listed in the *Braille Requisite Skills Inventory* (Labossiere, 1995). She worked well with a variety of manipulatives, enjoyed coloring, putting together puzzles, used a pincer grasp, and matched textures and shapes. She matched three-dimensional shapes to their same representation in tactile drawings. Rosy did not consistently correctly name the shapes, but when asked to point to shapes as they were named, she was able to do so.

Although Rosy has not had instruction in braille readiness, a 15 minute lesson of the *Mangold Developmental Program of Tactile Perception and Braille Letter Recognition* (Mangold, 1977) was carried out with her. Rosy was receptive to touching the braille. When asked, she located the top of the page and the first line of dots on each page. She was observed to prefer using only her right hand, but would use her left hand when encouraged to do so. With intermittent hand-over-hand assistance, Rosy made progress throughout the lesson in locating the top, bottom, and sides of the page; moving two hands together across the line; using left-to-right movement; locating the beginning and end of each line; putting push-pins in the corners; and locating the braille boxes on each line.

THE O&M SPECIALIST'S FINDINGS

The O&M specialist made the following observations:

When asked to perform various movements that involved the front, back, and sides, Rosy demonstrated some motor planning problems in addition to her difficulty understanding some of the body and positional concepts. At various times during the assessment she demonstrated extraneous motor movements, occasional problems with balance, and other motor planning difficulties.

Rosy was not consistent when asked to identify her left and right body parts. She correctly held up the requested hand or identified the requested body part in four of seven trials. She was inconsistent when asked to turn right or left when walking. Rosy demonstrated a very beginning level of understanding of positional and quantitative concepts.

Rosy is reported to be well oriented to her home, classroom, and general school layout. In the assessment classroom she was shown the various areas and she remained oriented throughout the week. Rosy became somewhat disoriented in large open spaces on the school campus and frequently turned in the wrong direction.

Rosy demonstrated difficulty when trying to follow directions, especially when she was to follow a specific route. Part of her difficulty occurred because she did not yet understand some of the common concepts needed for following directions, including right and left. In addition, Rosy demonstrated some difficulty in sequencing the directions.

Rosy traveled visually in her own school setting. She noticed brightly colored railings from a distance of one to two feet. She saw intersecting sidewalks from about the same distance. She eagerly moved about a playground and used the various parts of a climbing structure including stairs, slides, and tunnels without adult help.

When out in the community Rosy was inconsistent when in parking lots. At times she would begin to walk into a parking lot without looking or holding hands, while at other times she could verbalize that she was in a parking lot and that she should watch for cars. Rosy did not want to hold hands with adults when walking in the community; but seemed to prefer to follow them or to walk ahead. She was not usually impulsive but she would occasionally dart ahead of her companions as they walked.

Highlights of Recommendations

Following is an example of some of the recommendations made by the assessment team, illustrating how they can be organized into general areas of the expanded core curriculum:

LEARNING STYLE

From the Psychologist

Recommendations made by the psychologist about Rosy's learning style included the following:

- Provide learning environments where there is limited opportunity for distraction, to help Rosy maintain her focus.
- Give Rosy additional time to process information before expecting a response.
- Continue to enrich Rosy's life with experiential learning that will help her develop concepts and a meaningful vocabulary, while developing skills of independence.
- Provide repetition of learning routines, using a consistent approach and language.

COMPENSATORY OR FUNCTIONAL ACADEMIC SKILLS, INCLUDING COMMUNICATION MODES

From the Speech and Language Pathologist

- Teach Rosy about the properties of objects through sensorimotor-based activities that will allow her to explore independently the properties of objects and learn how to compare and contrast them to others.
- Provide Rosy with many experiences on errands and community outings and talk about the places, using descriptive words about what you feel, hear, smell, taste, and see.
- Provide opportunities to learn by doing, such as beginning household and cooking tasks.
- Help Rosy learn language by modeling it for her rather than by questioning her.
- Always check the understanding behind Rosy's rote learning.
- Capitalize on Rosy's strengths in imaginative play. She will learn new language best when it is modeled through play and role play.

From the Teacher of Students Who Are Visually Impaired

- Provide daily instruction in braille reading, making lessons fun and creative, emphasizing uncontracted braille and functional literacy skills.
- Continue instruction in print reading for short reading tasks, keeping in mind her visual requirements, which include attention to print size, spacing, format, and high contrast (also see section on Visual Efficiency Skills).
- In addition to emphasis on language structure, increase Rosy's language comprehension during reading activities by including a language experience approach in her reading and writing instruction.
- Through collaboration with Rosy's parents and the O&M instructor, tie Rosy's language experience approach to her real experiences in the community.
- Consult with the occupational therapist about ways to develop Rosy's fine motor skills, including finger strength, isolation, and motor planning as they apply to braille and skills of daily living.

- Help develop Rosy's listening comprehension by presenting new classroom information in a concrete manner. For instance, provide her with real objects presented in stories for hands-on exploration.
- When teaching math skills, use manipulatives to teach Rosy basic math concepts and connect math concepts to functional application whenever possible.
- Teach Rosy to write a legal signature.

SOCIAL EMOTIONAL SKILLS

Social Interaction Skills

FROM THE SPEECH AND LANGUAGE PATHOLOGIST

- Provide Rosy with scripted language that will help her express her needs and feelings when interacting with other children, and role-play with her to give her plenty of practice in using it.

FROM THE TEACHER OF STUDENTS WHO ARE VISUALLY IMPAIRED

- In the classroom, during small group activities, place Rosy with children who are likely to want to interact with her because of their similar temperament and interests.
- Teach Rosy turn-taking activities and games that she can participate in with other children during recess.
- Give Rosy gentle but straightforward feedback about any behavior of hers that might seem different to other children.
- Pair Rosy with other children when doing classroom jobs or participating in activities.
- Have Rosy help "teach" a beginning braille lesson to a small group of classmates who can share her "secret code."

Knowledge of Visual Impairment

- Provide Rosy with developmentally appropriate information about her visual impairment and teach her a verbal response to questions about it.

Knowledge of Human Sexuality

- Begin giving Rosy age-appropriate information about human sexuality, emphasizing privacy, personal rights, and family values.

RECREATION AND LEISURE SKILLS

- Introduce Rosy to many recreational activities such as swimming, dance, and children's theater that will provide her opportunities to expand her experiences for future choices in activities, and to socialize with other children.

O&M SKILLS

From the O&M Specialist

- A physical therapy evaluation is recommended to assess Rosy's abilities in motor planning.
- Continue instruction in the area of body concepts through direct instruction at school, using games and songs; and at home, during activities such as bathing and dressing.
- Continue instruction in concepts related to O&M, beginning with positional concepts.
- Give Rosy many experiences in the community that will enhance her understanding of environmental concepts.
- Help Rosy explore various community services such as the post office, grocery store, and fire house.
- Give Rosy continuing age-appropriate training in travel safety, such as following the "stop, look, and listen" rule at each curb.
- Teach Rosy, her family, and her school staff the human guide technique, which may be useful to her when traveling in crowded areas, in a large group, or in the dark.
- Increase Rosy's skills in the area of time, telephone use, and money through functional activities.

DAILY LIVING SKILLS

From the Teacher of Students Who Are Visually Impaired

- It will be important for the occupational therapist to help address the issues of fine motor skills as they apply to daily living skills as well as academics.
- Teach Rosy how to sort and put away her clothing items in a consistent place.
- Create a unit for Rosy on personal hygiene tools and products that could include organization and storage tips.
- Rosy can be an active participant within her family, by participating in a few household chores on a regular basis, such as making her bed, taking out the trash, and setting the table.
- Rosy can learn some simple cooking tasks, such as making juice, a peanut butter and jelly sandwich, or a glass of chocolate milk.

CAREER/VOCATIONAL SKILLS

From the Teacher of Students Who Are Visually Impaired

- Instill in Rosy, during activities at school and at home, the idea and practice of appropriate work habits including attention to task, following directions, and cooperative work with peers and adults.

- It is not too early for Rosy to have a job in her classroom. She can be regularly responsible for taking the attendance to the office or helping to maintain a class garden.
- When in the community with her parents or during O&M lessons, introduce Rosy to the variety of jobs that she encounters and, eventually, of the adaptations that people who are visually impaired make so that they can perform these jobs.

TECHNOLOGY

From the Teacher of Students Who Are Visually Impaired

- Presently, Rosy would benefit from learning beginning word processing skills on a computer with an adapted large print keyboard with voice output.
- As she gains proficiency on this type of device, she should learn to use keyboard commands for word processing rather than the mouse.
- A braille notetaking device with braille display and voice output should be considered for braille instruction once Rosy has learned to braille the alphabet.

VISUAL EFFICIENCY SKILLS

From the O&M Specialist and the Teacher of Students Who Are Visually Impaired

- Teach Rosy braille to give her reading options.
- Use the print size recommended by the low vision clinic (44 point) for all print presented to Rosy.
- Take care when using print to include adequate spacing between items on a page, on worksheets, and all other written assignments. Written materials should be as uncluttered as possible.
- It may be necessary to increase spacing between letters in words to offset the crowding effect that she experiences.
- Teach Rosy to use a line marker or her finger to help her keep her place under a line of print.
- Teach Rosy to use a specific scanning pattern consistently for all print materials.
- To reduce visual fatigue, visual tasks should be alternated with nonvisual tasks.
- Teach Rosy to use a closed-circuit television, beginning at first with exploration of highly motivating objects and fine detail in pictures.
- Be aware of and adjust for glare in Rosy's environment.

Summary

The story of Rosy's educational assessment illustrates the use of the expanded core curriculum as a framework for collaborative assessment. Although this example is related from the perspective of the teacher of students who are visually impaired, it is the sharing of information, with and from other team members, that makes a truly comprehensive assessment possible. Meaningful recommendations were possible from an approach that considered all of Rosy's needs within the expanded core curriculum. This was only possible by closely working with Rosy's parents, her classroom teacher, and all of the specialists who work with her.

References

Boehm, A. (2000). *Boehm test of basic concepts (3rd ed.) (Boehm-3)*. San Antonio, TX: The Psychological Corporation.

Brigance, A. H. *Brigance diagnostic comprehensive inventory of basic skills, revised (CIBS)*. North Billerica, MA: Curriculum Associates.

Dodson-Burk, B., & Hill, E. (1989). *Dodson-Burk and Hill preschool O&M screening—form B (for older, ambulatory children)*. Alexandria, VA: Division IX of Association for the Education and Rehabilitation of the Blind and Visually Impaired.

Erford, B. (1993). *The disruptive behavior rating scale*. East Aurora, NY: Slosson Educational Publications.

Gardner, M. F. (1996). *Test of visual–perceptual skills (non-motor) (TVPS) and TVPS, upper level*. Burlingame, CA: Psychological and Educational Publications, Inc.

Hanner, M. A. & Richard, G. J. (1995). *Language processing test revised*. East Moline, IL: LinguiSytems, Inc.

Harley, R. K., Long R. G., Merbler, J. B., & Wood, T. A. (1989). *Peabody mobility programs*. Wood Dale, IL: Stoelting Company.

Hauser, S., Levack, N., & Newton, L. (1999). *Functional academics: A curriculum for students with visual impairments*. Austin: Texas School for the Blind and Visually Impaired.

Hill, E. W. (1981). *The Hill performance test of selected positional concepts*. Wood Dale, IL: Stoelting Company.

Koenig, A. J. & Holbrook, M. C. (1993). *Learning media assessment of students with visual impairments*. Austin: Texas School for the Blind and Visually Impaired.

Labossiere, S. (1995). *Braille Requisite Skills Inventory*. Houston, TX: Special Education Region IV Education Service Center.

Mangold, S. (1977). *Mangold developmental program of tactile perception and braille letter recognition*. Castro Valley, CA: Exceptional Teaching Aids.

McCallum, B. J., and Sacks, S. (1994). *Social skills assessment tool for children with visual impairments (SSAT-VI)*. In S. Sacks (Ed.) *Santa Clara County social skills curriculum for children with visual impairments*. Santa Clara, CA: Score Regionalization Project.

Pogrund, R., Healy, G., Jones, K., Levack, N., Martin-Curry, S., Martinez, C., Marz, J., Roberson-Smith, B., and Vrba, A. (1993). *Teaching age-appropriate purposeful skills (TAPS): An orientation and mobility curriculum for students with visual impairments.* Austin: Texas School for the Blind and Visually Impaired.

Robertson, C., and Salter, W. (1997). *The Phonological Awareness Test.* East Moline, IL: LinguiSystems.

Slosson, R. L., Nicholson, C. L., & Hibpshman, T. H. (1991*). Slosson intelligence test—revised (SIT-R).* East Aurora, NY: Slosson Educational Publications.

Spache, G. (1981). *Diagnostic reading scales.* Monterey, CA: McGraw-Hill.

Sparrow, S. S., Balla, D. A., and Cicchetti, D. V. (1985). *Vineland Adaptive Behavior Scales.* Circle Pines, MN: AGS Publishing.

RESOURCES FOR EDUCATIONAL ASSESSMENT

Sources of Information and Tools for Assessing Children with Severe Multiple Disabilities

Educating Students Who Have Visual Impairments with Other Disabilities
Editors: Sacks, S. Z., and Silberman, R. K.
Publisher: Paul H. Brookes Publishing
P.O. Box 10624
Baltimore, MD 21285-0624
www.pbrookes.com
Date: 1998

Comments: Written by leaders in the fields of visual impairments and severe disabilities, this book is an excellent resource for teachers, specialists, and families. It includes information about the knowledge bases and practices that can contribute to collaboration among all members of the team that serves these students.

Education of Children with Multiple Disabilities: A Transdisciplinary Approach, Second Edition
Authors: Orelove, F. P., and Sobsey, D.
Publisher: Paul H. Brookes Publishing
P.O. Box 10624
Baltimore, MD 21285-0624
www.pbrookes.com
Date: 1993

Comments: This book emphasizes the transdiscipinary team model when assessing and designing programs for children with multiple disabilities. Includes information and guidelines for assessment, intervention, and program planning for students with severe or profound cognitive delay who also have sensory and/or motor impairments.

Future Planning, and New Hats for Special Educators
Authors: Curtis, E., and Dezelsky, M.
Publisher: New Hats, Inc.
HC 64 Box 2509
Castle Valley, UT 84532-9606
(435) 295-9400
www.allenshea.com/
newhats.html
Date: 1997

Comments: These workbooks are designed for families and special education teachers as guides for facilitating students' successful transitions from school to adult life. The questionnaires included could be used as part of the assessment process for young adults who are visually impaired and have multiple disabilities.

Hand in Hand: Essentials of Communication and Orientation and Mobility for Your Students Who Are Deaf Blind
Editors: Huebner, K. M., Prickett, J. G., Welch, T. R., and Joffee, E.
Publisher: AFB Press
American Foundation for the Blind
11 Penn Plaza, Suite 300
New York, NY 10001
(800) 232-3044
www.afb.org
Date: 1995

Comments: This four-component resource was designed for educators of children who are visually impaired, hearing impaired, and severely disabled. The materials emphasize communication and mobility skills that are crucial for independence and include a two-volume, self-study text explaining how deaf blind students learn; a trainer's manual that provides guidelines for using the *Hand in Hand* materials during workshops; and a collection of selected reprints, including an annotated bibliography, on the topics of working with students who are deaf blind.

Teaching Students with Visual and Multiple Disabilities:
A Resource Guide
Authors: Smith, M., and Levack, N.
Publisher: Texas School for the Blind
        and Visually Impaired
        1100 West 45th Street
        Austin, TX 78756-3494
        (800) 872-5273
        www.tsbvi.edu
Date: 1996

Comments: This user-friendly resource provides an abundance of information and tools for assessing the needs of and developing meaningful programs for students with visual and multiple impairments. Assessors will find the chapter on assessment especially helpful because it includes a list of assessment tools, sample assessments, and often-asked questions about assessment. The assessment tools include a vision screening form, picture assessment, informal assessment of tactual symbol use, assessment of auditory functioning, assessment of biobehavioral states and analysis of related influences, and the infused skills assessment by Susan Hauser and Linda Hagood.

Assessment Tools for Skill Areas of the Expanded Core Curriculum

The following is a list of instruments, including standardized assessments, criterion-referenced checklists, and observational checklists, that can be used to assess students in all areas of the expanded core curriculum and the core curriculum areas of reading, writing, and mathematics. While not exhaustive, the list includes assessments that are the favorites of the authors as well as tools that are commonly used in the field. Psychological assessments, including cognitive and psychosocial assessments are listed in the Resources section for Chapter 7.

COMPENSATORY OR FUNCTIONAL ACADEMIC SKILLS, INCLUDING COMMUNICATION MODES

Assessment Kit: Kit of Informal Tools for Academic Students with Visual Impairments
Editor: Sewell, D.
Publisher: Texas School for the Blind
        and Visually Impaired
        1100 West 45th Street
        Austin, TX 78756-3494
        (800) 872-5273
        www.tsbvi.edu
Date: 1997
Ages: Preschool through grade 12

Comments: This kit contains checklists that cover all areas within academic skills that should be considered when developmentally appropriate for students who are visually impaired. The lists are well designed and comprehensive, and cover all areas in compensatory academic skills.

Assessment of Braille Literacy Skills
(1995)
Authors: Koenig, A., and Farrenkopf, C.
Publisher: Special Education—VI
        Region IV Education
        Service Center
        7145 West Tidwell
        Houston, TX 77092-2096
        (713) 744-6368
Date: 1995
Ages: Preschool through adult

Comments: Provides teachers of students who read braille with a tool to assess their literacy skills and is organized into three sections: emergent literacy, academic literacy, and functional literacy. It can be used as a continuing assessment to track a student's progress.

Boehm Test of Basic Concepts,
Third Edition

This assessment is described in the Resources section of Chapter 7.

Braille Requisite Skills Inventory
Editor: Labossiere, S.
Publisher: Special Education—VI
        Region IV Education
        Service Center
        7145 West Tidwell
        Houston, TX 77092-2096
        (713) 744-6368
Date: 1995
Ages: Beginning and prereaders

Comments: An assessment tool designed to assess pre-braille, reading-requisite skills. Cognitive and fine motor/tactile skills are assessed. It can be used to assist teachers in selecting the appropriate reading medium for their students.

Functional Academics: A Curriculum for Students with Visual Impairments
Authors: Hauser, S., Levack, N., and Newton, L.
Publisher: Texas School for the Blind
        and Visually Impaired
        1100 West 45th Street
        Austin, TX 78756-3494
        (800) 872-5273
        www.tsbvi.edu
Date: 1999
Ages: 12 years and older

Comments: A curriculum focusing on basic academic skills at a kindergarten through second grade level for students who are 12 years or older, and for whom a developmental or academic approach is no longer effective. It includes assessments in all areas of the curriculum: social skills, cognition/thinking, O&M, English/language arts, math, career education, science, home economics and management, personal fitness, and use of free time.

Learning Media Assessment of Students with Visual Impairments
Authors: Koenig, A. J., and Holbrook, M. C.
Publisher: Texas School for the Blind
        and Visually Impaired
        1100 West 45th Street
        Austin, Texas 78756-3494
        (800) 872-5273
        www.tsbvi.edu
Date: 1993
Ages: Preschool through adult

Comments: Described by its authors as a resource guide for teachers, this work contains six chapters that outline the essential elements of learning media assessment. The appendices include a number of checklists and forms that provide a specific assessment procedure to help determine a student's optimal learning medium. This practical guide helps to demystify learning media assessment.

Minnesota Braille Skills Inventory
Authors: McNear, D., and Sharpe, M.
Publisher: Minnesota Resource Center
for the Blind & Visually
Impaired
615 Olof Hanson Drive
P.O. Box 308
Faribault, MN 55021-0308
(507) 332-5494
http://cfl.state.mn.us/
SPECED/Blind/blindindex.
html
Date: 1996
Ages: Preschool through adult

Comments: The purpose of the *MBSI* is to document a student's knowledge and progress in reading and writing braille. It focuses on the braille code and assesses areas including literary, basic Nemeth, advanced Nemeth, computer, music, dictionary, and foreign language.

Tools for Selecting Appropriate Learning Media
Editor: Caton, H.
Publisher: American Printing House
for the Blind
1839 Frankfort Ave.
P.O. Box 6085
Louisville KY 40206-0085
(800) 572-0844
www.aph.org
Date: 1994
Ages: Preschool through adult

Comments: A manual intended for use by an interdisciplinary team in learning media assessment. It describes the roles of various team members, and provides questionnaires, checklists, and report forms that can be used by various members of the team during assessment.

INDEPENDENT LIVING SKILLS

Independent Living
Authors: Loumiet, R., and Levack, N.
Publisher: Texas School for the Blind
and Visually Impaired
1100 West 45th Street
Austin, TX 78756-3494
(800) 872-5273
www.tsbvi.edu
Date: 1993
Ages: 5 through 21 years

Comments: A curriculum written in three volumes, covering social competence, self-care and maintenance of personal environment, and play and leisure. It is a criterion-referenced curriculum designed for students with visual impairment and includes assessment and instruction materials.

Vineland Adaptive Behavior Scales

This assessment is described in the Resources section of Chapter 6.

SOCIAL INTERACTION SKILLS

Independent Living—Volume I: Social Competence

This volume is part of Loumiet and Levack's *Independent Living* described in the section on Independent Living Skills.

Social Skills Rating Scale
Authors: Brown, L., Black, D., and Downs, J.
Publisher: Slosson Educational
Publications

538 Buffalo Road
East Aurora, NY 14052
(716) 652-0930
www.slosson.com

Date: 1990

Ages: 5 to 18 years

Comments: This is a criterion-referenced assessment instrument that evaluates students in four categories—adult relations, peer relations, school rules, and classroom behavior—in the form of a questionnaire about students filled out by their teachers. Although the normative sample does not include students who are visually impaired, when cautiously used, information can be gained about a student's skills in the areas assessed.

For other assessment tools, see the Resources section of Chapter 6.

RECREATION AND LEISURE SKILLS

Functional Academics: A Curriculum for Students with Visual Impairments

This is described in the section on Compensatory or Functional Academic Skills, Including Communication Modes.

Independent Living

See Loumiet and Levack's *Independent Living*, Volume III: *Play and Leisure*, described in the section on Independent Living Skills.

USE OF ASSISTIVE TECHNOLOGY

See the Resources section of Chapter 8.

CAREER EDUCATION

Career Occupational Preference System
Authors: Knapp, R., and Knapp, L.

Publisher: Edits
P.O. Box 7234
San Diego, CA 92107
(800) 416-1666
www.psychtest.com

Date: 1995

Ages: High school through adult

Comments: An interest inventory designed to help students define the type of work they are interested in doing. It is a norm-referenced instrument, and although the normative sample does not include students who are visually impaired, when this assessment is cautiously used, information can be gained about a student's skills in the areas assessed.

COIN Basic Skills and Career Interest Survey
Authors: Durgin, R., Ryan, J., and Ryan, R.
Publisher: COIN Educational Products
3361 Executive Parkway
Suite 302
Toledo, OH 43606
(800) 274-8515
www.coin3.com

Date: 1995

Ages: Grades 10 through 12

Comments: This includes the *Wonderlic Basic Skills Test* assessment based on the test of general education development that measures basic math and language skills needed for the workplace. Following the skills test is a career interest survey that helps students to explore their occupational interests, values, and aptitudes. While this assessment was not designed for students who are visually impaired, when used with care it can provide useful information for some students who are visually impaired.

O&M

See the Resources section of Chapter 9.

VISUAL EFFICIENCY SKILLS

See the Resources section of Chapter 4.

The area of visual perception should be assessed when it is suspected that a student who uses vision for learning may have learning disabilities. Tests of visual perception can be found in the Resources section of Chapter 4.

Core Curriculum: Reading, Writing, and Mathematics

Brigance Diagnostic Comprehensive Inventory of Basic Skills, Revised
Author: Brigance, A. H.
Publisher: Curriculum Associates
      153 Rangeway Road
      P.O. Box 2001
      North Billerica, MA 01862
      (800) 225-0248
      www.curriculumassociates.
      com
      cainfo@curriculum-
      associates.com
Date: 1999

Brigance Diagnostic Comprehensive Inventory of Basic Skills, Revised: Student Braille Edition
Author: Brigance, A. H.
Publisher: American Printing House
      for the Blind
      1839 Frankfort Ave.
      P.O. Box 6085
      Louisville KY 40206-0085
      (800) 223-1839;
      (502) 895-2406
      www.aph.org
Date: 1999

Ages: prekindergarten through ninth grade.

Comments: The Brigance *Inventory* has been adapted by APH in a braille edition that includes tactile representations of diagrams where appropriate. This criterion-referenced inventory can be used to assess basic skills in the areas of reading, listening, research and study skills, spelling, language and mathematics. Although the normative sample does not include students who are visually impaired, when this assessment is cautiously used, information can be gained about a student's skills in the areas assessed.

Burns Roe Informal Reading Inventory, Fifth Edition
Authors: Burns, P., and Roe, B.
Publisher: Houghton Mifflin
      222 Berkeley Street
      Boston, MA 02116
      (800) 733-1717
      www.hmco.com/college
Date: 1999
Ages: Preprimer to grade 12.

Comments: This informal reading inventory can be used to assess the reading skills, abilities, and needs of students in order to help design a reading program. The inventory can provide information about a student's independent reading level, instructional reading level, frustration level, listening comprehension, word recognition, and miscue analysis.

Diagnostic Reading Scales
Author: Spache, G. (adapted by Duckworth and Caton)

Publisher: American Printing House
for the Blind
1839 Frankfort Ave.
P.O. Box 6085
Louisville KY 40206-0085
(800) 572-0844
www.aph.org

Date: 1992

Ages: 6 to 12 years and adolescents 13 to 18 years who do not read at grade level.

Comments: Available in both braille and large print, it is a norm-referenced assessment that identifies the strengths and weaknesses in a student's reading proficiency within grade levels in the following areas: oral reading skills, silent reading skills, reading comprehension, word analysis, and behaviors related to reading. Although the normative sample does not include students who are visually impaired, when this assessment is cautiously used, information can be gained about a student's skills in the areas assessed.

KeyMath Revised: A Diagnostic Inventory of Essential Mathematics
Author: Connolly, A. J.
Publisher: American Guidance Service
P.O. Box 99
Circle Pines, MN 55014-1796
(800) 328-2560
www.agsnet.com

American Printing House
for the Blind
1839 Frankfort Avenue
P.O. Box 6085
Louisville, KY 40206-0085
(800) 223-1839;
(502) 895-2405
www.aph.org

Date: 1988

Ages: 4 to 14 years.

Comments: Available also in braille from the American Printing House for the Blind, this powerful test is norm-referenced. While the braille version was designed specifically for braille readers, the print version, when used and interpreted with caution, can be used with some students who are print readers. When it can be used, it will provide information about a student's strengths and weaknesses in the areas of basic concepts, operations, and applications.

The Phonological Awareness Test

See the Resources section of Chapter 7.

Test of Written Spelling, Fourth Edition
Authors: Larsen, S. C., Hammill, D. D., and Moats, L. C.
Publisher: Pro-ed
8700 Shoal Creek Blvd.
Austin, TX 78757
(800) 897-3202
www.proedinc.com

Date: 1999

Comments: A norm-referenced test of spelling used to assess skill level in spelling and to measure progress in spelling ability over time. It assists teachers and specialists in learning more about the nature of a student's spelling difficulties when it is used with other assessment procedures.

Wechsler Individual Achievement Test-Second Edition (WIAT-II)
Author: Wechsler, B.

Publisher: The Psychological
Corporation
555 Academic Court
San Antonio, TX 78204
(800) 228-0752
www.tpcweb.com

Date: 2001

Ages: 4 years and older

Comments: The WIAT-II is a norm-referenced assessment that can be used to assess educational achievement. It has nine subtests: oral language, listening comprehension, written expression, spelling, word reading, pseudoword decoding, reading comprehension, mathematics, reasoning, and numerical operations. It can be administered in its entirety or select subtests may be used for partial assessment. Although the normative sample does not include students who are visually impaired, when this assessment is cautiously used, information can be gained about a student's skills in the areas assessed.

Wide Range Achievement Test 3
Author: Wilkinson, G.
Publisher: Wide Range, Inc.
P.O. Box 3410
Wilmington, DE 19804-1314
(800) 221-9728
www.language-usa.net/
WRAT

Date: 1993

Ages: 5 to 75 years

Comments: A norm-referenced assessment with three subtests: reading, spelling, and arithmetic. It can be effectively used as a screening tool to help determine the need for further testing. Although the normative sample does not include students who are visually impaired, when this assessment is cau-tiously used, information can be gained about a student's skills in the areas assessed.

Woodcock-Johnson Psychoeducational Battery—Revised
Authors: Woodcock, R., and Johnson, M. B.
Publisher: Riverside Publishing
Company
425 Spring Lake Drive
Itasca, IL 60143
(800) 323-9540
www.riverpub.com/
products/clinical/wjr

Date: 2000

Ages: 2 to 90 years

Comments: This norm-referenced assessment measures cognitive abilities, scholastic aptitudes, and achievement. The Tests of Cognitive Abilities must be administered by a psychologist, but the Tests of Achievement can be administered by an educator with training in assessment. The Tests of Achievement include: reading (letter-word identification, word attack, passage comprehension, reading vocabulary, and reading fluency), mathematics (calculation, math fluency, quantitative concepts, and applied problems), written language (spelling, editing, writing samples, and writing fluency), and oral language (story recall, picture vocabulary, understanding directions, and oral comprehension).

Preschool Assessments

Carolina Curriculum for Infants and Toddlers with Special Needs—2nd Ed.
Authors: Johnson-Martin, N., Attermeier, S., and Hacker, B.

Publisher: Paul H. Brookes Publishing
P.O. Box 10624
Baltimore, MD 21285-0624
(800) 638-3775
www.pbrookes.com

Date: 1986

Ages: Birth to 2 years

Comments: A criterion-referenced, assessment-focused, teaching curriculum. It includes five domains: cognition, communication, social adaptation, fine motor skills, and gross motor skills. This curriculum is designed for students who are visually impaired.

The INSIGHT Model: Resources for Family-Centered Interventions for Infants, Toddlers, and Preschoolers Who are Visually Impaired
Author: Morgan, E.
Publisher: SKI HI Institute, Hope, Inc.
1856 North East
North Logan, UT 84341
(435) 245-2888
www.skihi.org/Research

Date: 1992

Ages: Birth to 6 years

Comments: Designed for students who are visually impaired and who have additional disabilities. While it is not designed as an assessment but as a teaching tool for home teachers, it covers skills in the following areas: communication, gross motor, O&M, vision, hearing and listening, tactile activities and getting ready for braille, cognition, and getting ready for school.

Oregon Project for Visually Impaired and Blind Preschool Children
Authors: Brown, D., Simmons, V., and Methvin, J.
Publisher: Jackson Education Service District
101 N. Grape St.
Medford, OR 97501
(541) 776-8580

Date: 1991

Ages: Birth to 6 years

Comments: This curriculum is not assessment focused, but it includes a large list of skills to be mastered in the following areas: cognition, language, socialization, vision, compensatory skills, self-help skills, and fine and gross motor skills. It was designed for students who are visually impaired or who have multiple disabilities and provides resources and teaching strategies for all areas listed.

Reynell-Zinkin Developmental Scales for Young Visually Handicapped Children

See the Resource section for Chapter 7.

6 Psychological Assessment

J. Richard Russo

IN THIS CHAPTER:

- The role of the school psychologist
- Conducting a collaborative psychological assessment of a student who is blind or visually impaired
- Choosing assessment instruments and interpreting the results
- Adapting instruments designed for sighted students
- Vision characteristics and their implications for learning
- Meeting and working with a student who is blind or visually impaired

---

This chapter presents a brief overview of assessment as a "first read" for the psychologist about to conduct an assessment of a student who is visually impaired. Many of the issues discussed in this chapter are presented more fully in other chapters in this book.

For others who will be collaborating with the school psychologist, this chapter will show areas in which the school psychologist might benefit from assistance from a person knowledgeable about students who are blind or visually impaired. For example, the teacher of students who are visually impaired can easily identify the types of information the psychologist will need in order to understand the nature of the student's vision and other characteristics that might be associated with the cause of the vision loss.

Other members of the assessment team unfamiliar with the role of the school psychologist might find this chapter useful in learning more about the potential contribution of the school psychologist to collaborative assessment.

Throughout this chapter, the reader will be introduced to the uniqueness of students who are blind or visually impaired. It should be kept in mind that for the student who is visually impaired without other disabilities, the potential for accomplishment and life success is little different from that for sighted students. With advancements in technology and miniaturization (the ability to make very complex electronic equipment small enough to be of practical use), the differences between sighted students and students who are visually impaired are rapidly diminishing.

For purposes of assessment, however, the psychologist accustomed to using instruments that rely on vision, or examine information garnered through visual experiences, must either reconsider those instruments, substitute for them, or interpret them in the light of the student's history of visual functioning.

THE ROLE OF THE PSYCHOLOGIST IN COLLABORATIVE ASSESSMENT

The role of the school psychologist varies from district to district, and even state to state. In some situations, the school psychologist conducts most if not all assessments of a student. In other situations, the assessment function is shared with other specialists. In all cases, the school psychologist is the specialist who assesses a student's cognitive functioning and emotional/psychological functioning. In the collaboration model described here, the psychologist is the primary specialist responsible for cognitive and emotional/psychological assessment of students. With a student who is blind or visually impaired, as with all other students referred to the school psychologist, assessment of his or her cognitive skills, strengths and weaknesses, mental processing skills, general knowledge, and memory functions is well within the domain of the school psychologist. When collaborating with other specialists, such as the teacher of students who are visually impaired, the speech and language pathologist, and the orientation and mobility (O&M) specialist, the assessment results obtained by the school psychologist from a student who is visually impaired can be as meaningful as those obtained from any sighted student assessed.

In the area of emotional and psychological functioning, feelings, attitudes, and behaviors, students who are blind or visually impaired are more similar to than different from sighted students referred to the school psychologist. Since many of the same assessment skills are required, it will not take long for the qualified school psychologist to discover that he or she has much to offer to the student who is visually impaired and the team providing service to him or her.

With the Teacher of Students Who Are Visually Impaired and the Functional Vision Assessor

Since school psychologists are usually not trained specifically in visual impairment, it is crucial that they not only become familiar with the specialists working with students who are blind or visually impaired but also take advantage of the opportunities and benefits of collaboration. The teacher of students who are visually impaired and the functional vision assessor (who may be the same person) can be especially helpful to the school psychologist. They can provide information on the exact cause of the student's visual impairment, the extent of his or her current visual functioning, and what additional disabilities might be associated with this type of vision loss. These specialists can provide information to help the school psychologist determine which assessment instruments could be used (or at least tried). These specialists can also provide information on setting up the assessment environment, lighting, enlargement of materials, and use of adaptive devices including magnifiers and enlarging equipment. In addition, these specialists can alert the school psychologist about the need to position stimulus material to maximize the use of the student's remaining vision (if any).

Visual fatigue must often be considered in the assessment of students who are visually impaired. It is important that the school psychologist knows how long a student can be expected to participate in visual activities before he or she experiences headaches or visual fatigue. The teacher of students who are visually impaired or the assessor of functional vision can provide this information (see Chapters 4 and 5 for more information).

With the Orientation & Mobility (O&M) Specialist

Psychologists typically assess a student's ability to understand space and the relationship of objects and themselves within that space. Understanding space and spatial concepts is a key ingredient for success in many academic activities. Since assessment instruments that require vision often cannot be used with students who are blind or visually impaired, that information must be gathered in other ways. The O&M specialist can provide much of the information usually gathered by the school psychologist through standardized testing.

Understanding space and acquiring a spatial mental map can be a primary determinant of how independent a student who is visually impaired can become. However, spatial concepts such as up, down, right, left, and between often have to be actively taught to children who are visually impaired, whereas sighted children learn much of this information spontaneously. Therefore, it is particularly important to obtain an accurate assessment of a student's grasp of such concepts. Assessing the student's understanding of the space around him or her, understanding the sequencing necessary for travel through space, and knowing how an environment is organized are all reflections of brain function.

How well a student travels in his or her environment is usually the domain of the O&M specialist. He or she not only teaches these skills but also assesses them. The O&M specialist can provide important information to the psychologist on how well a student performs in these important areas (see Chapter 9 for more information).

With the Speech and Language Pathologist

The speech and language pathologist and school psychologist often collaborate when working with students who are not blind or visually impaired, and this collaboration becomes required when working with a student who is blind or visually impaired. In the academic setting, language often is the greatest reflection of cognitive functioning. Issues specific to the student who is blind or visually impaired, including language development, the existence of verbalisms (use of words whose meaning is not truly known, often through lack of experience), depth of language understanding, and memory, are all areas that the speech and language pathologist can evaluate.

Immediate and delayed echolalia (parroting or repetitive speech) are often characteristics of students who are blind and visually impaired. Verbalisms and echolalia are often associated with the student's developmental level and are seen in some students who have neurological deficits. Collaboration between the psychologist and the speech and language pathologist can frequently yield information crucial to understanding the language functioning of the student who is visually impaired (for more information, see Chapter 7).

With Parents

When assessing students who are blind or visually impaired and may also have other disabilities, standardized assessment procedures often play a less central role than with sighted students. Since there are fewer instruments appropriate for use with students who are visually impaired, knowledge of many areas of the student's history become very important. Chapter 10 details the many areas that require exploration when compiling the report of the assessment of a student who is visually impaired. The other chapters in this book give detailed information about how the various areas are assessed. The California School for the Blind's Parent Inventory and History Form is provided in Appendix B as an example of an instrument that is helpful in gathering some of the information necessary.

Chapter 5 explains the importance of assessing daily living skills and the role of practical, concrete experiences in helping the stu-

Frances K. Liefert

Including parents in the assessment process from the beginning enriches the results.

dent who is blind or visually impaired to improve his or her independent skills and develop a more meaningful understanding of the world. Assessment of these areas is a perfect opportunity for collaboration between the teacher of students who are visually impaired, the student's family, and the school psychologist. Take, for example, the assessment of adaptive behavior skills. Instruments such as the *Vineland Adaptive Behavior Scales* (see the Resources section of this chapter) can be conducted jointly with the teacher of students who are visually impaired and the parents. The psychologist gains information on a student's adaptive skills, the teacher gains information on the student's daily living skills, and the interview is a perfect opportunity to help parents learn of the adaptive techniques available to help students improve their living skills.

For example, sighted students learn adaptive behavior and living skills incidentally, mostly by casual observation. Students who are blind and cannot visually observe the habits of others, must be actively taught these skills. Often the techniques are as directive as hand-on-hand, in which the teacher guides the student to perform a particular task or gesture. Collaboration is a perfect opportunity for the teacher, school psychologist, and parent to not only assess the student's skills but to determine areas where special adaptations are appropriate.

LEARNING AND VISION

The most important consideration for the school psychologist is to understand that a vision loss deprives the individual student of important environmental experiences. According to Ashcroft and Zambone-Ashley (1980), 90 percent of what fully sighted persons learn is through the use of vision. A vision loss reduces the opportunities to gain information and understanding through that sense. Vision is the best sense to learn about the world by casual observation. What is often referred to as incidental learning is greatly diminished without vision. Vision is also the fully sighted person's most important sense for experiencing things at a great distance. Even the stars and planets of the solar system can be experienced through vision.

Vision also gives meaning to what is heard, smelled, or touched by integrating the other senses and making what is heard, smelled, or touched more meaningful. Although the other senses—hearing, touch, smell, taste—of a person who is blind or visually impaired are still intact and functional, without vision they may not be fully integrated.

Vision gives perspective. It enables the sighted student quickly and easily to experience the environment as a whole without having to piece information together over time or through many attempts.

A vision loss therefore has a profound impact on the opportunity to gain information about the environment; the greater the vision loss, the greater the impact on information gathering. For this reason, the student who is blind has a different understanding of the world from a student who is sighted. The student who is blind or visually impaired may not understand concepts of color, perspective, and space or may understand them very differently than a sighted student does.

The world can be understood through channels other than vision, at least to a large extent. However, learning through seeing is often the most efficient method for acquiring information about the world.

Learning through hearing alone is extremely limited, as is learning through touch alone. Combining hearing and touch provides a richer experience of the environment, but may cause dependence on others to guide tactile exploration and to provide the necessary aural input. This greater dependence on others and the need to combine hearing and touch to develop the fullest experience possible requires considerable time and guidance.

To understand the effects of vision impairment, it is important to understand the degree of impairment, the current vision characteristics of the person who is blind or visually impaired, and the age of onset of vision impairment. Students who have sight until four, five, or six years of age have had the opportunity to learn much about the world through vision. They will have a visual reference for basic cognitive and development concepts and, even though they may experience complete visual impairment, they will still think about the world in visual terms.

A detailed vision history that documents when the vision impairment occurred, and the degree of impairment is crucial. The vision history of a student can be very complicated as, for example, in the case of cataracts. A student who has cataracts may have experienced full vision, which may then diminish gradually over a long period of time as the cataracts ripen, to the point where a substantial vision loss is evident. Surgery and corrective lenses can then restore much, if not all of the student's vision. The teacher of students who are visually impaired or the teacher doing the functional vision assessment can be excellent resources for this information. Another resource is the list of common causes of visual impairment in Appendix A of this book.

PREPARING FOR THE ASSESSMENT

Learning about the Student's Vision

After understanding the cause of a student's visual impairment, it is important to understand what a student is able to see. Some students have no vision at all (no light perception; NLP), others might have light perception (LP). Students with low vision may have unique vision characteristics, such as impaired near vision or distance vision. Some students may have significant reduction in their visual fields, or holes in their vision (scotomas), in which blotches of vision may be missing. Sometimes those missing sections can move, causing blind spots that travel.

Some students may have a loss of central vision (damage to the section of the retina responsible for seeing detail). Such students may not look directly at an object but may view objects from the side of their eyes (eccentric gaze).

The most difficult vision to understand is variable and fluctuating vision. In students with certain visual impairments, vision can vary with their level of tiredness, time of day, or for no apparent reason at all. For example, students with cortical visual impairment (see Appendix A) have variable and fluctuating vision. If this is not understood, they may be accused of malingering or be misdiagnosed as having hysterical blindness (loss of vision due to extreme emotional trauma).

All these characteristics of vision can have major effects on a student and his or her functioning and performance. Some professionals who lack experience in working with students who are blind or visually impaired may think that the student is not paying attention because he or she appears to not be looking directly at a stimulus. Usually, students who are visually impaired will position themselves and the objects at which they are looking so that their vision is used to best advantage. Asking students questions about their vision is appropriate. The examiner may learn that students see best when looking out of the side of their eyes or by adjusting the distance to a stimulus. The parent or the teacher assessing functional vision can often provide necessary information on what to expect in order to understand the reasons for a student's visual behavior. Chapter 4 provides more details that can help the assessment team to understand a particular student's visual impairment.

Elements of the Assessment

As mentioned in Chapter 2, the appropriate assessment for a student who is blind or visually impaired often takes substantially longer than the same assessment for a student who is sighted. Because processing by auditory and tactile channels is less efficient than processing by vision, it can take longer and be more difficult to assess. Especially with students who have some vision, a degree of trial and error in the assessment process is required. As with the assessment of sighted students, it is sometimes easier to trust higher scores than lower scores. With students who are visually impaired, it is important to consider whether their lack of vision prevented them from performing the task or deprived them of the background experience that sighted students have that enables them to perform the task. Sometimes comparing scores on tasks that require vision with tasks that do not, can provide useful information on a student's loss of effectiveness when they use vision to process information and solve problems.

CHARACTERISTICS OF STUDENTS WHO ARE BLIND OR VISUALLY IMPAIRED

Most assessments include observation of the student in a familiar environment. If the school psychologist conducting the assessment is familiar with some of the behavioral characteristics of students who are blind or visually impaired or those who are thought to have visual impairments, the results of the observation can be more meaningful. Visual impairment is diagnosed by an eye care specialist, but often parents or school personnel can be the first to suspect that a student has a vision loss. Sidebar 6.1 lists some of the behavioral characteristics of students who are visually impaired. As noted in the sidebar, some vision-related behaviors are associated with specific causes of vision loss. Stereotyped behaviors are most often seen in students who are cognitively impaired, those with neurological as well as visual impairments, and students who are stressed, bored, or overstimulated.

Everyone engages in some form of self-stimulatory behaviors (Moss, 1993). Most do it in such a subtle way that it is usually not noticeable to others. Persons who are sighted are usually more aware of such behaviors in themselves than are persons who are visually impaired and are able to hide their behaviors when necessary.

Sidebar 6.1   SOME BEHAVIORAL CHARACTERISTICS OF STUDENTS WITH A VISION LOSS

Behavior	Possible Cause
Overreaching or underreaching of objects	Eyes not working in coordination
Holding reading material extremely close to the eyes	Poor vision, attempt to enlarge visual target and/or reduce the distraction of other items in the visual field
Having an eccentric gaze, or not looking at objects straight on	Characteristic of students with central vision loss or cortical visual impairment.
Displaying jerky eye movements	Nystagmus, usually associated with early vision loss and characteristic of students with visual impairment associated with the eye itself (ocular visual impairment)
Roving eye movement	Problems with eye muscles or inability to focus
Responding to movement and not to static objects	Cortical visual impairment
Squinting	Photosensitivity seen in various eye conditions, or refractive problems
Matching problems with colors or shades	Impaired color vision or contrast sensitivity difficulties
Showing unusual behavior in extreme lighting conditions (e.g., bright light or reduced lighting conditions)	Cataracts, cortical visual impairment, and albinism. Some students do better in more subdued lighting conditions
Rubbing eyes	Eye fatigue or a self-stimulatory behavior that can produce the experience of light in students with retinal disease
Tilting head to see better	Field losses, or attempts to steady jerky eye movements

(continued)

| Sidebar 6.1 | SOME BEHAVIORAL CHARACTERISTICS OF STUDENTS WITH A VISION LOSS *(continued)* |

Behavior	Possible Cause
Bumping into obstacles or tripping frequently while moving about the classroom or playground	Poor vision or poor motor planning or difficulty using multiple senses simultaneously
Difficulty in eye-hand coordination	Cortical visual impairment or other neurological difficulties
Resisting or avoiding using vision for normal tasks (looking at the blackboard, reading, etc.)	Vision provides erroneous or confusing information.
Excessive blinking	Eye fatigue often seen in individuals with poor vision
Light gazing	Cortical visual impairment or other ocular diseases. Can provide self-stimulation
Rocking and other excessive movements such as hand flapping	Self-stimulation related to boredom is often excessive in visually impaired individuals. Can be perseveration as seen in those with neurological deficits, or obsessive behavior to reduce anxiety

Activities such as foot tapping, finger drumming, gazing, and knuckle cracking are common examples. Persons who are blind or visually impaired can have these and many other self-stimulatory behaviors. The more severe the vision loss and the more severe the neurological impairment, the more pronounced the self-stimulatory behaviors tend to be.

For all people, self-stimulatory behaviors can increase with tension, stress, boredom, or fatigue. For persons who are sighted, glancing around, observing others, and staring in the distance are everyday behaviors that can reduce boredom. Such visual behaviors are not available to many people who are blind or visually impaired. Therefore, their self-stimulating behaviors take a different, more observable, form.

These behaviors, sometimes termed blind mannerisms, can include rocking, finger flicking, eye poking, light gazing, hopping or jumping, and vocalizing. With the proper interventions, these behaviors can be refocused, modified, or directed to a different, more private environment (McAdam et al., 1993). Students who exhibit self-stimulating behaviors are often (questionably) diagnosed as being autistic or autistic-like. The teacher of the students who are visually impaired can provide valuable information to the psychologist on the nature of self-stimulatory behaviors.

Self-stimulatory behaviors should be differentiated from obsessive-compulsive behavior and perseveration. Although self-stimulatory behavior can increase with stress and can reduce tension for some, its primary purpose is to relieve boredom. Obsessive-compulsive behaviors are primarily designed to reduce anxiety, while perseveration will evidence itself in many other tasks and is usually defined as continuing an activity long after it continues to be appropriate.

INTERACTING WITH STUDENTS WHO ARE BLIND OR VISUALLY IMPAIRED

The Initial Meeting

Many persons who are disabled, and most students both disabled and not, are cautioned about strangers and can become suspicious of them. When first meeting the student to be evaluated, it is a good idea to have someone with whom the student is familiar to introduce you. This can take place anytime from several days to immediately before the assessment. Many students who are blind or visually impaired, especially those with other disabilities, are disturbed by changes in routine. Helping the student anticipate a new and unfamiliar activity with an unfamiliar person can improve rapport and foster trust. Many techniques can be useful in helping the student who is visually impaired adjust to the intrusion of an assessment, including orally informing him or her of what to expect, and performing the assessment in short segments. A cooperative and relaxed subject will provide much more valid assessment.

Communicating with Students Who Are Visually Impaired

Psychologists not accustomed to working with students who are visually impaired are sometimes uncomfortable at first. Sighted persons' everyday vocabulary contains many vision-related words and expressions: "look at this," "the way I see it . . . ," "it looks like . . . ," "I see what you mean." Students who are blind or visually impaired use these terms as well.

Vocabulary develops best when words and phrases are associated with the visual image of the object or action associated with the word. Students who are blind or visually impaired often hear words but do not have the opportunity to associate the words with the object or actions being addressed. Thus, they may use words without knowing their meaning or full meaning. Some visually impaired students have prodigious auditory memory skills, achieved by practice using their auditory memory but resulting in their using words they have heard but whose meanings they do not know. Such so-called verbalisms (also called hollow language) can mislead sighted persons. It is often useful to investigate more fully the meaning intended by the student who is visually impaired.

Traveling with Students Who Are Blind or Visually Impaired

Traveling from the classroom to the testing room with a student who is blind or visually impaired can require skill. Many inexperienced persons working for the first time with such students either hold their hands or push or pull them. This can be degrading and confusing for many students who are visually impaired. The preferred technique of human (or sighted) guide is simple and can be demonstrated to the psychologist by the teacher of students who are visually impaired or the O&M specialist and is described in Chapter 9. The student who is visually impaired takes the guide's arm just above the elbow and the guide leads the student by walking one step ahead of him or her. It is also necessary for the guide to describe orally where he or she is going, what obstacles might be

Frances K. Liefert

Comfort and ease in travel can be maximized for both the student who is blind or visually impaired and the guide when the student holds the guide's arm and walks slightly behind him or her.

anticipated (such as ramps or stairs), and what changes in direction are ahead. Traveling through doorways can be tricky, but can be done safely and with dignity with instruction from one of the specialists mentioned here.

The Testing Site

When the assessor and student arrive at the testing site, it is a good idea to describe where they are, and even to allow the student a moment of exploration. If there are sounds in the area, the assessor can inform the student about them. The assessor's voice will not replace the student's vision, but keeping the student informed as to what could affect him or her will go a long way toward establishing rapport and helping the student feel comfortable.

Touching Students Who Are Blind or Visually Impaired

Testing a student who is blind or visually impaired often requires the examiner to touch the student or to guide the student's hands to explore stimulus items. Such contact can be startling or make the student feel that his or her space has been violated. Many students who are visually impaired are tactilely defensive: they are highly sensitive to touch and may react adversely.

The teacher of students who are visually impaired and family members can provide advance warning if touch is an issue with the student. The assessor can ask the student's permission to touch him or her and communicate the purpose of the contact: "I'd like to guide your hands over these designs to show you what I want you to do. Is it OK to touch you?" Seeking permission and alerting the student communicates respect for the student, helps him or her anticipate what is about to happen, and gives the student control.

Students who are tactilely defensive feel uncomfortable being touched or with certain aspects of touch or touching. Some students can feel pain when touched or can be easily subject to extreme tactile overload. Tactile defensiveness can take many forms; if the examiner is not sensitive to this issue, it can severely damage rapport. For students with tactile defensiveness, a heavier touch may be better tolerated than a light touch, or vice versa. Guiding the student's hand to the intended target with the technique known as "hand under hand" is often more tolerable. Again, the assessor needs to ask permission and inform the students when, where, and why one is planning to touch him or her (Kranowitz, 1998).

Some students who are blind or visually impaired, and especially those with associated brain damage, can have significant tactile insensitivity. Their families report that they do not cry when physically injured. Such students can have difficulty learning through touch, impairing not only acquisition of braille skills but also any learning that involves touch. Performing motor tasks that require tactile feedback of any kind can be affected, and sensitivity can be reduced for textures, shapes, temperature, and other sensory experiences.

PSYCHOLOGICAL ASSESSMENT

The Testing Environment

When tests are referred to in this section, the author is referring to standardized tests. As described by Lewis and Russo (1998), standardization as it applies to tests refers to two basic components. The first involves a defined procedure for administration and scoring. Standardized tests must be administered by all who use them in exactly the same way, using the same instructions, materials, intonation, and timing on each administration (see Chapter 5 for a discussion of testing). Probing for clarification of ambiguous responses must be conducted precisely so as not to hint at an answer. Thus, a standardized test administered in one part of the country is exactly comparable to one administered in another part of the country.

The second component in standardization refers to the normative sample. The proper use of a normative sample gives meaning to the resulting scores. A raw score of 10 on a math test may not tell very much. Knowing that a raw score places the student at the 90th percentile puts that score into a meaningful framework for correct interpretation.

Assessing the student who is blind or visually impaired requires many of the same considerations as assessing sighted persons, with some important differences. Lighting can be a critical consideration. The lighting needs of many visually impaired students may not appear logical to the novice assessor of visually impaired students. For many students who have photosensitivity, too much light can impair their visual functioning. The source and direction of lighting can be important. Usually lighting from behind or over the shoulder is preferable. Glare or shadows may cause difficulty. Stimulus items that are easy for sighted persons to perceive can cause glare for the person with limited vision. The teacher who is assessing the student's functional vision can provide valuable information on modifying the test environment appropriately. Appendix A of this book also provides valuable information.

Students who are visually impaired may position themselves in unusual ways in relation to stimulus items in order to maximize their vision. Holding items extremely close to their eyes may improve their ability to see. For other students, doing so might reduce their visual field; items requiring such students to look at a wide field may be difficult. Such stimulus items as Picture Arrangement (which requires the subject to rearrange a series of small pictures to tell a logical story) and Picture Completion (which requires a subject to identify missing parts of pictures) can become inordinately difficult. See the Resources section of this chapter for more information on these and other assessment tools.

Adaptations such as the use of closed-circuit television equipment and magnifiers (described thoroughly in Chapter 4) that enlarge material being viewed should always be considered. The teacher of students who are visually impaired will know if the particular student being assessed is experienced enough with such devices to use them during assessment. If used, they should be described in the report. Use of such devices can be a tradeoff in many cases: some aspects of vision might be improved, but perspective may be lost and often the timing of timed items is affected.

A simple rule of thumb for many assessors is to try an approach. The outcome could be surprising, and provide useful and unexpected information. For example, some students who are visually impaired can be effective visual processors when the materials on which they are working are appropriately accessible. Limited vision does not mean ineffective vision. The discovery that a visually impaired student prefers his or her vision over other sensory modalities can have significant implications for program planning.

Assessment of Cognitive Functioning

Cognitive functioning is significantly influenced by opportunities for learning. Vision loss can greatly reduce such opportunities; the greater the vision loss, the greater the loss of learning opportunity. Also true is that many students who are blind or visually impaired have additional impairments, some neurological, that can interfere with functioning of all types.

Few assessment instruments are designed for and normed on students who are blind or visually impaired. Those with design and normative information based on visually impaired students are often not updated or revised in a timely fashion. In addition, they are often developed for a particular subgroup of visually impaired persons, such as students in special schools or centers.

Scales of cognitive ability or development designed for sighted persons can often provide meaningful information even when used with the student who is blind or visually impaired. Instruments that require vision can be useful even for those who have limited vision.

There are many opinions regarding the modification of instruments designed for individuals who are sighted to make them more suitable for persons who are blind or visually impaired. Such modifications should be described in the report. It must be borne in mind that when an evaluation is repeated, there is no guarantee that the modifications can be exactly replicated, permitting accurate comparisons of results.

The issue of reference group can be of critical importance. Some tests that are standardized on individuals who are fully sighted can easily be used without modification with students who are blind or visually impaired. Will the standard score results carry the same meaning as they would for a sighted individual? Can tests such as the *Blind Learning Aptitude Test (BLAT)*, standardized on blind students, be compared with the results of a *Wechsler Intelligence Scale for Children, Third Revision*, which was standardized on sighted subjects? Comparison of the results of various instruments that utilize different sensory modalities can provide helpful diagnostic information. Such comparisons can provide important information on the relative processing skills and modality strengths of students, leading to helpful recommendations for teaching. (See the Resources section of this chapter for detailed descriptions of these assessment tools.)

Stepping out of the box of traditional assessment is to be expected when assessing any student with a low incidence disability such as blindness or visual impairment. Often it is necessary to use instruments whose norms are not appropriate for the student being assessed. Objects can be substituted for printed pictures in counting activities. Objects of all types can be used to assess understanding of size, shape, texture, and other values. It is important to understand that replicas of real objects do not always have the same meaning for an individual who is blind or visually impaired. Plastic fruit does not smell, feel like, or taste like real fruit. One teacher working with a blind student was observed using a small plastic replica of a container of french fries. A sighted student would recognize the replica immediately. To the blind student, it bore no resemblance to the real thing.

Assessment of Emotional Functioning

Assessment of emotional status should be a component of every assessment of a student who is blind or visually impaired. Issues such as self-esteem, depression, and anxiety are often a part of the clinical picture of a student who is blind or visually impaired. Guilt can take many forms in students who are disabled. They often require greater care than nondisabled siblings and their needs can be a stressor on family functioning.

As with cognitive and other types of assessment, choice of assessment instruments greatly depends on the extent of the student's vision loss and severity of any associated disabilities. If vision is severely impaired or absent, instruments requiring vision are inappropriate. Student-read inventories or checklists can be translated into braille for students with sufficient braille reading skills, when translation services are available. The teacher of students who are visually impaired is a good resource to describe the student's reading level. Reading inventories or checklists aloud to students, then requiring a simple true or false, or yes or no response is a possibility, but the privacy of the student's response is compromised. Word association tests or sentence completion tests carry the same risk. Whatever approach is used should be described in the report, and any time infringements noted. It should be kept in mind that reading braille usually takes most students longer than reading the same material in print. In addition, brailling responses may take longer.

With these considerations in mind, many inventories, checklists, association tests, and sentence completion tests are useful in assessing students who are blind or visually impaired. Checklists and other instruments completed by parents, teachers, or other caregivers can also be valuable.

As with all instruments, creativity on the part of the examiner is often needed. Instruments designed for sighted students can be useful, and instruments normed on older or younger students can provide valuable information. Results can be reported in nonstandard formats such as age or grade equivalents when standard scores or percentiles are typically used. Any modifications of techniques must be adequately described so that the reader can more accurately understand the results.

CASE STUDIES

The following case studies are examples of assessments of students with two types of visual impairment: cortical visual impairment and retinopathy of prematurity. These two types of visual impairment combined compose nearly 40 percent of the cases of vision loss among children in the United States (Ferrell, 1998). Students with these conditions are among the most likely to have additional disabilities. They are also examples of the type of student most likely to be evaluated by school psychologists.

The excerpts from various sections of Gerry's and Mary Ann's psychoeducational reports are presented to give the psychologist a general introduction to some of the issues relevant in assessing students with these visual impairments. The excerpts presented are small portions of various sections of the entire reports.

Gerry: A Student with Cortical Visual Impairment

The following summary is exerpted from Gerry's final psychoeducational report. Some modifications have been made for clarity.

Reasons for Referral

At about 5 years of age Gerry sustained serious head injuries when he was run over by a car driven by a neighbor. Gerry was in a coma for two months and had 17 fractures to bones in his head and face. He was hospitalized for 5 months and was unable to speak during much of that time. At the time of this assessment, Gerry was 8 years, 9 months, and 26 days old.

As a result of his head injury, Gerry sustained severe cortical visual impairment and significant orthopedic impairments.

When he was referred to the assessment clinic, concern was expressed by his parents and teachers that his progress in print reading was exceedingly slow, compared with the general impression that his cognitive functioning was at least average. A recommendation was requested for an appropriate reading medium for Gerry, and if an investment should be made in talking books for him.

Gerry's Vision

The following is excerpted from Gerry's vision report from the visual assessment clinic. Note the complexity of his visual functioning.

Gerry has low vision due to head trauma, which caused damage to his visual pathways and oculomotor cortical system.

Gerry's contrast sensitivity (the ability to detect subtle shades of gray) was tested using the Mr. Happy test. His contrast sensitivity of 3.2 percent was found to be a moderate reduction from the normal 1 to 0.05 percent.

Gerry has damage to his visual pathways and his oculomotor cortical system, more commonly referred to as a cortical visual impairment (CVI). This damage has caused a disruption in the visual processing areas of Gerry's brain.

Gerry's distance visual acuity was measured with an illuminated Bailey-Lovie chart at 20/400 OD (right eye) and 20/640 OS (left eye) without correction. His uncorrected near visual acuities were measured with the Bailey-Lovie word chart at 20/1000 OD and 20/1600 OS.

The muscles of the eye control eye movement and Gerry's eye movements were substantially restricted. The right eye had very limited eye movement. He was especially limited in abduction and upgaze (upward rotation of the eye). (The abductor muscle of the eye allows you to move the eye away from the nose.) The left eye had better lateral eye movement but upgaze was also significantly restricted.

Gerry's visual field showed binasal hemianopsia. Hemianopsia is the nonseeing area of the visual field, which in Gerry's case was binasal (affected both sides of his nose). Field loss produces a nonseeing area between the right eye's and left eye's lines of fixation. The size of this nonseeing area depended on the direction of the right eye and the left eye gaze.

Gerry is legally blind due to his visual acuity measure. His near visual acuity measure along with his significant field loss binasally and the eye muscle restrictions make reading print, even very large print, extremely challenging for Gerry. (See Sidebar 6.2 for a discussion of learning media assessment.)

School-Related Aspects of CVI

When working with students who have CVI it is important to understand some of the associated conditions that can occur. CVI is sometimes associated with other neurological disorders, including

---

Sidebar 6.2   PRINT OR TACTILE LEARNING MEDIA

Based on the vision examination, Gerry's vision deficits alone suggest a reading medium other than print. Students with usable vision might be recommended for normal sized print, enlarged print, or print with the assistance of enlargers or magnifiers. Those without usable vision might receive a recommendation for braille, or talking books, or both. It is also not unusual for several reading media to be recommended, depending on the task. Those with even barely usable vision can benefit from learning some print reading as a convenience. (See Chapter 5, "Expanded Core Curriculum: Education," for a detailed discussion of learning media assessment.)

seizures, cerebral palsy, learning disabilities, deafness, and hydro-cephalus. Spatial confusion is common in students with CVI.

CVI causes vision to fluctuate throughout the day or the week. Each individual is different; Gerry may have had times of the day when he saw better than at others. These "good vision" times may vary from day to day or even minute to minute. It is possible that Gerry may have been visually locating or identifying items and then a short time later would have been unable to perform the same task. Some students learn to recognize that they are having a difficult time with their vision, but others are oblivious to discrepancies in their visual functioning. Gerry frequently rubbed his eyes during his assessment period. During the vision clinic evaluation, Gerry complained of itchy eyes. A fresh abrasion of his lid due to frequent rubbing was noticed.

Fluctuation in performance may also have an affect on other abilities, including spatial awareness, motor control, and memory. Fatigue and distractions can influence the fluctuation of vision. It is important for staff and families to realize that the student is not being stubborn or malingering, but rather may have no control over his or her visual functioning. It is not uncommon that an individual with CVI will become frustrated over the fluctuating nature of his or her vision. Due to the fluctuation that occurred with Gerry's vision, his performance on other tasks may have been affected. Students with CVI frequently prefer to use touch rather than use vision as their primary exploratory sense.

Fluctuation in performance can sometimes be reduced by elim-inating tiredness, extraneous noise, and other distractions. Some-times darkening the room slightly or providing diffuse lighting can encourage a student to concentrate on the task at hand.

Movement frequently triggers the ability to use vision in students with CVI. Movement can be either the person moving or the target object moving. Many students with CVI see better while walking than while standing still.

Visual field difficulties are often associated with CVI. Some-times visual fields may be symmetrically reduced, producing what is termed tunnel vision, but in many cases visual field losses are greater on one side than the other. Another type of visual field loss called scotomas can occur. These are blind spots that may be scattered throughout the visual field in a random pattern. It is important to realize that students with visual field deficits probably do not realize that they are missing portions of their surroundings, even if those portions are substantial.

In students with CVI, recovery can continue to occur in visual performance, as well as in the performance of mental and physical skills. There is, however, no way to predict the speed and scope of such recovery. Repetition and practice of activities are vital in promoting learning. It is also important to return to activities that have previously seemed too difficult, since sufficient recovery in a particular area may make performance of the task possible later.

The brain is a necessary component in interpreting and understanding a visual message. For students with neurologic damage, disruptions in visual functioning cannot be considered in isolation from other functions. Visual attention does not automatically mean cognitive understanding. The use of vision is also an emotional process. Students with CVI tend to use the visual system more if they feel confident about what is expected, have previously experienced the activity and enjoyed it, or find the task interesting.

Formal Psychoeducational Assessment

As part of Gerry's assessment, he was administered various tests without modification from standardized procedure. (These tests are described in more detail in the Resources section for this chapter.) On the *Wechsler Intelligence Scale for Children, Third Revision (WISC-III)*, he achieved a verbal score of 99. A listing of his subscale scores is provided in Table 6.1 (subscale average is 10). On the *Slosson Intelligence Test Revised (SIT-R)* he achieved a standard IQ score of 111. On the *Test of Nonverbal Intelligence, 3rd revision (TONI-3)*, Gerry achieved a standard IQ score of 83. On *The Blind Learning Aptitude Test (BLAT)*, Gerry earned a standard IQ score between 115 and 130.

There were no test results available from before Gerry's accident, so no determination can be made about what changes have taken place as a result. The profile from his results, however, was

Table 6.1	GERRY'S SCORES ON THE *WECHSLER INTELLIGENCE SCALE FOR CHILDREN*		
Verbal Subscales	**Scaled Score**	**Percentile Rank**	**Description of Subscales**
Information	11	63	Measures general knowledge and facts
Similarities	10	60	Finding commonalities between words
Arithmetic	11	63	Mental arithmetic
Vocabulary	8	25	Knowledge of word meanings
Comprehension	9	37	Social information: what should we do in certain situations
Digit Span	12	75	Remembering number sequences forward and reversed

one of several sometimes seen in students with CVI. As indicated by his scores on the *WISC-III* and the *SIT-R*, his verbal reasoning skills were within average range. His memory skills seemed intact from the test results presented here and from information provided during interviews. These would suggest that his auditory input channels were functioning effectively. Talking books would be an appropriate information gathering medium for Gerry, if sufficient environmental experiences are provided to help him gain meaning to what he hears.

The results of the *TONI-3* suggested that his visual processing has been impaired (this conclusion was supported by scores on other visual processing measures). The eye report indicated that he had experienced a significant loss of visual acuity, but his visual processing was also significantly disrupted.

The results on the *BLAT* suggest that Gerry's tactile sensitivity was unimpaired and his ability to process tactile symbols was at least above average. Braille rather than print would serve Gerry best as a primary reading modality. For students with suitable vision, some print reading skill is desirable even though print might not be their primary reading medium.

The results of this assessment suggested that Gerry received injury to his brain as a result of his accident. His verbal processing and memory skills seemed very functional as were his tactile abilities. His visual processing skills, on the other hand, showed significant damage. The assessment team agreed with the psychologist's recommendation that talking books, which use auditory channels of learning, would be desirable as long as Gerry is provided the real life experiences to make what he hears meaningful, and that braille is likely to be his primary reading medium.

Mary Ann: A Student with Retinopathy of Prematurity

Part of Mary Ann's assessment report is presented here. She is a good example of students who have retinopathy of prematurity (ROP) which can be very complicated and varied (see Appendix A for a complete description of ROP). She was a 12-year-old sixth grader at the time of this assessment.

Reason for Referral

Mary Ann was jointly referred for assessment to the vision assessment clinic by her school district and her parents. The school district identified evaluation of assistive technology, transition services, academic achievement, and mobility needs as their highest priorities for this assessment. They were also interested in finding ways to help Mary Ann work more independently, and more quickly, to keep up with regular schoolwork and assignments. They stated that she did very well, but needed to be pushed all of the time to keep up with her classmates and assignments. They were interested in an assessment program's opinion of her skills and recommendations for improvements.

Mary Ann's parents identified evaluation of mobility needs, assistive technology, academic achievement, and transition services as their highest priorities for the assessment. They were also interested in making sure all her needs were currently being met in the school district.

Mary Ann's Vision

Mary Ann was born prematurely and, when she was three months old, was found to have stage V retinopathy of prematurity. Stage V is the complete detachment of the retina, which consists of the layers in the back of the eye where the nerves should receive visual information and transmit it to the brain. Mary Ann had surgery in an attempt to reattach her retina in the right eye. At the time of this assessment, Mary Ann claimed to have some light perception, presumably in her right eye. None of the assessment team members noticed her using that light perception in any of the activities provided. Mary Ann held her head down much of the time during the assessment and poked her eyes frequently. Eye poking is one of the behavior mannerisms often seen in students with retinal damage.

Vision-Related Recommendations

The teacher assessing Mary Ann's functional vision recommended that Mary Ann would benefit from an education program that addresses all areas of the expanded core curriculum for students who are blind or visually impaired. She noted that the expanded core curriculum includes many areas beyond the curriculum followed by sighted students and frequently takes more time to complete than the 13 years of elementary and secondary school expected. (More information about the expanded core curriculum can be found in Chapters 5, 8, and 9.)

Ms. Emery, Mary Ann's teacher, had developed a good plan for helping Mary Ann to reduce her eye poking. By giving her a verbal cue that was not embarrassing, she reminded Mary Ann to alter her habit in a way that may eventually lead to Mary Ann reminding herself. Eye poking is a difficult habit to break because it is apparently very compelling for people with retinal disorders. The primary reasons to stop eye poking are visual; not to look strange when socializing with others and to keep from having strange-looking eyes. It was important to give Mary Ann gentle assistance in breaking this habit so that the rewards for stopping it were greater than the incentives for continuing.

Mary Ann's Other Disabilities

Mary Ann was born extremely prematurely and was hospitalized for about three months after birth. She had some of the heart and lung problems associated with prematurity. She has certain muscle tone problems, toe walks, and may have certain information processing difficulties.

Behavior During Assessment

Mary Ann worked for long periods of time without breaks during the assessment and without complaint. When she tired, she would "phase out," but would not ask for a break. When a break was suggested in order to revive her, she responded appropriately and usually in the affirmative.

Mary Ann's motor movement was somewhat awkward. She showed excessive limb movements and toe walked. When talking, she held her head in a downward position, talking into her chest. Her sitting posture was excessively slumped over her work area and, at times, her speech was difficult to hear. When requested to sit up, she responded appropriately, at least for a while.

Mary Ann was very slow in making her responses, which sometimes elicited a prompt to determine if she was still attending. She usually was attending properly, and often was mulling over previously asked questions while simultaneously attending to the current item. When not prompted for a response, she usually responded eventually, and appropriately. She was just very slow.

Mary Ann showed an element of passivity, usually holding back while waiting for a prompt, even when it seemed she knew what was expected of her. This passivity impaired her productivity, interfered with her initiative, and usually led to a prompt from the adult working with her.

Mary Ann seemed to have difficulty learning her way around the testing environment. Typically, a student of her age and cognitive ability would quickly learn her way around the assessment classroom and travel to the testing table, conference table, or bathroom independently. Mary Ann usually needed assistance of some kind or other to navigate the assessment classroom, even after several days' experience in that environment.

Cognitive Functioning

The following psychological assessment techniques were used without modification (see the Resources section of this chapter for further information on these tools): *Wechsler Intelligence Scale for Children, Third Revision (WISC-III)* (verbal subtests only), *Blind Learning Aptitude Test (BLAT)*, and *Peabody Individual Achievement Test, General Information Subtest*.

On the *WISC-III*, Mary Ann achieved a verbal IQ of 93, within the average range. Her scores can be found in Table 6.2.

Table 6.2	MARY ANN'S SCORES ON THE WECHSLER INTELLIGENCE SCALE FOR CHILDREN		
Verbal Subscales	**Scaled Score**	**Percentile Rank**	**Description of Subscales**
Information	8	25	Measures general knowledge and facts
Similarities	8	25	Finding commonalitites between words
Arithmetic	8	25	Mental arithmetic
Vocabulary	8	25	Knowledge of word meanings
Comprehension	12	75	Social information: what we should do certain situations
Digit Span	16	98	Remembering number sequences forward and reversed

On the BLAT Mary Ann generally had a light touch on the braille-like designs. She used the index fingers of both hands. She lost concentration, especially as tasks became difficult, and her tactile memory seemed to lapse on occasion. On some types of tasks, Mary Ann had difficulty remembering the expectation and had to be given the instructions again. Some "scrubbing" was noticed as her fingers tried to "read" the designs (defined as movement of the fingers heavily and repeatedly over braille or braille-like designs). Scrubbing can be seen in many students including those with neurologic difficulties with reduced tactile sensitivity.

Mary Ann was a very slow processor, taking somewhat longer to complete this test than other blind or visually impaired students of similar age and cognitive level. There were times when she "drifted off" and on one occasion was taken for a walk to restimulate her. Even at her best, however, her processing time was longer than is typical.

Mary Ann's errors frequently involved reversals or rotations of the correct answer, and when suggestions were made about techniques that would be helpful, she sometimes did not use them. Mary Ann achieved a standard score of 97, which is in the average range and commensurate with her score on the *WISC-III*, a measure of verbal skills.

The *Peabody Individual Achievement Test, General Information Subtest*, assesses a student's general information, which is the type of information usually learned in school. It reflects long-term memory usually for meaningful information. For students who are blind or visually impaired, it can reflect exposure to learning opportunities. This is often a problem for students who are visually impaired because vision loss deprives them of important environmental experiences and opportunities for incidental learning. Mary Ann achieved a grade equivalent of 3.8 (equivalent to the latter part of third grade). Her score is substantially below her current placement of sixth grade.

Students born with extreme prematurity often have a cluster of characteristics. Mary Ann showed some, but certainly not all, of those characteristics, in her cognitive processing. She was within the average range in most areas of thinking and reasoning, showing relative strength in her knowledge of social/interpersonal processes. She showed strength in auditory memory and short-term memory skills. Her ability to concentrate seemed good, especially when activities were not too frustrating for her.

Mary Ann showed reduced long-term memory. This may be related to limited environmental experience, as is often the case with students who are blind or visually impaired. Often, simple exposure is not sufficient to develop understanding. Exposure must be repetitive and is best when combined with multiple sensory modalities to provide optimal learning. Without vision, Mary Ann's other sensory channels must work harder and none of them is more efficient than vision for learning about the world.

Mary Ann's tactile sensitivity may have been reduced, which is not unusual for students with motor and/or muscle tone issues. This could inhibit her learning through the use of touch. Braille reading in particular requires a sensitive touch that might be affected by her reduced tactile sensitivity.

SUMMARY

This chapter is provided as an introduction to the assessment of students who are blind or visually impaired for the school psychologist, and to provide the nonpsychologist with some information on the type of assessment a school psychologist might perform. As noted, the two cases presented highlight some of the characteristics seen in students in addition to their visual impairment. Other types of visual impairment and their associated characteristics are discussed throughout this book and particularly in Appendix A, "Common Causes of Visual Impairment."

As noted in various places in this chapter, other chapters of this book should be reviewed for more in-depth information on assessment components, curriculum for visually impaired students, and vision. Chapter 7 will provide a description of how the speech and language pathologist on the assessment team works with the rest of the team members, as well as on his or her own, to assess students who are blind or visually impaired.

REFERENCES

Bradley-Johnson, S., & Harris, S. (1990). Best practices in working with students with a vision loss. In Thomas & Grimes (Eds.), *Best practices in school psychology, II*. National Association of School Psychologists, 4340 East West Highway, Bethesda, MD 20814.

Ferrell, K. A. (with A. R. Shaw & S. J. Deitz). (1998). *Project PRISM: A longitudinal study of developmental patterns of children who are visually impaired. Final report* (Grant H023C10188, US Dept. of Education, Field-initiated research, CFDA 84.023). Greeley, CO: University of Northern Colorado. Available at http://vision.unco.edu/Faculty/Ferrell/PRISM/default.html

Hall, A., Scholl, G. T., & Swallow, R. M. (1986). Psychoeducational assessment. In G.T. Scholl (Ed.), *Foundations of education for blind and visually handicapped children and youth: Theory and practice*. New York: American Foundation for the Blind.

Kranowitz, C. S., (1998). *The out-of-sync child*. Arlington Heights, IL: Skylight Press.

Lewis, S., & Russo, R. (1998). Educational assessment for students who have visual impairments with other disabilities. In S. Z. Sacks & R. K. Silberman (Eds.), *Educating students who have visual impairments with other disabilities*. Baltimore, MD: Paul H. Brookes.

McAdam, D. B., O'Cleirigh, C. M., & Cuvo, A. J. (1993). Self-monitoring and verbal feedback to reduce stereotypic body rocking in a congenitally blind adult. *RE:view, 24*(4), 163–172.

Moss, K. (1993). Looking at self-stimulation in the pursuit of leisure or I'm okay, you have a mannerism. *P.S. NEWS, 5*(3).

RESOURCES FOR PSYCHOLOGICAL ASSESSMENT

The following list of tests does not include all the tests available or useful for the assessment of students with visual impairment. It is a sampling of instruments that the typical school psychologist might find useful. Many of them are readily available in most school districts; others might be borrowed from agencies who serve students who are visually impaired, and others might be purchased.

Blind Learning Aptitude Test (BLAT)
Author: Newland, T. E.
Ages: 6 to 16 years
Publisher: University of Illinois Press
             118 University Press Bldg.
             1325 S. Oak Street
             Champaign, IL 61820
Date: 1971
Type of instrument: Normative-referenced assessment instrument.

Qualifications to administer: Graduate training in tests and measurement, with relevant clinical experience.
Stated purpose: To obtain a picture of the learning potential of young blind children.
Comments: This can be seen as a culture free test of learning aptitude and a good predictor of the potential to learn braille. Students with usable vision may try to use their vision in completing the test. The examiner may want to experiment with procedures such as lowering the lights in the test environment. Encouraging the student to use only their hands is also helpful. Students with some familiarity with braille may feel more comfortable with the stimulus items. Users should be cautious as this test has not been renormed for a long time and the distribution of scores in the normative sample may be somewhat skewed. The test may be hard to obtain. Students with tactile insensitivity such as those with neurological damage may have difficulty with the stimulus items.
Normative data: The normative sample was large and representative of the blind population as a whole. It is not clear if the BLAT assesses aptitude equivalently in those with low vision and those who are blind. Reliability and validity data for the BLAT, however, are poor and incomplete.
Standardization: The BLAT was designed for those without vision. The manual states that aptitude is reliably discerned only up to 12 years of age.
Adaptation: As an instrument designed for students with visual impairment or multiple disabilities, the BLAT does not require adaptation.

Child Anxiety Scale (CAS)
Author: Gillis, J. S.

The listings in this section are adapted with permission from Keith Benoff, Mary Ann Lang and Michelle Beck-Viisola, *Compendium of Instruments for Assessing the Skills and Interests of Individuals with Visual Impairments or Multiple Disabilities* (New York: Lighthouse International, May 2001). Available free in electronic format by visiting <http://www.visionconnection.org/> www.visionconnection.org, search term,"Assessment Compendium."

Ages: 5 to 12 years
Publisher: Institute for Personality and
Ability Testing
1801 Woodfield Drive
Savoy, IL 61874
Date: 1980
Type of instrument: Normative-
referenced assessment instrument.

Qualifications to administer: Master's
degree in psychology, counseling, or
social work, with relevant courses in
tests and measurement.
Stated purpose: To detect anxiety-based
disturbances in young children.
Comments: A brief screening instrument that assesses anxiety experienced
by children. It is intended to identify
adjustment problems at an early stage.
It is administered by audiocassette, and
children are asked to mark a response
sheet. For each item, the response sheet
has a picture surrounded by a red circle on one end of a line and a blue
circle on the other. Students are in-
structed to mark closer to the red circle
or the red circle itself if they feel more
anxiety or closer to the blue circle or
the blue circle itself if they feel less
anxiety. Students are asked to mark
their feelings about each statement
based on their present feelings. This
format was selected for its nonverbal
response pattern.
Normative data: The publisher states
that the normative data collected assessed only those without visual impairment, and no set of data was collected
for administration to students who are
visually impaired or with multiple disabilities. It is unclear how applicable
the available normative data may be for
those with visual impairment or multiple disabilities.

Standardization: The CAS has not been
standardized in administration procedure and interpretation for individuals
who are visually impaired with multiple disabilities. Testing students who
are blind is clearly impossible. Children
who are visually impaired may have
difficulty discerning the colored circles
or be unable to mark a particular point
on a line appropriately. An additional
consideration applies to children with
multiple disabilities who may be unable
to complete the task because of motor
problems. Ruling out these problems
may permit the use of the CAS.
Adaptations: The publisher states that
the CAS has not been formally adapted
for students with visual impairment
or multiple disabilities. Any informally
adapted items require standardization
and normalization before comparison of
performance on adapted items to existing normative data.

*Columbia Mental Maturity Scale
(CMMS)*
Authors: Burgemeister, B. B., Blum,
L. H., and Lorge, I.
Ages: 3 to 10 years
Publisher: The Psychological
Corporation
19500 Bulverde Road
San Antonio, TX 78259
Date: 1972
Type of instrument: Normative-
referenced assessment instrument.

Qualifications to administer: Completion of advanced training in psychology
or education, with relevant clinical experience and appropriate state licensure or certification.
Stated purpose: To provide an estimate of the general reasoning ability
of children.

Comments: It consists of 92 pictorial and figural classification items arranged in a series of eight overlapping levels. Children are asked to look at a selection of drawings presented on a card and point to the one that is different from the others. For younger children, the distinctions are based on color, size, and form. For older children, the distinctions are related to more abstract elements. The CMMS was not designed to be an authoritative intelligence quotient test, but a screening test providing nonspecific information about a child's reasoning abilities.

Normative data: The publisher does not specify whether individuals who are visually impaired or have multiple disabilities were included in the normative studies conducted. It is unclear how applicable the available normative data from these studies may be for drawing conclusions about those with visual impairment or multiple disabilities.

Standardization: The CMMS has not been standardized in administration procedure and interpretation for individuals with visual impairment and multiple disabilities.

Adaptations: No adaptations are referenced for this instrument. It can only be used with students with usable vision. Students with restricted fields may be at a disadvantage.

Cognitive Test for the Blind and Visually Impaired (CTB)
Author: Dial, J. G.
Ages: 13 years to adult
Publisher: McCarron Dial Systems
P.O. Box 45628
Dallas, TX 75245
Date: 1992

Type of instrument: Normative-referenced assessment instrument.

Qualifications to administer: Graduate training in tests and measurement, with relevant clinical experience.

Stated purpose: To measure cognitive, intellectual, and information processing skills.

Comments: Consists of a verbal scale and a nonvisual performance scale, from which a total score is derived. There are six verbal subtests: auditory analysis and sound repetition, immediate digit recall, language comprehension and memory, letter-number learning, vocabulary, and abstract reasoning. There are five nonvisual performance tests: category learning, category memory, memory recognition, pattern recall, and spatial analysis. Six factors are derived from both the verbal and performance tasks: conceptual, learning, verbal memory, nonverbal memory, language, and spatial. The CTB differs from most measures of intelligence, claims its author, in that it focuses on active problem solving, learning, and memory.

Normative data: A separate set of normative data is available for those who are visually impaired and those who are blind. The publisher does not specify whether individuals with multiple disabilities were included in studies resulting in the available normative data.

Standardization: The CTB is a central component of the comprehensive vocational evaluation system, an assessment curriculum designed specifically for individuals who are blind or visually impaired. Standardization procedures have been established separately for individuals with visual impairment, as well as those who are blind.

Adaptations: There is no need for any adaptation.

Developmental Profile II (DP-II)
Authors: Alpern, G., Boll, T., and Shearer, M.
Ages: Birth to 9 years
Publisher: Western Psychological
          Services
          12031 Wilshire Boulevard
          Los Angeles, CA 90025-1251
Date: 1986
Type of instrument: Normative-referenced assessment instrument.

Qualifications to administer: Graduate training in tests and measurement, with relevant clinical experience and appropriate licensure.
Stated purpose: To assess a child's functional, developmental age level.
Comments: Composed of five scales: physical age, self-help age, social age, academic age, and communication age. The test manual states that the functional utility is reliable only until seven years of age, despite a stated upper age limit of nine years.
Normative data: Although the publisher specifies the inclusion of students with impairments, no psychometric information is provided for the establishment of norms for them, nor is there mention of including students who are visually impaired or with multiple disabilities. It is unclear how applicable the available normative data may be for those with visual impairment or multiple disabilities.
Standardization: The DP-II may be administered as an interview with parents, a combination of an interview and direct testing of the student, or an interview completed by the teacher. There is a set of administration procedures for students who are visually impaired or have multiple disabilities.
Adaptations: As an instrument that may be given to a student's parents or teacher, there is no need to adapt.

Developmental Test of Visual-Motor Integration, 4th Edition (VMI)
Authors: Beery, K. E. and Buktenica, N. A.
Ages: 3 to 18 years
Publisher: Modern Curriculum Press
          135 South Mount Zion Road
          P.O. Box 2500
          Lebanon, IN 46052
Date: 1997
Type of instrument: Normative-referenced assessment instrument.

Qualifications to administer: Graduate training in tests and measurement, with relevant clinical experience.
Stated purpose: To screen for visual-motor problems.
Comments: Evaluates a child's ability to copy a series of geometric designs presented in order of increasing difficulty. Includes 24 items, which yields a developmental age score and a standard score from which a percentile is derived. It is meant to assess children with neurological impairments, learning disabilities, and motor/perceptual problems. The performance score is based on the number of correct reproductions.
Normative data: The publisher states that the normative data collected assessed only those without visual impairment, and no set of data was collected for administration to students who are

visually impaired or have multiple disabilities. It is unclear how applicable the available normative data may be to those students.

Standardization: The VMI has not been standardized in administration procedure and interpretation for individuals who are visually impaired or have multiple disabilities. The publisher states that the VMI is not suited to students with significant visual impairment, since they likely will have difficulty recognizing fine details of the more complex figures, and the quality of their reproductions may be adversely affected. An inability to view a figure clearly does not imply a lack of motor reproductive ability, and a student's abilities may be underestimated.

Adaptations: The publisher also states that no adaptations have been made specifically for such individuals who are visually impaired or have multiple disabilities. Any informally adapted items require standardization and normalization before comparison of performance on adapted items to existing normative data.

Peabody Individual Achievement Test-Revised (PIAT-R)
Author: Markwardt, F. C.
Ages: Five to eighteen years.
Publisher: American Guidance
　　　　　Service
　　　　　4201 Woodland Road
　　　　　Circle Pines, MN 55014-1796
Date: 1989
Type of Instrument: Normative-referenced assessment instrument.

Qualifications to Administer: Completion of graduate training in tests and measurement, with relevant supervised clinical experience.

Stated Purpose: An individual measure of academic achievement.

Comments: There are eight scores to the Peabody Individual Achievement Test-Revised (PIAT-R), which are General Information, Reading Recognition, Reading Comprehension, Written Expression, Mathematics, Spelling, Written Language Composite, and Total Reading. All tasks of the PIAT are untimed, and, with the exception of the Written Expression subtest, can be completed without writing. These two factors are significant advantages over most achievement tests when evaluating students with visual impairment or multiple disabilities.

Normative Data: The publisher states that the normative data collected assessed only those without visual impairment, and no set of data was collected for administration to students with visual impairment or multiple disabilities. It is unclear how applicable the available normative data may be for those with visual impairment or multiple disabilities.

Standardization: the PIAT has not been standardized in terms of administration procedure and interpretation for individuals with visual impairment or multiple disabilities. However, the publisher states that the visual stimuli are not well suited for use with students with visual impairment.

Adaptations: The publisher also states that no adaptations have been made specifically for individuals with visual impairment or multiple disabilities. Any informally adapted items require standardization and normalization before comparison of performance on adapted items to existing normative data.

Perkins-Binet Tests of Intelligence for the Blind
Author: Davis, C. J.
Ages: 3 years to adult
Publisher: Perkins School for the Blind
175 North Beacon Street
Watertown, MA 02472
Date: 1980
Type of instrument: Normative-referenced assessment instrument.

Qualifications to administer: Completion of graduate training in tests and measurement, with relevant supervised clinical experience.
Stated purpose: To measure verbal reasoning, quantitative reasoning, and short-term reasoning in individuals who are blind.
Comments: An adapted version of the *Stanford Binet Intelligence Scale, 3rd Revision*, forms L and M for children with no or low vision. The Perkins-Binet is constructed so that serial tasks come first. Two forms of the test were developed. Form N was designed for those who are blind and aged 4 years and older, consisting of 94 items. Form U, designed for those with low vision, is for students aged 3 years and older and consists of 99 items.

Reynell-Zinkin Scales: Developmental Scale for Young Visually Handicapped Children
Authors: Reynell, J. and Zinkin, P.
Ages: Birth to 5 years
Publisher: NFER-Nelson Publishing
Company, Ltd.
Dorville House
2 Oxford Road East

Windsor, Berkshire SL4 IDF, UK
Available in US through Stoelting
620 Wheat Lane
Wood Dale, IL 60191
Date: 1979
Type of instrument: Norm-referenced assessment instrument.

Qualifications to administer: Graduate training in tests and measurement, with relevant clinical experience.
Stated purpose: To provide guidelines for assessment and developmental advice to professionals working with young children who are visually impaired.
Comments: The six scales included are social adaptation (self-help), sensorimotor understanding, exploration of environment, response to sound and verbal comprehension, expressive language, and communication. This instrument was designed for those with multiple disabilities, not only visual impairment. Based on the severity of the visual impairment, performance in each of the areas may be converted to an approximate age equivalent, which is reported in years and months. A new version of this tool is being reviewed for publication.
Normative data: It has recently been re-evaluated psychometrically, and a manual with new developmental age levels has been published by the Bartimeus Foundation (P.O. Box 1003, 3700 BA Zeist, The Netherlands). The new age levels address complaints about the original data based on overestimating the abilities of children who are visually impaired.
Standardization: Standard procedures for administration and scoring are ap-

propriate, since this was designed specifically for students who are visually impaired or have multiple disabilities. Adaptations: No adaptations are necessary.

Scales of Independent Behavior-Revised (SIB-R)

Authors: Bruininks, R. H., Woodcock, R. W., Weatherman, R. E., and Hill, B. K.
Ages: Birth to adult
Publisher: Riverside Publishing
        Company
        425 Spring Lake Drive
        Itasca, IL 60143-2079
Date: 1996
Type of instrument: Normative-referenced assessment instrument.

Qualifications to administer: Completion of graduate training in adaptive/maladaptive behavior testing, or special appraisal methods appropriate for this test.
Stated purpose: To assess behaviors needed to function independently in home, social, and community settings.
Comments: Includes fourteen scales: gross-motor function, fine-motor function, social interaction, language comprehension, language expression, eating and meal preparation, toileting, dressing, personal self-care, domestic skills, time and punctuality, money and value, work skills, and home/community orientation.
Normative Data: The publisher states that the normative data collected assessed only those who are not visually impaired, and the set of data provided in the test manual is only for the longer form not to be administered to students who are visually impaired. It is unclear how applicable the available normative data may be for those with visual impairment or multiple disabilities.
Standardization: Individuals with many types of impairments were considered during the design phase of the SIB-R, which provides a short form specifically for the assessment of those with visual impairment or multiple disabilities.
Adaptations: Adaptations for the short form are specified in the test manual.

Slosson Intelligence Test-Revised (SIT-R)

Authors: Slosson, R. L., Nicholson, C. L., and Hibpshman, T. H.
Ages: 4 years to adult
Publisher: Slosson Educational
        Publications
        538 Buffalo Road
        East Aurora, NY 14052
Date: 1991
Type of instrument: Normative-referenced assessment instrument.

Qualifications to administer: Completion of graduate training in tests and measurement, with relevant supervised clinical experience.
Stated purpose: A quick estimate of general verbal cognitive ability.
Comments: This gives a total score only. Areas assessed include general information, similarities and differences, vocabulary, comprehension, arithmetic, and auditory memory. This brief intelligence test is best used as a screen of verbal intelligence.
Normative data: The author states that it was intended for use with students who are mentally retarded, visually impaired, have minimal brain dysfunction, or learning disabilities. However, a separate set of normative data to provide

more accurate interpretation of data from individuals with visual impairment or multiple disabilities is necessary.

Standardization: Standard administration and scoring procedures are appropriate for individuals who are visually impaired or have multiple disabilities, as items are presented verbally and responses recorded by the administrator. However, assessing intelligence only verbally is theorized to fail to test certain nonverbal abilities unique to those with visual impairment or multiple disabilities, thus underestimating their overall abilities.

Adaptations: Supplementary materials are available from the publisher for use with students with limited but usable vision. For those without usable vision, blocks for items which require counting can be used instead of printed items.

Test of Auditory Perceptual Skills-Revised (TAPS-R)
Author: Gardner, M. F.
Ages: 4 to 13 years
Publisher: Psychological and
             Educational Publications
             P.O. Box 520
             Hydesville, CA 95547-0520
Date: 1996
Type of instrument: Normative-referenced assessment instrument.

Qualifications to administer: Occupational therapists, speech-language pathologists, psychologists, audiologists, learning specialists, and teachers.
Stated purpose: To measure a student's functioning in various areas of auditory perception.
Comments: There are seven scores to the test of auditory perceptual skills-

revised (TAPS-R): auditory number memory-digits forward, auditory number memory-digits backward, auditory sentence memory, auditory word memory, auditory interpretation of directions, auditory word discrimination, and auditory processing (thinking and reasoning). A Hyperactivity Rating Scale is a parental questionnaire designed by Keith Beery as a separate part of the TAPS-R.

Normative data: The publisher states that the normative data collected assessed only students who are not visually impaired, and no set of data was collected for administration to individuals with visual impairment or multiple disabilities. It is unclear how applicable the available normative data may be for those students.

Standardization: Standard administration and scoring procedures are appropriate for individuals with visual impairment or multiple disabilities: the TAPS-R is read to the student, who responds verbally.

Adaptations: Specific items of the TAPS-R do not require adaptation, because oral presentation of items and verbal recording of responses by the assessor suit a student who is visually impaired or has multiple disabilities.

Test of Auditory Perceptual Skills-Upper Level (TAPS-UL)
Author: Gardner, M. F.
Ages: 12 to 18 years
Publisher: Psychological and
             Educational Publications
             P.O. Box 520
             Hydesville, CA 95547-0520
Date: 1994
Type of instrument: Normative-referenced assessment instrument.

Qualifications to administer: Occupational therapists, speech-language pathologists, psychologists, audiologists, learning specialists, and teachers.
Stated purpose: To measure a student's functioning in various areas of auditory perception.
Comments: Includes seven scores: auditory number memory-digits forward, auditory number memory-digits backward, auditory sentence memory, auditory word memory, auditory interpretation of directions, auditory word discrimination, and auditory processing (thinking and reasoning). This instrument was designed as an upper extension of the original *Test of Auditory Perceptual Skills.*
Normative data: The publisher states that the normative data collected assessed only students who are not visually impaired, and no set of data was collected for administration to individuals with visual impairment or multiple disabilities. It is unclear how applicable the available normative data may be for those students.
Standardization: Standard administration and scoring procedures are appropriate for individuals with visual impairment or multiple disabilities, because the TAPS-UL is read to the individual, who responds verbally.
Adaptations: Specific items of the TAPS-UL do not require adaptation, because oral presentation of items and verbal recording of responses by the assessor suit an individual with visual impairment or multiple disabilities.

Test of Nonverbal Intelligence, 3rd Edition (TONI-3)
Authors: Brown, L., Sherbenou, R. J., and Johnsen, S. K.

Ages: 6 to 90 years
Publisher: Pro-ed
        8700 Shoal Creek Boulevard
        Austin, TX 78757-6897
Date: 1997
Type of instrument: Normative-referenced assessment instrument.

Qualifications to administer: Completion of graduate training in tests and measurement, with relevant supervised clinical experience.
Stated purpose: A language-free measure of abstract/figural problem solving.
Comments: Gives a total score only, from which standardized deviation scores and percentiles can be computed. According to the test manual, the TONI-3 was designed for use with disabled or minority populations, requiring a nonverbal format. All the items require the student to identify the most salient relationship among several abstract figures. Each item contains a figure drawing, and the subject is asked to complete the set from among several options. A set is defined by shape, position, direction, shading, size, length, movement, or pattern within the figure.
Normative data: The publisher states that the normative data collected assessed only students who are not visually impaired, and no set of data was collected for administration to students with visual impairment or multiple disabilities. It is unclear how applicable the available normative data may be for those students.
Standardization: The TONI-3 has not been standardized in terms of administration procedure and interpretation for individuals with visual impairment or multiple disabilities. Although the

stimuli are moderately sized and clear, the use of the TONI-3 may not be appropriate for use with many individuals with visual impairment. The TONI-3 is not appropriate for those who are blind or have little useful vision. Students with limited visual fields may also be at a disadvantage in using this test.

Adaptations: The publisher also states that no adaptations have been made specifically for individuals with visual impairment or multiple disabilities. Any informally adapted items require standardization and normalization before comparison of performance on adapted items to existing normative data.

Vineland Adaptive Behavior Scales
Authors: Sparrow, S. S., Balla, D. A., and Cicchetti, D. V.
Ages: Birth to 19 years
Publisher: American Guidance
          Service
          4201 Woodland Road
          Circle Pines, MN 55014-1796
Date: 1985
Type of instrument: Normative-referenced assessment instrument.

Qualifications to administer: Completion of graduate training in tests and measurement, with relevant supervised clinical experience.

Stated purpose: To assess personal and social sufficiency of individuals from birth to adulthood.

Comments: This has thirteen scores: communication (receptive, expressive, and written), daily living (personal, domestic, and community), socialization (interpersonal relationships, play and leisure time, and coping skills), motor skills (gross and fine), adaptive behavior composite, and maladaptive behavior. The instrument was designed to assess both students who are visually impaired and those who are not. The primary focus of the scales is on activities of daily living, including communication, living skills, socialization, and motor skills. The scales can be very useful when a psychologist AND a teacher of the visually impaired conduct this interview collaboratively. While the psychologist is gathering data about the student's adaptive behavior, the teacher can gain information regarding daily living skills.

Normative data: Separate normative data are provided for the assessment of both students with visual impairments and those without. The publisher states that normative data are available for students with visual impairment who attend residential schools, but no normative data has been collected for students with visual impairment or multiple disability residing outside residential school environments.

Standardization: The Vineland Adaptive Behavior Scales has specific instructions for administration to individuals with visual impairment or multiple disabilities.

Adaptations: The publisher states that no adaptations have been made specifically for individuals with visual impairment or multiple disabilities. Any informally adapted items require standardization and normalization before comparison of performance on adapted items to existing normative data.

Adaptations: The publisher also states that no adaptations have been made specifically for individuals with visual impairment or multiple disabilities. Any informally adapted items require standardization and normalization before comparison of performance on adapted items to existing normative data.

Wechsler Adult Intelligence Scale, 3rd Edition (WAIS-III)
Author: Wechsler, D.
Ages: 16 to 89 years
Publisher: The Psychological
             Corporation
             19500 Bulverde Road
             San Antonio, TX 78259
Date: 1997
Type of instrument: Normative-referenced assessment instrument.

Qualifications to administer: Completion of graduate training in psychology or education, with relevant clinical experience and appropriate state licensure.
Stated purpose: To assess the intelligence of adults.
Comments: Perhaps the most widely used intelligence test for adults, this has a verbal scale and a performance scale (each of which yields an intelligence quotient), which together yield a full scale intelligence quotient. The verbal scale has seven subtests: vocabulary, similarities, arithmetic, digit span, information, comprehension, and letter-number sequencing. The performance scale has seven scales: picture completion, digit symbol, block design, matrix reasoning, picture arrangement, symbol search, and object assembly.
Normative data: The publisher states that the normative data collected assessed only those who are not visually impaired, and no set of data was collected for administration to those with visual impairment or multiple disabilities. It is unclear how applicable the available normative data may be for those students.

Standardization: The WAIS-III is administered to those with visual impairment or multiple disabilities by reading aloud verbal tasks only, and recording of responses by the assessor. Standard scoring procedures are used.
Adaptations: The WAIS-III is generally adapted for adolescents and adults with impaired vision by the administration of the verbal scale only. However, this adjustment is unfair because numerous verbal subtest items are visually oriented and thus not appropriate for use by those who are visually impaired. In addition, those with visual impairment develop unique, nonverbal intellectual abilities that are not assessed through verbal subtests. Thus, the lack of performance-oriented questions fails to assess aspects of intellectual development of students with visual impairment or multiple disabilities.

Wechsler Intelligence Scale for Children, 3rd Edition (WISC-III)
Author: Wechsler, D.
Ages: 6 to 16 years
Publisher: The Psychological
             Corporation
             19500 Bulverde Road
             San Antonio, TX 78259
Date: 1991
Type of instrument: Normative-referenced assessment instrument.

Qualifications to administer: Completion of graduate training in psychology or education with relevant clinical experience and appropriate state licensure.
Stated purpose: To assess the intelligence of children.
Comments: Perhaps the most widely used intelligence test for children, this has a verbal scale and a performance

scale (each of which yields an intelligence quotient), which together yield a full scale intelligence quotient. The verbal scale has six subtests: information, similarities, arithmetic, vocabulary, comprehension, and digit span. The performance scale has seven scales: picture completion, coding, picture arrangement, block design, object assembly, symbol search, and mazes.

Normative data: The publisher states that the normative data collected assessed only students who are not visually impaired and no set of data was collected for administration to those with visual impairment or multiple disabilities. It is unclear how applicable the available normative data may be for those students.

Standardization: The WISC-III is administered to those with visual impairment or multiple disabilities by reading aloud verbal tasks only, and recording of responses by the assessor. Standard scoring procedures are used.

Adaptations: The WISC-III is generally adapted for students who are visually impaired by the administration of the verbal scale only. However, this adjustment is unfair because numerous verbal subtest items are visually oriented and thus not appropriate for use with those who are visually impaired. In addition, students who are visually impaired develop unique, nonverbal intellectual abilities that are not assessed through verbal subtests. Thus, the lack of performance-oriented questions fails to assess aspects of intellectual development of students with visual impairment or multiple disabilities.

Digit Span is a supplementary test and not always given. It should be given to all students with visual impairment.

Auditory memory is a critical skill for visually impaired students and should be assessed from many perspectives. Visually impaired students often have high auditory memory because they get lots of practice. In students with retinopathy of prematurity and cortical visual impairment, elevated scores on this subtest can be a positive sign suggesting that the neurological damage did not diminish this skill. High auditory memory is often seen as evidence of "smartness" in a blind student whose overall scores and functioning are reduced. The auditory memory can include memory for music lyrics, nursery rhymes, prayers, phone numbers, etc. Elevated auditory memory skills, by themselves, while desirable in students with neurological injuries, should not be confused with overall high cognitive ability.

Wechsler Preschool and Primary Scale of Intelligence-Revised (WPPSI)
Author: Wechsler, D.
Ages: 3 to 7 years
Publisher: The Psychological
             Corporation
             19500 Bulverde Road
             San Antonio, TX 78259
Date: 1989
Type of instrument: Normative-referenced assessment instrument.

Qualifications to administer: Completion of graduate training in psychology or education with relevant clinical experience and appropriate state licensure.
Stated purpose: To assess the intelligence of children.
Comments: Perhaps the most widely embraced intelligence test for young children, this has a verbal scale and a

performance scale (each of which yields an intelligence quotient), which together yield a full scale intelligence quotient. The verbal scale has six subtests: information, comprehension, arithmetic, vocabulary, similarities, and sentences. The performance scale has six scales: object assembly, geometric design, block design, mazes, picture completion, and animal pegs. Many of the verbal subtests require the use of vision.

Those subtests may be inappropriate for students with no usable vision.

Normative data: The publisher states that the normative data collected assessed only students who are not visually impaired, and no set of data was collected for administration to young children with visual impairment or multiple disabilities. It is unclear how applicable the available normative data may be for those students.

Speech and Language Assessment

Marsha A. Silver

IN THIS CHAPTER:

- The impact of visual impairment on communication

- Language issues common to students who are visually impaired, with and without multiple disabilities

- How to collaborate with professionals and families while assessing communication skills

- How to design an assessment battery for students who are visually impaired

- How to modify speech and language tests for students who are visually impaired

- How to interpret assessment results

This chapter illustrates how speech and language assessment of a student who is blind or visually impaired must take place through a collaborative approach. Only through the contribution of the other professionals and family can a picture of the whole student emerge within a realistic time frame. The contribution of communication skills cannot be separated from a student's cognition, social development, and behavior and the multiple contexts in which they are observed. Therefore, the speech and language pathologist's findings can help interpret other observations as well as offer practical solutions and interventions that can be incorporated into the curriculum.

ASSESSING COMMUNICATION

The observation and assessment of communication are frequently shared by many professionals working with the student who is blind or visually impaired. The comprehensive domain of language naturally intersects and overlaps with assessments in cognition, orientation and mobility (O&M), vision, occupational and physical therapy, and general and special education domains at many levels. For example, the abilities to follow verbal directions, to express one's opinions, to read and write, and to play interactively with other students are all skills whose development have relevance to many professionals and all families of students who are visually impaired children. Nevertheless, it is the primary responsibility of the speech and language pathologist, in conjunction with the family and assessment team, to identify the presence or absence of a communication delay or difference.

As defined by the National Joint Committee for the Communicative Needs of Persons with Severe Disabilities (1992), "Communication is any act by which one person gives to or receives from another person information about that person's needs, desires, perceptions, knowledge, or affective states. Communication may be intentional or unintentional, may involve conventional or unconventional signals, may take linguistic or nonlinguistic forms, and may occur through spoken or other modes."

The Challenge for the Speech and Language Pathologist

Speech and language pathology focuses on the identification of delayed, or different, aspects of communication development, how these relate to the total student, and the formulation and administration of an intervention plan to remediate or compensate for them. Although the speech and language pathologist is well trained in assessment of the speech and language development of students with neurologic or developmental impairments or learning disabilities, he or she may not be as equipped to isolate the role of the visual impairment in an individual student's particular pattern of communication. Because of the low incidence of visual impairment and its unclear impact on the development of communication, visual impairment has not been central in training programs for speech and language pathologists. It is more often the student who is visually impaired whose multiple disabilities include hearing loss, cerebral palsy, delayed cognitive development, or autistic-like behaviors who will be referred for assessment.

Speech and language pathologists have been taught that in order to determine the presence of delayed or disordered language, they must be familiar with normal language acquisition. Typical sequences in the development of semantics (words and their meanings), grammar and syntax (how words are combined to make sentences), morphology (the application of the smallest parts of meaningful speech such as word endings and pronouns), phonology (the speech sound system) and pragmatics (the social use of language) have been well established through years of linguistic research (Pinker, 1994; Locke, 1993; Brown, 1976; Snow & Ferguson, 1977).

The literature includes differing opinions as to the impact of visual impairment on speech and language development in students who are blind or visually impaired and have no additional disabilities. Nevertheless, differences in the rate and sequence of language development have been found in typically developing visually impaired youngsters. The specific challenge for the speech and language pathologist is to discover what are to be considered the norms with respect to the sequence and rate of development of language comprehension and verbal expression in students who are visually impaired, with or without multiple disabilities. Warren (1994), addresses these issues with the premise that "it is the variation within the population of children with visual impairments that we should be studying, not the norm. . . . I believe that a truly useful body of research-based knowledge about this population must focus not on the norm, or the usual, but on the unusual." Warren goes on to say that research should focus on the factors in students' experience that have caused their development to vary in a positive or negative direction. Warren states that, "Only with that kind of knowledge base will we be prepared to intervene in the lives of children with visual impairments in order to allow them to achieve their optimal potential."

Professionals in the field of visual impairment have developed many tools appropriate for assessing specific aspects of language and literacy that are included in Chapter 5. Checklists, questionnaires, criterion-referenced and normative-referenced tests have been developed over many years. Speech and language assessment tools are filled with pictures and objects that may have little or no relevance to a student who is visually impaired. Even when tests require aural input (listening) and oral output (speaking), the norms do not typically include students who are blind or visually impaired. Collaboration with family and teaching staff is therefore imperative from the start of any evaluation of the speech and language development of a student who is visually impaired.

How Vision Loss Affects Communication

To tackle this challenge, it is helpful to have a clear concept of the role that vision plays in language learning. It is estimated that for sighted children 80 to 90 percent of early learning is based on visual input (Ashcroft & Zambone-Ashley, 1980). Vision serves as a primary stimulus for learning as well as an integrator of input from other sensory channels. Without vision as a central integrator, children who are blind or visually impaired rely on the remaining senses of hearing, touch, motor–kinesthetic feedback, and smell to help them assign order and meaning to their world. In the absence of vision, the world can potentially be perceived as a great number of disjointed sounds and events. The opportunities to learn through imitation of adult or child behavior are significantly reduced. Many more deliberate exposures including direct, hands-on experiences are required to piece together the parts of a sequence when vision is diminished. Many developmental delays may be avoided by appropriately structuring the experiences of a student who is visually impaired. Chapters 1 and 6 provide additional information on the impact of visual impairment on learning.

Vision also plays a significant role in the development of early parent–child interaction and of attachment. Auditory and tactile stimuli do not present a problem for an infant who is blind or visually impaired. However, if the parent's responses to infant behavior are primarily visual, there is a potential for lack of effective interaction. On the infant's part, vocalization, smiling, and a system of body language involving reciprocal eye gaze and shared attention help to engage the parent. Warren's review of the literature (1994, p. 216) revealed that "there is no question whether the visually impaired infant is at risk for inadequate attachment. Nevertheless, the risks are not necessarily consequences of the infant's visual impairment. They can be avoided in a social-interactive environment in which the infant's interactive behaviors are encouraged and are responded to."

Without the benefit of mutual or reciprocal eye gaze, shared attention, and affect, caregivers tend to ask many questions of their children who are blind or visually impaired. Comments, when they are made, are centered upon the child or objects within his or her reach. This may support a cycle of interaction that is high risk for creating a passive communicator. Kekelis and Andersen (1984) found that, "Parents provided more labels and requests for labels of objects to blind children but, unlike parents of sighted children, did not follow up with comments and questions for new information concerning these objects." According to Kekelis and Prinz (1996), the majority of studies have examined the attainment of language milestones by children who are visually impaired that were derived from developmental scales designed for sighted children (Hall et al., 1984; Mills, 1983; Bigelow, 1987; Dunlea, 1989; Urwin, 1983; Dunlea & Andersen 1992, 1992; Fraiberg, 1977; Wilson & Peters, 1988). Kekelis & Prinz (1996, p. 424) states that

> Although studies have documented that children with visual impairments can achieve a number of language milestones in a timely manner [such as the content of early vocabularies

and the emergence of two and three word utterances], their results have not substantiated claims by some researchers that the language development of blind children is advanced or, at least, comparable to that of sighted children.

Many factors converge that affect social development and the language accompanying it in students who are visually impaired. From the start, development of play is significantly influenced by vision loss. Students who are blind or visually impaired do not typically re-enact familiar play schemes with toys or engage in role playing to the extent that fully sighted children do. They may have difficulty entering a play group because of reduced play skills. Vision allows sighted students to read facial expressions and body language that help them to interpret verbal messages. Without vision, it is more difficult to know who is being addressed in a crowd, what the emotional intent of the message is, or when the right time is to make comments or ask questions.

Sight contributes enormously to concept and vocabulary development. Asking students who are blind or visually impaired to define words can be an enlightening window into their world. For one child who is blind, a garage may be "where you park the car, take the seatbelt off, and go into the house." An airplane may be "something noisy in the sky that takes people places."

Language Form, Function, and Content

Another way to conceptualize how vision affects communication is to look at the model designed by Bloom and Lahey (1978) which organizes language into the three dimensions of form, function/use, and content. This model has been adapted to emphasize the patterns of development observed in children who are visually impaired or have multiple disabilities (Rowland & Stremel-Campbell, 1987; Siegel-Causey & Downing, 1987).

Language Form

The form of utterances can be described in terms of their units of sound (phonology), units of meaning that are words or word endings (morphology), and the way in which units of meaning are combined with one another (syntax). Form can also refer to the specific behavior used to communicate, whether nonsymbolic—such as the use of an object or body movement—or symbolic/linguistic—such as the use of words, sign language, or tactile symbols.

Language Function

Language function and use have to do with the reasons why people speak. Reasons range from intrapersonal (i.e., vocal play or problem-solving) to interpersonal (i.e., making requests or obtaining information). The social aspects of communication fall in this realm, including communicative intentions (i.e., requesting, rejecting, or commenting).

Language Content

Content is the aspect of communication that deals with objects, actions, and relations in the world. The content of language is cumulative and continuous as it evolves in the course of development. The accumulation of knowledge of objects and actions and the relations between events and objects are learned through exposure, experience, and personal interests. Topics of language are variable, however, with respect to age and culture. For example, 2-year-olds might talk about "bouncy balls," 5-year-olds might talk about "baseballs," and adults might focus on "golf balls." Knowledge about topics in the world is highly interrelated with vision.

The Impact of Multiple Disabilities on Communication

Assessment team members are aware of the difficulty in assessing children who have multiple disabilities. Most tests require an understanding of spoken language, the ability to see stimuli, a means of responding either verbally or motorically, or all three (Fewell, 1991).

For children who are visually impaired and have multiple disabilities, including those affecting hearing or motor development, sensorimotor integration, language or cognitive delay, or learning disabilities, the task of gaining meaning from the world is even more demanding.

The Goal of a Speech and Language Assessment

The goal of a speech and language assessment is to determine whether the student has a weakness or deficit in language processing, verbal expression, or speech relative to their skills in other areas. The speech and language pathologist can make a significant contribution to assessment by defining the student's individual profile of strengths and weaknesses in communication and identifying how the environment interacts with him or her. The speech and language pathologist must also determine whether the student has a speech and language problem independent of vision issues. Once these conclusions have been made, the speech and language pathologist, in conjunction with the individualized education program (IEP) team, can write short- and long-term recommendations for how to capitalize on the student's strengths and improve upon or compensate for his or her weaknesses.

Communication Characteristics of Students Who Are Blind or Visually Impaired

As discussed in Chapter 1, the student who is blind or visually impaired may develop communication differently from students who are fully sighted. The degree and character of these differences will also be related to the student's level of cognitive development, environmental and academic exposure, other disabilities, the fit between the parent and child, as well as between the educational program and the student's learning style.

Even assuming that students who are blind or visually impaired and with no additional disabilities do not exhibit long-term language delays, it is still important for the speech and language pathologist to recognize the short-term characteristics of the language associated with visual impairment. Sidebar 7.1 lists language characteristics typical of children who are blind or visually impaired.

Language characteristics of children who are blind or visually impaired may include but are not limited to those described here.

Receptive Language

- A knowledge base centered on personal, hands-on experience without the benefit of incidental learning.
- Gaps or delays in general knowledge and concept development.
- Gaps or delays in vocabulary development or limited understanding of the full meaning of some words (particularly ones they have not had hands-on contact with).
- When students are in a group, they may not know who is being addressed or what the topic of conversation is, if it is not stated explicitly.

Expressive Language

- Extended periods of echolalia
- Pronoun confusion
- Overuse of questions
- Verbalisms (use of expressive language without complete receptive understanding)

Practical Difficulties in Students Who Are Blind or Visually Impaired

- May tend to be passive communicators with infrequent topic initiations.
- May have difficulty taking turns in conversation.
- May dominate the conversation by asking a series of questions.
- May play with language as a form of entertainment, for example, may repeat television commercials, radio advertisements, other people's voices, rhymes, and jingles.

Practical Difficulties More Frequent in Students Who Are Blind or Visually Impaired and Have Multiple Disabilities

- May engage in perseverative language about personal topics of interest.
- May use language for a narrow range of intentions, for example, primarily to ask repetitive questions or to perseverate upon favorite topics.

(continued)

- May talk to himself or herself.
- May display many language characteristics common to students with autism including immediate and delayed echolalia, perseveration, and pronoun confusion.

Oral/Motor Development/Eating

- It takes longer to learn independent eating skills without vision. A student who is visually impaired will be taught to use their fingers to locate items on the plate.
- Students with multiple disabilities such as cerebral palsy often have motor strength and coordination issues that affect speech and eating.
- Children born prematurely may have been tube fed. Aversion to eating solid foods, tactile defensiveness, and deficient eating patterns, including chewing and swallowing, is common in this population.

Speech and language areas that are minimally affected by visual impairment in the absence of additional disabilities include the following.

Articulation

Acoustically similar phonemes such as f/th or m/n are often confused because they are difficult to differentiate without vision. Articulation is otherwise unaffected by visual impairment unless the student has additional disabilities.

Expressive Morphology and Syntax

Students with visual impairment tend to develop this area of language in the same sequence as their sighted peers.

Auditory Processing/Memory

Difficulties in this area are important to diagnose. However, they may be a result of learning problems associated with vision impairment or exist independent of it. For example, if the topic under discussion revolves around a visually based experience, the student who is blind or visually impaired will most likely have difficulty following the topic. Nevertheless, visual impairment in and of itself does not cause problems in this area.

AREAS INCLUDED IN SPEECH AND LANGUAGE ASSESSMENT

Important Receptive Language Areas to Assess

Auditory Processing

An efficient system for processing verbal information is helpful for all students. For those who are visually impaired, good verbal processing skills are crucial. Visual impairment in and of itself does not have a negative impact on auditory processing. However, it is not uncommon for the multiple impairments or the neurological damage that caused the visual impairment to also cause impairment in auditory processing. In addition, learning disabilities, such as attention deficits, may coexist with visual impairment and affect the auditory processing domain. Quality and length of attention as well as the perceived rate of verbal processing are important factors to be documented.

Phonemic Awareness

For the most part, phonemic awareness is not directly affected by visual impairment. Minor exceptions include auditory discrimination of speech sounds that are very close acoustically such as *f* and *th*. For the child who is having difficulty learning to read with large print, braille, or audiotape, the identification of difficulty in this area will lead the assessment team to prescribe additional educational modifications, interventions, or compensations.

Many students who are blind or visually impaired rely heavily on paralinguistic cues from language, such as vocal intensity, rate of speech, and intonation, to interpret the message or to gain additional information about the speaker's personal characteristics.

Auditory Memory

Even with availability of assistive technology, including braille notetakers and miniature handheld tape recorders, successful students who are blind or visually impaired rely heavily on their auditory memory. The identification of an auditory memory problem, short- or long-term, is best assessed in collaboration with the psychologist and family. Many students who are blind or visually impaired have well-developed auditory memory skills. This is an excellent resource for them, but should always be viewed in relationship to their level of true verbal comprehension.

Semantic Knowledge

The comprehension of words and their meanings is greatly affected by visual impairment. Therefore, great caution must be taken when assessing this area. In general, it is best to avoid measures of quantity of vocabulary acquired. Semantic testing must take into account the student's previous exposure to the concept being assessed. Undergeneralization, in which the word may be defined by a limited set of factors based upon individual experiences, or tactile, olfactory, and auditory qualities, is common.

Teachers of students who are visually impaired and orientation and mobility (O&M) specialists test concept development. Therefore, the speech and language pathologist will have the advantage of consulting with these professionals while assessing in this area. The speech and language pathologist may find that enough testing has been done or may provide additional data that does not duplicate what has already been accumulated.

Important diagnostic questions to answer include the following: What are the underlying reasons for delayed vocabulary and concept development? Are there additional difficulties in auditory processing, auditory memory, or cognition, or are gaps in semantic knowledge associated more directly with vision loss?

Verbal Problem Solving

Collaboration with the psychologist who may be conducting concurrent assessment will prove very helpful in assessing verbal problem-solving ability. Many formal assessment tools include areas of verbal problem solving that have significant overlap with speech and language assessment.

Paragraph and Story Comprehension

Good listening skills are critical for the learner who is visually impaired. Students with average ability in this area should still work on improving their skills. Therefore, the speech and language pathologist must keep in mind that listening for meaning is of paramount importance. Even for the student with average skills, recommendations for improved skill development in this area are beneficial.

Teachers of students who are typically visually impaired also assess listening comprehension. Collaboration in advance of the assessment will help streamline the speech and language pathologist's efforts and add a new dimension of information to the assessment data.

Assessing Expressive Language Skills

Because the development of word and conceptual knowledge is so connected to visual input, the student who is visually impaired is likely also to experience delayed or uneven expressive language development. The degree to which expressive language developed is dependent on a cluster of factors that include but are not limited to:

- The student's previous academic instruction (was it hands-on, functional, experiential, or more didactic?)
- The student's verbal memory
- The student's cognitive level (ability to abstract and learn from verbal input)
- The coexistence of specific receptive, expressive, oral–motor, or hearing deficits

Ability to Describe and to Define Words

By asking the student to define and describe words, the assessor will gain insight about what the student is learning from his or her environment and how well he or she can put that knowledge into words. For example, one student with visual impairment might define a window as, "something that you open and close," while another with a similar level of vision might say, "It has glass, a screen, it can break if you hit it with a ball, people look out of it."

Ability to Give Clear Directions

Students who are blind or visually impaired, especially those receiving O&M training, are exposed to many verbal directions in natural contexts. For students with an adequate amount of language, it is worthwhile to perform a barrier games task in which a screen is placed between the examiner and the student. Each person would be given identical materials and the student would be asked to give clear directions about how to assemble them to create a matching design. Another useful task would be to have the student tell a naive listener the sequence of an activity they have recently performed, such as cooking.

Ability to Formulate Thoughts into Words

It is always important to assess the degree of ease and fluency with which a student can express his or her thoughts. Behaviors such as false starts, decreased grammatical complexity when generating novel utterances, and word retrieval difficulties are warnings that may suggest the presence of verbal formulation problems.

Storytelling Ability

Stories are often read to students who are blind or visually impaired. If the stories are within students' realm of cognitive ability and experience, they should be acquiring storytelling abilities, including awareness of different types of narratives, such as scripts about familiar, recurring events or fictional stories such as those that begin "Once upon a time." Students should demonstrate awareness of the concept of story structure, character development, and setting.

Many types of stimuli, from unstructured to partially structured to highly structured, can be used to collect stories. In addition, many of these can omit the need for vision, such as in the cue, "Tell me a story," by giving story starter lines, or by playing a tape and then having the student retell the story after it is finished.

Grammar and Morphology

Standard language sampling procedures that tally mean length of utterance and subsequent analysis of the presence and use of grammatical and morphologic markers appropriate to that mean length of utterance are appropriate for use with students who are blind or visually impaired.

In keeping with all good language sampling procedures, the speech and language pathologist must choose the conversational partners, setting, activity, and stimuli carefully so that they will yield language that best represents the student's typical or optimal level of performance.

Pronoun usage is an important area to assess because many students who are blind or visually impaired experience confusion with their use for a longer time than students who are fully sighted. Without vision, it is difficult to know who is being referred to with the words "he," "she," or "they." In addition, visually impaired students who have additional disabilities often demonstrate pronoun reversals (for example using "you" for "I") similar to those documented in children with autism.

Pragmatic and Social Language

As previously stated, social interaction and the development of social language are clearly affected by visual impairment. This can be a difficult area to assess; it may be hard to differentiate which behavior relates to vision loss, to additional disabilities, or to a deficit in communication. An accurate picture of the whole student can only be gained through close collaboration with family and other assessment team members to make these difficult determinations. The speech and language pathologist, as a crucial player on the team, can help to identify specific problem areas with respect to pragmatic language development which includes the following aspects.

Degree and Type of Echolalia

Immediate echolalia is an echoing back of what the student has just heard. Delayed echolalia occurs when language that was heard some time in the past is "played back." Functional delayed echolalia refers to the use of a language segment that has been acquired as a whole in a particular context and then has become overgeneralized. For example, one student sang, "If you're happy and you know it" to communicate that she was happy and sang, "Silent night" to communicate

J. Richard Russo

The speech and language pathologist can observe and record conversational skills in a natural setting while accompanying the student and his or her O&M specialist on a community outing.

she was sad. Nonfunctional delayed echolalia is delayed echolalia, such as a favorite phrase that has no apparent bearing on anything. For example, a student with a Spanish-speaking caretaker would say, "Oh, Carolina!" with a perfect Spanish accent.

For some students who are blind or visually impaired, the presence of echolalia, especially functional echolalia, may indicate that the environment is not providing adequate multisensory support to allow them to make sense of the language they are hearing.

Verbal Perseveration or Highly Repetitive Verbal Behaviors

These behaviors persist or re-emerge with high frequency in a different form and can be an indication of additional cognitive delays, mental retardation, or autism. Prizant and Rydell (1993) and Rydell and Prizant (1995), when describing children with autistic spectrum disorders, place echolalia, perseverative speech, and incessant (repetitive) questioning under the umbrella of "unconventional verbal behaviors." For some children who are blind or visually impaired, verbal perseveration may also serve as a form of self-stimulation or play.

Variety in Language Use

Because of the effects of visual impairment on language and social development described in Chapters 1 and 6 and in this chapter, students who are blind or visually impaired may express a narrower range of communicative intentions than their sighted peers. For example, students may often make *requests* to gain information or actions, voice *protests* to express disapproval or resistance, use *greetings* to perform a social ritual, or *answer* as a response to a request for information or action. However, they may demonstrate reduced use of the intent to *label* objects, actions, or feelings; make *comments* about the past or future; or *describe* objects or events around them.

Turn-taking Skills

Many aspects of verbal and nonverbal turn-taking can be difficult for the student who is blind or visually impaired. These include learning how to follow a partner's turn with an appropriate utterance, when to yield a turn in the conversation, and how to avoid interrupting. Practice with taking turns during interactive play can be reduced by lack of vision in the absence of specifically engineered environments and activities to foster these skills.

Because symbolic and interactive play is difficult for students who are visually impaired, many feel more comfortable in the presence of adults rather than their sighted peers. It is important to observe the student's interactions with peers and family members, as well as with adults, to gain information on the student's functioning in this area.

Topic Continuation/Initiation Skills

In order to maintain a conversation successfully, the speaker often needs to understand subtle cues such as signals for a topic shift, how to make contingent comments or responses, or when to acknowledge the partner's comments. Lack of visual cues create a greater demand on the speaker to understand these signs.

Clarification Strategies

It is important for the student who is blind or visually impaired to know how to request clarification when necessary in an appropriate manner. Recognizing when a breakdown in communication has oc-curred and having strategies to repair it are extremely useful tools that allow the student to engage in pleasurable social interactions.

Self-Advocacy Skills

Wolffe (1999) notes that "Students with visual impairments need to learn self-advocacy early in their lives. Because they may find them-selves in educational settings where the teachers have not spe-cialized in the education of children with visual impairment, these youngsters may need to articulate reliable information about their abilities and needs." Knowledge of the student's ability to advocate for himself or herself, such as knowing how to explain his or her visual impairment to others or knowing how to refuse an offer for help politely is an important aspect of the communication assess-ment of students who are blind or visually impaired.

Augmentative and Alternative Communication

According to the American Speech-Language-Learning Association (1989, p. 107), "Augmentative and alternative communication (AAC) is an area of clinical practice that attempts to compensate (either temporarily or permanently) for the impairment and disability pat-terns of individuals with severe expressive communication disorders (i.e., the severely speech and language and writing impaired)" (see Sidebar 7.2). AAC systems include gestures, signs, and communica-tion boards, as well as computer-based voice output communication aids. For a student who is blind with accompanying disabilities, an AAC system may include a board with real objects or parts of ob-jects that allows him or her the opportunity to make choices throughout the day by touching the object or giving the object to another. It is the position of the National Joint Commitee for the Communication Needs of Persons With Severe Disabilities (2002, p. 1) "Communication services and supports should be evaluated, planned, and provided by an interdisciplinary team with expertise in communication and language form, content, and function, as well as in augmentative and alternative communication."

Sidebar 7.2 AUGMENTATIVE AND ALTERNATIVE COMMUNICATION

The following are important considerations when assessing the need for augmentative and alternative communication system for students who are blind or visually impaired.

- Does the student require an augmentative and alternative communication (AAC) system in place of or in addition to speech output?

- What has already been attempted? How was the system introduced, who was involved in implementing it, what kind of success or failure did it yield?

- Through observation, interview, and consultation, determine the student's motor and visual abilities that can be used successfully to access a communication system.

- Assess the student's receptive language abilities and cognitive level through collaboration with the family and all relevant school personnel.

- Determine the types of messages the student wants to communicate. If an alternative communication system is unsuccessful, poor or inappropriate vocabulary selection is frequently the culprit. Students will not find a communication system useful unless it allows them to express their own needs, feelings, and desires.

- How does or can the AAC system interface with other technology the student may be using such as a braille notetaker or screen-reading program?

- How should the AAC system be most appropriately modified to take the student's visual limitations into consideration? Can an object exchange system replace a picture exchange system? Can the keys of a dedicated voice output device be modified with tactile markers?

Oral–Motor Development and Feeding

A complete oral–motor and feeding evaluation is advised for any student for whom there are concerns or questions about the integrity of the oral mechanism as it relates to eating or speech. This may include students with a history of tube feeding or prolonged ventilator support, early sucking or swallowing problems, or difficulty adjusting to eating solid foods. An oral–motor and feeding evaluation is also recommended for students who demonstrate difficulties in sensory–motor integration, motor coordination, motor strength or tone, motor planning, or sensory defensiveness. Students with a syndrome that involves oral–facial or oral–pharyngeal anomalies should also undergo an assessment of this area. Students with a speech delay or disorder including articulation, voice, fluency problems, or delays in expressive language should also undergo oral–motor assessments.

Medical complications associated with prematurity and cerebral palsy often contribute to oral–motor and feeding complications in students who are blind or visually impaired.

Voice

A tracheostomy is an artificial opening between the cervical trachea and the neck. Some children with tracheostomies also receive mechanical ventilation. Conditions that may be present in students who are blind or visually impaired that result in the creation of tracheostomy include bronchopulmonary dysplasia associated with prematurity, neuromuscular disorder, head trauma, and craniofacial anomaly.

Voice problems associated with cerebral palsy, neuromuscular problems, or craniofacial anomalies may also be present. In addition, functional voice problems caused by vocal abuse may present as they would in sighted students.

Fluency

Students with complaints regarding speech fluency should be fully assessed with accompanying interviews of family members, teachers, and classmates. Dysfluencies may stem from neurologic, developmental, or psychological causes, or a combination of factors.

Articulation

For students who have articulation difficulties, a phonological analysis based on whole word production is recommended. When pictures cannot be used, word or sentence repetition or word elicitation strategies can be used. The nature of the articulation disorder must also be identified. Do the patterns stem from difficulties in motor planning (apraxia), muscle tone or coordination (dysarthria), or an anatomical anomaly? Is the student's articulation delayed or does he or she have a specific deficit? Students who are blind or visually impaired may have neurologic, anatomical, or developmental delays that contribute to difficulties in speech sound production.

Hearing

A hearing screening should be performed on all students who can cooperate with such a procedure. For those who cannot, behavioral observations and parent interviews should be documented in the report. Any child who fails to meet the qualifications of the screening or in whom any hearing problem is suspected should be referred to an audiologist for testing.

Deaf-Blindness

Hagood (1997, p. 14) reports that "In many ways, the child with deaf-blindness is experiencing ongoing sensory deprivation. Even students who have adequate vision or hearing to detect and discriminate visual or auditory stimuli may not get enough incidental information from the environment to communicate about it." Communicative form is almost always difficult for students with deaf-blindness. They often have difficulty with the social aspects of communication because their interactions with people have often been unannounced and unanticipated. At both the prelinguistic and early linguistic levels, the student with deaf-blindness is at risk for restricted communicative content because his or her experiences are frequently limited and fragmented.

Multicultural and Bilingual Issues

The relationship between communication and culture is reciprocal: culture and communication influence each other. Therefore, one cannot understand communication by a group of individuals without a thorough understanding of the ethnographic and cultural factors related to communication in that group. Bilingual students are defined as those who have been exposed to two languages in natural speaking contexts and who come from families who speak a language other than that of the dominant culture. Communication assessment of the bilingual multicultural student who is blind or visually impaired must include nonbiased procedures conducted in a nondiscriminatory manner, that are culturally and linguistically appropriate. This will inevitably include non-standardized assessment measures in addition to questionnaires, interviews, and checklists.

THE SPEECH AND LANGUAGE ASSESSMENT

Preparation

A complete description of how to prepare for an assessment is provided in Chapter 3. Critical steps include the following:

- Carefully read the student's educational and medical records.
- Consult with the vision and O&M specialists to determine specifically the student's vision, so that testing materials and environmental conditions can be properly selected and modified.
- Become knowledgeable about the student's vision diagnosis and its potential effects on learning and communication. This allows the assessor to differentiate the impact of vision loss from that of the coexisting conditions.
- Interview the parents, other involved teachers, and specialists in order to understand clearly their concerns and what they wish to gain from the assessment.

Materials Preparation and Test Modification

Chapter 3 describes possible modifications to the assessment site, including appropriate lighting, enlarged print, and an organized work space. In addition to environmental modifications, some tests and/or subtests can be modified from one type of stimuli to another.

J. Richard Russo

Through close collaboration between the teacher of students who are visually impaired and the speech and language pathologist, formal tests can be adapted for some students.

This is often necessary in order to make materials accessible to a student who is visually impaired. With such modifications, formal test scores are invalid; however, much descriptive information can still be gleaned by observing the student's performance and describing it clearly. Areas which can be modified include test stimuli and test directions.

Test Stimuli

An oral directions subtest or concept test with visual stimuli might be modified by substituting three-dimensional objects. When using three-dimensional objects to replace pictures, real objects or parts of real objects must be used. Miniature objects or plastic replicas have no tactile or olfactory resemblance to a real object and therefore can only confuse or underestimate the student's performance. For example, a piece of a swing chain will relate to the real object or activity of swinging, while a plastic toy swing will have no tactile relationship to it.

Test Directions

Directions can be modified to adapt for visually related descriptors such as "white" and "black" by adding textures to stimuli and using tactile terms such as "rough" and "smooth" instead.

Observation

Observing the student in all of his or her typical environments—at home, during an O&M lesson in the community, in class, during a lesson with the teacher of students who are visually impaired, or during recess—gives the speech and language pathologist a fuller picture of how that student is functioning in the real world. It will also help the speech and language pathologist to appreciate the communication demands being placed on the student on a daily basis.

Frances K. Liefert

Observation of actual classroom activities such as reviewing the daily calendar will give the speech and language pathologist valuable information about the language a student is expected to understand and use in the classroom.

Observation of assessments performed by psychologists, O&M specialists, and teachers of students who are visually impaired provide useful information about a student's concept development, ability to follow oral directions, and ability to manipulate language (e.g., formulating similarities and differences).

Interviews with parents or other caregivers and professionals will help the speech and language pathologist gain insight into discrepancies between the caretakers' and the teachers' perceptions of the student's performance.

Questionnaires and Checklists

Communication questionnaires and checklists are useful tools for collecting behavioral information. Few communication questionnaires and or checklists have been formulated specifically for students who are visually impaired. Nevertheless, the speech and language pathologist can use questionnaires successfully by keeping the cognitive, communication, and social issues associated with a visual impairment in mind. There are numerous published speech and language checklists, interviews, and observation forms. Several useful resources are those by Huisingh (1993), Academic Communication Associates (1995, 1989), Mattes (1996), Musslewhite and King-DeBaun (1997), Hagood (1997), and Smith and Levack (1996). Chapter 1, Chapter 6, and the Resources section of this chapter provide more information and specific reference citations. In addition, the Checklist for Classroom Observation of Communicative Behavior that appears in Appendix E to this book can serve as a tool to assist the speech and language pathologist in observing a student's communicative behavior in the classroom.

Collaborative Model

Through collaborative assessment, a student's profile of strengths and weaknesses becomes rapidly apparent. Particular areas of overlap in language between disciplines include concept development, learning style, reading and writing, receptive/expressive language, social language, verbal problem solving, and daily living skills (including feeding).

The informal assessment can revolve around a community outing or food preparation activity, during which the true picture of the whole student emerges. Students who are otherwise at grade level can surprise assessors with very low performance during activities of daily living. Students who are less proficient academically may excel in their social abilities outside of the school environment.

Choosing Assessment Tools

With few exceptions, no published speech and language tests are normed for students who are blind or visually impaired. Nevertheless, many tests or individual subtests can yield meaningful descriptive information and contribute to a larger picture of the student's relative strengths and weaknesses. There are several rules of thumb that can be followed when selecting tests or subtests.

- Look for tasks that use a verbal input/verbal output modality.
- When pictures or printed words are used, look for visual stimuli that are uncluttered, high in visual contrast, and lend themselves to enlargement using a copy machine or closed-circuit television (see Chapter 4 for a description of low vision devices).
- Choose receptive and expressive language tests that emphasize investigation of learning styles and processing rather than testing of acquired vocabulary or information. Students who are blind or visually impaired are often lacking in these areas due to sensory deprivation.

Informal testing often yields the most helpful information about students who are blind or visually impaired. Various strategies are successful in this respect. Language sampling can be accomplished in a variety of natural settings. Scripted sampling is an additional procedure described in *Communication: A Guide for Teaching Students with Visual and Multiple Impairments* (Hagood, 1997):

"Scripted sampling involves following a specified procedure for performing a meaningful activity." Both quantitative and qualitative information can be obtained from this procedure: "As the examiner uses the scripted situation repeatedly with different students, the standard context provides a nice way to compare responses and levels."

Several informal assessment tools have been published, including *Evaluating Communicative Competence* (Simon, 1994), which yields meaningful information about pragmatic language, verbal problem solving, and verbal processing through a similar type of scripted format.

Report writing is an important vehicle for compiling information and stating interpretations and conclusions (see Chapter 10). Recommendations for communication must be functional and infused into the student's curriculum. When designing goals for this population the question to be asked must always be "How will this skill lead to a more independent life?"

The speech and language pathologist needs to decide carefully about his or her service delivery model. Collaboration with the teacher of students who are visually impaired, the O&M specialist, parents, and other professionals is always the key to a successful intervention plan.

Informal assessment and diagnostic teaching can simulate activities ranging from daily living to specific academic skill learning. Community outings or hands-on projects can easily be incorporated into the assessment to gain a view of the student's functioning during a real-life activity.

Formal tests can also be used. Assessment tools for speech and language, and suggestions for their adaptation, are found in the Resources section of this chapter.

Assessment techniques standardized on sighted students can be useful when used for students who are visually impaired if interpreted cautiously and in light of the student's visual impairment. They should be interpreted by persons knowledgeable about the effects of a visual impairment on students' growth and development and on test performance. Such instruments are best utilized when they can be repeated and results compared over time. According to

Benoff, Lang, and Beck-Viisola (2001), "Any informally adapted items require standardization and normalization before comparison of performance on adapted items to existing normative data."

Meeting the Student who is Blind or Visually Impaired

Before assessing a student who is blind or visually impaired, it is important to help the student anticipate a new and unfamiliar activity, with an unfamiliar person. It is a good idea to have someone with whom the student is familiar introduce the assessor to the student. When communicating with the student, the assessor needs to introduce himself or herself each time. In a group, it is always best to refer to the student by name so he or she knows who is being addressed. It is best to avoid using abstract directional words such as "here" or "there" and to substitute descriptions such as "at the corner of the table" or "on the tray." It is not necessary to avoid visually related words and terms such as "I see," because students hear these words in everyday conversation and use them. Chapter 6 provides a detailed description of tips for communicating, touching, and traveling with a student who is blind or visually impaired.

SUMMARY

Equipped with the information provided in this book, the speech and language pathologist with a background in assessment and differential diagnosis will be well prepared to perform a speech and language assessment with a student who is blind or visually impaired. Through the process of team collaboration, a true perspective on the student's communication findings and needs can be gained. Speech and language recommendations can be prioritized and integrated into the student's curriculum to help him or her achieve a maximum level of independence and rewarding social interactions.

In the next chapter, assistive technology devices and their use in the assessment of students who are blind or visually impaired are discussed.

REFERENCES

Academic Communication Associates. (1995). *Classroom Language and Learning Checklist*. Oceanside, CA.

Academic Communication Associates. (1989). *Pragmatic Communication Skills Protocol*. Oceanside, CA.

American Speech and Language-Hearing Association, Committee on Augmentative Communication. (1989). Competencies for speech and language pathologists providing services in augmentative communication. *Asha, 31*, 107–110.

Asha. http://www.proffessional.asha.org/NJC/njcguidelines.cfm. Guidelines for meeting the communication needs of persons with severe disabilities. *Asha* (2003).

Ashcroft, S. C., & Zambone-Ashley, A. (1980). Mainstreaming children with visual impairments. *Journal of Research and Development in Education, 13*(4), 21–35.

Benoff, K., Lang, M. A., Beck-Viisola, M. (2001). *Compendium of instruments for assessing the skills and interests of individuals with visual impairments or multiple disabilities*. New York: Lighthouse International. www.lighthouse.org/assessment

Bigelow, A. (1987). Early words of blind children. *Journal of Child Language, 14*, 47–56.

Bloom, L., and Lahey, M. (1978). *Language Development and Language Disorders*. New York: John Wiley & Sons.

Brown, R. (1976). *A First Language*. Cambridge, MA: Harvard University Press.

Drezek, W. (1995). *Move, Touch, Do*. Louisville, KY: American Printing House for the Blind

Dunlea, A. (1989). *Vision and the emergence of meaning*. Cambridge, England: Cambridge University Press.

Dunlea A., & Anderson, E. S. (1992). The emergence process: Conceptual and linguistic influences on morphological development. *First Language, 12*, 95–115.

Fewell, R. R. (1991). Trends in the assessment of infants and toddlers with disabilities. *Exceptional Children, 58*, 166–173.

Fraiberg, S. (1977). *Insights from the blind*. New York: Basic Books.

Hagood, L. (1997). *Communication: A resource guide for teachers of students with visual and multiple impairments*. Austin: Texas School for the Blind and Visually Impaired.

Hall, A., Kekelis, L., & Bailey, I. L. (1984). *Identifying developmental patterns of normal and high risk visually impaired infants: Development of an assessment protocol*. Final report prepared for the California

State Department of Education, Special Needs Division. Berkeley: University of California, Berkeley, School of Optometry.

Huisingh, R., Barrett, M., Zachman, L., Orman, J., & Blagden, C. (1993). *The Assessment companion.* East Moline, IL: Linguisystems.

Kekelis, L. S., & Prinz, P. M. (1996). Blind and sighted children with their mothers: The development of discourse skills. *Journal of Visual Impairment & Blindness, 90*(5), 423–436.

Kekelis, L. S., & Andersen, I. S. (1984). Family communication styles and language development. *Journal of Visual Impairment & Blindness, 78,* 54–65.

Locke, J. L. (1993). *The child's path to spoken language.* Cambridge, MA: Harvard University Press.

Mattes, L. J. (1996). *Sourcebook for speech and language assessment.* Oceanside, CA: Academic Communication Associates.

Mills, A. E. (1983). Acquisition of speech sounds in the visually-handicapped child. In A. E. Mills (Ed.), *Language acquisition in the blind child* (pp. 46–56). San Diego, CA: College-Hill Press.

Musslewhite, C., & King-DeBaun, P. (1997). *Emergent literacy success: Merging technology and whole language for students with disabilities.* Park City, UT: Creative Communicating.

National Joint Committee for the Communication Needs of Persons With Severe Disabilities. (2002). Adults with learning disabilities: Access to communication services and supports: Concerns regarding the application of restrictive "eligibility" policies. *Communication Disorders Quarterly, 23*(3), 143–144.

Pinker, S. (1994). *The language instinct.* New York: Harper Perennial.

Prizant, B., & Rydell, P. (1993). Assessment and intervention strategies for unconventional verbal behavior. In S. Warren & Reichle, J. (Eds.), *Communicative approaches to challenging behavior: Integrating functional assessment and intervention strategies.* Baltimore, MD: Paul H. Brookes.

Rowland, C., & Stremel-Campbell, K. (1987). Share and share alike: Conventional gestures to emergent language for learners with sensory impairments. In L. Goetz, D. Goess, & K. Stremel-Campbell (Eds.), *Innovative program design for individuals with dual sensory impairments.* Baltimore, MD: Paul H. Brookes.

Rydell, P., & Prizant, B. (1995). Educational and communicative approaches for children who use echolalia. In K. Quill (Ed.), *Teaching children with autism: Methods to increase communication and socialization.* Clifton Park, NY: Delmar.

Siegel-Causey, E., & Downing, J. (1987). Nonsymbolic communication development: Theoretical concepts and educational strategies. In L. Goetz, D. Goess, & K. Stremel-Campbell (Eds.), *Innovative program design for individuals with dual sensory impairments.* Baltimore, MD: Paul H. Brookes.

Simon, C. (1994). *Evaluating Communicative Competence (ECC).* Tempe, AZ: Communi-Cog Publications.

Smith, M., & Levack, N. (1996). *Teaching students with visual and multiple impairments: A resource guide.* Austin: Texas School for the Blind and Visually Impaired.

Snow, C., & Ferguson, C. (1977). *Talking to children.* London, England: Cambridge University Press.

Urwin, C. (1983). Dialogue and cognitive functioning in early language development of three blind children. In A. E. Mills (Ed.), Language acquisition in the blind child (pp. 142–161). San Diego: College Hill Press.

Warren, D. (1994). *Blindness and children: An individual differences approach.* New York: Cambridge University Press.

Wilson, B., & Peters, A. (1988). What are you cookin' on a hot? *Language, 64,* 249–273.

Wolffe, K. (1999). *Skills for success.* New York: AFB Press.

RESOURCES FOR SPEECH AND LANGUAGE ASSESSMENT

Auditory Continuous Performance Test (ACPT)
Author: Keith, R. W.
Ages: 6 through 11 years
Publisher: The Psychological
   Corporation
   19500 Bulverde Road
   San Antonio, TX 78259-3701
   (800) 872-1726
   www.PsychCorp.com
Date: 1994
Type of instrument: Normative-referenced assessment instrument

Comments: Designed to indicate whether a student's performance matches that of children with normal attention skills or children identified as having attention deficit-hyperactivity disorder. The student listens to single words presented on tape or CD through earphones and raises a thumb when the target word is heard. This tool can be used with students who are blind or visually impaired who have adequate cognitive and physical skills to perform the task.

Boehm Test of Basic Concepts-Third Edition (Boehm-3)
Author: Boehm, A.
Ages: 5 to 9 years
Publisher: The Psychological
   Corporation
   19500 Bulverde Road
   San Antonio, TX 78259-3701

(800) 872-1726
www.PsychCorp.com
Date: 2000
Type of instrument: Normative-referenced assessment instrument.

Comments: Designed as a screening instrument for the identification of relational concepts of space, quantity, and time, it has not been standardized for administration procedures and interpretation for individuals who are blind or visually impaired. It is unclear how applicable the available normative data may be for them.
Adaptations: Assessors can modify this test informally in two ways. For some students with low vision, pictures can be enlarged to an adequate size. Consultation with the teachers of students who are visually impaired is critical before this adaptation is made. For other students, pictures can be replaced with objects that are then manipulated by the student.

The CELF-3 Observational Rating Scales
Authors: Semel, E., Wiig, E., and Secord, W.
Ages: 6 through 21 years
Publisher: The Psychological
   Corporation
   19500 Bulverde Road
   San Antonio, TX 78259-3701

The listings in this section are adapted with permission from Keith Benoff, Mary Ann Lang, and Michelle Beck-Viisola, *Compendium of Instruments for Assessing the Skills and Interests of Individuals with Visual Impairments or Multiple Disabilities* (New York: Lighthouse International, May 2001). Available free in electronic format by visiting <http://www.visionconnection.org/> www.visionconnection.org, search term "Assessment Compendium."

(800) 872-1726
www.PsychCorp.com
Date: 1996
Type of instrument: Observational rating scale

Comments: Includes a set of three parallel forms for teachers, parents, and students. Each contains 40 statements that measure listening, speaking, reading, and writing. Also available is an observational rating scales guide and summary forms. These interview-formatted scales are a useful addition to direct testing. The statements provided target communication issues that can be readily differentiated from difficulties associated with visual impairment.

The Classroom Language and Learning Checklist
Author: Academic Communication Associates
Ages: 4 through 11 years
Publisher: Academic Communication
        Associates
        4149 Avenida de la Plata
        P.O. Box 4279
        Oceanside, CA 92052-4279
        (760) 758-1604
        www.acadcom.com
Date: 1995
Type of instrument: Observational record form

Comments: Designed for use when deficits in attention, language comprehension, or oral communication are observed in the classroom setting. Problems in articulation, fluency, voice, and language can also be recorded.
Adaptations: This can be a very useful tool when used with a student who is blind or visually impaired. For example a student's ability to "Make relevant comments during classroom discussions" may be dependent upon the nonvisual topic support he or she is offered, such as guided experience or holding the real object under discussion. "Appears to be motivated to learn" can likewise be deceiving if the student has not been provided with adequate curricular adaptations that help him or her to stay engaged with the task.

Clinical Evaluation of Language Fundamentals-3rd Edition (CELF-3)
Authors: Semel, E., Wiig, E. H., and Secord, W. A.
Ages: 6 to 21 years
Publisher: The Psychological
        Corporation
        19500 Bulverde Road
        San Antonio, TX 78259-3701
        (800) 872-1726
        www.PsychCorp.com
Date: 1995
Type of instrument: Normative-referenced assessment instrument

Comments: Eleven subtests are categorized according to receptive and expressive language. Several of these have verbal input only and require a verbal output response: word classes, recalling sentences, word associations, and listening to paragraphs.
Adaptations: Several subtests can be modified for students who are blind or visually impaired by enlarging text stimuli or converting text to braille: sentence assembly and semantic relationships. The concepts and directions subtest pictures can be enlarged for use by some students who are visually impaired. Consultation with the teacher of students who are visually impaired regarding size, contrast, and possible crowding concerns is critical.

An informal modification for the concepts and directions subtest can be made by substituting three-dimensional shapes with different textures in place of pictures and black and white for colors. In addition, in place of a pointing response, the student can be required to name the target shape once he or she has scanned the array. Placing the shapes on a tray with hook and loop fasteners helps the student and examiner stay organized. No formal scoring can be made; however, this adaptation can give the assessor a good measure of the student's ability to follow oral directions.

Although no formal scoring can be used, the formulated sentences subtest can be administered with pictures to determine how well the student can construct novel sentences when given one word or phrase.

Communication Matrix
Author: Rowland, C.
Ages: Birth to 24 months in the typically developing infant
Publisher: Design to Learn Projects
          1600 SE Ankeny St.
          Portland, OR 97214-144
          (503) 238-4030
          www.designtolearn.com
Date: 1996
Type of instrument: Record form

Comments: Designed for use with children functioning at the earliest stages of communication who use any form of communication, including presymbolic and augmentative or alternative forms. The instrument is organized into four major reasons for communicating: to obtain, to refuse, to engage in social interaction, and to provide or seek in-formation. The matrix is a useful tool for assessing early communication in students who are blind or visually impaired.

Communication Screening Questionnaire
Author: Hagood, L.
Ages: Not specified
Publisher: Texas School for the Blind
          and Visually Impaired
          1100 West 45th Street
          Austin, TX 78756-3494
          (512) 454-8631
          www.tsbvi.edu/publications
Date:1997
Type of instrument: Questionnaire

Comments: Can be used to structure an interview with parents and instructors and to provide information about skills that may not be observed during direct assessment. This questionnaire addresses the areas of communicative form, social aspects of communication, and communicative content.

Evaluating Communicative Competence (ECC)
Author: Simon, C.
Ages: 10 years through high school
Publisher: Communi-Cog Publications
          P.O. Box 27771
          Tempe, AZ 85285
          (602) 839-5507
          www.speechpath.com/
          academic.com-cog/
Date: 1994
Type of instrument: Scripted language sampling procedure

Comments: A series of 21 informal probes presented in two categories: auditory tasks and expressive tasks. The author states that it is most appropriate for use with students in the middle and upper grades (grades 4 to 12), who have subtle but significant communication difficulties. The cognitive level of the tasks is appropriate for students who have reached or are entering Piaget's concrete operational state and who have a mean length of utterance of at least 4.5 words. Ten of these probes are accessible for students who are blind or visually impaired. For students with sufficient vision, additional tasks using the pictorial stimuli may be appropriate. Tape recording student responses is essential for all expressive tasks. Accessible tasks include: the interview, comprehension and memory for facts, comprehension of a paragraph, comprehension of story inferences, comprehension of directions, and twenty questions.

Adaptations: The sequential directions for using a pay telephone can be administered with or without picture stimuli; creative storytelling printed stimuli may be enlarged, provided in braille, or presented orally; expression and justification of an opinion can be presented without picture stimuli; and the barrier games tasks can be adapted with textured blocks of various shapes and sizes, if the provided materials are not accessible to the student visually.

Goldman-Fristoe 2 Test of Articulation
Authors: Goldman, R., and Fristoe, M.
Ages: 2 to 21 years
Publisher: Western Psychological
            Services
            12031 Wilshire Boulevard
            Los Angeles, CA 90025-1251
            www.wpspublish.com

Date: 2001
Type of instrument: Normative-referenced assessment instrument

Comments: Includes three subtests: sounds-in-words, sounds-in-sentences, and stimulability. The visual stimuli are large, colorful pictures, which may be accessible to some students who are visually impaired.

Adaptations: The sounds-in-words subtest can be used in an imitative mode, although the speech and language pathologist must remember that imitated productions may be different from those produced spontaneously. The sounds-in-sentences subtest can likewise be used without pictures. If the student's memory does not permit the entire story telling (especially in absence of picture stimuli), this author has reduced the length of input to one or two pictures at a time. The stimulability subtest can be administered as described in the manual. Although no standard scores can be derived if the test administration has been modified, the speech and language pathologist can still perform a phonologic analysis using his or her system of choice. Many articulation tests may be used when adapted and accompanied by a phonologic analysis.

The HELP Test—Elementary
Author: Lazzari, A.
Ages: 6 through 11 years
Publisher: LinguiSystems
            3100 4th Avenue
            East Moline, IL 61244-9700
            (800) 776-4332
            www.linguisystems.com
Date: 1996

Type of instrument: Normative-referenced assessment instrument

Comments: A diagnostic test of basic language skills in semantic and grammatical areas. Useful subtests for students who are blind or visually impaired include specific vocabulary, in which the student is asked to give two pieces of information about different common situations; word order, in which the student must rearrange words to form a sentence; and general vocabulary, in which the student must state a verbal response after being given verbal clues about daily experiences or curriculum content. Results must be interpreted cautiously because all of these items assume the presence of vision in the student's learning process.

Adaptations: Word order has printed stimuli that can be enlarged or used in braille for students who can read.

The Language Processing Test—Revised
Authors: Richard, G., and Hanner, M.
Ages: 5 through 11 years
Publisher: LinguiSystems
       3100 4th Avenue
       East Moline, IL 61244-9700
       (800) 776-4332
       www.linguisystems.com
Date: 1995
Type of instrument: Normative-referenced assessment instrument

Comments: This battery includes six subtests: associations, categorization, similarities, differences, multiple meanings, and attributes arranged from simple to complex processing tasks. The picture stimuli may be accessible to some students who are visually impaired. Many of the test items are within the experiential realm of students who are blind or visually impaired. Therefore, this instrument gives the examiner a good idea of the student's ability to process and manipulate language.

Adaptations: Objects may be substituted for pictures for the majority of items. For five subtests, the directions are only verbal.

The Listening Test
Authors: Barrett, M., Huisingh, R., Zachman, L., Blagden, C., and Orman, J.
Ages: 6 through 11 years
Publisher: LinguiSystems
       3100 4th Avenue
       East Moline, IL 61244-9700
       (800) 776-4332
       www.linguisystems.com
Date: 1992
Type of instrument: Norm-referenced assessment instrument

Comments: This test measures five listening behaviors: main idea, details, concepts, reasoning, and story comprehension. With the exception of the concepts subtest, all input is oral with a verbal response output. The test is accessible for students who are blind or visually impaired. Nevertheless, caution must be used in interpreting these results, because many items are based upon visually based concepts and experiences.

Oregon Project for Visually Impaired and Blind Preschool Children, 5th Edition
Authors: Anderson, S., and Davis, K.
Ages: Birth to 6 years

Publisher: Jackson County Education
        Service District
        101 N. Grape Street
        Medford, OR 97501
        (541) 776-8555
        www.jacksonesd.k12.or.us/
        or_project
Date: 1986
Type of instrument: Non-assessment-focused teaching curriculum

Comments: Provides a list of teaching activities for developing cognition, language, socialization, vision, compensatory skills, self-help skills, and fine and gross motor skills. Developmental skills and the way in which visual impairment may affect them is discussed. This instrument was designed specifically for students who are visually impaired or have multiple disabilities.

The Phonological Awareness Test
Authors: Robertson, C., and Salter, W.
Ages: 5 through 9 years
Publisher: LinguiSystems
        3100 4th Avenue
        East Moline, IL 61244-9700
        (800) 776-4332
        www.linguisystems.com
Date: 1997
Type of instrument: Norm-referenced assessment instrument

Comments: This test assesses phonological processing and phoneme-grapheme correspondence. Eight subtests with an optional tenth are included. The first five subtests—rhyming, segmentation, isolation, deletion, and substitution—require oral input and verbal output. Graphemes, decoding, and invented spelling require reading or writing.

Adaptations: Graphemes and decoding can be adapted for students who read by enlarging text or offering it in braille. Invented spelling can be offered in braille or spelled orally.

The Pragmatic Communication Skills Protocol
Author: Academic Communication Associates
Ages: Preschool through elementary school grades
Publisher: Academic Communication
        Associates
        4149 Avenida de la Plata
        P.O. Box 4279
        Oceanside, CA 92052-4279
        (760) 758-1604
        www.acadcom.com
Date: 1989
Type of instrument: Observation record form

Comments: A form that can be used to record observations of children's pragmatic use of language in the classroom setting, during testing sessions, and generally during conversational speech. This type of record form can also be a guide for interviewing family and staff who are familiar with the student.

Adaptations: This can be a very useful guide for the observation of students who are blind or visually impaired if the examiner uses common sense in omitting inappropriate items such as, "Uses appropriate eye contact." For other items, such as "Follows verbal directions," it can provide an opportunity to record visual clues that other classmates are given, which may not be accessible to the student who is visually impaired.

Reynell-Zinkin Scales: Developmental Scale for Young Visually Handicapped Children
Authors: Reynell, J., and Zinkin, P.
Ages: Birth to 5 years
Publisher: NFER-Nelson Publishing
        Company, Ltd
        2 Oxford Road East
        Windsor, Berkshire SL4 1DF,
        UK
Date: 1979
Type of instrument: Norm-referenced assessment instrument

Comments: The six scales are social adaptation (self-help), sensorimotor understanding, exploration of environment, response to sound and verbal comprehension, expressive language, and communication. The instrument was designed for students with multiple disabilities.

SCAN-C: Test for Auditory Processing Disorders in Children-Revised
Author: Keith, R. W.
Ages: 5 to 11 years
Publisher: The Psychological
        Corporation
        19500 Bulverde Road
        San Antonio, TX 78259-3701
        (800) 872-1726
        www.PsychCorp.com
Date: 1999
Type of instrument: Normative-referenced assessment instrument

Comments: This test can be administered to a student with normal peripheral hearing who appears to have poor listening skills, short auditory attention span, or difficulty understanding speech in the presence of background noise. The test is administered using a portable CD player through headphones. The student repeats the words and sentences he or she hears on the CD. This test can be used for students who are blind or visually impaired who have achieved an adequate cognitive and language level to perform the task.

The Sourcebook for Speech and Language Assessment
Author: Mattes, L.
Ages: Not specified
Publisher: Academic Communication
        Associates
        4149 Avenida de la Plata
        P.O. Box 4279
        Oceanside, CA 92052-4279
        (760) 758-1604
        www.acadcom.com
Date: 1996
Type of instrument: Collection of checklists, record forms and criterion-referenced assessment.

Comments: Provides speech and language pathologists with a comprehensive collection of procedures, assessment tasks, and record forms for use in the assessment of communication disorders. The resources can be used to assess language, voice, and fluency. A section on assessing multicultural students is included. Case history forms, criterion-referenced assessment tasks, observational checklists, and language sample record forms are included.
Adaptations: Many of the informal screening tasks, such as articulation, oral directions and giving explanations, and bilingual language usage evaluation are picture-free and therefore useful for students who are blind or visually impaired.

Test of Auditory-Perceptual Skills Revised (TAPS-R)
Author: Gardner, M.
Ages: 4 through 12 years
Publisher: Psychological and Educational Publications, Inc.
P.O. Box 520
Hydesville, CA 95547-0520
(800) 523-5775
Date: 1996
Type of instrument: Normative-referenced assessment instrument

Comments: Designed to measure seven areas of auditory-perceptual skills. Auditory number memory forward, auditory number memory reversed, auditory sentence memory, auditory word memory, and auditory word discrimination can be easily used with students who are blind or visually impaired. Auditory interpretation of directions requires vision and mobility skills that make it inappropriate for them. Auditory processing (thinking and reasoning) must be interpreted very cautiously because it measures general information, much of which is acquired through visual experience. The parent questionnaire can be helpful if the speech and language pathologist collaborates with the teacher of students who are visually impaired in order to understand the answers within the context of visual impairment.

Test of Problem Solving (TOPS)— Adolescent
Authors: Zachman, L., Barrett, M., Huisingh, R., Orman, J., and Blagden, C.
Ages: 12 through 17 years
Publisher: LinguiSystems
3100 4th Avenue
East Moline, IL 61244-9700

(800) 776-4332
www.linguisystems.com
Date: 1991
Type of instrument: Norm-referenced assessment instrument

Comments: The test examines the language-thinking connection and the student's ability to develop higher-level thinking skills that affect his or her quality of life in and outside of the academic setting. Items are presented verbally, with the printed stimulus from the manual visible to the subject.
Adaptations: The printed stories, which are mostly one to three paragraphs long can be enlarged or printed in braille for students who read at this level. Caution is advised when interpreting test results, however, because many of the topics (i.e., football) presuppose visual experiences. Social experiences that the student who is visually impaired may not have been part of are assumed as well. A further adaptation that cannot be formally scored would be to provide the stories verbally with no visual counterpart.

Time to Learn
Authors: Rowland, C., and Schwiegert, P.
Ages: 3 to 21 years
Publisher: Design to Learn Projects
1600 SE Ankeny St.
Portland, OR 97214-1448
(503) 238-4030
www.designtolearn.com
Date: 1999
Type of instrument: Book and inventory

Comments: These materials were developed for use with children who are deaf-blind or who have other multiple disabilities. The inventory contains 70 items in eight categories: transitions, activity, adult's interaction, student's communication system, peer interaction, opportunities to communicate, opportunities to use objects, and materials. The instrument was designed to help teachers assess the degree to which a specific activity encourages learning and independence for a specific student.

Vineland Adaptive Behavior Scales
Authors: Sparrow, S. S., Balla, D. A., and Cicchetti, D. V.
Ages: Birth to 19 years
Publisher: American Guidance Service
P.O. Box 99
Circle Pines, MN 55014
(800) 328-2560
www.agsnet.com
Date: 1985
Type of instrument: Normative-referenced assessment instrument

Comments: Includes 13 scores: communication (receptive, expressive, written), daily living (personal, domestic, and community), socialization (interpersonal relationships, play and leisure time, and coping skills), motor skills (gross and fine), adaptive behavior composite, and maladaptive behavior. This structured interview is often administered by a psychologist. However, this interview with the parent can provide a wealth of information regarding the student's daily skills for other assessment team members. It is recommended that the speech and language pathologist and teacher of students who are visually impaired team to administer this interview in absence of a psychological assessment.

Adaptations: The *Vineland* has specific instructions for administration to students who are visually impaired or have multiple disabilities.

Wide Range Assessment of Memory and Learning (WRAML)
Authors: Sheslow, D., and Adams, W.
Ages: 5 to 17 years
Publisher: Wide Range Inc.
P.O. Box 3410
Wilmington, DE 19804-0250
(800) 221-9728
www.widerange.com
Date: 1990
Type of instrument: Normative-referenced assessment instrument

Comments: Assesses primarily short-term memory, but some tasks assess long-term delayed memory (30 minute recall). The verbal memory subtests are accessible to students who are blind or visually impaired: verbal learning, story memory, delayed recall-verbal learning, sentence memory, number/letter memory, delayed recall-story memory, recognition task-story memory.
Adaptations: When omitting the visual memory tasks, the length of time before the delayed recall tasks will not be standard.

WORD Test-R—Elementary
Authors: Huisingh, R., Barrett, M., Zachman, L., Blagden, C., and Orman, J.
Ages: 7 through 11 years
Publisher: LinguiSystems
3100 4th Avenue
East Moline, IL 61244-9700
(800) 776-4332
www.linguisystems.com
Date: 1990

Type of instrument: Normative-referenced assessment instrument

Comments: A diagnostic test of expressive vocabulary and semantics. All of the subtests may be useful for students who are blind or visually impaired, especially associations, synonyms, semantic absurdities, and antonyms. Definitions and multiple definitions test skills that rely on having access to vision.

WORD Test—Adolescent
Authors: Zachman, L., Huisingh, R., Barrett, M., Orman, J., and Blagden, C.
Ages: 12 through 17 years
Publisher: LinguiSystems
          3100 4th Avenue
          East Moline, IL 61244-9700
          (800) 776-4332
          www.linguisystems.com
Date: 1989
Type of instrument: Normative-referenced assessment instrument

Comments: A test of expressive vocabulary and semantics for secondary students. The authors state that they have attempted to create tasks relevant to the real verbal world of the adolescent. Several subtests can be useful for students who are blind or visually impaired: brand names, synonyms, and definitions.

Adaptations: All printed stimuli can be enlarged or printed in braille for students who can read.

8 Expanded Core Curriculum: Technology

Joan Anderson

IN THIS CHAPTER:

- Why assistive technology is essential
- Overview of assistive technology devices
- Keys to a successful assessment

The purpose of assessment in the area of assistive technology is to determine which technology tools or devices will increase, maintain, or improve the functional capabilities of the student being assessed. For a student who is blind or visually impaired, assistive technology—equipment and methods used to make the environment and printed information accessible—includes everything from a slate and stylus or handheld magnifier, on the low technology end, to an electronic notetaker with a refreshable braille display or screen magnification program on the high technology end. This chapter will focus on the assessment of the student's ability to use devices that fall into the category of high-end technology.

WHY IS ASSISTIVE TECHNOLOGY ESSENTIAL?

Certain skills are necessary for any student to be successful. These abilities are not different for a student who is visually impaired. Therefore, in order to ensure student success it is first necessary to make certain students acquire these abilities. A successful student has the ability to:

Read material
Produce written material
Complete written assignments on time
Take notes
Listen in class
Ask questions for clarification
Study what he or she has read
Study what he or she has written
Demonstrate an understanding of the material through testing

Access to the printed word for students who require materials in braille or large print is crucial to their success. Nowhere has the impact of assistive technology played a more important role. Greater access to the printed word is attainable with the use of various types of assistive technology. In addition, student success is directly linked to timely access of printed materials distributed in class (see Sidebar 8.1). Providing textbooks in the appropriate format on time is a primary goal and responsibility of the school system.

OVERVIEW OF ASSISTIVE TECHNOLOGY

It is important to determine which of the different types of assistive technology devices currently available might be advantageous for a particular student. It is imperative to search for assistive technology devices that facilitate independence and assist in the overall development of successful, confident learners. The following is an overview of assistive technology devices and software used in the classroom. Appendix 8.1 at the end of this chapter provides additional details about the impact of assistive technology on access to the printed word in the education of students who are blind or visually impaired.

Accessible Computer System

There are two key considerations for a computer that will be used by a student who is blind or visually impaired. The first is the amount

Sidebar 8.1   PROVIDING ACCESSIBLE TEXTBOOKS ON TIME

In an ideal world, every student who is visually impaired would start the first day of class with braille or large print textbooks for every subject. In the real world, this is often not the case.

A student can experience a greater level of success in the classroom when he or she can independently access and manipulate both print and electronic information. Assistive technology can play a major role in providing printed materials in the preferred medium so that a student who is visually impaired can have the same opportunity for success as other students. There are groups and organizations whose primary focus is working with publishing houses to provide textbook materials in accessible formats for students. In the foreseeable future, a braille reader might log on to the publisher's Web site, enter an identifying number to indicate that he or she is a braille user, download a text version of a history book, save a copy onto a memory card, load it into an electronic notetaker with a refreshable braille display, and be ready for the first day of class. Until then, assistive technology offers means to assist teachers in providing accessible materials.

of random access memory (RAM) and the second is the processor speed. The combination of these two components affects the efficiency of the computer, specifically, how quickly it can process information and respond to commands. A computer being set up for a visually impaired student will require not only the software that his or her sighted peers are currently using but also any extra software to make the computer accessible. The computer will be expected to perform double duty, handling all of the commands of the regular software while simultaneously performing the functions required by the adaptive software. Generally speaking, braille users will not rely on the screen for accessing information and a standard monitor that comes with the system is sufficient. If students with low vision are going to use the same system or require a system of their own, then the size of the monitor used should be determined according to their needs.

Students may have to work with either the Windows or the Macintosh operating system. The assessor needs to know the accessibility options for each system. There are more accessibility options for the Windows environment than for the Macintosh environment. While the Macintosh environment depends primarily on pointing and clicking the mouse, which is difficult or impossible for many individuals who are blind or visually impaired, many Windows applications provide keyboard commands to control the hardware and software.

Regardless of which operating system is used, a person who is blind or visually impaired requires software or a combination of software and hardware that will provide access to the information on the screen. Access to the computer screen can be accomplished using the following:

- Screen magnification and/or enlargement without speech (see the sections on Screen Enlargement and Screen Magnification)
- Screen magnification and/or enlargement with speech (see the section on Specialized Software)
- Synthetic speech output (see the section on Specialized Software)
- A combination of synthetic speech and braille output
- Specialized self-voicing optical character recognition (OCR) software providing screen access within the program

Specialized Hardware

Screen Enlargement

In general, the more vision a student has the easier the solution for accessing the computer. Sometimes providing the student who is visually impaired with a large monitor is a simple and effective way for the student to have access to the information on the screen. Seventeen-inch monitors are now the norm for a standard off-the-shelf computer system. Nineteen- and 21-inch monitors can be purchased for an additional charge. Some visually impaired students can access the computer by using cursor enhancement software. This software enables the user to make adjustments to the type, size, color and overall visibility of the cursor. Accessibility features built into Windows 98 and later editions, simple shareware screen magnification programs, or a combination of these adaptations with a larger

Frances K. Liefert

Screen enlargement is enough to give some students who are visually impaired access to the computer.

monitor may be all that is needed for some visually impaired students. Screen magnification software is discussed in the next section.

Refreshable Braille Devices

A refreshable braille device can be connected to the computer and enables the user to access information on the screen with braille output. The braille display consists of an array of pins arranged in the shape of braille cells that can raise and lower to form braille characters. It works in conjunction with a screen reader and usually comes in 40 or 80 cell widths. It is designed for use with a desktop or laptop computer and has built-in commands for navigating through menus and documents and provides quick braille access to the computer. This device should not be confused with an electronic notetaker with a refreshable braille display.

Electronic Notetakers

Electronic notetakers are among the most popular devices available for braille users. They do not offer the navigation capabilities of the refreshable braille devices described above. The main purpose of an electronic notetaker is as a portable notetaker, but it is the closest thing to a personal digital assistant designed for users who are visually impaired. It works as a stand-alone unit that provides word processing, e-mail, planner/organizer, calculator, and a Web browser. Electronic notetakers are generally small, portable, lightweight, and battery operated. They either have speech output or a combination of speech output and a refreshable braille display. Input can be either through a braille keypad or a standard alphanumeric keyboard. They can also connect to a computer to transfer files to and from the computer. Electronic notetakers with refreshable braille displays can also connect to the computer using a screen reader to enable the user to access information on the screen with braille output. See Appendix 8.1 for more information about the impact of electronic notetakers on the education of students who are blind or visually impaired.

Braille Embossers

A braille printer, referred to as an embosser, produces a hard copy of a braille document. It can be connected to a computer to emboss formatted braille files, or connected to electronic notetakers to produce a hard copy of documents created using the notetakers. Most embossers have the ability to produce interpoint braille (braille embossed on both sides of the paper).

Video Magnifiers

A video magnifier or closed-circuit television (CCTV) allows the student who is visually impaired to use a camera to magnify a document and view the image on a screen. There are many types of CCTVs: some can connect to a regular television, some can use a computer monitor, some are stand-alone units with their own monitor. Features include autofocus on newer models, line markers, lighting adjustment, zoom features, and contrast controls. Color CCTVs are also readily available.

One exciting development that bears mentioning is the auto focus and zoom features of portable video magnifiers. Although originally designed as a portable CCTV that can connect to any TV, they can now be connected to a laptop computer with a special video card. The camera can view images at a near distance or be rotated and directed to view objects across the room. These images could be viewed on the laptop and magnified to suit the viewer. The invaluable benefit of this device for students is the ability to view information written on the blackboard or an overhead projector. The image is stationary and steady, unlike that viewed through handheld telescopic devices. A snapshot of the images can be saved on the computer for future reference.

Adaptive Input Devices

A variety of input devices can be used to access the computer: expanded keyboards, mini keyboards, track balls, joysticks, switches, and others. Students who cannot read or write can enjoy participating in computer activities using these devices. For example, a single switch may provide a solution for a student with multiple disabilities to access a simple cause and effect program; a more complex keyboard overlay may solve access issues for another student. The occupational therapist, physical therapist, or assistive technology specialist is an excellent resource for more information on alternative input devices.

Augmentative and Alternative Communication Devices

According to the American Speech-Language-Hearing Association (ASHA, 1989, p. 107), augmentative and alternative communication (AAC) is an area of clinical practice that attempts to compensate (either temporarily or permanently) for impairment and disability patterns of students with severe expressive communication disorders. A speech and language pathologist can design an AAC system that integrates a group of components, including symbols, devices, strategies, and techniques used by a student with a severe expressive communication disorder, to enhance communication. The devices used range in complexity from a simple two-choice option to very complex devices with layers of programming. (See Chapter 7 for more information.)

Specialized Software

Screen Magnification

If the solutions mentioned earlier for screen enlargement are not sufficient, a screen magnification program is the next choice. It will magnify the information on the screen, allowing the user to see an enlarged portion of this information on his or her monitor. It is necessary to use movement commands or the mouse to view the rest of the information on the screen. The screen can be magnified in varying powers from a small degree to a large degree, depending on the preferences of the user and the software chosen. With each magnification, a smaller percentage of the entire screen is available on the monitor. After 5x magnification a screen magnification program is usually contraindicated because too little of the original screen is viewable. In this case, a screen reader may be more efficient.

Screen Readers

A screen reader is software that provides access to the computer screen through synthetic speech output, providing students with extremely low vision or no vision with access to the computer. It works with an internal speech synthesizer and the computer's sound card. Information on the screen is read aloud. Screen readers run simultaneously with other software applications, such as those that access the Internet or a word processor. Screen readers can also provide output to refreshable braille displays, either those designed to work only with a computer or those that are electronic notetakers as well.

Braille Translation

Braille translation software allows the user to take a document prepared in a word processor, translate it into braille, and emboss it with a braille embosser. To ensure that information is formatted correctly, a certified braille transcriber will need to proofread material. One of the features that teachers and transcribers appreciate is the ability to use the computer keyboard as a six-key braille keypad. The letters *f*, *d*, *s* and *j*, *k*, *l* become the six braille keys when the six-key entry mode is turned on. Teachers and transcribers can also use a software program, Scientific Notebook, for creating linear mathematical equations. Once files are created with this program, they can be opened in Duxbury (a braille translation program) and translated into Nemeth braille (a special braille code for mathematic and scientific notation).

Self-voicing Optical Character Recognition Software

Specialized self-voicing optical character recognition (OCR) software works in conjunction with a computer and scanner. It is also available as a stand-alone unit known as a reading machine. These enable a user to scan information from a book, magazine, or any clear typewritten document and have it read aloud through synthesized speech or saved. Even beginners find this software easy to use. Once the program is started, a readable document is placed on the scanner. The scan key is pressed and within minutes students have accessed the printed word. The program can be set to begin reading the document immediately or ready to scan another page. The accuracy of what is read depends on the clarity or complexity of the document scanned, but it is not generally 100 percent accurate. Documents or books can be scanned, saved as text files or document files for word processors, or saved and read using the program's features. Once files have been saved, they can be used with a word processor, translated into braille with a braille translation program, or copied into an electronic notetaker with a refreshable braille display and read in braille. Many books of classic literature are now available in electronic format and can be read using the synthesized speech output of the reading machine.

Specialized self-voicing OCR software programs have features that allow users with low vision to change the font size and color, background color, spacing between words and lines, and the way that the material and cursor are displayed on the screen. Some specialized self-voicing OCR software programs also have a built-in dictionary that enables a student to look up a word with a few simple keystrokes, highlight the definition, and copy and paste it into a word-processing document.

KEYS TO A SUCCESSFUL ASSISTIVE TECHNOLOGY ASSESSMENT

The purpose of assessment in the area of assistive technology is to determine which technology tools or devices will increase, maintain, or improve the functional capabilities of the student being assessed. It is important to determine the following:

What tasks the student needs to accomplish

What skills are necessary for the student's success

What assistive technology devices can best meet the student's needs to complete the tasks

The Assessor

The first step in the assessment process is to determine who will administer the assessment of assistive technology devices for the visually impaired. A good assessor is one who is knowledgeable and proficient with computers, possesses expertise with the assistive technology devices used in the assessment, has a knowledge of visual impairment, and is objective. Along with gathering information about the student, the assessor will need to know the most current types of assistive technology devices available for students today and how these devices enhance a student's learning. It is important to know where to look and whom to ask.

Where to Look?

The information in this field is constantly changing. Building a list of favorite Web addresses of organizations, vendors, distributors, and other sites that offer technical support on assistive technology is a good starting point. Publications such as *Access World: Technology and People with Visual Impairments* published by the American Foundation for the Blind, provide valuable information about assistive technology designed for users who are blind or visually impaired. Vendors' Web sites are also a good source of information for their products. See Sidebar 8.2 for additional information about keeping up with changing technology.

Whom to Ask?

Create a list of local contact people with whom to network. Professional and consumer organizations, a local rehabilitation agency, the local education agency, schools for the blind, or other groups and organizations in your area that provide services for people who are visually impaired are also an excellent resource. The local community college can be a good source of information if they have an assistive technology laboratory on their campus. The Rehabilitation Engineering Society of America (www.resna.org/taproject) has a Technical Assistance Project that provides assistance throughout the country and offers assessment services. Some centers will loan equipment on a trial basis to schools and districts.

Locate others who have an interest in or are users or trainers of assistive technology. Distributors who sell many competing products can explain the advantages and disadvantages of each. It is always helpful to ask someone who is not involved with selling the product to provide unbiased information. (See the Resources section at the end of this book for information about specific agencies.)

Choosing the Assessor

Each school district must determine who will perform the assessment. The size of the district and its special education budget may also be factors in deciding how a district will approach assistive technology. A larger school district might hire a special education assistive technology specialist to perform assessments, make recommendations for equipment, and provide teacher and student training. This is an enormous task if the specialist is expected to cover all areas of special education. Depending on the size of the district,

It is a always a challenge to keep abreast of the changing world of assistive technology devices. Before purchasing any hardware or software, it is helpful to consider the following questions:

- What new products are available?
- What is the latest version of the software?
- Is a new version of the software going to be released soon?
- Are free upgrades included in the purchase price?
- Is it best to purchase an upgrade agreement when you first buy the product?
- What are the computer requirements to run the program?
- Is the assistive technology compatible with the computer system the student will use?
- Is a demonstration version of the program available that the student can try?

Attending local and national conferences offers opportunities to see new products being demonstrated and receive experience. Local service and professional organizations will have information on local conferences that may be of interest. Three national conferences on assistive technology are held each year. Closing the Gap is held in Bloomington, Minnesota, in the fall, CSUN is held in Los Angeles, California, in the spring, and Assistive Technology Industry Association Conference and Exhibition is held in Orlando, Florida, in January.

For more information, contact:

- Closing the Gap
  526 Main Street, Box 68
  Henderson, MN 56044
  (507) 248-3294
  www.closingthegap.com

- CSUN
  18111 Nordhoff Street
  Northridge, CA 91330
  (818) 677-2684
  www.csun.edu/cod

- Assistive Technology Industry Association
  526 Davis Street, Suite 217
  Evanston, IL 60201
  (847) 869-1282
  www.atia.org

several people may be involved in assistive technology assessments: specialists in alternative and augmentative communication, visually impaired, orthopedically impaired, and multiply impaired, or one person could be assigned to cover all areas. Another district might delegate this task to their staff of teachers of students who are visually impaired. Rural districts might share a specialist in assistive technology with another district or group of districts. In some states, the state school for the blind may provide assistive technology assessments through their outreach programs.

The Student

The assessment team will need to meet and collaborate as information is gathered before administering the assessment. The following information needs to be collected before an assistive technology assessment is performed: vision information (if appropriate to eye condition) including results of ophthalmologic, low vision, and functional vision examinations and learning media assessment; results of medical, psychological and cognitive examinations; academic assessments; tasks to be completed by the student being assessed; and information about the environment where tasks are completed. See Chapters 1 and 3 for more information on collecting these data.

Vision Information

Understanding a student's eye condition, its implications, as well as how the student uses remaining vision are prerequisites to the technology assessment. Whether the student's vision is stable on a day-to-day basis as well as any degenerative aspect of the visual condition are critical for the assessor to consider. The assessor should also be aware of any symptoms that will affect how efficiently the student is able to use a given assistive device. Environmental concerns such as lighting and glare often affect performance. Often during the assessment, the student's strengths and weaknesses with regard to his or her visual condition become apparent. (See Appendix A of this book, "Common Causes of Visual Impairment," for more details.)

Present Level of Performance

It is important to ascertain how motivated the student is to learn and work with assistive technology devices. The assessor gathers information regarding any previous experience with or exposure to assistive technology devices, whether this experience was positive or negative, how recent the experience was, and how in-depth. The assessor will need to know how the student is presently producing written material and if the student is able to read his or her own writing. Also important to note would be any activities in which the student is not participating because of his or her disability. It is particularly important for the assessor to know if the student's previous experience with technology was frustrating and what caused the frustration.

Primary and Secondary Learning Media

Determining the appropriate learning media for a student is crucial when deciding the specific devices to consider. The student's individual needs and preferences will determine which medium or combination of media will be most effective for him or her. If information on the student's preferred learning medium is not available, request that a learning media assessment be conducted. (See Chapter 5 for further information on learning media assessment.)

Cognitive Ability

Assistive technology can help a student to become more independent, efficient, and organized. However, if students do not have the cognitive ability to read and write, access to and training with an assistive technology device will not give them this ability.

Physical Considerations

Students who have multiple disabilities may require additional hardware or software to accommodate their specific needs. For example, using a device one-handed or providing a student with a one-handed keyboard may be crucial for a student with limited or no use of one hand. Ergonomic issues should also be addressed. The body position should be comfortable, with arms and legs bent at right angles. The feet should be grounded; if not in direct contact with the floor, a foot rest should be provided. Most critical for students with low vision is the position of their head in relation to the monitor. The monitor must be close enough for comfortable viewing. This distance will vary according to eye condition and personal preference. The keyboard needs to be level so that the wrists can rest lightly on a padded surface in front of the keyboard. An adjustable chair can ensure proper positioning.

The Assessment Tool

The tool chosen for assessment will vary depending on the skill level of the student and whether the assessment is the student's initial assistive technology assessment (demonstration and exploration) or a continuing assessment of specific skills.

Demonstration and Exploration

When working with students who have had little or no exposure to assistive technology, a demonstration/exploration approach works well. For example, when assessing a fourth grade student with excellent braille skills who has no experience with assistive technology, the assessor might have the student perform some tasks using an electronic notetaker with a refreshable braille display to determine if the student has the physical and cognitive skills needed to use the device. Under the direction of the assessor, the student can explore the device while the assessor describes the purpose and location of all the keys, braille display, printer ports, card slots, headphone jack, power supply, and on/off switch. A discussion of using the backspace key/command and the new line command/return key are also included. The student can then be given an opportunity to pretend to write something with the device still in the off position, make a mistake, correct the mistake, and continue. The exploration process and discussion will vary with each student. The student can then be directed to turn the device on, braille his or her name and a few sentences, and read back what he or she has written. The

Frances K. Liefert

Using diagnostic teaching to help a student explore a device helps the assessor determine whether the student will be able to use the device effectively.

assessor assists the student during this time, giving as much feedback as is necessary to make certain the experience is positive.

Specific Skills

When assessing specific skills, the assignment approach is reliable. When assessing a student with low vision who is a skilled computer user with a system that has screen magnification software installed, assignments can be given in various areas such as word processing, performing an Internet search, and using e-mail. The assessor can observe the student's skills while performing the assignments and determine the ability of the student to complete tasks independently.

Using forms with checklists and checkboxes allows the assessor to minimize writing time needed for recording details and observations and maximize time spent observing the student working with the device. A variety of forms and checklists are available, and the time allotted for assessment and personal preference will determine which, if any, is chosen. The Resources section for this chapter provides a selected list of assistive technology assessment forms and checklists that have been chosen for their ease of use.

Matching Technology to Students' Needs

Matching the appropriate device with the needs of a specific student is a challenging task. With the high cost of hardware and software for this low incidence population, it is important to look at the big picture. (See Sidebar 8.3 for information on obtaining funding for assistive technology as well as training in its use.) Addressing the student's present day needs as well as the usefulness of the device in the future are important considerations.

If the student prefers braille, and uses auditory or taped materials only when absolutely necessary, purchasing an electronic notetaker with a refreshable braille display might be a good match. Likewise, an academically advanced student whose primary learning medium is auditory and who has excellent keyboarding skills would be a good candidate for a laptop computer with a screen reader or an electronic notetaker with an alphanumeric keyboard and speech output.

Other Considerations

Age of Student

Is there an age when the child is too young to work with assistive technology? If a child is trained with equipment from a very young age, the devices become very much a part of their everyday life. However, each case must be looked at individually.

For example, the author worked with a 4-year-old child who was blind using a Braille 'n Speak electronic notetaker. She was bright and eager to learn to read and write. She specifically wanted to learn to write her name, as several other students in her preschool class were doing. Her fingers were so small that it was difficult for her to use a Perkins braillewriter when letters contained more than one dot that needed to be pressed with each hand. She was highly motivated to learn and the auditory feedback of the Braille 'n Speak device confirmed when she had correctly written a letter. If she wrote a letter incorrectly, she learned to erase and correct the mistake. She demonstrated skills that showed her readiness to use an assistive technology device.

Although funding to purchase assistive technology and training students in its use are not part of an assistive technology assessment, they are key issues that affect the recommendations the assessor can make and that each school district will have to address. How successfully a school district implements assistive technology in their special education services is tied directly to issues of funding and training.

Funding

Some of the most exciting products available that can improve the level at which students can compete with their sighted peers are expensive. The cost must be weighed against the benefits of the device and how well it addresses the Individuals with Disabilities Education Act's purpose for assistive technology, which is to increase, maintain, or improve the functional capabilities of a student with a disability. In California, the state has established low incidence committees to address the issue of purchasing equipment for students, such as those who are visually impaired, who have a low incidence disability. Each state addresses this issue differently, and the special education department must seek funding sources available through the state. Most states have also developed Technology Centers, which are excellent resources for information and may know of funding sources. Grant writing is a source for funding that is often overlooked because of the paperwork involved. Lions Clubs are a well-known service organization whose primary focus is providing assistance to people who are visually impaired students. Some nonprofit organizations like the Braille Institute in Southern California have a distinguished record of providing equipment and training for the visually impaired. You must seek in order to find.

When a school or district is spending a considerable amount of money, the device should match the student's learning style, preferences, and provide years of service. Many products are available. Between two similar products it is best to choose the one with the best technical support and from the most reputable company. When equipment is purchased from a local distributor, they may provide technical support directly as well as the vendor who supplies the product.

Training

Training needs to be addressed prior to the purchase of any device. A successful teacher has a firm grasp of the subject matter he or she is teaching.

(continued)

Sidebar 8.3   IMPLEMENTING ASSISTIVE TECHNOLOGY *(continued)*

Teachers of students who are visually impaired must become ready to teach students to use equipment.

A survey course on assistive technology is now included in some teacher training programs. It is designed to give an overview of all the types of assistive technology available for persons who are visually impaired. In order for a teacher to feel competent in teaching a specific piece of technology or software program, however, further training is required.

Various training opportunities are available at universities and schools for the blind. At the California School for the Blind, an Outreach Program for Assistive Technology provides training for teachers and students in their own districts. The Summer Technology Academy offers students an opportunity to learn technology and socialize with other students during two week-long sessions offered every June. The state school for the blind may offer similar services. If not, perhaps they may provide a contact list of local trainers.

The distributor or vendor of the product may include training and set-up with the purchase of a device. If they are available at an additional cost, they need to be included in the purchase request to prevent equipment from sitting unused or unopened for lack of training in its use.

During our initial training session, a list of rules for using the device were discussed. Of course, the rules were immediately tested. The consequence for breaking the rules was to wait a week before she used the device again. That worked so effectively there were only a few instances when she broke the rules after that. Motivation played a major role in the student's success. She wanted to print out what she had written to take home and show to her parents. Her preschool teacher also appreciated the printed copy.

Equipment Location

A little preplanning can go a long way in finding the appropriate location for equipment. In an elementary school setting the best solution is usually to place equipment in the regular classroom or resource room. As students advance in school, they have classes in different sections of the school building or campus. Providing accessibility for the student, secure location, and Internet access need to be considered before determining the best location. If the student is in a mainstream program and receives services from a teacher of students who are visually impaired in a resource room setting, the resource room may be the most logical placement for the equipment, unless it is portable. If the student uses an electronic notetaker with a refreshable braille display, a portable printer might work better than setting up a printer in one location. If the student is served by an itinerant teacher, the library or computer room may be more useful. Easy access to the equipment is most important for student success.

Current Services

The current level of services the student receives may need adjusting when assistive technology devices are included in the student's program. The use of assistive technology devices can be extremely valuable for the student, regular education teachers, and the teacher of students who are visually impaired. The initial period of training will require a commitment by those involved until the device becomes second nature to the student. For some students, this happens quickly; for others, the training period may take longer. Adjustments to specialists' caseloads may be necessary initially in order to provide adequate time for training.

Future Needs

Another key to a successful assessment is recognizing the student's potential and the path he or she is most likely to follow. A student following an academic path who is fully included in the mainstream program will have different needs from a student whose program is nonacademic. It is important to be aware of the goals of the student and examine the impact of assistive technology on his or her future. Students in transition and high school programs who will move into employment or on to higher education will need to graduate knowing which equipment works best for them.

Recommendations

When the final recommendations are in, there are two absolutes. The device must accomplish its intended purpose for the student and the student must be willing to use it. There is no need to spend money on equipment that a student does not want to use. If a student has low vision and prefers a large monitor with no screen enlargement software, the assessor needs to pay attention to that. It is difficult to know for certain what is best for someone else. In the end, the students are the ones who will embrace the technology.

SUMMARY

The use of technology is a necessity for children and older students who are blind or visually impaired. Supplying technology which is appropriate is just as important as supplying pencils and pens to students who are not visually impaired. Appropriate assessment is the right first step for determining what specific technology needs a student has, as well as that student's capability for learning to use more sophisticated technology.

The next chapter turns to another aspect of the expanded core curriculum for students who are blind or visually impaired. This is the area of orientation and mobility, the curriculum for learning to get around safely. Students can use some of the technology discussed in this chapter to enhance their knowledge of the community, but they must be out and about in order to learn to travel safely and efficiently. A thorough description of orientation and mobility and its place in collaborative assessment can be found in the next chapter.

APPENDIX 8.1

THE IMPACT OF ASSISTIVE TECHNOLOGY ON ACCESS TO THE PRINTED WORD

Assistive technology has changed the way braille and large-print readers access the printed word. Two of the most exciting developments are Internet access and electronic notetakers. These technologies are described briefly in this chapter. This appendix provides additional details on the extraordinary impact of access to the Internet and electronic notetakers.

Internet Access

In the past, when students who were braille readers were required to write a research paper, material on their subject was not likely to be available in braille. Obtaining information on a research subject required assistance from others. Students could get assistance in the library and find printed information on the subject, but then required the services of a reader or a transcriber to produce the material in braille or large print. Although braille copies of encyclopedias and dictionaries are available, they are few and far between, cumbersome, difficult to store and use, and often outdated. Students who required large print have had other options not available to braille readers. Hand magnifiers and large print typewriters became available in the 1960s and 1970s. More options for obtaining large print became available as CCTVs and copy machines that enlarge became available.

Today, in theory, a properly trained and equipped student who is visually impaired can complete a research assignment independently. For example, a student could be assigned to research the contributions of a famous American of the 18th century. After doing an Internet search to find useful information, the information can be saved to a disk and downloaded into an electronic notetaker with a refreshable braille display. The information can then be read in contracted braille using the braille display or it can be embossed if hard copy braille would be more effective. This process can be completed in one class period for a skilled user.

At this point, the student is ready to read the information and write the report. All of this can be accomplished independently. This material could also be saved in a word processing program, accessed with a screen reader or screen magnification program, or enlarged in a font size useful for students with low vision. However, although Internet access is now possible for users who are visually impaired, it can be frustrating, particularly for beginning users. Unfortunately, some Web sites are still inaccessible for a screen reader user, because they may be very poorly designed, links may be labeled using numbers and codes, and information may appear on the screen in graphic format for sighted users. Unless that information is clearly defined and labeled, the screen reader user has no useful information. For example, a "Click Here" link does not provide the screen reader user with enough information to make an informed decision. Pop-up windows can be annoying for sighted users but are particularly aggravating for screen reader users.

E-mail is a common form of communication today. Students can be highly motivated to learn keyboarding and specific screen reader commands knowing eventually that these skills will allow them to access the Internet and use e-mail.

Electronic Notetakers

The impact electronic notetaking devices can have on the student, the teacher of students who are visually impaired, and the classroom teacher is extraordinary. The development of a relationship between the classroom teacher and the student who is visually impaired is important to the success of any inclusion program. Anything teachers of students who are visually impaired can do to encourage this growth and development to occur as it does with other students in the classroom should be encouraged. The availability of notetaking devices can be very helpful to students in mainstream classrooms.

When discussing the assistive technology needs of students whose primary reading medium is braille, it is important to consider the role an electronic note-taker with a refreshable braille display can play. In the past, a teacher responsible for three students who use braille could expect to spend several hours interlining braille (writing print letters above braille) on a daily basis depending on the age and grade level of the students. The regular classroom teacher was dependent on the availability of the teacher of students who are visually impaired or another professional who knew braille to see in print what the student had written.

A student with an electronic notetaker, however, could complete the assignment in class, print a copy, and turn it in at the same time as other students do. This enhances the inclusion process while fostering independence. It gives the regular classroom teacher the opportunity to give immediate feedback to the student. Personal digital assistants such as the Palm Pilot connect to notetakers and enable a classroom teacher to view work the student is currently writing on a notetaker. An electronic notetaker provides more opportunities for the classroom teacher to involve the student who is blind or visually impaired in day-to-day classroom activities, which enhances the student's sense of belonging.

YOUNG BRAILLE READERS

An electronic notetaker with a refreshable braille display can be particularly useful for young braille readers because it provides immediate auditory and tactile feedback of what has been written. When students are just learning to read braille, it is vital to provide them with as many opportunities as possible throughout the day to be exposed to braille. The dots on these notetakers are crisp and clean, which is fundamental for beginning braille readers, and will not flatten after repeated use. The notetakers are small, lightweight, quiet, portable, and easy to operate. Students can write as soon as they are turned on.

Electronic notetakers with refreshable braille displays supply young braille readers with the ability to hear the letters as they braille them, and then to hear the words spoken when they are finished writing. Auditory feedback, coupled with the tactile feedback from the braille display, can help a student learn braille, improve spelling and writing skills, as well as build confidence about using braille. These devices are also excellent tools to assist students in learning braille contractions and short form words. For example, if the student wants to use the /st/ sign and writes the /ch/ sign instead, the notetaker can be set to speak characters and say /ch/. Using this mode, the student will immediately know if the sign was written correctly, and it can be erased and rewritten if needed.

Another handy feature allows users to turn off the speech entirely and use only braille output. This can be particularly helpful during test-taking. However, if some students prefer to have both the speech and braille output simultaneously, they can plug in headphones to listen to what they have written and avoid disturbing other students in the class. Some electronic notetakers with refreshable braille displays feature a scrolling option that is available when the speech is turned off. By automatically scrolling through a document, it allows the reader to set the pace and read without using the advance key to continue. This feature can also be useful for improving braille reading speed. A student can also use the headphones when giving an oral presentation from the notetaker.

A text file of a book or a formatted braille file can be downloaded onto a notetaker and read using the electronic notetaker as can information from a Web site. Files are usually automatically saved on notetakers when the user exits; a backup file can also be saved to a storage card or floppy disk using the disk drive. Students can contact their local Library for the Blind to get a user name and password to download Web braille books. (Contact the Web site of the National Library Service for the Blind and Physically Handicapped at the Library of Congress for local branches, http://www.loc.gov/nls/).

PRODUCING WRITTEN MATERIAL

The electronic notetaker with a refreshable braille display can be connected to a braille embosser to print a hard copy of the braille file or to a standard printer for an inkprint copy. Some notetakers require a specific cable and do not work with all inkprint printers. It is important to determine what is needed prior to ordering a device. With the proper cables, an inkprint copy of any file can be printed for the regular classroom teacher immediately after a student has completed working on it.

One of the difficulties encountered by regular education teachers who have students who are visually impaired in their classrooms is reading what students have written. Students with low vision often have difficulty making handwriting legible enough to read back either themselves or by others. Or they can read back what they have written immediately after writing, but cannot do so when asked to read the same material later. Teachers often have difficulty deciphering the handwriting of a student with low vision and prefer to receive assignments in typewritten format.

The electronic notetaker and printer solves these problems. Its editing features are more efficient than correcting what is written using a braillewriter or a handwritten document. With braille, it is difficult to erase an embossed dot completely using a braille eraser (or fingernail as many students do). Once a cell is erased and rewritten, the new character may retain shadows of the erased character. Inserting and deleting text on a document embossed with a braillewriter is almost impossible. Most students who are required to edit their work simply rewrite the entire document using a fresh sheet of braille paper. Although it may be easier to erase a hand-written document, it may not be very legible. Using the editing features on the electronic notetakers, mistakes can be easily corrected without rewriting the entire document and another copy can then be printed.

RESOURCES FOR ASSISTIVE TECHNOLOGY ASSESSMENT

Tools for Assessing Assistive Technology Needs

Assessment Kit: Kit of Informal Tools for Academic Students with Visual Impairments
Author: Sewell, D.
Age/grade level: Preschool through grade 12
Publisher: Texas School for the Blind
　　　　　and Visually Impaired
　　　　　1100 West 45th Street
　　　　　Austin, TX 78756-3494
　　　　　(512) 454-8631
　　　　　www.tsbvi.edu

Comments: This kit contains the following checklists, among many others: Braille 'n Speak/Braille Lite checklist, assessment of keyboarding skills, assessing typing skills, and report and recommendations for assistive technology. The checklists are organized, logical, and easy to use. They are best used as a continuing assessment tool for students already using assistive technology.

Assistive Technology Assessment Summary
Authors: Georgia Project for Assistive Technology
Publisher: Georgia Project for Assistive Technology
　　　　　528 Forest Parkway, Suite C
　　　　　Forest Park, GA 30297
　　　　　(404) 362-2024
　　　　　www.gpat.org

Comments: This comprehensive form is also available on the Web site of the Texas School for the Blind.

Assistive Technology Assessment for Visually Impaired Students
Authors: D'Andrea, F. M., and Barnicle, K.
Published in: "Access to Information: Technology and Braille," *Instructional Strategies for Braille Literacy,* pp. 298–303
Publisher: AFB Press
　　　　　11 Penn Plaza, Suite 300
　　　　　New York, NY 10001
Editors: Wormsley, D. P., and D'Andrea, F. M.
Date: 1997

Comments: This is a modified version of the *Assistive Technology Assessment Summary* of the Georgia Project on Assistive Technology.

Skills Needed to Operate Equipment
Author: Presley, I.
Published in: "Access to Information: Technology and Braille"
Date: 1997

Comments: This is included in the chapter by D'Andrea and Barnicle detailed above.

Technology Assessment Checklist for Students with Visual Impairments
Author: Presley, I.
Published in: "Specialized Assessment for Students with Visual Impairments," *Foundations of Education, 2nd ed. Vol. II: Instructional Strategies for Teaching Children and Youths with Visual Impairments,* pp. 157–169
Editors: Koenig, A. J., and Holbrook, M. C.

Publisher: AFB Press
        11 Penn Plaza, Suite 300
        New York, NY 10001
Date: 2000

Comments: This is another modification of the *Assistive Technology Assessment Summary* of the Georgia Project on Assistive Technology.

VI Technology Assessment
Publisher: Texas School for the Blind
        and Visually Impaired
        1100 West 45th Street
        Austin, TX 78756-3493
        (512) 454-8631
        www.tsbvi.edu

Comments: The Texas School for the Blind's Web site (www.tsbvi.edu/technology/tech-assess.htm) offers an excellent list of forms and checklists on technology assessment, including but not limited to the following: VH technology evaluation checklist, ABILITYs in technology decision making, skills needed to operate equipment, student's computer abilities, and environmental considerations for assistive technology.

Additional Resources for Assistive Technology

Adaptive Technology Services

P.O. Box 22504
San Francisco, CA 94122
(415) 564-6650
(866) 564-6650
www.adaptivetec.com

Although many companies offer assessment and training services, the vast majority of them are associated with a company that also sells a product. Adaptive Technology Services offers computer evaluations, installation, training, and on-site technical support. It does not sell products.

Braille Institute
Los Angeles Center
741 N. Vermont Ave.
Los Angeles, CA 90029
(323) 623-1111

Braille Institute offers a Youth Subsidy Program for college-bound teenagers who are blind or visually impaired. This special program alows recipients to borrow note-taking devices and other technology that will assist them with their students at school and home.

Note: The Braille Institute Subsidy Programs are for Southern California residents only.

Visit the Institute's Web site for futher information. http://www.braille-institute.org/Serv-Adaptive.html

9 Expanded Core Curriculum: Orientation and Mobility

Frances K. Liefert

IN THIS CHAPTER:

- Introduction to the field of orientation and mobility (O&M)

- The place of O&M in a collaborative assessment

- What is assessed by an O&M specialist

- Available assessment tools for O&M

People who are blind or visually impaired have always found ways to travel. Some of those techniques have fostered independence and others have fostered reliance on sighted people. After World War II, when many young men returned from war without vision, the U.S. Veterans Administration rehabilitation workers decided to take the most successful methods, standardize them, and consolidate them into a body of knowledge about traveling without sight. This was the beginning of the systematic teaching of travel skills to people who are blind or visually impaired. In the 1960s, once adults who were blind or visually impaired had proven the effectiveness of such training, orientation and mobility (O&M) became part of the curriculum for children who are blind or visually impaired. The original

J. Richard Russo

Orientation and mobility specialists work with one student at a time to ensure the student's safety.

methods of traveling and of teaching have since then been adapted to meet the needs of children who have been visually impaired since birth, of people who have low vision, and people who have multiple disabilities.

O&M is a small field usually known only to people who are blind or visually impaired or those who have direct contact with people who are blind or visually impaired. It is an area of the expanded core curriculum for students who are blind or visually impaired (see Chapter 5) that has become a professional specialty due to the complexity of the issues it addresses.

O&M specialists usually work with one student at a time to ensure his or her safety. Lessons include learning to travel in many environments, including crossing all sorts of streets and using public transportation. Specialists in O&M work with people of all ages to develop as much travel independence as possible. Training to be an O&M specialist involves learning about independent travel from beginning to end, from the spatial concepts and body image development needed by young children to the steps needed by an adult who is blind or visually impaired to be independent when traveling to work or even across the country and beyond.

THE ROLE OF O&M IN A COLLABORATIVE ASSESSMENT

Families and Caregivers

Interviewing the child and family members is a good first step in an O&M assessment. Parents and caregivers can usually provide accurate information about how their child travels in the familiar environment of the home; how far the student can, or is allowed to, venture outside the home alone; and how he or she moves in new, unfamiliar, or less protected environments, such as on a trip to the grocery store. Sometimes answering the questions asked by an O&M specialist starts parents and caregivers thinking about possibilities for independence for their child that they had not previously considered. Brainstorming with caregivers about what the child can already do leads naturally to working together on deciding what the next steps will be for the child. This collaboration sets the scene for practical, workable recommendations to emerge from the assessment process.

School Psychologists

O&M is often the practical application of the skills assessed and taught by professionals in other domains. Having a sense of space, understanding verbal directions, and remembering a series of numbers—such as a telephone number to use in a travel emergency—

are examples of items typically assessed by a school psychologist that find application in various levels of independent travel. It is helpful to both the psychologist and the O&M assessor to discuss findings in these areas with each other. This will confirm that both disciplines are discovering similar patterns or will allow assessors to discover areas that warrant further assessment.

Speech and Language Pathologists

Communication skills assessed and taught by speech and language pathologists are put to use in O&M lessons: asking for or turning down travel assistance, gathering travel information such as bus schedules and the hours a business is open, and maintaining appropriate conversation with store personnel, bus drivers, and other members of the public. By observing the part of the O&M assessment that takes place in the community, a speech and language pathologist has a chance to see a student in one more natural environment, where there is a real-life use for communication skills.

Collaboration between the speech and language pathologist and the O&M specialist on the team also results in a fuller picture of the student's spatial concept development. Speech and language pathologists typically assess spatial concepts on a two-dimensional plane. The O&M specialist more often assesses those concepts using the student's body and familiar environment. Noticing how the student responds to the different types of assessment can give a more complete picture of how he or she functions. When a speech and language pathologist and an O&M specialist work with a student at the same time, the net result is often more accurate information than either one would have garnered alone. There is also the advantage that while one of the adults engages the student in an activity, the other can be recording how he or she responds to the directions.

Classroom Teachers and Teachers of Students Who Are Visually Impaired

Using money for bus fare or to make a purchase in a store, and budgeting time for a trip, are examples of how the math skills taught by a classroom teacher or a teacher of students who are visually impaired may be used in O&M. Reading also undergoes a functional test as the O&M specialist assesses the student's skills in community travel. Reading directions, using the telephone book to gather travel information, and reading signs in stores and on public transportation are all observed by the O&M assessor. Writing shopping lists, recording information gathered by telephone, and writing down directions given by a friend may all be part of an O&M assessment. Sharing assessment findings related to reading media, use of low vision devices, and the practical applications of reading can help to create an accurate assessment of skills that will be of interest to the special day class teacher, the teacher of visually impaired students, and the O&M specialist.

Occupational and Physical Therapists and Adapted Physical Education Teachers

Other professionals who frequently consult with the O&M specialist during an assessment, as well as during instruction, include occupational and physical therapists whose expertise has an important relationship to both orientation to space and physical mobility. Teachers of adapted physical education may also consult with an O&M specialist about a student's gross motor ability and how vision loss may affect the student's recreation and leisure skills.

Consultation with an occupational therapist trained in sensory integration therapy is helpful for O&M specialists assessing students who are chronologically or developmentally young. Students who are blind or visually impaired, especially those with cortical visual impairment or retinopathy of prematurity, often have an impaired sense of space and ability to take in tactile information, which affects their orientation (Strickling, 1998).

Sensory integration therapy is an area of specialization for occupational therapists from which many young students who are blind or visually impaired can benefit. Sensory integration therapy addresses the needs of students who overreact to sensory stimuli and those who underreact. If there is no occupational therapist on a student's assessment team, it is often the responsibility of the O&M

specialist to decide if a referral is needed for such assessment. Sidebar 9.1 lists findings that indicate the need for a referral for assessment by an occupational therapist with a specialty in sensory integration therapy. This list can be copied for use as a checklist while observing students during assessment.

It is apparent from the list in Sidebar 9.1 that sensory integration therapy problems affect many of the activities in which students engage during preschool, elementary, and secondary school. Having someone who specializes in the area of sensory integration therapy giving direct service and acting as a consultant both during assessment and continued work with some students is necessary to meet their educational needs.

Consultation with a physical therapist and an adapted physical education teacher may also be needed for an O&M specialist assessing a child who has physical disabilities that affect his or her mobility. Unless the O&M specialist is also trained as a physical therapist, he or she does not have the information and experience needed to prescribe corrective equipment and exercises for students with orthopedic impairments. O&M specialists depend on collaboration with physical therapists, teachers of adapted physical education and occupational therapists to solve many mobility challenges for their students. Consultation with physical therapists and occupational therapists often results in travel styles and devices tailored for a specific student's needs.

Occupational and physical therapists who are assessing a student who is blind or visually impaired benefit from consultation with the O&M specialist. They often need information about what techniques are used by people who are blind or visually impaired for safe travel. By learning what kinds of motions are required to use a white cane effectively or what arm positions are commonly used to trail a wall or to protect the head, occupational therapists and physical therapists can collaborate with O&M specialists to serve best the students' specific O&M needs. The O&M specialist may know of adaptive equipment of use for travelers who are visually impaired such as a wheelchair that can be maneuvered with one hand, freeing the other hand to use a white cane or a support cane colored white and red as a signal that the user is legally blind.

Sidebar 9.1 INDICATIONS OF SENSORY INTEGRATION PROBLEMS

The following findings indicate a student needs a referral for assessment by an occupational therapist with a specialty in sensory integration therapy.

Overreactions:

- ☐ Dislikes being touched. Squirms and pulls away when anyone attends to him or her physically.
- ☐ Very picky about clothing and how it feels.
- ☐ Dislikes a variety of food textures.
- ☐ Hates lotion, glue, or food on his or her skin. Avoids messy tasks.
- ☐ Seems afraid to move, has shaky balance.
- ☐ Falls out of his or her chair throughout the school day.
- ☐ Clings to walls, fences, and railings rather than walking alongside them.
- ☐ Has stiff posture.
- ☐ Locks his or her joints as he or she moves or tries to stay still.
- ☐ If sighted, watches everyone who moves in the room.
- ☐ Easily startled by unexpected sounds.
- ☐ Distracted by background noises or others' conversations.
- ☐ Detects scents sooner and more accurately than most people.
- ☐ Intolerant of unpleasant smells.

Underreactions:

- ☐ Mouths and chews objects frequently.
- ☐ Has no reaction or a delayed reaction when touched.
- ☐ Leaves the clothes he or she is wearing bunched or twisted without trying to pull them straight.
- ☐ Leaves food, drool, or mucus on his or her face without attempting to wipe it off.
- ☐ Cannot differentiate between textures with his or her fingers.
- ☐ Touches items to his or her face when first exploring them.
- ☐ Gets too close to others when playing or talking.

(continued)

Sidebar 9.1   INDICATIONS OF SENSORY INTEGRATION
PROBLEMS *(continued)*

- ☐ Takes a long time to react to physical contact or to his or her cane contacting an object.
- ☐ Is clumsy or lethargic.
- ☐ Tires easily, has poor stamina.
- ☐ Rocks when sitting and standing.
- ☐ Gets turned around easily, even when traveling in familiar places.
- ☐ Craves swinging.
- ☐ Has a weak grasp.
- ☐ Cannot lift heavy objects or maintain his or her arm in raised positions, such as those used for trailing, protective arm techniques, or classic cane techniques.
- ☐ Moves body parts in different rhythms; has difficulty moving a cane in time with his or her feet.
- ☐ Leans on things when trying to sit or stand still. Hangs on people when being guided.
- ☐ Slow to respond when his or her name is called.
- ☐ Seems overwhelmed or oblivious in a noisy environment.
- ☐ Frequently makes nonsense noises.

AREAS ASSESSED BY THE O&M SPECIALIST

Body Image

How does an assessment of O&M skills begin? It usually begins in the same place where students' awareness of space and movement in their environments begin: with their own bodies. O&M specialists assess infants, preschoolers, and school-age children who are blind or visually impaired to determine if they need help to develop gross motor skills, an adequate body image, and a sense of themselves in space. Assessing for the development of a good body image involves discovering which body parts a student can touch when they are named and which ones he or she can name when they are touched. Identifying the periphery of the body is also important. Can the child touch the top of his or her head, the bottom of his or her foot, the sides, front, and back of his or her body on request? Even this basic part of the assessment can yield interesting replies. One student, when asked to touch his forearm, replied, "I only have two!" The student's body image may also be a concern of the preschool teacher and the teacher of students who are visually impaired. Assessment in this area may be shared by these teachers. Tools for assessing body image are included in the annotated list of O&M assessment tools listed in the Resources section for this chapter.

Motor Skills

The O&M specialist can assess the development of a young student's motor skills as he or she learns to roll, crawl, and walk in open space. The O&M specialist is also interested in the motor skills an older student uses for walking on different terrains, up and down stairs, when holding something such as a cane, and when walking with someone else. Moving in time to the assessor's or the student's favorite music can be a good indication of whether the student will be able to move the cane in time with his or her feet. Stamina and comfortable posture may be assessed. An assessment of the fine motor skills needed for moving a white cane in an adequate arc to give good information about the environment or for focusing a monocular is indicated. As mentioned in previous sections, an occupational therapist or physical therapist may be valuable as collaborators in these areas.

Spatial Concept Development

As mentioned in previous chapters, students who are blind or visually impaired do not develop spatial concepts in the same way that students who are sighted do. Depending on their experiences exploring space and whether or not they have had help putting their experiences into words, for children who are blind or visually impaired spatial concept development may be delayed or occur out of the sequence that is usual for their sighted peers. The O&M specialist's role is to assess the need to provide experiences, first through play and then through travel in the student's natural environments, that will encourage the development of spatial concepts. The O&M specialist joins the student's parents and other caregivers, the speech and language pathologist, the school psychologist, and the classroom teacher in assessing the student's concept development and in recommending ways to help him or her have the kinds of experiences that promote the development of spatial concepts and learning how to follow directions.

As students become more independent in their travel skills, their spatial concepts become more sophisticated. Concepts such as parallel and perpendicular and north, south, east, and west become part of the O&M assessment. The O&M specialist assesses whether children who are blind or visually impaired understand how streets are laid out, how traffic flows, why we walk on the right, where homes are in relationship to the sidewalk, and the different layouts of business areas. All of these environmental features might be learned by observation by students who are sighted, but must be deliberately taught to students who are visually impaired.

Family members may not be fully aware of their children's educational needs and may not realize how much information children who are blind or visually impaired miss. Even if families do know what is needed, frequently they do not have time to allow their children who are blind or visually impaired the depth of experience required in order to understand their homes, their neighborhoods, and their communities. O&M assessments include determining whether students know what is available in various businesses, how to get assistance in stores, and whether they have the social skills for making a purchase. Recommendations may include an educational component for the student's family so that they can help the student to be ready for future independence in the community.

A variety of tools described in the Resources section of this chapter include ways of assessing spatial concepts.

Orientation in Space

Orientation in space is assessed in various ways by an occupational therapist, a school psychologist, a speech and language pathologist, a teacher responsible for reading instruction, as well as an O&M specialist. It is interesting for the assessment team to compare how the student manages space in the different activities presented by specialists in different disciplines. A complete picture of the student's comprehension of space can often best be uncovered by such a comparison.

The O&M specialist and the occupational therapist are frequently the only assessors who emphasize three-dimensional rather than two-dimensional space. Activities such as making different degrees of turns on request or turning back toward an object after being turned away from it are examples of ways to assess orientation to three-dimensional space. Another piece of information is gained by asking the student to identify left and right body parts on his or her own body, to follow directions using both a left and a right body part, to turn left and right on request, and to identify left and right body parts on someone facing the student. An occupational therapist specializing in sensory integration may have other ways to assess orientation to space and will be a valuable resource for recommending remedial therapy for students experiencing disorientation.

As children grow, the O&M specialist assesses travel in larger and larger areas. He or she recommends how to help young children with orientation in their own environments, from getting around their own homes to finding their way from the school bus to the classroom door. Students who are blind or visually impaired are typically taught by an O&M specialist much of the information about the environment that children who are sighted pick up incidentally as they travel at school with their friends or in the community with their families. During an initial assessment it is important for the O&M specialist to determine whether a student notices certain features in the environment that can be used as landmarks and cues while traveling. Picking out landmarks that are meaningful and memorable for a specific student and recommending how the student can work on enlarging the number of landmarks to which he or she responds are recommendations an O&M specialist might make.

Use of Vision for O&M

Virtually any amount of vision may be useful for O&M, even when an eye care specialist may have determined that a student has "no usable vision." When walking down the block in a city on a sunny day, a person who has light perception only can still see when he or she has reached the end of the buildings on the block and is approaching the curb at the corner. A person who has an extremely limited field of vision may be able to identify who is approaching in the hallway or determine whether a pedestrian sign is indicating "walk" or "don't walk." A person whose visual acuity does not allow him or her to read print for learning in school may be able to read signs in public, to see whether cars are moving or still, or to find landmarks visually on familiar routes. Eye care specialists and teachers of students who are visually impaired frequently discount vision that is valuable for O&M. It is important for the O&M specialist to review eye reports and to collaborate with the teacher of visually impaired students to get an accurate picture of how the student can be encouraged to use his or her vision.

Tools for assessing functional vision are listed in the Resources to Chapter 4. A few of the tools listed in the Resources for this chapter also include checklists for assessing a student's use of vision for O&M.

Basic O&M Techniques

Various O&M techniques have been developed to be taught by an O&M specialist in order to help people who are blind or visually impaired to travel with the most independence possible. Observing a student's familiarity with and use of these techniques is part of an O&M assessment.

Basic O&M techniques involve using the visually impaired person's own arms to protect his or her face and groin (protective arm techniques) and using an extended hand to follow a wall (trailing).

Holding another person's elbow, in a technique called human guide (formerly called sighted guide, but sight is not necessary to be a fine guide) is a practical way of traveling that is assessed and taught by O&M specialists. O&M lessons in using human guide technique may be recommended to allow a student to develop ease in walking slightly behind a guide responding to the guide's movements. Human guide technique is used commonly by adults who are blind or visually impaired when visiting unfamiliar areas or when using assistance solicited from strangers. It is a practical technique to use when walking with another person or in a group. Visually impaired people who have other disabilities may find it helpful to use a human guide for much of their travel. An O&M assessor may recommend practicing techniques that make the guide, as well as the person following the guide, comfortable. Learning to be assertive yet polite with guides may also be recommended, especially when a young student is being assessed.

O&M specialists assess the use of sounds, smells, and tactile input as assistants in travel. Many people who are blind or visually impaired devise their own techniques of making specific sounds with their feet, fingers, or tongues in order to use the different-sounding echoes from nearby obstacles to help with orientation. O&M specialists may assess the use of such an echolocation system or whether a student might respond well to help in developing one. Giving feedback on what noises are discrete enough for this purpose may also be part of an O&M assessment. More commonly, O&M specialists assess whether students make use of existing environmental sounds, smells, and textures, identifying their causes, and using them for orientation and to avoid danger.

Cane Skills

The white cane is recognized widely as a symbol of independent mobility for people who are blind or visually impaired. It is used to detect changes in terrain, to signal others that the user is blind or visually impaired, and to find specific landmarks used in orientation to a given location. O&M specialists assess the use of white canes in techniques that optimize safety and good orientation. The most widely taught, classic, white cane technique is called two-point touch. The cane is held out in front of the traveler with his or her index finger pointed down the shaft and the hand centered. The cane is moved from side to side, moving only the hand at the wrist, to form an arc a little wider than shoulder width. With each step the cane is moved in front of the foot that is farthest back. The cane's tip is kept low to the ground. Other cane techniques have also been developed for special situations such as walking up and down stairs, looking for landmarks on a specific route, and for the various components of street crossing.

Cane techniques must frequently be adapted to meet the needs of people with multiple disabilities, such as low muscle tone or spatial confusion. An O&M specialist can assess the usefulness of adaptive techniques, and may benefit from consultation with a physical therapist when deciding which adaptations to try for a specific student.

Part of the O&M assessment involves deciding which travel tools to recommend, if any. A variety of canes in different weights and that fold differently are available in many different lengths. Several types of cane tips have also been designed to allow the cane to slide easily on the ground at all times, to make movement easier, and to give weight to the cane, thus increasing the feedback received by its user.

People working with students on travel skills have also created alternative tools for toddlers and children with multiple disabilities that may be easier to use. Sometimes these adaptive mobility devices are referred to as precane tools, but at times these tools serve a student's needs best on a long-term basis. They include the Pushpal (available from Exceptional Teaching Aids) and devices made of hula hoops or plastic pipe (Pogrund et al., 1993) that can be custom-fit to their users. Toys designed for toddlers to lean on and push as they are learning to walk are sometimes useful for young children who are blind or visually impaired for exploring an area without changes in its levels of terrain. An O&M specialist, perhaps in consultation with a physical therapist, can assess which device suits the child's level of gross motor skill and awareness of the environment.

Although O&M specialists are the only professionals trained to assess and teach white cane skills, it is often helpful for an O&M specialist to consult with a physical or occupational therapist when deciding the type of cane and technique modifications that would be most suitable for a given student. As mentioned earlier, the physical therapist and occupational therapist can gain more understanding of how the student who is blind or visually impaired will get around by participating in the assessment with an O&M specialist.

Most of the assessment tools described in the Resources section of this chapter include information about white cane skills.

Street Crossings

Many of the concepts referred to in previous sections are necessary for safe street crossings, including understanding left and right, sound location, parallel and perpendicular, and street layouts. An O&M specialist must find ways to determine whether a student can hear traffic sounds, locate their origin, and understand the pattern that traffic is making. To cross a variety of intersections safely, a person who is blind or visually impaired needs skills for analyzing intersections in order to determine what type of traffic control is present, if any, and the shape of the intersection. Also to be assessed is whether the student can walk down a sidewalk and through the open space of an intersection without getting turned around and without veering too severely to recover safely. Street-crossing skills are assessed only by an O&M specialist, but the assessment's results may provide valuable information for other team members assessing spatial concepts and orientation and problem-solving skills.

Since many O&M assessment tools do not include a section concentrating on the concepts needed for street crossings, a checklist of these concepts is included in Figure 9.1.

Making Appropriate Judgments

Determining whether a student is ready to take responsibility for aspects of travel that he or she cannot do independently is another aspect of an O&M specialist's assessment. It is important for the

O&M specialist to find out whether a student can determine when assistance is needed, knows where to ask for the kind of assistance needed, and is assertive in asking for it. When trying to cross at an intersection where construction noises mask the sounds of traffic, does the student realize that being independent needs to take a back seat to being responsible? Can the student make the judgment to walk to the next intersection where it might be quieter, or wait until another person will give him or her some help crossing the street?

Judgment is an important factor in taking responsibility. Students who have congenital brain damage or who have sustained a traumatic brain injury are particularly at risk for poor judgment. A school psychologist may be the best collaborator with the O&M specialist to determine whether a specific student's judgment is intact enough to allow independent community travel. Parents and other caretakers and other members of the assessment team will also have valuable input in this area. Recommendations for accommodating difficulties with judgment often require a team effort.

Soliciting, Accepting, and Refusing Assistance

Using an assertive and polite manner to ask for assistance is a helpful skill for any traveler who is blind or visually impaired. Finding items in stores, getting around in an unfamiliar subway station, and recovering orientation once it has been lost are all common occurrences requiring assistance from strangers for a visually impaired traveler. The O&M specialist assesses whether a student is able to determine his needs, find an appropriate person to ask for assistance, and ask in a clear, articulate way. It is often helpful for the speech and language pathologist to observe a student in public during the O&M assessment, or to at least hear from the O&M specialist about the experience.

It is equally important to assess whether the student knows how to refuse unnecessary or potentially unsafe assistance assertively. Many years ago students at the California School for the Blind had a group discussion about the differences between friends, acquaintances, and strangers. One of the O&M specialists asked what the students would do if a shopkeeper they had met before asked them

FIGURE 9.1

CHECKLIST FOR ASSESSING STREET CROSSINGS AND COMMUNITY ORIENTATION

This checklist is meant as a supplement to other O&M assessment tools that may not include items specifically about the concepts needed for safe street crossings.

The items on this checklist can be assessed before a student goes out into the community. To use this assessment checklist, you will need a tactile map on which the student can move toy cars and/or a large model of a grid area made with gym mats or tables between which the student can move on foot or on a scooter board.

Date _____

Student _____

Assessor _____

Directionality
____ Identifies left and right sides of someone facing him or her.
____ Identifies which side of the hallway we walk on.
____ Explains why we walk on the right side of the hallway.

Cardinal Directions
____ Identifies opposites of cardinal directions.
____ Identifies all cardinal directions when given one direction.
____ Explains the difference between cardinal directions and left and right.

The following questions are to be answered using a *tactile map* or *a model of a grid pattern* made from gym mats or tables. (Circle which was used.)

Parallel and perpendicular
____ Demonstrates the meaning of parallel using the edges of a table or a gym mat.
____ Demonstrates the meaning of perpendicular using the edges of a table or gym mat.
____ Demonstrates the meaning of parallel using toy cars or scooter boards moving parallel to each other.
____ Demonstrates the meaning of perpendicular using toy cars or scooter boards moving perpendicular to each other.

Describes what is meant by "going around the block":
____ What shape is a block?
____ How many streets do you walk on when you walk around the block?
____ How many corners do you come to?
____ How many streets do you cross when you walk around the block?

Describes what is meant by "walking one block," "walking two blocks":
____ How many streets do you walk on when you walk one block?
____ When you walk two blocks?

Source: California School for the Blind Assessment Program, Fremont, CA. Reprinted with permission.

___ How many streets do you cross when you walk one block?
___ How many streets do you cross when you walk two blocks?

Identifies shapes of
___ Blocks
___ Intersections (*T*, +, *offset*)
___ How many corners are there at a *plus* intersection?
___ How many corners are there at a *T* intersection?

How is traffic controlled? (or) How do drivers know when it is their turn to go?
___ Describes stop signs
___ Identifies traffic lights
___ Describes yield signs
___ Describes purposes of traffic controls
___ Demonstrates how cars move down the same street going in opposite directions without crashing.
___ Describes the danger of walking in a street.

Using a tactile map, demonstrates how cars move through an intersection with different traffic controls:
___ No control
___ Stop sign
___ Four-way stop
___ Simple light
___ Light with left turn arrows
  ■ Including right turners ___
  ■ Including left turners ___
  ■ Going in opposite directions ___
  ■ Going perpendicular to each other ___
  ■ Free right turn lanes ___

Uses cardinal directions:
___ Identifies three cardinal directions on the map or model when given one.
___ If you are walking north, which side of the street is on your right, the east side or the west side? (East)
___ If you are walking west, which side of the street is on your left, the north side or the south side? (South)
___ Identifies corners at a plus intersection using northwest, southwest, northeast, and southeast.
___ If you are on the southeast corner of a + intersection facing west, which corner are you facing?
___ If you are standing at a light-control intersection on the northeast corner, facing west and you hear the traffic surge, where should you look before crossing? Why?

Addresses:
___ If you are outside of 1423 Orange Street what do you expect the addresses of the houses next door to be?
___ What do you expect the address of the house across the street to be?

_____

Source: California School for the Blind Assessment Program, Fremont, CA. Reprinted with permission.

out for a Coke. One student's hand shot up in the air. He said, "I would say, 'I am a Mormon, so I don't drink Coke, but I'll have a root beer!'" Although this student had mistaken what the discussion was truly about, the others went on to say that it might be okay to go out for a soda at the shopping center, but it would not be a good idea to get into a car with the acquaintance. This kind of judgment is sometimes difficult to assess in a short, initial assessment. It needs to be watched for during continuing work with the student and in consultation with family and other individualized education program (IEP) team members.

Public Transportation

Students who are older and continuing to develop independence may be assessed by the O&M specialist in the area of more advanced travel skills. The specialist can spend time looking at such skills as gathering information about the locations to which the older student would like to travel, connecting with resources such as public transportation and paratransit service, scheduling all aspects of a trip, and learning to navigate in unfamiliar areas of the community.

When looking at the student's ability to use public transportation, an O&M specialist may assess everything from whether or not a student has heard of buses to whether a student knows how to call the bus company, record or remember the travel information obtained, find the desired bus stop, communicate appropriately with the driver, transfer as needed, get off the bus at the appropriate stop, and find the location to which he or she is traveling. The student's knowledge of and experience with other types of transportation is also assessed by an O&M specialist, including the use of taxis, paratransit, subways and hired drivers. Checklists for assessing a student's ability to use public transportation are included in many of the tools listed in the Resources for this chapter.

Dog Guides

O&M specialists may also assess a student's readiness to work with dog guides. They may need to assess whether a dog guide handler who is blind or visually impaired is using the dog in the most effective way. Dog guides are available from private schools that breed and train the dogs, select eligible people to handle the dogs, and train those people to use the dogs for travel. Adults, and sometimes older teenagers, who are blind or visually impaired are typically selected to become dog handlers if they have adequate O&M skills and if they travel enough to keep the dog well-exercised and trained. Younger children are not usually eligible to become dog handlers because the dogs need a high level of consistent use to maintain their intensive and expensive training. Several dog guide schools train dogs specifically to work with visually impaired people who have additional disabilities. Schools that train dogs for people who have multiple disabilities usually assess the individual in detail in order to train a dog specifically for him or her. Dog school personnel are usually ready to advise O&M specialists on how to assess the appropriateness of a dog handler's work with a dog from their school.

Other O&M Devices

Low vision devices may be important for O&M. Monoculars and binoculars are frequently used by travelers with low vision, and O&M specialists help people select such low vision devices if they do not have access to a low vision examination from an eye care specialist (see Chapter 4). Assessing the use of such devices for travel is part of the O&M specialist's job, even if the monocular was selected by an eye care specialist. Assessment might include whether a student can use a monocular to scan to find a traffic signal or to recognize the signs needed when using public transportation. The use of pocket magnifiers, which may also be useful when traveling in the community, may also be assessed. Handheld magnifiers may be used to read bus schedules, labels on food products, and price tags.

There are increasing efforts to make communities in the United States accessible to people who are blind or visually impaired, especially since passage of the Americans with Disabilities Act in 1990. Traffic signals, particularly in urban areas, more frequently have an auditory component with one auditory signal for north–south traffic and another for east–west traffic. Assessing a student's concepts of

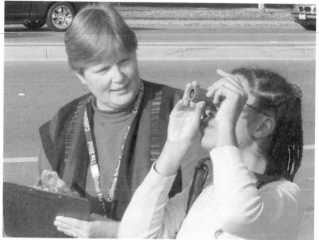

J. Richard Russo

The orientation and mobility specialist assesses whether a student can use a low vision device, such as a monocular, out in the community.

the cardinal directions and whether he or she understands the meaning and the limitations of the auditory signals are included in the O&M specialist's domain.

"Talking Signs" are becoming a feature of the urban environment. These radio devices are installed in transportation depots and other public areas. They send spoken auditory signals to handheld receivers to provide people who are blind or visually impaired with information helpful for orientation. Assessing the use of the receiver and of the information available through a talking sign may be an objective of an O&M assessment.

Electronic travel aids are available for use by people who are blind or visually impaired. These help people to detect obstacles in the environment by projecting laser light or ultrasound waves that bounce back to the device from any obstacles present, creating a sound or vibration. Electronic devices are not widely used because many of them are expensive and difficult to maintain. As this technology improves and becomes more affordable, more and more travelers who are blind or visually impaired are finding electronic travel aids that are practical for them. O&M specialists who assess the usefulness of an electronic travel aid for a particular student are usually trained and certified by the companies producing these devices.

Ancillary Skills for O&M

Four primary areas of skills that are part of the expanded core curriculum addressed by a teacher of students who are visually impaired are among those also important for O&M: shopping, time, money, and using the telephone. Some proficiency in each of these areas is necessary to travel with independence.

Shopping

Sometimes O&M specialists are referred to as shopping teachers, because a trip to a store is often used as a motivator to learn travel skills. O&M specialists may consult with parents and other caregivers, speech and language pathologists, and teachers of students who are visually impaired to assess how much independence a student has for accessing goods and services in the community. Skills to assess include knowing what goods and services are available in various places in the community, organizational skills for planning a trip, as well as public behavior and the ability to communicate with strangers. Checklists for assessing shopping skills are included in many of the assessment tools listed in the Resources for this chapter.

Time Concepts

Being able to use time concepts has a crucial impact on being able to plan all kinds of travel, from getting from the classroom to lunch and back efficiently to using the bus to get to an extracurricular activity across town on time. In conjunction with the parents and caregivers, classroom teacher, and teacher of students who are visually impaired, the O&M specialist assesses, teaches, and reinforces time concepts. The use of watches, timers, school bells, and bus schedules may all be assessed as aspects of becoming a reliable traveler. Figure 9.2 provides a checklist for assessing time concepts in relation to O&M. The need to create a calendar box (Blaha, 2001) to help children who are deaf-blind or who have multiple disabilities to learn about their daily routines may also become apparent in the course of an O&M assessment since anticipating when to go somewhere is nearly as important as knowing how to go somewhere.

FIGURE 9.2
CHECKLIST FOR ASSESSING TIME CONCEPTS

Date _____

Student _____

Assessor _____

Early/late

Which happens earlier in the day? (Circle the correct answer in each pair)

Breakfast/lunch   Going to bed/going to school

Getting up/eating dinner   Leaving school for the day/getting dressed

Which time is later in the afternoon? (Circle the correct answer in each pair)

12:50/1:20   4:30/12:15   2:45/2:40

4:35/1:28   2:20/3:15   6:15/1:55

Awareness of daily schedule

Around what time do you

Get up? _____   Eat breakfast? _____

Eat lunch? _____   Eat dinner? _____

Go to school? _____   Go to bed? _____

Watch your favorite show on TV? _____

Estimating the length of a task

How long would it take you to do the following things?

Walk from class to the restroom _____

Brush your teeth _____

Go into a store, buy a bag of chips, and go out of the store _____

Eat dinner _____

Get dressed in the morning _____

Telling time

What do you do when you want to know what time it is? _____

Do you have a watch or a clock? _____ What kind? _____

Using _____, tell me what time it is now. _____

Comments: _____

_____

Source: California School for the Blind Assessment Program, Fremont, CA. Reprinted with permission.

Time intervals

The buses come every _____. The last bus came at _____. When will the next one come?

hour/1:30 _____   15 minutes/12:03 _____

½ hour/12:15 _____   15 minutes/8:45 _____

½ hour/8:43 _____   10 minutes/6:12 _____

½ hour/4:10 _____   10 minutes/12:55 _____

Allowing time

The bus leaves at _____. You need _____ to get to the bus stop. What time do you need to leave to catch the bus?

3:15/5 minutes _____   2:10/15 minutes _____

1:20/20 minutes _____   8:32/15 minutes _____

11:45/15 minutes _____   6:04/10 minutes _____

Source: California School for the Blind Assessment Program, Fremont, CA. Reprinted with permission.

A calendar box may be a series of objects associated with an activity which are presented to the student slightly ahead of an activity. A more sophisticated calendar box may have objects or pictures arranged in the order of the activities with which they are associated. The student uses the box by finding the next object, doing the activity and then depositing the object in the "finished" basket.

Telephone Use

Using the telephone may not seem like an O&M skill since (at least until recently) most people are fairly sedentary when talking on the phone. However, the telephone allows access to the community that cannot be obtained as easily in any other way. Assessing a student's skills for telephone use ranges from observing whether he or she can remember his or her own telephone number and talk to a familiar person on the phone, to assessing an older student's ability to ask for bus information and record that information efficiently and in a way that can easily be retrieved later. Recommendations in the area of telephone skills may be for work at home or in the classroom, but the actual skills are likely to be used eventually as part of community travel. A checklist for assessing telephone skills is provided in Figure 9.3.

FIGURE 9.3
CHECKLIST FOR ASSESSING TELEPHONE SKILLS

Date _____

Student _____

Assessor _____

What is your home phone number? _____

What is your mother's/father's work phone number? _____

Dial your home phone number on this unplugged phone. Comments: _____
_____

Identify the noises that the telephone makes. (Either listen to the telephone make the sounds, imitate the sounds, or have the student imitate the sounds. Circle the method used.)

___ Dial tone

___ Busy signal

___ Ringing signal

___ Not in service

What number do you call in an emergency? _____

In what kinds of emergencies do you call 911? _____
_____

What kinds of emergency vehicles come when you call 911? _____
_____

How do you find a telephone number if you don't know it? _____
_____

Have you ever called 411? ____ Role play calling 411 and comment: _____
_____

_____

Source: California School for the Blind Assessment Program, Fremont, CA. Reprinted with permission.

How do you get a telephone number for a business if you don't know the name of the business? For example, how would you get a number for a drug store near your home? Role play asking for Yellow Page assistance. The student can choose how to identify herself as having a disability that allows access to this service. Comment:

_____

_____

How do you record a telephone number when you get it? _____

_____

How do you keep track of telephone numbers you use frequently? _____

_____

What is a pay telephone? How is it different from other telephones? _____

_____

How much do local calls cost on a pay telephone? _____
_____

Source: California School for the Blind Assessment Program, Fremont, CA. Reprinted with permission.

Handling Money

The use of money is another area where the O&M specialist may do an assessment in collaboration with parents and caregivers, the classroom teacher, and the teacher of students who are visually impaired. Although many people who are blind or visually impaired use coins with ease, recognizing each and identifying their values— the first step usually learned by many children whether they are sighted or visually impaired—may be irrelevant for many students who are blind or visually impaired, especially when other disabilities such as fine motor impairment or cognitive impairment make the use of coins difficult. Together with other teachers, including parents and caregivers, the O&M specialist may recommend that the student learn to use paper money only when making a purchase. Learning to offer the clerk an appropriate number of one dollar bills to make a purchase frequently requires a lot of repetition. Students are taught to fold bills of different denominations in different ways and to keep track of their money at home and while shopping. A checklist for the assessment of money skills is provided in Figure 9.4.

FIGURE 9.4

CHECKLIST FOR ASSESSING MONEY SKILLS

Date _____

Student _____

Assessor _____

Identifying coins and their values (Indicate how the coins were presented)

Coin	Name	Value
Penny	_____	_____
Nickel	_____	_____
Dime	_____	_____
Quarter	_____	_____
Dollar	_____	_____

Identifying bills visually or by folding method

Bill	Visual identification	Method of folding
One	_____	_____
Five	_____	_____
Ten	_____	_____
Twenty	_____	_____

Costs of common items: How much do you think each of these items costs?

Pack of gum _____   Half-gallon of milk _____

Can of soda _____   Clock radio _____

Hamburger _____   TV set _____

CD _____   New car _____

More or less

Which costs more? (Circle one in each pair)

Apple/TVset   Candy bar/hair brush

Hot dog/pair of pants   Tape recorder/new car

Bus ride/taxi ride   New shoes/a pair of socks

Source: California School for the Blind Assessment Program, Fremont, CA. Reprinted with permission.

Which is more money?

$.50/$1.00	$.65/$3.00
$.47/$.12	$8.45/$1.90
Quarter/nickel	Dime/penny
3 dimes/6 nickels	10 pennies/one dime

Next highest dollar

You are going to buy some things at the store and pay the clerk using only one dollar bills, no coins. If the total is _____, how many dollars will you give the clerk?

Fifty cents _____	A dollar ninety-nine _____
Twenty-four cents _____	Two twenty-five _____
Six dollars and fifty cents _____	Three eighty-nine _____
Two dollars and forty-two cents _____	Eight fifty _____
A buck and a quarter _____	Three dollars, six cents _____

How many cents?

Either give student the coins or have the student answer without coins. (Circle the method used)

1 quarter, one dime _____	3 nickels _____
5 dimes _____	3 quarters _____
2 dimes, three pennies _____	2 quarters, one dime _____

Relative values

Either give the student the money or have the student answer without the money. (Circle the method used)

You want to buy something that costs _____, and you have _____. Do you have enough money?

$.50/$.75 _____	$1.50/$1.10 _____	$4.00/$2.50 _____
$1.67/$3.00 _____	$.25/$.40 _____	$1.89/$5.00 _____
$.25/2 dimes _____	$.42/2 quarters _____	$.80/1 dollar _____
$3.59/4 dollars _____	$2.50/3 dollars _____	$.52/5 dollars _____

Source: California School for the Blind Assessment Program, Fremont, CA. Reprinted with permission.

ELIGIBILITY FOR O&M SERVICES

O&M is listed as a "related service" under the federal Individuals with Disabilities Education Act (IDEA). An O&M assessment usually makes clear which students require the services of an O&M specialist to experience successful involvement and progress in the general curriculum and to increase their independence in travel. Nearly all children and young adults who are totally blind can benefit from the services of an O&M specialist. Most students who have some vision but whose visual impairment interferes with other areas of their education can also benefit from O&M services.

It is ultimately up to the IEP team to decide whether O&M services have a place in a student's program. Other professionals may act as consultants to the O&M specialist or may have parallel and collaborative activities in their programs for students who are visually impaired. However, direct services from an O&M specialist are needed when an assessment shows that a student has deficits and can benefit from instruction in the areas listed in Sidebar 9.2.

Sometimes it is less clear whether services of an O&M specialist are needed or whether instruction can be provided by other teachers, including the family and other caregivers. For example, when the student's primary need in the areas covered by an O&M assessment is to develop better use of spatial concepts, especially if the student is already receiving services from a speech and language pathologist, it may not be to his or her advantage to have another service added to the IEP. Young children or students receiving many educational and therapy services may benefit more from O&M consultation to their other specialists than from direct O&M services.

Instruction in the following areas of need, which may become apparent through an assessment by an O&M specialist, can be addressed in a number of ways by other members of the team:

- body image development
- spatial concept development
- fine and gross motor skills
- basic O&M skills (may be taught by a teacher of students who are visually impaired, an O&M specialist, or someone trained by either of those)
- exposure to the community, available goods and services, and public transportation
- communication with the public

Sidebar 9.2   INSTRUCTIONAL NEEDS THAT CALL FOR DIRECT O&M SERVICE

- Using pre-cane devices and alternatives to canes
- Learning cane skills
- Using echolocation and other sound cues
- Orientation to protected environments and to the community
- Following verbal and/or written travel directions
- Developing advanced travel concepts, such as cardinal directions and traffic patterns
- Trip planning
- Street crossings of all kinds
- Use of monoculars for travel
- Use of public transportation and other alternatives to driving

These skills and concepts may be taught by a special day class or regular education teacher, by the teacher of students who are visually impaired, by an occupational or physical therapist, by parents and other caregivers, or by any of these with consultation from or in conjunction with direct service from an O&M specialist.

ASSESSMENT TOOLS FOR O&M

There are many tools available for the assessment of O&M skills. Most are used to assess strengths and weaknesses in the various skills needed for O&M. Most O&M assessment tools are comprehensive, covering almost all of the areas mentioned in this chapter. In addition, checklists and assessment tools are available to assess specific areas, such as concept development, various living skills, and the use of vision for O&M. Other assessment tools are listed and described in the Resources for this chapter.

SUMMARY

The assessment of O&M skills is the last area of the expanded core curriculum covered in this book. This discussion of O&M has shown how important collaboration is to both professionals trained to work regularly with students who are blind or visually impaired and those who may evaluate very few blind or visually impaired students in their careers. O&M skills offer a practical expression of many of the skills taught by other professionals. As students become more independent in their academic pursuits, communication skills, and living skills, O&M becomes more and more essential to allow them access to the world where they can apply those skills.

The next step in collaborative assessment is to put the information the assessment team has gathered into a comprehensive report that reflects the student's current level of abilities. The next chapter looks at how reports can be written to reflect a collaborative assessment and how priorities can be established as recommendations for the student's future goals emerge from the assessment findings.

REFERENCES

Blaha, R. (2001). *Calendars.* Austin: Texas School for the Blind and Visually Impaired.

Pogrund, R., Healy, G., Jones, K., Levack, N., Martin-Curry, S., Martinez, C., Marz, J., Roberson-Smith, B., & Vrba, A. (1993). *TAPS, an orientation and mobility curriculum for students with visual impairments.* Austin: Texas School for the Blind and Visually Impaired.

Strickling, C. (1998). *Impact of vision loss on motor development.* Austin: Texas School for the Blind and Visually Impaired.

RESOURCES FOR O&M

Tools for Assessing Spatial Concepts and Body Image

The comprehensive O&M assessment tools listed in other sections also include checklists of spatial concepts. Those listed here assess only spatial concepts and body image.

Body Image of the Blind Child Checklist
Authors: Cratty, B. J., and Sams, T. A.
Published in: *The Body Image of the Blind Child*
Ages: Preschool through 8 years, and for older students who have cognitive disabilities
Publisher: American Foundation for
   the Blind
   11 Penn Plaza, Suite 300
   New York, NY 10001
   (212) 502-7600
Date: 1968
Type of instrument: Checklist

Comments: An extensive list of body parts and positional concepts that the student is asked to demonstrate using his or her own body parts and by positioning himself or herself in relation to walls and the floor. The list is extremely detailed, and parts of it have been reproduced in composite assessment checklists, such as the Los Angeles Unified School District's Orientation and Mobility Assessment. It is particularly good for use with young children, who often enjoy moving in accordance with the directions. The portion involving the concepts of left and right is designed for children over the age of 6 or 7 and is quite sophisticated. This book is currently out of print but may be available in some libraries.

Boehm Test of Positional Concepts
See the description of this tool in the Resources for Chapter 7.

The Hill Performance Test of Selected Positional Concepts
Author: Hill, E. W.
Ages: 6 through 10 years
Publisher: Stoelting
   620 Wheat Lane
   Wood Dale, IL 60191
   (708) 860-9700
Date: 1981
Type of instrument: Norm referenced

Comments: This may be the only standardized tool designed for use by O&M specialists. It consists of 75 items that ask students to identify the relationships of various body parts, to move body parts into certain positions, to move themselves into certain relationships to objects and, finally, to move objects in relation to each other. Standardized for children who have been legally blind since before the age of 5, have receptive language abilities, are flexible and mobile, have a basic knowledge of body parts, and are from 6 through 10 years old.

Peabody Developmental Motor Scales and Activity Cards.
Folio, M. R., and Fewell, R. R.
Ages: Birth to 7 years
Publisher: Pro-ed
   8700 Shoal Creek Blvd.
   Austin, TX 78757
   (800) 897-3202
   www.proedinc.com
Date: 1983

Comments: Includes items to assess both gross and fine motor skills with plans for instruction as well. Adaptations are offered for students with visual impairments, hearing impairments, and multiple disabilities.

Tools for Assessing the Use of Vision for O&M

See the description of tools used for assessing functional vision in the Resources for Chapter 4.

Tools for Assessing the O&M Skills of Infants and Preschoolers

Peabody Mobility Kit for Infants and Toddlers
Authors: Harley, R. K., Long, R. G., Merbler, J. B., and Wood, T. A.
Ages: Birth to 3 years
Publisher: Stoelting
        620 Wheat Lane
        Wood Dale, IL 60191
        (708) 860-9700
Date: 1981

Comments: Designed for use with young children who are blind or visually impaired who may have other disabilities as well. This tool lists the skills by developmental level, leading directly to recommendations for O&M objectives.

Preschool Orientation and Mobility Screening
Authors: Dodson-Burk, B., and Hill, E. W.
Ages: Birth through 5 years
Publisher: Association for Education and Rehabilitation of the Blind and Visually Impaired

4600 Duke Street, #430
P.O. Box 22397
Alexandria, VA 22304
(703) 823-9690
www.aerbvi.org/
publications/books.htm
Date: 1989
Type of instrument: Checklists

Comments: This assessment is organized into two parts: one for younger, delayed, or nonambulatory students and the other for older, ambulatory, preschool students. The tool includes questions for parents and caregivers and spaces to record medical information, as well as tasks the student is asked to perform. These checklists record valuable information about how the student is functioning in O&M, which points to what service(s) may be needed from an O&M specialist.

Tools for Comprehensive O&M Assessments

Many unpublished checklists have been compiled by O&M specialists to assess each aspect of O&M. The available comprehensive tools for O&M assessments are essentially compilations of such checklists. They start with very basic skills, such as identifying body parts, and continue to such complex independent tasks as planning trips across town by public transportation. The wide range of skills makes them appropriate for students with a wide range of abilities as well as a wide age range. These tools provide directions for the student to perform a task that can be observed and evaluated by the O&M specialist.

Orientation and Mobility Assessment for Blind, Low Vision, and Multi-handicapped Students
Authors: Orientation and Mobility Teachers of Los Angeles Unified School District
Ages: Preschool through high school, including students with other disabilities
Publisher: Los Angeles Unified School District
     Frances Blend School
     5210 Clinton St.
     Los Angeles, CA 90004
     (323) 464-5052
Date: 1989

Comments: Items are arranged in developmental order as much as possible, beginning with attending to noises, following one-step directions, and body image, and ending with independent travel in a business area.

Peabody Mobility Programs
Authors: Harley, R. K., Long, R. G., Merbler, J. B., and Wood, T. A.
Ages: 3 years old to adult
Publisher: Stoelting
     620 Wheat Lane
     Wood Dale, IL 60191
     (708) 860-9700
Date: 1981

Comments: Includes tasks for students to perform while the O&M specialist observes. There are separate tools for assessing students who have some vision and students who have no vision. The items are delineated into very small steps for each area. Items assess such skills as whether a student locates a sound source, whether he or she turns back toward an object after being turned away from it, and his or her level of proficiency with basic O&M skills. Using this tool to supplement the concept areas of other comprehensive assessments is effective, especially with students who are young or cognitively disabled.

Teaching Age-Appropriate Purposeful Skills (TAPS): An Orientation and Mobility Curriculum for Students with Visual Impairments
Authors: Pogrund, R., Healy, G., Jones, K., Levack, N., Martin-Curry, S., Martinez, C., Marz, J., Roberson-Smith, B., and Vrba, A.
Ages: 3 to 21 years
Publisher: Texas School for the Blind and Visually Impaired
     1100 West 45th St.
     Austin, TX 78756
     (512) 454-8631
     www.tsbvi.edu/
     publications/index.htm
Date: 1993

Comments: *TAPS* can be used for students who are visually impaired and have other disabilities and includes a section to assess students who use wheelchairs for mobility. A screening assessment is included as well as a comprehensive assessment. The assessment tools are incorporated into a curriculum book that includes teaching strategies and directions for making adaptive equipment as well as developmentally arranged curriculum ideas.

Report Writing

*J. Richard Russo and
Frances K. Liefert*

IN THIS CHAPTER:

- Purpose of the assessment report

- Report components

- Collaborative and comprehensive method of writing reports and recommendations

- How to use the assessment report to establish educational priorities

---

This chapter details how the collaborative assessment team can best report its results in writing. It provides detailed descriptions of the report's constituent parts and discusses its role in determining further evaluation and services.

The assessment report serves a variety of purposes: primarily, it is the device used to communicate information from one person or group to another. The report can take a wide variety of forms, including an oral report, simple checklists, or more comprehensive reports prepared by a variety of professional experts. The authors have found that the most effective reports are those that include a collaborative approach, which can take various forms as described in this chapter.

FUNCTIONS OF THE ASSESSMENT REPORT

Any assessment report, in whatever form, should answer the referral questions, document assessment results, provide baseline data, identify and justify the need for services, and provide information about the student's disability.

Answering the Referral Questions

The goal of an assessment report is to respond to the concerns that motivated the referral for the assessment in the first place. However, parents and school districts often have vastly differing referral questions. Sometimes the differences in the questions reflect conflict between parents and school officials, which lead to requests for further assessment and may even lead to a referral to an independent assessment service. Often too, once the assessment has begun, assessors discover information thought to be vital to the student's success in school that was not requested in the initial referral.

Sometimes the referral questions cannot be answered either because they are outside the scope of the assessment services available or because the assessment technology is not advanced or sophisticated enough. For example, if the student is too young or too disabled to respond to formal testing, no standardized scores or IQ numbers will be assigned. If the student's disability is in a state of flux, the snapshot view that assessors take of the student may not be relevant for very long. Addressing specific concerns expressed by the referring individuals is nevertheless an important goal of the report.

Documentation of Assessment Results

The assessment report needs to document the results of all the assessments performed. It also provides an excellent opportunity to document information such as the student's history and background. More and more frequently, parents and other caregivers take time to compile their child's medical, developmental, and educational histories since they are asked for that information repeatedly by various assessors and agencies. The assessment report should include pertinent background information to help readers understand events that have contributed to the student's present level of functioning. If the parents or caregivers have not provided background information, it is important to glean pertinent information from medical and social workers' reports, as well as educational reports (see Chapter 3), in order to document the student's history as fully as possible.

Providing Baseline Data

The assessment report is a document against which future assessments can be compared. Rates and patterns of growth can prove to be extremely useful information. For students who are visually impaired they can be critical, because often the validity of individual assessments can be challenged, particularly in the areas of psychological assessment and speech and language assessment. Looking at the results of a series of assessments done periodically during the student's education helps to clarify which behaviors are a result of visual impairment and which are the result of other factors. Comparing test scores over time can increase the accuracy of the individualized education program (IEP) team's picture of a student who is visually impaired.

Identifying and Justifying the Need for Services

The written assessment report conveys information about the student's present level of functioning in a valid and objective way, for the review of those who make program decisions, as well as for those who will work with the student. Documentation can include information needed for the IEP team to determine whether he or she is eligible for services from the district's special education department. The documentation is intended to lead the IEP team to create a program that includes the types of interventions and accommodations appropriate for the particular student. In the case of a student who is visually impaired, the documents provided by an eye care specialist, either an ophthalmologist or an optometrist, are also central to determining eligibility for services. (See Chapter 4 for more information.) The outcome of an appropriate assessment should be a map of the scope and types of services that will benefit an individual child, which will be provided in the assessment report.

Providing Information about the Student's Disability

Sometimes it is important to give a general description of the particular eye condition or the concomitant disabilities the student has, in order for the report reader to understand how this particular student is affected by these conditions. For example, students with severe cortical visual impairment (CVI) can display confusing and misleading symptoms. General information about CVI should be included in the report as well as the particular aspects of CVI observed in the student being assessed. Some eye conditions are not well known and may need to be described in order for readers to understand the report. Providing this specialized information makes the background information more meaningful and supports the role of the assessment report in documenting the student's present level of functioning.

COMPONENTS OF THE ASSESSMENT REPORT

The report on a collaborative assessment must reflect the collaborative approach. Typical areas for assessment, as discussed elsewhere in this book, include psychology, vision, O&M, speech and language, technology needs, and education (which examines the broad area referred to as the expanded core curriculum). Some assessment teams will include professionals from the areas of adapted physical education, occupational or physical therapy, social work, and school nursing. The comprehensive report format can follow a traditional form, frequently seen in the fields of education and psychology. The report may be designed to be reviewed as a whole, as well as to have sections removed and provided to particular specialists who will be charged with implementing the recommendations in those sections. Report sections may vary in length and detail, depending on the nature of the findings and the need for emphasis. A typical report format would have the following sections:

- Background information
- Behavior during assessment
- Assessment procedures

- Findings
- Recommendations

These areas are described in more detail in the following sections.

Background

Before the results of the assessment are reported, background information about the student and about the referral for assessment needs to be stated. This background information is much the same as the information collected during the preparation for assessment, discussed in Chapter 3. The information to be included in the background section, especially if the student is a new referral to special education services or is new to a particular school situation, includes the following:

- Identifying information
- Reasons for referral
- Vision information
- Hearing information
- Other disabilities
- Medical history and current medical status
- Personal history and current living environment
- Educational history
- Current placement and services
- Agencies serving the child
- Family language and ethnic background
- Validity of assessment

What follows is a description of all the components. Some of the descriptions are longer than some of the sections will be in an actual report and are offered to give a complete picture of what may need to be included. A vehicle for gathering much of the information contained in the report is the Parent Inventory and History Form, a copy of which is provided in Appendix B of this book.

Identifying Information

This section provides information on the student's date of birth, parents, and school district. It can be presented in a table format to make gathering information easy on the assessment team, telephone numbers, addresses, and other personal information. In addition, key contact persons are identified to reduce time spent searching when specific information is needed.

Reasons for the Referral

The reasons for referral are drawn from a variety of sources. A formal referral form may have sections that are completed by the parents and the school district. In a less formal assessment referral, report writers will rely on notes from interviews with school staff and family members that took place before the assessment began (see Chapter 3). Questions that arose during the assessment may be included here, but will more likely find a place in the body of the assessment report.

Vision

The vision report can vary in length and depth. Assessors may prefer to include all information about vision in a separate section of the final report or it may be included in the background section. The type of vision information reported in this section reflects the results of vision examinations conducted by ophthalmologists, optometrists, optometrists who specialize in low vision, and teachers of students who are visually impaired specializing in functional vision assessment. Each of these types of assessment provides specialized information. (See Chapter 4 for detailed information about optometrist's and ophthalmologist's reports, as well as functional vision assessment.) The information from the eye care specialist is interpreted here to be helpful to parents and education personnel, who are expected to understand and accommodate the child's vision and vision needs.

Hearing

The hearing section of the report may be a simple statement of the child's hearing gathered from information provided in the referral packet or the results of an audiological screening. It may be included in the speech and language section of the report if the speech and language pathologist prefers. If a hearing disability is suspected or discovered during the assessment processes, a more in-depth audiological examination needs to be conducted or recommended as a follow-up. Referral for assessment by a teacher of students who are hearing impaired or a teacher of students who are visually impaired who specializes in the needs of students who are deaf-blind is appropriate when a hearing impairment is discovered during the assessment of a child who is blind or visually impaired.

Other Disabilities Section

It is important to describe any other disabilities in addition to the student's visual impairment. Included in this section will be a description of any neurological deficits, learning disabilities, cerebral palsy, seizure disorders, emotional problems, and other disorders known at the time of the referral for assessment. This information is gleaned primarily from the reports submitted by the parents, medical professionals, and the school district as part of the supportive documentation supplied with the referral information. It does not include additional diagnoses or disabilities identified during the course of this assessment. Those are reported in the findings section of the report.

Medical History and Current Medical Status

The section of the report concerning medical information contains critical data gathered from various sources including the referral form, if completed by both the family and the school district, the Parent History and Inventory form presented in Appendix B of this book, and medical reports collected as part of the referral information. In addition, it is informative to interview parents or other caregivers to help review and clarify their child's medical history.

The medical history is central to understanding the student who is blind or visually impaired. In many cases, whatever caused the visual impairment also caused other disabilities. Appendix A of this book describes many causes of childhood visual impairment, with information about their implications for assessment, including other disabilities that often accompany specific visual conditions.

Key areas in the medical history include the following:

- Mother's pregnancy and delivery including:
- Any illnesses or injuries experienced by the mother during pregnancy
- Mother's work history during pregnancy
- Any use of alcohol, tobacco, and drugs (prescription, non-prescription, or illicit)
- Delivery, including duration of labor, type of delivery, and any complications during delivery
- Condition of baby after delivery including Apgar scores, breathing, cry, other relevant findings
- Childhood illnesses or injuries, especially any that might have caused the visual impairment
- Child's development including milestones
- Child's current health including current medical treatments or medications

Personal History and Current Living Environment

Personal information is gathered from many of the same sources as that of the medical history. The purpose of this section is to gather information regarding the student's heredity and the environment in which he or she was raised. Information is gathered about both the birth parents and the caregivers who raised the student, if they are not the same. If social workers have been involved with the student, it is helpful to interview them or, with the current caregivers' permission, request any reports they may have written.

Major areas of this section include the following:

- Age of biological parents at student's birth
- Educational background of parents (and caregivers, if different) and current employment status
- Parents' or siblings' learning or other disabilities
- Family history of use of illicit drugs or alcohol
- Family socioeconomic status, including income, if available

It is helpful to describe the student's current living environment. Included here is general information on where the student lives, the adults in his or her life and other siblings or relatives living in or frequenting the environment.

Educational History

The educational history section elucidates the student's school or school-related experiences. Especially important for this section is the age at which formal educational interventions began. Also included are dates and types of placements the student has had; grade level, if appropriate; and any specialized interventions in the past, such as physical therapy, occupational therapy, speech and language therapy, psychotherapy or counseling, and orientation and mobility (O&M) services. Academic progress is discussed in the appropriate section of the body of the assessment report, along with the findings of the academic assessment.

Current Placement and Services

It is very important to include information about the student's current educational placement and any school- or family-supported related services. This section includes a description of current services to the student or family, both direct and indirect, and the time and duration of the services. For example, if the teacher of students who are visually impaired provides two hours of direct instruction and one hour of consultation to the classroom teacher and one hour of family consultation, those times are stated here.

Other Agencies Serving the Student

A brief statement of the other agencies serving the student, and a brief description of those services, is also included. This section should not only list the agencies and services but might also be a preliminary discussion about other services to which the family might be entitled. For example, children who are disabled might be eligible for Supplemental Security Income (SSI) benefits and services from specialized social work or educational agencies for children who are disabled in specific ways. The parents might be asked about or informed of parent or other organizations that can provide support or educational services.

Family Language or Culture

Federal law requires a statement about the child's language or ethnic background that might have a bearing on his or her education. This information can be gathered from school records or parent history. When a child's primary language is other than English, the assessment implications can be significant.

Validity of Assessment

The validity statement is also required by law. Since a vision loss can seriously impair a student's ability to gather environmental experiences, the possible effects of that loss should be described. The following is a sample validity statement:

> Assessment techniques standardized on sighted children can be useful when used for students who are visually impaired if the results are interpreted cautiously and in light of the student's visual impairment. Results should be interpreted by persons knowledgeable about the effects of a visual impairment on child growth and development, and test performance. Such instruments are best utilized when they can be repeated and results compared over time.
>
> The results reported below were obtained through one-to-one interaction with the student in a distraction-free environment. The assessment setting often elicits higher performance and better attending behavior than might be observed in the student in a typical classroom or other school environment.

Body of the Report

Once preliminary information has been provided, the body of the report should contain the assessment's findings. Each assessor needs to report on what was found in his or her area of expertise. An outline of possible headings for each section of the findings in specific disciplines is found in Sidebar 10.1. In a collaborative assessment, the various areas are sometimes less distinct than in assessments in which professionals of each discipline conduct separate assessments. Discussion at this time is appropriate to decide who will cover certain parts of the assessment for purposes of the report, to reduce redundancy and ensure complete coverage of significant findings. For example, both the teacher of students who are visually impaired and the O&M specialist are trained to assess living skills; they need to agree on how the living skills observed will be reported and by whom. Likewise, the speech and language pathologist and the psychologist may both be concerned with the student's concept development and may want to avoid repeating the information in their respective sections. What follows are some suggestions for what to include in the section on each area on which the team is reporting.

Behavior During Assessment

It is important to describe the student's reaction to being assessed; whether he or she cooperated with the assessors, maintained an alert posture or gave answers indicating attentiveness, or whether his or her caregiver reported that the student had not slept at all the previous night and had eaten only sugar for breakfast, lunch, and last night's dinner. This section could be written by each person conducting the assessment. To reduce this duplication of effort, the collaborative report approach can include a major discussion of testing behavior in the Psychological Assessment section and not be repeated for each of the other disciplines. However, brief behavior statements can be made by each assessor, especially as needed to clarify assessment results.

Assessment Procedures Used

Each assessor needs to list the procedures he or she used to obtain the assessment results being reported. These vary according to the individual student and include interviews with those who have lived and worked with the child, review of records, assessment tools used,

The following outline shows how the findings section of an assessment report might be organized:

Functional Vision Findings

  I. Review of eye care specialist's report
    A. Diagnosis
    B. Acuity/visual fields
    C. Contrast sensitivity
    D. Color vision
    E. Prescribed devices
 II. Observations in natural environments
    A. Effects of various lighting on vision
    B. Optimal learning media
      1. Braille/tactile materials
      2. Print
        a. Symbol size
        b. Crowded symbol acuity
    C. Use of prescribed devices
    D. Figure/ground discrimination
    E. Fluctuation in vision
    F. Postural concerns

Physiological Assessment Findings

   I. Cognitive functioning: test results
  II. Discussion of cognitive functioning
 III. Adaptive behavior
 IV. Emotional and behavioral functioning: test results
  V. Discussion of social–emotional and behavior functioning
 VI. Summary and conclusions

Speech and Language Findings

   I. Auditory attention/processing
  II. Phonological awareness
 III. Receptive language
 IV. Expressive language/communication
  V. Speech
 VI. Oral motor–feeding

(continued)

Educational Findings

   I. Reading
      A. Braille
      B. Print
  II. Listening comprehension
 III. Writing
      A. Braille
         1. Spelling
         2. Composition
      B. Print
         1. Spelling
         2. Composition
  IV. Mathematics
   V. Access technology
  VI. Social emotional skills
      A. Interaction with others
      B. Knowledge of visual impairment
      C. Knowledge of human sexuality
 VII. Recreation and leisure
VIII. Living skills
      A. Personal hygiene
      B. Dressing
      C. Food preparation
      D. Household management
  IX. Career/vocational skills

O&M Findings

   I. Motor skills
  II. Body image/orientation in space
 III. Use of vision for O&M
 IV. Spatial concept development
  V. Basic O&M techniques
 VI. Cane use
VII. Use of other O&M devices

(continued)

Sidebar 10.1 SAMPLE OUTLINE FOR THE FINDINGS SECTION OF AN ASSESSMENT REPORT *(continued)*

VIII. Community travel
- A. Concepts about the community environment
- B. Street crossings
- C. Interacting with the public; exercising judgment
- D. Using public transportation

IX. Ancillary skills
- A. Shopping/handling money
- B. Time concepts
- C. Telephone skills

---

and informal types of assessment such as observation in particular environments. This is a good place to describe any modifications that have been made to the standardized procedures: if items have been enlarged, if magnifiers were used, or if braille versions were substituted for the standardized print format, for example. Sometimes a version of an instrument designed for younger children is used because it is more appropriate for the particular student being assessed. These variations should be explained and described so that the instruments can be interpreted properly, and so that the next time an assessment is conducted, examiners can consider the modifications made for this assessment.

Findings

In a collaborative assessment the same assessment event may be reported on several times from the point of view of different assessors. To take an example from the assessment of Henry (see Chapter 11), the speech and language pathologist would report on Henry's experience making a peanut butter and honey sandwich by discussing how well Henry was able to describe his experience to the "naive" listener. The O&M specialist might use the same activity to describe how well Henry remembered where things were while he made the sandwich, enhancing information about Henry's spatial orientation.

The teacher of students who are visually impaired would write about how well Henry read the braille story about peanut butter and honey that was eventually written during the assessment.

Likewise, the teacher of students who are visually impaired might assess daily living skills (see Chapter 5) at the same time that the school psychologist assesses adaptive behavior. The daily living skills assessment might examine what a student is capable of doing, and an assessment of adaptive behavior might suggest what he or she typically does. Similar procedures might be used for both assessments; interviews, observations of the student, and the use of checklists or inventories. In working collaboratively, the psychologist and teacher of students who are visually impaired could describe what a student is capable of doing, what is expected of the student in various environments (diagnosis), and at the same time identify areas requiring remediation, adaptations, and other recommendations.

It is important to remember when writing reports that the student's behavior is what was observed, and provides the data that is the basis for the report. Descriptions of how the student felt, what he or she noticed, could or could not do, or did and did not understand all involve some conjecture on the part of the assessor. It is not possible to observe what a student understands, only how he or she responds to questions and to situations. Reporting on what actually happened and what was actually observed may have implications about what the student can or cannot do. But what actually happened during the assessment is not the only behavior in which the student engages. He or she may be able to perform behaviors which were not elicited during the assessment. Responses and other assessment behavior must be reported as a snapshot of the period of time in which the student was observed and assessed. The use of "behavioral language," that is, language that describes only the student's actual behavior is of paramount importance in this section of the report.

Recommendations

In a collaborative assessment there is the possibility of overlap in the area of recommendations. In fact, the more effective the collab-

J. Richard Russo

Collaboration on an assessment does not end until the report is finished.

oration, the more likely it is that the recommendations generated from the assessment will fit together, indicating the direction of a comprehensive program for the particular student. Further discussion among assessment team members about how best to present recommendations for specific aspects of the child's program will take place at the time of report writing. Including parents and other caregivers in this aspect of the assessment is often useful, in order to provide recommendations that encourage participation from the family, as well as to make sure the parents understand what is being recommended and why.

Many examples of recommendations from several disciplines are included in Chapter 11. Please note that behavioral language needs to be used in the recommendations, just as it was used in the assessment findings. Rather than describing what the student should understand or how the teacher should teach, it is useful to describe specific goals and methods for accomplishing them and to use language that encourages both the teachers and the student to respond creatively to suggestions about the next steps in the student's education. Rather than recommending what should happen, it is better to recommend what would be beneficial, useful, the next step, or helpful for the student.

WRITING THE REPORT

The collaborative assessment report may be written with different degrees of collaboration, depending on the assessment information included and the time available for collaboration among the professionals. Many assessment team members feel most comfortable writing their own section of the report, which includes everything but the Background section. These separate reports are then collected and incorporated into a report that is easy to separate according to the disciplines that have been covered.

The report may also be written in a more collaborative style, especially if its participants represent fewer disciplines. Headings may be selected by the team members, and each member may contribute the findings from his or her discipline that fit each heading. A report might have these headings: cognitive ability, communication, academics, motor skills, self-help skills, and O&M. The recommendations of the team would be grouped in a similar way to cover each area.

ESTABLISHING PROGRAM PRIORITIES

Once the assessment is finished, the work of the student's education begins. The ultimate purpose of the assessment is to describe the student in a way that will lead to appropriate programming. When all the findings are described and all the recommendations have been put forward, it is time to begin planning how to structure or improve the structure of the student's school program. The assessment team may not be the same team that decides on the actual program, unless the assessment team members are the same as the IEP team members.

The IEP team must take many things into consideration that are not as important during the assessment phase. Choosing which recommendations can be followed and which ones are appropriate for any given school year involves a number of factors. For the student to be successful in the school program it is essential that the IEP team evaluate each recommendation for its contribution to the program in several ways. First, is this a recommendation for which the student is immediately ready? This should be easy to determine by reading the assessment findings. Next, is this a recommendation that will increase the student's independence, either for academic work or for life outside of school?

Making sure that the school and the family feel that a recommendation is a priority is also an important criterion for the IEP team. Discovering whether the student is motivated or can be motivated to work on the area that is recommended is also important. If the goal of the recommendation was addressed unsuccessfully earlier in the student's education, it is important for the IEP team to discover why it was unsuccessful and remove impediments, where possible, before suggesting that the recommendation be implemented again.

Using the collaborative approach for implementing the recommendation is often important. If teachers, family members, and therapists all work in similar ways on the same goals, the collaborative approach often results in more effective education than each working separately.

Finally, it is important that the IEP team establish the appropriate setting for the student to follow any recommendation. Regular opportunities to practice a skill in the context where the skill is appropriate can be written into the IEP. For example, tooth brushing becomes an appropriate part of the school day if it occurs after a meal or a snack. Likewise, functional reading is done appropriately while following a recipe or sorting labeled items used in the classroom. Money skills are meaningful only when opportunities to exchange money for purchases are available.

SUMMARY

From the initial referral of a student who is blind or visually impaired for assessment to the writing of the IEP can be a journey requiring the efforts of the student, family members, and professionals from many disciplines. An important part of the journey is the writing of the assessment report in which all of the preparation, observation, and formal assessment come together as a comprehensive document describing how the student's disabilities affect his or her learning and how his or her strengths can be used to increase independence and contentment both in an academic milieu and in the world outside of school. Writing the report and the accompanying recommendations as a collaborative team can lead to a more cohesive program for a student who is blind or visually impaired.

The next chapter provides an example of how collaboration worked for a particular student. The story of Henry's assessment is presented to illustrate how collaboration is actually used at the California School for the Blind. It is the team's hope that the collaborative model can find a home in school districts as well as other centers serving students who are blind or visually impaired.

Collaboration in Action: Henry

Lizbeth A. Barclay,
Frances K. Liefert,
and Marsha A. Silver

IN THIS CHAPTER:

- An illustration of all parts of a collaborative assessment: referral, preparation, and collaboration
- Presentation of findings and recommendations
- A review of collaborative assessment

This chapter tells the story of a collaborative assessment. It is impossible to choose a typical student to present, since each student assessed presents a unique combination of problems and strengths. This story is based on an actual assessment, embellishing from experience with other students as well. The assessment story told in this chapter is entirely typical and factual in one aspect: the ways in which the process of collaboration is used.

PARTS OF A COLLABORATIVE ASSESSMENT

Referral

The receipt of a referral for assessment by school personnel begins the clock ticking on the federally mandated time lines. Typically,

Henry's Medical History

Henry had an eventful medical history. His mother reported that she had an unidentified virus when she was one month pregnant, which may have been what is termed walking pneumonia or cytomegalovirus (CMV). When she was three months pregnant, she was involved in a car accident in which the car rolled.

At birth, Henry weighed nine pounds, requiring a difficult forceps delivery. Although his Apgar scores were eight and nine at one and five minutes respectively, he was jaundiced and nystagmus was noted at birth. Henry remained in the neonatal intensive care unit of the hospital for 11 days, where he was diagnosed with septo-optic dysplasia, as well as hypoglycemia and galactosemia (lactose intolerance).

Septo-optic dysplasia, which involves abnormalities in how the brain is formed and how it functions, was responsible for Henry's substantial visual impairment. It also was the cause of abnormal cognitive development, including problems with gross and fine motor skills, speech and communication, and the ability to regulate basic body functions (see Appendix A).

Henry's pituitary gland was affected, which is common in cases of septo-optic dysplasia, resulting in problems with growth, metabolism, the intake and voiding of fluids, weight gain, the perception of heat and cold, and sexual development. Henry experienced seizures, also associated with the condition. As may be guessed, Henry was required to take a variety of medications to regulate these conditions.

Henry's Vision

Optic nerve hypoplasia is a hallmark of septo-optic dysplasia. As mentioned, Henry's visual impairment was apparent at birth because of nystagmus. His vision history included many reports from eye care specialists over the years. Information gleaned from these reports described low visual acuity (his ability to see details), which ranged from 20/400 to 20/200; esotropia (the eyes turn in), with an absence of binocularity (ability of the eyes working together), and field deficits (described in Chapter 1). All previously written reports stated that the visual acuity measures were estimates because Henry's responses were difficult to interpret accurately.

(continued)

Sidebar 11.1 **HENRY'S HISTORY** *(continued)*

Henry's Educational History

The assessment team learned that Henry had consistently received a high level of special educational services, beginning with in-home infant intervention. He was currently enrolled in a special day class for children with learning disabilities and was receiving beginning braille instruction two times per week from an itinerant teacher of students who are visually impaired. He was also served by a speech and language pathologist, an occupational therapist, a physical therapist, and an adapted physical education specialist. Because of his continuing medical needs, Henry had a nurse with him throughout the day at school.

The team had access to information regarding prior assessments of Henry. Very little formal testing of Henry had been done in the past, but observational records described a medically fragile child who had many delays in communication, motor, and academic areas.

---

federal law mandates that when an assessment of a student who is disabled is requested, and an assessment plan has been signed by the student's parents, the appropriate professionals conduct the assessment in a timely manner.

Henry was an 11-year-old boy who had septo-optic dysplasia (see Sidebar 11.1 for more details on Henry's medical history). He lived with his parents and his sister and attended public school in a special day class. His mother was not satisfied with the service Henry was getting at school, and his teacher of students who are visually impaired believed that the direction of Henry's education could use improvement.

Henry was referred for formal assessment to the California School for the Blind. The referral included information from Henry's parents, his teachers and therapists, his doctors, and his eye care specialist. Henry's current individualized education plan (IEP) was also included in the referral packet.

The referral questions were considered first. These questions, as well as the student's history, help to determine the focus of the assessment. Henry's teachers and parents each asked somewhat different questons. Henry's parents asked:

- What should the focus of Henry's education be?
- What is the best reading medium for Henry?
- If braille is needed, what is the best way for Henry to learn it? Can he still learn to read print as well?
- What technology could help Henry learn?

Henry's teachers asked:

- How much vision does Henry have?
- How much potential does Henry have for academic learning?
- What kind of program would best suit Henry?
- What is the best reading medium for Henry?
- How can we help Henry develop better language skills?

The teacher on the assessment team contacted Henry's mother and Henry's special day class teacher and discovered that they did not completely share common goals for the assessment. Henry's mother was concerned with Henry's primary learning medium and his academic progress. His teacher's interest in those aspects of his assessment took a backseat to other issues such as augmenting Henry's language acquisition and whether an emphasis on academics was appropriate.

After reading through the material in the referral packet, and conferring with the teacher of students who are visually impaired, who had also read the referral packet, the director of the Assessment Program scheduled the time for Henry's assessment and called his parents to see if it would fit into their calendar. He did the necessary research to make sure that the assessment personnel who were needed had the time and flexibility in their schedules to do a comprehensive, collaborative assessment.

Henry was assigned a team of assessors who would be appropriate to answer all the questions that his parents and teachers had asked. Reading media, vision needs, assistive technology, and an appropriate education program were the priorities. The team included a psychologist to focus on Henry's cognitive development and ability to meet academic standards; a teacher of students who are visually impaired to investigate Henry's learning styles and his current skills in various areas of the expanded core curriculum; a speech and language pathologist to assess Henry's current ability to express himself, to understand others, and who could offer suggestions for improving his language; a teacher of students who are visually impaired who specializes in technology to answer questions about Henry's readiness to use various types of technology; and an orientation and mobility (O&M) specialist, who is also certified as a low vision therapist, to evaluate Henry's functional vision, as well as his skills for getting around, which are important for any program to work. If this assessment had been done in Henry's local public school district, the team might have had additional members, including his special day class teacher, an occupational therapist, and an adapted physical education teacher.

Determining the Team Leader

As discussed in Chapter 3, one member of each assessment team usually takes the lead. The first step in preparing for Henry's assessment was to choose the school psychologist as the team leader. He had had a great deal of communication with Henry's mother prior to the assessment. This connection developed over time, as preparations were made for the assessment through telephone discussion. The psychologist also used the Parent Inventory and History Form (see Appendix B of this book) to gain crucial background information.

Involving Henry's Family

Thorough preparation for Henry's assessment could not have taken place without his mother's full participation. Henry's mother shared valuable information about his medical, visual, and educational history. She completed a family and medical history interview with the psychologist, and she provided work samples and anecdotal information about Henry's progress in school. Furthermore, she had organized a support group for parents of children with septo-optic dysplasia, and her enthusiasm and knowledge were extremely helpful to the assessment process.

Henry had a three-year-old sister, Grace, who was observed interacting with Henry throughout the assessment, which was another source of information that could not have been reproduced in a formal assessment setting.

Consultation with Henry's Classroom Teacher

Henry's special day class teacher was consulted during the preparation stage of Henry's assessment since she would not be taking part in the assessment itself. She was asked to provide the assessment team with essential information about his daily performance in a variety of academic and social skills. His teacher's concerns about his behavior and performance at school helped focus the questions that guided the assessment. She was worried about how to adapt class work for him, given his low reading level and extremely low vision. She shared her concerns about Henry's inability to connect socially with classmates and his seemingly "goofy" behavior. She invited members of the assessment team to observe Henry in class during the assessment.

Formulating Assessment Team Questions

In addition to the broad questions regarding Henry's development and his progress in school, after reviewing his background information the assessment team members had additional questions to consider during testing.

Functional Vision Assessor

- To what extent does Henry use his vision during traveling and during close tasks in learning, and how much should he be expected to do so?
- If Henry is going to use print to read, what size would be optimal?

Psychologist

- Given the neurological implications of Henry's septo-optic dysplasia, how does he process information, and what is the nature of his distinctive learning style and learning disabilities?

O&M Specialist

- How much does septo-optic dysplasia affect Henry's ability to travel independently, given that difficulties in orientation are typical for students with this condition?
- Given Henry's motor skills impairment, how effective is the cane as a tool for him?

Speech and Language Specialist

- How do Henry's communication skills affect his social interaction?

Teacher of Students Who Are Visually Impaired

- Given Henry's visual challenges and his tactile approach to many tasks, should a shift to a higher emphasis on braille be considered in his literacy instruction?
- Would a functional academics program be appropriate? What would be emphasized?

Technology Specialist

- What assistive technology can be considered as an appropriate support to Henry's curriculum?

Determining the Mode of Assessment and Observational Environments

The assessment team decided that a multimodal approach would be used to assess Henry. While some formal assessments could be used with Henry, his unique constellation of disabilities required that they be used and interpreted with caution. The assessment team believed that much more information about Henry could be gained by observing him in as many natural environments as possible. In order to obtain a complete picture, information from formal and criterion-referenced assessment should be seen in light of observational information obtained about him.

The team decided that some members should observe Henry's day at school, as well as his daily routines at home, such as dressing and tooth brushing. A trip to the grocery store to make a purchase of ingredients for a cooking experience would yield information about Henry's familiarity with the community, as well as his communication skills with the public. A cooking experience would give many team members information regarding his communication, daily living skills, fine motor skills, and functional vision. By having Henry dictate the sequence of activities that he did during the cooking experience once it was completed, the team hoped to garner information about his learning style. This would suggest potential adaptations and learning activities that could be utilized.

These various modes of assessment would give the assessors many opportunities for coassessment, observation of each other working with Henry, and collaboration in discussing the findings. It would provide rich sources of information about Henry and his learning style.

Low Vision Examination

Once the preparation had been done, the assessment team was ready to begin working with Henry. Henry and his mother were taken by the O&M specialist to an appointment at an optometry clinic that specializes in low vision examinations of students who are visually impaired and have other disabilities. Since the O&M specialist was taking responsibility for the assessment of Henry's functional vision, it was important for her to accompany the family to the clinic appointment. Henry's mother and the assessor were able to ask questions of the eye care practitioners while Henry was available to help them determine the answers. While waiting for Henry's eyes to dilate, the O&M and functional vision assessor had time to ask Henry's mother questions about how she noticed Henry using his vision and about his O&M skills. The eye care practitioners tailored the low vision examination to the needs that Henry's mother and the assessor indentified. Sidebar 11.2 presents the results of the low vision examination. The result was not only a better picture of what Henry could see, but also a way to solidify the inclusion of Henry's mother in the assessment process.

**Sidebar 11.2   RESULTS OF HENRY'S LOW
VISION EXAMINATION**

Henry's mother was an excellent source of information about how Henry was currently using his vision and in discussing the variability of his vision. She noted that Henry's vision had always been hard for his teachers to understand because he sometimes appeared to gain information visually and at other times he seemed to ignore or not have access to visual input. She observed that Henry approached many tasks tactilely, and that although he could read print that was two inches in height from a distance of three inches, he tired quickly and was very inaccurate.

Henry's low vision examination showed that his current visual acuity was around 20/700, using both eyes with best correction. Henry primarily used his right eye. He viewed objects eccentrically from a spot on the right side of his eye rather than from the center. He tended to bring objects very close to his eye when viewing.

Henry used his eyes independently of each other. His visual fields were restricted, with field loss in the upper and side areas of his vision. The optometrist reported that she suspected that there might be other blind spots scattered within Henry's restricted fields as well.

Henry's contrast sensitivity—his ability to differentiate between shades of gray—was reduced, as well as his ability to discern color, especially pastels or muddy colors in the red/green spectrums.

The eye care specialist's recommendations are included in Appendix 11.1 to this chapter.

The educationally focused low vision examination contributed an abundance of information that was applied during the assessment preparation and process. The information about Henry's visual functioning discovered during the examination was immediately e-mailed to all the other team members so that they could use the information to modify their assessment plans as needed. When the information was shared with all team members, assessment materials and settings could be chosen and adapted with Henry's visual requirements in mind.

Collaboration During the Assessment

As noted throughout this book, there are many issues that the professionals of each discipline must address during the assessment. In an assessment done with collaboration in mind, it is still important that each professional be given time to work with the student to discover what his or her skills are in the specific areas of that professional's discipline. The psychologist, the speech and language specialist, the O&M specialist, and the teacher of students who are visually impaired all needed to schedule individual time with Henry to do activities that would provide assessment information. Using collaboration as the model minimized the individual time. Here are some of the ways in which the assessment team collaborated as it assessed Henry.

Observations in Henry's Home and School

Functional Vision Assessment

The functional vision assessment included many examples found throughout the assessment week that illustrated Henry's areas of visual strength and deficit. Henry was observed in many settings, both at home and at school, during all kinds of activities to discover information about his visual functioning. By sharing the information and providing suggestions to team members, the functional vision assessor helped each member of the assessment team determine how to choose and modify assessment materials. Sometimes it was not possible for the functional vision assessor to observe Henry while another professional was assessing him. By asking the other team members how they saw Henry using his vision, she was able to get a more complete picture of Henry's functional vision.

At Home

The teacher of the students who are visually impaired visited Henry and his family at home before school one day. The purpose of the visit was twofold: to observe Henry's morning routine as part of the living skills assessment, and to involve Henry's family further as collaborators in the assessment. Although the visit was early in the morning, the teacher thought it was worthwhile to work into her schedule. Afterwards she understood better how Henry interacted with his family and the degree to which he was able to take care of his own personal needs. She also established a rapport with Henry's mother, helping her to feel, once again, included and listened to in the assessment process.

In School

As was decided during the preparation for assessment, several team members scheduled time to observe Henry in the special day class he attended regularly. The teacher of students who are visually impaired and the O&M specialist observed Henry in his classroom for an entire morning. The teacher of students who are visually impaired watched for adaptations in the schedule and materials for Henry's vision and for how well Henry used those adaptations. The O&M specialist took the opportunity to observe Henry's travel skills in a familiar environment. She was particularly attuned to how Henry handled transition times and how well oriented he was in space. Sidebar 11.3 provides detailed lists of what these two specialists looked for in their assessments. These lists can be used as guidelines for specialists making these types of school observations.

In the afternoon, the teacher of visually impaired students was joined by the speech and language pathologist to observe Henry with his own speech and language pathologist. They observed Henry in a small group of students working on listening and comprehension by answering questions about a story that was read to them. The speech and language pathologist's lists of questions is provided in Sidebar 11.4.

Collaborative Assessment Activities

Community Experience

The O&M specialist and the speech and language pathologist took Henry into the community as the first part of a series of collaborative assessment activities. Before leaving his school, Henry made a

The teacher of students who are visually impaired focused on the following:

- Are all curricular materials and information adapted and made accessible throughout Henry's day?
- What alternatives are used for providing access to information on boards and walls throughout the classroom?
- What adaptive strategies work well for Henry and what strategies do not?
- What does Henry do when the other students are reading information that is inaccessible to him because of his much lower reading level?
- How long can Henry maintain a visual activity before he begins to tire visually?
- What adaptations can be made so that Henry can be a full participant in his class?
- Where does Henry sit during various classroom activities? What are the best seating strategies to maximize Henry's attention and participation in class?
- Is braille being integrated into classroom activities?
- What is Henry's level of independence and proficiency while handling curriculum materials?
- How independent is Henry within his classroom, given that he has a nurse who assists him in many activities throughout the day?
- Is Henry "tuned in" to what is happening in the classroom?
- What is Henry's behavior throughout the day and what situations are most likely to prompt Henry's "goofy" behavior?
- How is Henry's posture with relation to balance and physical support during learning activities?
- How do Henry's difficulties in motor skills affect his ability to participate in classroom activities and activities in self-care at school?
- Who does Henry communicate with in school and what is the level of his social interactions? What happens socially during recess and during mealtimes?

(continued)

- Is there a difference in the way Henry participates and interacts during small and large group activities?
- What is Henry's level of assertiveness or passivity within the class?
- How do transitions affect Henry?

The O&M specialist focused on the following:

- What kind of transportation did Henry use to get to school? Where was he dropped off when he arrived at school? Did he walk to his classroom on his own, use human guide, follow other students, or was he led in some other way by an adult?
- Did Henry store his jacket and backpack himself without prompting? Did someone else put them away? Did he require assistance to store them?
- Did Henry find his seat on his own?
- When asked to find the top, bottom, or left or right sides of a page or a desk top, did Henry follow directions?
- At recess did Henry retrieve his own jacket and put it on? Did he find his way around the play yard? Did he use any O&M devices or assistance from other students or from adults?
- How did Henry handle any stairs or other changes in elevation?
- What was the adaptive physical education teacher working on with Henry? How was Henry responding?
- What did Henry work on with the occupational therapist? How did he do on those tasks?
- At lunch time did Henry require assistance to get his lunch and find a place to eat it? Could he manage wrappers and utensils himself or did he need assistance?
- Did Henry ask for assistance when he required it or did he wait for someone to notice that he was in need of assistance? Was he assertive, passive, or aggressive about asking for and refusing assistance? Was he more likely to get assistance from classmates or from adults?
- How did different lighting conditions affect Henry's travel? Did he have trouble with glare? Did he move from a dimly lit to a brightly lit space with ease or was there an adjustment period?

Sidebar 11.4 QUESTIONS ASKED BY THE SPEECH AND LANGUAGE PATHOLOGIST

- What quality of attention did Henry give to the language of the teacher and the other students?
- What was the level of language Henry was expected to understand to participate successfully in the activity?
- What was the level of language used during verbal directions?
- What types of additional stimuli were presented to support language comprehension? How successful were they for Henry?
- Which oral directions did Henry comprehend? With which did he have difficulty?
- To what degree was there consistency in the language used by various staff members?
- What modes did Henry use in his verbal interactions: spontaneous, prompted, echolalic, perseverative modes? (The speech and language pathologist transcribed what Henry said to review later.)
- Were there discrepancies in Henry's communication with different teachers and specialists?
- Were there discrepancies in Henry's level of comprehension during tasks of daily living/hands-on activities and listening only?
- How was Henry's social interaction and communication with peers? (Again, these interactions were transcribed.)
- Were there any oral–motor/articulation issues?
- Were there any questions regarding Henry's hearing or his ability to focus in the presence of background noise?

---

plan with the O&M specialist and the speech and language pathologist about what he would like to prepare for lunch. Henry chose to make a peanut butter and honey sandwich and have milk to drink. The speech and language pathologist asked him to list the ingredients, and the O&M specialist wrote out the list in inch-high letters. Henry could read this list by holding it within an inch or two of his face, a position he preferred when reading letters of any size. The O&M specialist also asked Henry to estimate how much each item would cost and gave Henry money to make the purchase. Henry was observed storing the money and the list in preparation for the trip. This part of the collaboration took about half an hour.

In the community the O&M specialist used the *TAPS* checklist (Pogrund et al., 1993) to record observations about how Henry traveled and how he used his vision, O&M devices, and orientation skills. Henry was given a chance to compare how his estimates of prices related to the actual prices. The speech and language pathologist observed how Henry interacted with the public in an unfamiliar environment. His ability to handle money was also observed. The trip to the store lasted about 45 minutes.

Preparing to Fix Food

Upon returning to school, Henry was asked to store his purchases in the teachers' lounge kitchen. Although Henry was unfamiliar with that kitchen, the teacher of students who are visually impaired, the O&M specialist, and the speech and language pathologist observed that he knew which item needed to be refrigerated (the milk) and which items could be stored in a cupboard. Five minutes at most was spent on this activity.

The speech and language pathologist asked Henry to describe how he was planning to make a peanut butter and honey sandwich while the teacher of visually impaired students took notes. She spent about 15 minutes eliciting and listening to Henry's general knowledge of the process sequence and the language he used to describe it. During Henry's assessment, the O&M specialist stayed during the food preparation part of the experience to observe his living skills and to set up a video camera to tape the activity for later reference by the whole assessment team.

Food Preparation

Henry began to make a peanut butter and honey sandwich following his own directions, which had been printed out in two-inch-high letters by the speech and language pathologist. The O&M specialist took over directing the task so that the speech and language pathologist could join the teacher of visually impaired students in taking

---

Sidebar 11.5   SPEECH AND LANGUAGE PATHOLOGIST'S OBSERVATIONS DURING HENRY'S FOOD PREPARATION ACTIVITY

- Henry's attention was very well focused while he was involved in making the peanut butter and honey sandwich.

- During food preparation, Henry's comments were relevant to the topic. He made significantly fewer extraneous verbalizations when compared to activities performed without hands-on exposure.

- Before making it, Henry's description of how to make a sandwich was lacking in detail and poorly sequenced.

- After the sandwich was completed, Henry was asked to tell the steps to another examiner not present during the activity. This was most challenging for him, and he was only able to complete it when given a high degree of prompting.

---

notes of the skills salient to each of their assessments. The teacher of visually impaired students and the speech and language pathologist observed Henry's tactile skills and food preparation skills as he made his sandwich and then observed his eating skills. Items observed by the speech and language pathologist are listed in Sidebar 11.5. This part of the assessment lasted almost an hour, which included time to clean up.

Some teaching of daily living skills was involved in the process, and the assessment team members observed how well Henry responded to both verbal and physical prompting. The skills observed included sequencing tasks; opening jars, a bag, and a milk carton; scooping and spreading; pouring; setting the table; and putting leftover ingredients away.

Eating

While Henry ate his peanut butter and honey sandwich and drank his milk, the speech and language pathologist had the opportunity to observe how he used his lips, tongue, teeth, and jaw for eating, as well as how he related to the assessment team members in a more social setting around the table. The teacher of students who are visually impaired was also interested in how Henry held a conversation.

Cleanup

More living skills were observed as Henry was prompted to clean up after the lunch. Clearing the table, washing dishes, putting them away, wiping the table, and sweeping the floor were all included.

Telling the Story

During Henry's assessment the psychologist was available to come in after lunch to ask Henry about what he had just done. In other assessments any adult who had not been involved in the activities could be invited to be the so-called naive listener. Henry's ability to tell the story of his shopping trip and his food preparation was observed by the assessment team members.

The teacher of students who are visually impaired assisted Henry as he dictated his story for a tape recording. The speech and language pathologist observed as the teacher prompted Henry to tell the events in the actual sequence in which they took place. The teacher used the actual materials used in the activity to remind Henry of what he had done. Henry listened to his tape and grinned.

The teacher of students who are visually impaired transcribed the story into braille as Henry dictated it a second time. Henry was asked to read the story. His reading of this experiential story made an interesting contrast to the reading he did of test material stories. The reading and writing took about 45 minutes.

Midpoint Meeting

Once each assessor had had time to observe Henry, work with him on assessment tasks, and had had contact with his family, the team convened to discuss their findings thus far and to determine what else needed to be assessed. Each assessor learned something from what the other team members presented. The psychologist was interested in finding out from the O&M specialist and the speech and language pathologist how well oriented Henry was in space and how well Henry followed directions using spatial concepts. The teacher of students who are visually impaired let the team know what levels of academic skills had been demonstrated by Henry, which helped all the other team members put their findings into perspective. The psychologist discussed how his findings conflicted with what he knew about Henry's neurological impairment, leading to a discussion about how that type of impairment might influence Henry's performances in each domain being assessed.

During the meeting, the team realized that there was a need for more information on Henry's spatial concept development and orientation in space. It was decided that the assessment would be concluded with the administration of the *Blind Learning Aptitude Test (BLAT)* by the school psychologist and an adaptation of the *Boehm Test of Basic Concepts*, modified with objects, by the speech and language pathologist. (*The Blind Learning Aptitude Test* is described in the Resources for Chapter 6 and the *Boehm Test of Basic Concepts* is described in the Resources for Chapter 7.)

Observing Each Other's Assessments

It is possible to gather a lot of information about a student by observing another assessment team member administer a formal test. Sometimes the observing member can be helpful as a recorder as well. For example, the teacher of students who are visually impaired often administers the *Gardner Test of Visual Perceptual Skills, Non-motor, revised* (described in the Resources for Chapter 4), to students who have low vision with assistance from the team member responsible for the functional vision assessment. The first teacher sits across from the student, gives the student directions and turns the pages of the test booklet, while the other specialist records the student's responses and indicates when enough wrong responses have been given to warrant moving on to the next section. The notetaker can also record observational information, such as remarks the student makes during testing or the visual scanning style that he or she is using.

When Henry's use of technology was assessed by the specialist in assistive technology, it was important for the teacher of students who are visually impaired to observe. Henry was introduced to an electronic braille notetaking device, which is described in Chapter 8. He had difficulty generalizing what he knew about the keyboard of the Perkins brailler to the notetaker's keyboard. The assistive technology specialist brought a Perkins brailler over to show him the similarities, but Henry still did not make the connection. This was important information for the teacher of visually impaired students, who often recommends the electronic notetaker as a teaching tool for beginning braille students because of its auditory feedback and distinct braille display.

On the other hand, Henry was interested and talented in using the IntelliTools assistive technology hardware and software that includes IntelliKeys, a programmable alternative keyboard, and IntelliTalk, a word processor that utilizes speech. He responded well to the auditory and visual components and used the alphabetical keyboard with some facility, even though it was his first exposure. In addition to seeing which technology worked best, the teacher of students who are visually impaired confirmed that the print size recommended at the low vision examination, which was three times Henry's threshold print size of 1.8 inches from one foot away, was appropriate for Henry.

The results of two tests, which were decided on during the midpoint meeting, were each of interest to more than one assessor. The BLAT results were important to the teacher of students who are visually impaired, who was assessing Henry's use of braille, as well as to the psychologist who was assessing cognitive levels and administering the test. Seeing Henry's performance on the BLAT and discussing the results with the psychologist confirmed for the teacher of visually impaired students that Henry was indeed likely to succeed in using braille as his primary reading medium.

The Boehm test was administered by the speech and language pathologist and observed by the O&M specialist, who had already administered the *Hill Performance Test of Selected Positional Concepts.* (See the Resources for Chapter 9 for information on the Hill Test.) The O&M specialist had questions about Henry's responses to the Hill Test, which came up during the midpoint meeting. When the O&M specialist and the speech and language pathologist put the results of the two assessment tools together, they were astounded at Henry's orientation to space and ability to follow directions using spatial concepts. His actual behavior when taking the tests ran contrary to the behavior expected, considering Henry's brain damage, which had been well described in Henry's medical records and by the psychologist. The results of the tests meshed well with the psychologist's own assessment findings.

Final Assessment Team Meeting

When all the components of the assessment were complete, the team met once more to put the findings together and get an idea of which areas needed to become priorities for Henry's school program in the next few years. In an assessment that involves professionals from several disciplines as this one did, it is important to compile the results so as to avoid presenting a fragmented program that requires the student to be pulled from one area to another, adding unnecessary confusion to his or her school day.

The first agenda item in the final team meeting was to review the original questions asked by Henry's parents and his current educational team. Reading media, vision needs, assistive technology, and academic achievement had been the priorities when Henry was referred for assessment. All had been addressed by the collaborative team. The other concerns mentioned at the beginning of the assessment, including social and communication skills, emotional status, and functional skills, had also been assessed.

Although the assessment process tends to divide a student's skills into parts in order to have pieces small enough to examine, the needs of the whole student were considered in the final team meeting for Henry. The findings of various team members pointed to a school program that would emphasize functional academics—reading and math instruction—related to practical home, school, and community experiences that would be provided for Henry. By tying his math instruction into the use of time and money, the team suggested that the O&M specialist and the special day class teacher would both be responsible in the area of math, with support from the teacher of students who are visually impaired. By connecting literacy lessons to stories about real experiences, the team aimed to create an alliance among the special day class teacher, the teacher of visually impaired students (who would be responsible for braille teaching), and all the other specialists and family members who provided enriching experiences for Henry. The assessment team hoped that the family and the rest of Henry's individualized education program (IEP) team would be receptive to the idea of changing Henry's academic program to a more functional skills program, which would have academic learning embedded in it.

Sharing the Findings with Henry's Parents

The assessment team wanted to include Henry's parents in the process of developing recommendations stemming from Henry's assessment. The psychologist, who was the assessment team leader, arranged to meet with both of Henry's parents to present some of the team's findings and to get feedback from the parents about the team's suggestion that a functional academics approach be tried with Henry. The parents were receptive to meeting with the psychologist, having spent some time already answering questionnaires and chatting with him about their son and their concerns. They were particularly pleased to learn that braille could become Henry's primary learning medium, and that recommendations for delivering braille instruction would be made. When the idea of a functional academic program came up, they were skeptical because they feared that reading, writing, and math would be lost if functional skills were stressed. After further conversation, they grew more enthusiastic about the proposal, with the condition that the whole educational team would understand the continuing need to make sure that academic learning still took place.

PRESENTATION OF FINDINGS AND RECOMMENDATIONS

Oral Presentation and Discussion

The results of the collaborative assessment were presented formally to the district administrator, the IEP team members who were not part of the assessment team, and the parents in two ways. First, a meeting termed the exit conference was held at the end of the assessment week. It was similar to an IEP meeting in which triennial assessment results are reported. Each professional reported on the findings in his or her discipline, describing how the collaborative assessment experiences as well as other testing added to the information gained about Henry's skills. After each presentation, recommendations were made in each discipline area.

Participants were invited to ask questions and add comments when all of the presentations were finished. This format was followed to avoid asking questions that would be answered later in the presentations and to delay discussion of issues until all of the assessment results had been presented. The entire oral presentation was taped so that the IEP team would have an immediate record of the assessment results to which they could refer when deciding on goals and benchmarks for the IEP document.

Written Assessment Report

Since the assessment team had gotten permission from Henry's parents to waive the time lines legislated in federal law, a written report followed the oral presentation within 6 weeks. Had Henry's assessment been to fill the triennial requirements, the written report would have been due at the same time as the oral presentation (50 days after the assessment plan was signed). In this case, the time lag gave the assessment team time to assimilate the information discussed during the exit conference as well as to consider further the implications of the assessment results.

The written report format was designed to be similar to the oral report. Each assessor described his or her assessment procedure, the assessment results, and the recommendations for the various areas of assessment. Referrals to other sections of the report were made when domains overlapped or were informed by another discipline. The long, final report followed the outline of reports presented in Chapter 10.

Recommendations

The recommendations that each assessor wrote for Henry followed directly from the assessment findings and from discussion among the assessors, with Henry's parents, and with the IEP team members. These recommendations are included in the Appendix to this chapter. Specific products are often recommended along with information about how to purchase them. References to specific products have been removed from the recommendations in Appendix 11.1.

SUMMARY

There is no typical assessment of a student who is blind or visually impaired. Each student has unique strengths and weaknesses, even though he or she may share the same visual condition, the same IQ score or the same concomitant disabilities with other students. Each family has its own constellation of personalities and ways of incorporating a member who is blind or visually impaired. Despite the need to adhere to federal laws and state guidelines, each district also has a personality, its own way of administering the education of students who are blind or visually impaired, and an array of teachers and specialists who have their own styles within their specialties.

Henry's assessment is typical of the California School for the Blind's method in one way: it illustrates how assessment can be done by working together as a collaborative team. This collaboration is facilitated by all the specialists being headquartered at the same school, which may not be practical, or even desirable, in a public school district. Team members who previously worked in public school districts have also had the experience of successful collaborative assessments in that context, which we hope is reflected in the various chapters of this book.

With coordination from an administrator, it is possible for an assessment team to be put together that specializes in working with students who are blind or visually impaired. The team may have more than one psychologist, speech and language pathologist, teacher of students who are visually impaired, O&M specialist, adapted physical education teacher, or occupational therapist. It will take time and work for the team to learn to collaborate efficiently and effectively. The authors and editors hope that the information offered here will be helpful as teams set out to learn how to make comprehensive assessments of the educational needs of students who are blind or visually impaired, and that this model of collaboration will find a home in public school districts serving these students.

REFERENCE

Pogrund, R., Healy, G., Jones, K., Levack, N., Martin-Curry, S., Martinez, C., Marz, J., Roberson-Smith, B., & Vrba, A. (1993). *TAPS: An orientation and mobility curriculum for students with visual impairments.* Austin: Texas School for the Blind and Visually Impaired.

APPENDIX 11.1
SAMPLE RECOMMENDATIONS FOR HENRY

Vision

* WEAR GLASSES FOR SAFETY AND FOR DISTANCE VIEWING

Henry will benefit from following the eye care specialist's recommendation to wear his glasses for distance viewing and to keep his eyes safe from injury. He is more at risk for eye injury than most students because of his reduced fields and the limited use of his left eye. An injury to his right eye would leave him with very little vision. If he wants to remove his glasses for near work, the eye care specialist reported that this would be fine since his right eye is well suited for close viewing.

* WATCH FOR TROUBLE WITH GLARE AND LIGHTING CHANGES

Henry will do best if he is seated with light sources behind him or to his side. It is suggested that teachers and parents offer him caps and sunshades occasionally, to see if he is ready to use them, since bright light may reduce his acuity temporarily. It may also be important to eliminate glare from screens he views, such as televisions, computers, and closed-circuit televisions (CCTV). This can be done effectively by looking at the screen while it is still dark and adjusting its position to eliminate reflections. It would also be appropriate to be careful when presenting material with lamination or on shiny paper, making sure that the glare is not interfering with Henry's viewing. More recommendations regarding use of the CCTV and computer are included in the *Education* section of this report.

* MAKE GOOD FIGURE–GROUND DISTINCTIONS

Because Henry has some difficulty with contrast sensitivity and color vision, it is important to present materials with high contrast between the object and its background. For example, it will be helpful to wear a solid-color top if one is holding objects in front of oneself for Henry to view. Henry will benefit from having changes in terrain such as steps and curbs painted in high contrast, at least in areas where he travels regularly. The recommendations in the *Education* section of this report contain further information.

* ALLOW HENRY TO CHOOSE HOW TO LOOK AT MATERIALS

Henry depends on eccentric viewing and may not always look like he is looking in the right direction when he is observing objects. It is important to permit Henry to choose the angle at which he views and to view as closely as he needs to.

* DESCRIBE WHAT IS BEING VIEWED

Henry will benefit from verbal descriptions of pictures and objects he needs to see, especially when tactile input is unavailable. Encouraging Henry to describe what he is seeing himself will also help him remember what he has been shown.

* FOLLOW THE LOW VISION CLINIC RECOMMENDATIONS FOR SYMBOL AND LETTER SIZE

Although Henry can discern letters that are 1.8 inches high from a distance of one foot, it is important to offer him symbols three times that size when he is receiving new instructional materials or when he is expected to view material for a long period of time. Reading print this large may have a practical application for reading signs in the community and for labeling items for Henry at home and at school. Since this is not a practical size for sustained reading, see the *Education* section of this report for information regarding instruction in braille.

Psychology

* USE A FUNCTIONAL–ACADEMIC APPROACH

Given his cognitive abilities, Henry would benefit from a functional–academic approach, in which academic content is presented in a functional context. Such an approach will be most helpful to Henry if it emphasizes experiential, hands on learning and incorporates as many sensory modalities as possible (vision, touch, smell, sound). One goal of a functional–academic approach would be for Henry's somewhat stronger nonverbal skills to support the development of his language-based reasoning. (See the *Education* and *Speech and Language Sections* for specific recommendations.)

* PROVIDE SOCIAL EXPERIENCES FOR HENRY WITH OTHER STUDENTS WHO ARE VISUALLY IMPAIRED

It would be beneficial for Henry to have exposure to peers who are visually impaired and developmentally delayed. Information is available from the assessment team about camps that provide summer experiences for students who are visually impaired and their families. Students may attend alone or with their families and scholarships may be available. Given Henry's positive outlook on life and interest in interacting with others, it is likely that he would enjoy such a camp experience.

* INVESTIGATE SERVICES THAT WILL FOLLOW HENRY FOR LIFE

It is recommended that the Henry's family investigate what state services for people who are developmentally disabled may be available to Henry at this time and as he matures. Services may include respite for Henry's family, training toward independent living, vocational training, or social activities for developmentally disabled adults. The assessment team can provide names of services available and numbers to call.

Speech and Language

* RESCREEN HENRY'S HEARING

The results of the hearing screening during this assessment may not be reliable. Henry's hearing needs to be screened again. If he should fail the screening, Henry should receive a complete audiological evaluation.

* PROVIDE A THOROUGH ORAL–MOTOR AND FEEDING EVALUATION BY A SPEECH AND LANGUAGE PATHOLOGIST

It would be helpful for Henry to have more assessment in the area of oral–motor and feeding skills. A speech and language pathologist with expertise in this area would be the person to do the assessment and offer recommendations to the school and to Henry's family.

* IMPROVE THE USE OF MEANINGFUL, APPROPRIATE LANGUAGE

Henry needs to participate, in the most directly involved manner possible, in his daily living and educational activities. While Henry is involved in the activity, provide simple, repetitive, well-formed, scripted language to him. Over time, repeated exposure to language coupled with a real activity will allow Henry to make the appropriate connections between the two.

In addition to traditional reading and writing approaches, a whole language approach to language comprehension and literacy is recommended. When the concepts to be learned are experienced in a personal way first, they can be reinforced through multisensory input and repetitive exposure, as in Henry's sandwich-making activity.

After this type of exposure, discrete tasks such as spreading with a knife or reading specific words can be repeatedly practiced in a way that will make more sense to Henry.

* GIVE HENRY SCRIPTED LANGUAGE TO USE IN SOCIAL SETTINGS

Henry will benefit from being told what to say during routine social interactions. Telling him to ask someone their name or what to say to take another turn in the conversation will be worthwhile. After many repetitions, Henry will learn to incorporate these new sentences into his repertoire.

* USE REPETITIVE ROUTINES TO INCREASE HENRY'S USE OF LANGUAGE

Routines are very important to students who are visually impaired. It is important to involve Henry in the preparation or gathering of materials and in the cleanup phases of an activity. These ordered sequences allow active participation, provide predictability, and promote a sense of control over events.

Education

* GENERAL TEACHING STRATEGIES

Testing and observation indicate that Henry is a multimodal learner and will require a multimodal approach in acquiring information. He will learn optimally with hands-on experiences that will support his true understanding of concepts throughout life. Manipulation of objects, as well as experiences in the community and real life situations, will give meaning to what he sees and hears and facilitate true concept development and comprehension.

When he is learning new information, in addition to providing Henry with objects and experiences, allow him to use all modes of learning: vision, touch, movement, and self-talk to take it in.

Academic skills, especially reading, writing, and mathematics, will be best taught through a functional approach and community-based activities whenever possible. Language experience stories based upon Henry's experiences on mobility trips, cooking lessons, field trips, and family outings can be a rich source of concept and language development, as well as creating the reading and writing vocabulary that Henry will learn.

Curricular activities within Henry's classroom will need to be adapted with this in mind. It will be beneficial for Henry's teacher of students who are visually impaired to observe Henry's day in the classroom to note ways in which his curriculum can be adapted in order to make it more meaningful through a hands-on approach and experiential learning.

Repetition will also be a cornerstone of Henry's learning style. He will require many opportunities to experience new concepts over time.

* READING

Henry's reading program will require a balanced approach that emphasizes decoding as well as comprehension. To bring greater interest and meaning to Henry's reading vocabulary, a whole language approach should be incorporated into his reading program. The whole language approach integrates the development of reading skills with the development of listening, speaking, and writing skills. The basis for this type of reading program is the student's own experience.

Henry will benefit from having experiences in the community that will broaden his understanding of the world and will therefore become the content of his experiential stories. A trip to the post office in which he learns about the different jobs at the post office, the duties of a postal clerk, or the sequence of events that a letter goes through once it is mailed will be the basis for the type of story that will begin to accomplish this purpose. Activities in which Henry is the "doer," such as a cooking lesson or a trip to the store in which Henry makes a purchase, will also be useful activities on which to base Henry's stories.

Throughout Henry's reading instruction, in both print and braille, emphasis should still be given to phonics instruction taught within the context of his reading instruction. In addition, materials used for phonics drill can be adapted for Henry's use so that he can become more adept in recognizing word families and sound–symbol relationships.

Braille

Henry will benefit from daily braille instruction. He has made tremendous progress in braille reading, but he is still in the beginning phase of building his braille literacy foundation.

It is recommended that Henry build a more firm foundation in reading and writing uncontracted (grade 1) braille before moving on in contracted (grade 2) braille. He will benefit from this because it will more closely follow the same program as the primary reading program and because it will be much easier for him to mesh his tactile-perceptual skills with his auditory-perceptual skills. Phonemic awareness skills can be emphasized using uncontracted braille. Once he has acquired a firm foundation in reading and writing using uncontracted braille, he can then be taught contractions.

It will be beneficial to find ways to integrate braille into more of Henry's daily curriculum. One way to do this is for Henry to take his spelling tests in braille. He can also be given a braille schedule of his regular daily activities. Henry's teacher of students who are visually impaired can observe his daily schedule to help determine other opportunities for this.

At home, braille labels can be used to identify some of Henry's belongings, a braille telephone index box can be set up for Henry's use, and simple braille notes can be brailled back and forth between Henry and his parents. The most important aspect is increasing the amount of time that Henry has braille under his fingertips throughout the day in practical and meaningful ways. It will be important to use instructional strategies that will make braille lessons fun and rewarding to Henry.

Print

Henry will also be using print for academic tasks. Refer to the *Vision* section of this report for more information about his print reading requirements.

It will be difficult for him to work on both media at the same time. The instructional team should therefore decide when it is most appropriate to include braille as Henry gains more proficiency in reading braille.

Henry will require continued access to curriculum materials in print. His threshold print size, 1.8 inch letters when viewed from one foot, should be multiplied by three, giving him an optimal instructional print size of 5.4 inches at one foot or 1.35 inches at three inches. The large size will make it necessary either to custom produce his worksheets using the computer or for Henry to use the CCTV. When print is this large it is impossible to achieve high-contrast copies using a copy machine. Print size and contrast will be important for Henry, but it will also be very important to ensure simple format when reproducing print materials. If Henry is using the CCTV with materials that have a complex format, he will require instruction in accessing the material within that complex format. He should not be expected to handle complex formats independently at this point.

When using the CCTV, Henry found reverse polarity (white letters on black) to be helpful. Some CCTVs have line isolation and line marker capabilities, which would be helpful features for Henry. If the CCTV does not have this feature, it will be helpful to train Henry to read the current line at the bottom of the screen.

Henry will only be able to use print materials for short periods of time. When using print materials, it will be necessary to allow him to take breaks every

10 minutes. When taking a break, he should do something that does not require the use of his near vision. Of course, if Henry is doing something that is highly motivating, and he is sustaining the use of his near vision for longer periods of time successfully, that is fine. However, it will always be important to make sure that he is reading accurately under these conditions; when visual fatigue sets in, reading accuracy declines and with it goes comprehension.

* LISTENING COMPREHENSION

Listening to instruction in the classroom is very different from listening to some-one read a story. It will be very important to observe when Henry does not listen to classroom instruction. Is it when the information is too difficult? Is it when materials being discussed are not visually accessible? Is it when Henry has begun to focus on something in his near vision that is more interesting? The answers to these questions will determine what type of intervention is to be tried.

Henry's seating placement should be chosen with listening in mind. It will be important to teach Henry to choose the optimal placements himself. Activities often happen in a variety of locations in the classroom, and Henry will need to vary his seating position as these changes occur.

It will probably be necessary to provide a few listening prompts occasionally, to help Henry learn that his listening focus should be on his classroom teacher or the activity being presented.

When stories are read to the entire class, Henry should have an opportunity to go over pertinent information before or afterwards with an adult. It will often be necessary to provide Henry with objects and experiences that will give him a foundation for understanding what he hears.

* MATHEMATICS

It will continue to be important for Henry to use manipulatives to demonstrate math concepts. When choosing the manipulative tools, it is important to take into consideration Henry's motor and vision limitations. Manipulatives that require little movement and that are not plastic representations of real objects or animals will be the most practical. Plastic replicas are often confusing to students who are visually impaired, and may be more distracting than fun for Henry. Manipulatives that are difficult to keep track of tactilely or visually will tend to make Henry concentrate on motor planning rather than counting.

Henry will benefit from a math curriculum built around real life skills, such as time, measurement, money, and cooking. A hands-on approach should be used. Anytime that Henry can experience the math concept he is learning by using real objects, his true understanding of the concept will be enhanced. Math lessons that take place within the context of cooking or shopping activities and that can then be reinforced in the classroom will be beneficial.

* TECHNOLOGY

For more information about software that can be adapted and used by Henry for the development of language skills and early concepts, see the *Speech and Language* section of this report.

* KEYBOARDING

As Henry learns to use the computer keyboard it will be beneficial for him to learn the keyboard commands so that he will not have to rely heavily upon using the mouse with more sophisticated programs.

Social-Emotional Skills

* INTERACTIONS

Henry will continue to need to be given information about social interactions. This will include knowing who is involved, what they are doing, and why. This will be especially important in situations and with behaviors that can only be observed visually.

Henry will need honest and sensitive feedback about his behavior and its impact on social interactions. He will benefit from knowing if his behavior stands out from what is normal within his peer group. He should be given examples of how he might change it if he cannot devise his own solutions. Role playing might be beneficial to help him practice behaviors before attempting them in everyday situations.

It may be necessary for the adults in Henry's life to play an active role in orchestrating activities that involve Henry and his friends during recess and lunch time for a while, until social interaction begins to happen naturally. Activities and pieces of equipment that are fun for both Henry and other children can be provided to help him increase his social opportunities.

Henry will benefit from frequent opportunities to socialize with peers who are visually impaired. This will help ease the sense of isolation that a student who is visually impaired so often has and help him to experience belonging and connectedness to a peer group.

* KNOWLEDGE OF HUMAN SEXUALITY

Much of the information that students accumulate about sexuality and social mores is based on visual observation. Consequently, students who are visually impaired are at a disadvantage in learning about such things as displaying affection in an acceptable fashion, male and female body changes, relationships, culturally accepted gender roles, using a public restroom, and the intricacies of dating. Students who are visually impaired may also have limited access to incidental sources of information about sexuality such as movies, television, magazines, books, and community resources.

Consequently, a well-designed, systematic program of sexuality education is important. Many areas of this program are most appropriately addressed at home, but instructors should work closely with Henry's parents to ensure that a complete and appropriate education in this area is being provided. Values, societal attitudes, the issues of privacy and personal limits, and self-protection should all be addressed in tandem with Henry's age-appropriate knowledge about sexual functioning.

* KNOWLEDGE OF VISUAL IMPAIRMENT

This checklist was not used with Henry, but it will be included in the appendix of this report. This is an area of social/emotional development that is important as a young person is ready to understand and discuss his or her own visual impairment and visual impairment in general.

Just as it is necessary for Henry to have many opportunities for interaction with sighted peers and adults in the home, community, and school, having experiences with peers and adults who are visually impaired is also very important. As mentioned in the *Psychology* section of this report, we would refer the family to camps and other recreation activities available to children who are visually impaired, which will enable Henry to develop social competencies in a less threatening environment and provide him with a rich experience of sharing and support.

Henry might eventually benefit from having books read to him about students who are visually impaired or have other disabilities, to gain different perspectives of how young people contend with the demands of growing up and establishing their identity when challenged by a disability.

Henry will benefit from having regular opportunities to explore and share his feelings about his visual impairment with a caring adult who is knowledgeable about the emotional issues common among young people who are visually impaired.

* DAILY LIVING SKILLS

In addition to addressing the fine motor issues that affect Henry's progress, it will be important to help Henry learn the sequence of each of his daily living skills routines. This can be integrated into his functional academics program by creating with Henry some of his daily living routines in list form, which will be part of his reading and writing program. For instance, a sequence for brushing teeth might be written as follows:

1. Put water on the toothbrush.
2. Put toothpaste on the toothbrush.
3. Brush front teeth.
4. Brush one side of teeth.
5. Brush the other side of teeth.
6. Brush lower molars.

7. Brush upper molars.
8. Rinse toothbrush.
9. Rinse mouth.
10. Dry face.
11. Put away toothbrush and toothpaste.

Once this has been created, it can be used both at home and at school (in a routine journal) for a variety of purposes. Ultimately the goal would be for Henry to be able to refer to it during his routine, if needed, in order to reduce the number of personal prompts required during the activity. By learning and reading the sequence in school, Henry will be reinforcing it for home application.

It will be helpful to keep all of Henry's tooth brushing items together and in one place, perhaps on his own tray in the bathroom, for easy and consistent location. Henry can learn to apply the toothpaste by putting it first onto his finger and then from his finger onto the toothbrush.

It will be important for Henry to have instruction in the organization of his personal belongings so that he can maintain his highest level of independence. Henry will need to be taught how to sort and put away his clothing in an assigned place. Eventually it will be helpful for him to be taught laundry skills, which will include many aspects of clothing organization. At school, a unit on personal hygiene tools and products could include organization and storage tips.

It will be important for Henry to participate in a few more household chores on a regular basis. It is vital for him to learn how to be independent in everyday tasks such as making his bed, taking out the trash, and setting the table. It is important for him to be an active participant in his family and this is how he will best learn the tasks of household management.

Henry can learn some simple cooking tasks. He will benefit from learning how to make juice, a peanut butter and honey sandwich, or to open and heat a can of soup. These and other basic cooking tasks can be taught as part of Henry's curriculum and adaptations for Henry's visual impairment should be made. The teacher of students who are visually impaired will assist with these adaptations.

* CAREER AND VOCATIONAL SKILLS

It is never too early to begin thinking about career goals. Students who are visually impaired benefit from early exposure to the work world on many different levels.

It will be important to instill in Henry, throughout his education and at home, the idea and practice of appropriate work habits including attention to task, following directions, and cooperative work with peers and adults. Jobs at home will begin this process and vocational training at school will eventually be an important part of Henry's education.

As Henry matures, so will his interests and aptitudes, and these will need to be taken into account as he begins to explore work choices. The more interested

Henry is in a work or job option, the more likely that he will be successful in maintaining it.

It is not too early for Henry to have a job in his classroom. He can be regularly responsible for taking the attendance list to the office or helping to maintain a class garden. As he gets older, he will be eligible for special education vocational programs that will provide a variety of job opportunities at school and in the community.

Henry will benefit from becoming aware of the variety of jobs available in the world and of the adaptations that people who are visually impaired make so that they can perform these jobs. At this point, when Henry is out in the community with one of his parents or with a teacher, the adult can encourage this process by discussing with Henry the various workers they encounter. For example, discuss the kinds of work people do in commonly visited places such as the gas station. Does the attendant wear a uniform? What type of equipment does he or she use? Or, how many people work in a fast food restaurant? What are the different jobs involved there?

When he is older, Henry might eventually consider becoming involved in a work skills program offered through his school. A job coach can be provided to support his skill acquisition. These jobs provide the foundation of good work habits. They also provide an information bank that eventually helps lead an individual to a career choice.

O&M

The following recommendations are all related to Henry's O&M skills, but they do not all need to be addressed by an O&M specialist exclusively. It is up to the IEP team to decide who will be the primary person to address the recommendations the team chooses to put into practice.

* HAVE AN ASSESSMENT BY AN OCCUPATIONAL THERAPIST WHO WORKS ON SENSORY–MOTOR INTEGRATION

An occupational therapist may be helpful for filling in the gaps in Henry's body image as well as addressing Henry's resistance to crossing the midline of his body with either hand. The inability to cross the midline will make it difficult for Henry to use a white cane effectively, among other things.

* GIVE HENRY A TRIAL OF A FEW MONTHS OF LESSONS AND PRACTICE USING THE WHITE CANE

Henry may benefit from the safety of using a white cane to detect drop-offs and other changes in terrain as he travels. He will need help to respond to the cane contacting changes in terrain without watching the cane tip as much as he did during this assessment. Games can be played to have him meet the challenge of finding items with the cane alone, perhaps while he wears a blindfold if he is willing. Practice in judging how far away the item is that the cane is contacting will be beneficial. Fostering reliance on the cane to detect the top and bottom of staircases will make Henry a more efficient and safe traveler.

* GIVE HENRY RESPONSIBILITY FOR TRAVELING IN A PROTECTED ENVIRONMENT

Although Henry is easily oriented to new locations, his tendency to be distracted reduces his reliability for traveling without someone guiding him or prompting him frequently. If he could learn to walk, without adult prompts, from his classroom to the office to deliver messages, for example, this would be a step toward independent travel. Having Henry find locations at school when the other students are in class will reduce the distractions and increase the likelihood of his success. It may be necessary to set up a system of rewards to encourage Henry to pay attention to where he is expected to go. The route to a specific location can be divided into short segments, and Henry can be praised or given a reward for walking each segment without prompts. As he increases in independence, the segments can be lengthened until he is able to follow an entire route with only the supervision necessary for his health.

* PROVIDE QUALITY EXPERIENCES IN THE COMMUNITY

Increasing Henry's responsibility on community outings will also move him toward more independence. Giving him practice in estimating and then checking prices on common items will improve his awareness of the value of money. His use of money can be improved by letting him handle money; learning to get it out, hand it to the clerk, and hold his hand out for change. Assessing his knowledge of various types of businesses may lead to giving him more exposure to the businesses and services available in the community.

* INCREASE ACCESSIBILITY OF THE TELEPHONE

Henry showed good aptitude for using the telephone. This is an important skill for a traveler who is visually impaired because much of the information needed to take responsibility for planning a trip can be obtained over the phone. Giving Henry an enlarged keypad—either a phone with a large keypad built in or a device that can be placed over a standard phone—will allow him to dial numbers without having to concentrate as hard on reading the dial. A large keypad may also help Henry memorize the locations of the numbers eventually so that he can learn to transfer that knowledge to a regular keypad. Practicing making calls during the school day and at home will help Henry to become comfortable with talking on the phone, laying the groundwork for talking to clerks or public transportation operators eventually.

* WORK ON TIME CONCEPTS

Awareness of time and the sequence of events is an important factor in planning travel. Henry can begin to learn more about time by talking about his daily schedule each day. Perhaps pictures of his daily activities could be labeled, and Henry could be asked to put them in order according to when they occur in the day. Breaking a specific activity into its components and having Henry dictate their order will also help him to organize his concepts of time. Discussing an activity that he has recently done, from beginning to end, is another way to help him become aware of the sequence of events. (See the *Speech and Language* section of this report for more suggestions.)

Common Causes of Vision Loss in Children and Implications for Assessment

Frances K. Liefert

The structures of the eye are shown in Figure 1.1 in Chapter 1.

ACHROMOTOPSIA   See *Rod-cone dystrophy.*

ALBINISM   Albinism is an inherited condition causing a lack of pigment in the eyes, skin, and hair (oculocutaneous albinism) or in the eyes alone (ocular albinism). Students with type 1 oculocutaneous albinism have pale skin and light hair and moderate to severe visual impairment. Children with type 2 oculocutaneous albinism have some skin and hair pigment and less severe visual impairment.

Children with albinism have decreased visual acuity, which makes them less able to see detail. The reduction in acuity is due to a number of factors. They are usually very sensitive to light and glare. Frequently children with albinism have *astigmatism,* which is an irregular shape to the cornea of their eyes. Astigmatism causes visual blurring and more sensitivity to glare, which can be improved with prescriptive lenses.

Most children with albinism have full visual fields. Many have *strabismus,* which is a misalignment of the eyes. Most often there is an inward eye turn affecting one eye. The misaligned eye often has poorer vision. *Nystagmus,* which is a rapid, involuntary eye movement, is frequently present in people with albinism.

When Assessing a Child Who Has Albinism:

- Pay attention to lighting. Make sure that light sources such as windows or lamps are behind or next to the student. If the light source is behind the object or the person you want the student to view, the student will see only the silhouette. Reduction of lighting and glare may be helpful indoors. Sun protection from sunglasses and a cap with a dark brim may help outdoors.
- Enlarged materials may be helpful. Prescription eyeglasses and magnifiers may be needed.
- Using a template—a piece of cardboard, plastic, or metal with a window cut out—to frame what you want the student to view may be helpful.
- Telescopes (binoculars or monoculars) may be helpful for distance viewing.
- Let the student hold materials as closely as needed.
- Provide high-contrast markers and bold-lined paper when writing is required.
- Watch for visual fatigue.

AMBLYOPIA   Reduction of vision in one eye without detectable anatomical damage in the eye or the visual pathway is called amblyopia or "lazy eye." This condition must be treated in early childhood to avoid irreversible visual deficits including loss of depth perception, loss of binocularity, and cosmetic defects. Treatment is determined by an eye care specialist, an ophthalmologist, or an optometrist. It usually involves a prescription of eyeglasses and/or a schedule of placing a patch over the stronger eye for a certain period of time each day. Amblyopia is not an eye disease. It is usually correctable by early treatment and does not require the involvement of a teacher of students who are visually impaired if it is the student's only visual problem.

When Assessing a Child Who Has Amblyopia:

- Refer to the recommendations of the eye care specialist for use of glasses, patching schedule, or other treatment.

- Seek consultation from a teacher of students who are visually impaired if other eye conditions are present or to assess whether functional vision is affected.
- Allow frequent rest periods due to visual fatigue caused by using only one eye. The student may have difficulty keeping track of his or her place when reading.
- Present materials to the stronger eye.

ANIRIDIA   The total or partial absence of the iris, which is the colored part of the eye, is called aniridia. It is a hereditary condition. The iris is the muscle that controls the size of the pupil, which is the opening in the eye that lets in light. Without an iris to control how much light enters the eye, bright light and glare cause the reduction of vision due to sensitivity to light, which is called photophobia. It takes longer for students with aniridia to adjust to the change in visual stimuli when they move from one lighting condition to another, such as going outdoors or entering a darkened theater. Visual acuity, which is the ability to see details, and visual fields are usually reduced. Aniridia is frequently associated with *cataracts* and *glaucoma.*

When Assessing a Child Who Has Aniridia:

- Pay attention to lighting. Make sure that light sources such as windows or lamps are behind or next to the child. If the light source is behind the object or the person to be viewed, the child will see only the silhouette.
- Reduction of lighting and glare may be helpful indoors. Sun protection using sunglasses and a cap with a dark brim may help outdoors and may help reduce the adjustment time when coming back indoors.
- Give the student time to adjust to any changes in lighting.
- Enlarged materials and magnification may help for near viewing. Let the student determine the viewing distance.
- A telescope (binocular or monocular) may improve distance viewing.
- Because of the predisposition to glaucoma and cataracts, make sure that the student is being evaluated regularly by an eye care specialist.

ANOPHTHALMIA   Anophthalmia is the absence of one or both eyes. Some children are born without eyes or with only one eye. When this occurs, a prosthetic eye is usually inserted in the eye socket primarily for cosmetic reasons. In order to avoid infection, the prosthesis must be cared for similarly to contact lenses. Larger prostheses must be inserted as the student grows.

When Assessing a Child Who Has Anophthalmia:

- Follow the guidelines for assessment of a student with whatever condition exists in the remaining eye.
- If the student has neither eye, use tactile materials, including braille if appropriate, and use auditory modes. All assessors are advised to consult with a teacher of students who are visually impaired when preparing assessment materials. See Chapters 3, 5, 8, and 9 for details about assessing a student who is totally blind.

APHAKIA   When the lens of the eye is removed as it may be when *cataracts* are present, the condition is called aphakia. Students with aphakia cannot focus at different distances and may have problems with depth perception. They often use contact lenses, even as toddlers, and almost always depend on some kind of eyewear prescription to see at different distances. Sometimes both contacts and eyeglasses are used to reduce the thickness of the eyeglasses.

When Assessing a Child Who Has Aphakia:

- Pay attention to lighting. If a dimmer switch is available, the student may be able to adjust the light to the optimal level for his or her use. He or she may need to wear a sun visor both indoors and out to protect the eyes from bright light and glare.
- Make sure that light sources such as windows or lamps are behind, above, or—preferably—next to the student. If the light source is behind the object or the person you want the student to view, the student will see only the silhouette.
- Make sure that the student is using any prescribed lenses.

- Enlargement and/or magnification of materials may be helpful. Let the student determine viewing distance.
- A telescope (monocular or binocular) may improve distance viewing.
- Protect the student's eyes from the sun with sunglasses and/or a cap with a visor when outdoors. Students with aphakia are particularly vulnerable to the harmful rays of the sun.

ASTIGMATISM   When the cornea or, less often, the lens of the eye has an irregular shape, it does not refract light uniformly. The result is that the image is blurred. Astigmatism alone is rarely the cause of significant visual impairment, but it often is present with other conditions.

When Assessing a Child Who Has Astigmatism:

- Encourage the student to wear prescriptive lenses that correct the astigmatism.
- Protect the student from glare, especially if the astigmatism is not corrected.

CATARACTS   Clouding and hardening of the lens of the eye is called a cataract. It causes light entering the eye to be reduced and diffused. Students with cataracts have blurred vision or no vision, depending on the maturity of the cataract. They have reduced acuity (the ability to see details), poor color vision, photophobia (extreme sensitivity and discomfort from light), and may have *nystagmus.*

Cataracts are removed when they become mature: so opaque that the back of the eye cannot be seen through them by an eye care specialist. Once they are removed (creating **aphakia**), prescription lenses are used to replace the natural lens. An artificial lens may be implanted, creating a condition called pseudophakia. If congenital cataracts are not removed soon after birth, the child's vision will be reduced due to lack of early visual stimulation.

When Assessing a Child Who Has Cataracts:

- Pay attention to lighting. If a dimmer switch is available, the student may be able to adjust the light to the optimal level for his or her use. Students with central cataracts may benefit from low illumination. Those with peripheral cataracts may prefer high illumination to narrow their pupils out of the range of the cataracts.

- The student may need to wear a sun visor and/or tinted glasses both indoors and outdoors to protect his or her eyes from bright light and glare.
- Make sure that light sources such as windows or lamps are behind, above, or—preferably—next to the student. If the light source is behind the object or the person you want the student to view, the student will see only the silhouette.
- Enlargement and magnification of materials may be helpful.
- Let the student determine viewing distance. The student may find that tilting the head or looking out of the corner of the eyes makes visual material more accessible.
- Watch out for visual fatigue.

CONE-ROD DYSTROPHY   See *Rod-cone dystrophy.*

CORTICAL VISUAL IMPAIRMENT (CVI)   When a student is visually impaired due to damage to the visual cortex or the posterior visual pathway of the brain, it is called cortical visual impairment. CVI is part of a category of neurological visual impairments and is often just one part of global neurological problems. It is frequently seen in children with cerebral palsy. Children with CVI do not have dependable vision. They often seem to see things one day or one moment and not see the same things later on. They experience significant delays in reacting to most stimuli, including visual stimuli. Often children with CVI either recover more vision or learn to use the remaining vision better over time.

When Assessing a Child Who Has CVI:

- Be aware of glare. Make sure that light sources such as windows or lamps are behind or next to the student. If the light source is behind the object or the person you want the student to view, the student will see only the silhouette. If print material has a glossy surface, it will be difficult for the student to view the material. Glare from a window or from direct sunlight or hazy conditions will further reduce the student's ability to see.

- Avoid crowding. Students with CVI cannot differentiate between two objects if they are close together or touching each other. If you want the student to view a particular object, place it on a solid, high-contrast background by itself. If you want the student to identify symbols or letters, make sure there is adequate space between letters and between words on the page.

- Use color. Often students with CVI respond well to color coding and are especially attracted to red and yellow.

- Watch out for fatigue. Students with neurological impairments often need extra time and energy to respond to any stimuli. If the student you are assessing needs to work at holding his or her head up or keeping his or her legs and arms still, it will take more energy for that student to complete the assessment tasks. Try to position the student so that he or she is well supported, perhaps with consultation from a physical therapist.

- Typically students with CVI look at an object with their eyes, look away, and then move their hand or speak in response to the visual stimuli. It is important to allow time for this process. Once the student is working on a specific task, the lag time tends to decrease until he or she is tired and unable to continue.

- Accept eccentric viewing. Students with CVI often have large field losses. They may not face an object when they are looking at it.

- Use contrast between figure and ground. It is especially important for materials to have a clear distinction between the object to be viewed and the background.

- Avoid visual clutter by keeping backgrounds simple. For example, avoid wearing a print shirt, when holding objects for a student to view.

- Do not frame material to be viewed. Often students with CVI are unable to differentiate between a frame and the object inside it. They may just see the shape of the frame and miss the object altogether.

- Use movement. Students with CVI see better when they are moving or when the visual target is moving. Objects may disappear from view when they stop moving.

CYTOMEGALOVIRUS   See *Infections.*

GLAUCOMA   Too much pressure in the eye due to blockage of the normal flow of the fluid inside the aqueous humor results in glaucoma. Glaucoma is often associated with other eye conditions. It can lead to total blindness due to damage of the optic disc if untreated. (The optic disc is the head of the optic nerve that leads from the eye to the brain. See the diagram of the eye in Chapter 1.)

Students with glaucoma have fluctuating vision. Their loss of peripheral vision leads to poor vision in dimly lit areas and at night. They have photophobia, which is reduced vision and extreme discomfort in bright light. A sudden rise in pressure can cause eye pain or headaches. Chronic and acute pain should be reported to an eye care specialist: it may be a medical emergency. Students with glaucoma have reduced ability to see objects with low contrast to their background.

Glaucoma is frequently treated with medication directly applied to the eyes as eyedrops.

When Assessing a Child Who Has Glaucoma:

- Pay attention to lighting. Avoiding glare is important. If a dimmer is available, the student may be able to adjust the lighting to the optimal level.
- The student may need to wear a sun visor and/or tinted lenses both indoors and out to protect his or her eyes from bright light and glare.
- Make sure that light sources such as windows or lamps are behind, above, or—preferably—next to the student. If the light source is behind the object or the person you want the student to view, the student will see only the silhouette.

- Materials with high contrast between what is being viewed and the background are preferable.
- Enlargement of materials and magnification may be helpful.
- A telescope (binocular or monocular) may improve distance viewing.
- Watch out for fatigue from using vision while working and from possible pain caused by the glaucoma.

HERPES See *Infections.*

HYPEROPIA Hyperopia is often referred to as farsightedness. Children may be farsighted due to the shape of their eye, which causes the focal point of images to fall behind the retina. Students with hyperopia see better in the distance than up close. Hyperopia can usually be corrected by prescription lenses, which are convex and referred to as + (plus) lenses.

Students whose eyes are severely hyperopic may not be able to use lenses that correct their vision to 20/20. These students will need magnification for close work.

When Assessing a Child Who Has Uncorrectable Hyperopia:

- Enlargement and magnification may help.
- Watch out for fatigue. The strain of forcing their eyes to do close work for which they are not suited will be tiring for students with hyperopia.

INFECTIONS: CYTOMEGALOVIRUS (CMV), HERPES, *TOX-OCARA*, AND TOXOPLASMOSIS These infections, which can occur in utero or after birth, are all associated with damage to the retina and/or choroid in the back of the eye (see Figure 1.1 in Chapter 1). Infection scars the choroid and/or the retina, causing losses in the visual fields or blind spots. These blind spots are called *scotomas.*

The cornea may also be affected by infections. Extreme damage to the cornea may be surgically repaired with a corneal transplant. Less extensive scarring may be repaired by removal of only part of the cornea. Damage may be done to the central nervous system by these infections.

When the scarring is in the area of central vision, see the adaptation recommendations for *macular degeneration.* When peripheral vision is affected, see the recommendations for *retinitis pigmentosa.*

When Assessing a Child Who Has Visual Damage Due to Infection:

- Magnification or enlargement may be helpful, but care must be given not to enlarge items into the areas of the student's blind spots.
- Allow the student to view eccentrically. Sometimes students with peripheral field loss or central scotomas due either to retinal or corneal damage need to view a target using peripheral vision. They may not appear to be attending visually because they do not direct their central gaze at the target. They are looking around the scarring.
- High-contrast materials, including dark line markers may be helpful. A closed-circuit television with reversed polarity (white on black) may be helpful.
- Watch out for visual fatigue.
- Let the student adjust the lighting if possible.

LAURENCE-MOON-BEIDEL SYNDROME   See the section on *retinitis pigmentosa* for a description of the visual components of this syndrome. This condition may include visual impairment, obesity, hypogonadism (small genitals), cognitive disability, spastic paraplegia, and kidney problems.

LEBER'S CONGENITAL AMAUROSIS   Leber's congenital amaurosis is an inherited form of **retinitis pigmentosa** in which the central vision deteriorates at birth or in the first months after birth. Students with this eye condition have difficulty seeing colors and detail and have blind spots. They frequently have abnormal corneas and may have *cataracts. Nystagmus* accompanies Leber's congenital amaurosis. Eye pressing is common. This eye condition is sometimes, but not always, associated with cognitive disabilities. Severe visual impairment is possible and acuity is often affected. Typically these students have **hyperopia:** they see better at a distance than up close.

When Assessing a Child Who Has Leber's Congenital Amaurosis:

- Allow eccentric viewing. The student may be looking around the blind spots.
- Enlargement and magnification may be helpful, but be careful not to enlarge into the student's blind spots.
- Pay attention to lighting. Dim light will not be adequate for the peripheral vision on which students with Leber's congenital amaurosis frequently depend, but bright light may cause the pupils to constrict so much that peripheral vision is not available. Diffuse light may be best.
- Make sure that light sources such as windows or lamps are behind, above, or—preferably—next to the child. If the light source is behind the object or the person you want the student to view, the student will see only the silhouette.
- A closed-circuit television with reversed polarity (white on black) may be helpful.
- A monocular may be helpful for distance viewing.
- Adaptations for children who are totally blind may be appropriate. All assessors may need to consult with a teacher of students who are visually impaired while preparing assessment materials. See Chapters 3, 5, 8, and 9 for more information about assessing a child who is totally blind.

MICROPHTHALMIA   When a child is born with eyes that are too small, the condition is called microphthalmia. Students with this condition are sometimes fitted with prosthetic eyes to hold the shape of the eye socket. The prosthesis may have a clear center to allow the student to use any remaining vision. Other eye problems are likely to be present, including *cataracts, glaucoma, aniridia,* and *coloboma.*

When Assessing a Child Who Has Microphthalmia:

- Be aware of other conditions the student may have. Follow the guidelines for assessment under those conditions.
- Observe how lighting affects the student. If possible, let him or her adjust the lighting. Avoid glare.
- Enlarge and magnify material as needed.
- Use materials with good contrast between symbols or letters and the background.
- Use tactile materials and braille if necessary.
- Allow frequent breaks to avoid stress and fatigue.
- Expect fluctuating visual performance.

MYOPIA   When the image enters the eye and the focal point is in front of the retina, the condition is referred to as myopia or near-sightedness. Myopia is usually correctable by prescription lenses, but sometimes it is so extreme that it cannot be corrected to 20/20. Lenses to correct myopia are concave, and referred to as – (minus) lenses. Children with uncorrectable nearsightedness, or *high myopia*, cannot see well in the distance.

When Assessing a Child Who Has High Myopia:

- Provide good illumination.
- Enlargement and further magnification may help. Use of closed-circuit television may be helpful.
- Sometimes tactile materials and braille are necessary.

NYSTAGMUS   Congenital vision loss may result in nystagmus, an involuntary, rhythmic movement of the eyes. *Pendular nystagmus* refers to movement of equal speed and duration in each direction. *Jerky nystagmus* is when there are slower movements in one direction followed by a rapid return to the original position. Nystagmus itself does not interfere with vision. It is currently believed that the brain makes a perceptual adjustment when nystagmus is present so that fixing and focusing are not compromised. People with nystagmus are sometimes able to find a position, called the *null point*, at which the eye movement is reduced so that the brain is momentarily not required to make the adjustment.

When Assessing a Child Who Has Nystagmus:

- Follow the guidelines for any other eye condition present.
- Allow head tilting, which may help the student find the null point.
- Watch out for fatigue.
- Underlining items, providing a frame for the visual target, and increasing space between lines of print may improve the student's ability to keep track of what is to be viewed.

OPTIC NERVE ATROPHY   If the optic nerve atrophies, an eye care specialist can detect the pallor of the optic disk, which is the place where the optic nerve is attached to the retina. Students with optic nerve atrophy have fluctuating vision and often have a loss of color vision. Optic nerve atrophy compromises both the acuity and the visual fields. *Nystagmus* may accompany this condition, making it harder for the student to focus. Depending on the cause of the optic nerve atrophy, the student may have other neurological and visual impairments as well.

When Assessing a Child Who Has Optic Nerve Atrophy:

- Pay attention to lighting. Students with optic nerve atrophy often need high illumination, but have trouble seeing when glare is present.
- Avoid visual clutter. Make sure that backgrounds are plain and of good contrast with the target objects. For example, do not hold objects to be viewed against print clothing. Make sure there is adequate spacing between letters and between words.
- Enlargements and magnification may be beneficial.
- Braille and other tactile materials may be necessary.
- Expect fluctuating visual performance.

OPTIC NERVE HYPOPLASIA (ONH)   If the optic nerve fails to develop, the diagnosis is optic nerve hypoplasia. The optic nerve of a person who has ONH is so small that light cannot get to the brain and vision fails to develop typically. Visual acuities range from 20/20 to no vision at all. Visual fields and visual perception may be affected.

Students diagnosed with ONH may have a syndrome called *septo-optic dysplasia,* which is not always diagnosed in addition to ONH. The students are likely to have endocrine problems due to problems with the pituitary gland. They may need supplements of human growth hormone, thyroid and other hormones. Hormone problems may compromise their ability to fight off diseases, and simple cold viruses may endanger their lives. Low blood sugar may cause a drop in energy level. Students with ONH may have problems with orientation in space, stemming form disruption to the development of the middle portions of the brain. They may have varying degrees of cognitive disability or learning disabilities. Diabetes insipidus, which causes an inability to regulate fluids in the body, is also associated with ONH.

The cause of ONH is unknown. Often mothers of children with ONH are very young. There are clusters of babies born with ONH in agricultural areas in the United States.

When Assessing a Child Who Has Optic Nerve Hypoplasia:

- Pay attention to lighting. High illumination is likely to be helpful.
- Enlargement and magnification may be helpful.
- Tactile and braille materials may be necessary.
- Avoid visual clutter. Make sure that backgrounds are plain and of good contrast with the target objects. Do not hold objects to be viewed against print clothing, for example. Make sure there is adequate spacing between letters and between words.
- Expect fluctuating visual performance.
- Watch out for fatigue. Often children with optic nerve hypoplasia may need frequent snacks to maintain an adequate blood sugar level. They may crave water if they have concomitant diabetes insipidus.

RETINITIS PIGMENTOSA (RP)   This is a disorder affecting the peripheral vision. Students with RP have difficulty seeing movements and obstacles outside of their narrowed visual fields. Their vision may be severely compromised in dimly lit areas and at night. They may have *myopia* and other eye anomalies as well. This condition is degenerative and may result in total blindness. RP is associated with several syndromes, including *Laurence-Moon-Beidel syndrome, Usher syndrome,* and *Leber's congenital amaurosis.*

When Assessing a Child Who Has Retinitis Pigmentosa:

- Make sure there is adequate lighting. In dimly lit areas, be sure to watch for changes in visual ability and make sure the student moves safely. Wearing a cap with a dark brim and/or tinted glasses to reduce glare may help to minimize transition time between brightly and dimly lit areas.
- Enlargement and magnification may be helpful, but be careful not to enlarge items so much that they cannot fit in the student's field of vision. Use of a closed-circuit television may be helpful.
- Tactile materials and braille may be useful.
- Use of a monocular for distance viewing may be helpful.

RETINOBLASTOMA   This is the most common malignant tumor of the eye among children. Students with retinoblastoma usually have the affected eye removed. They are at risk for tumors in the other eye as well as in other locations of their body. The condition is usually discovered because the pupil looks white and the eyes are not moving in conjunction with each other *(strabismus).* Other neurological impairments may be present due to tumor growth.

Students with one eye have no real depth perception, although they can learn to use other visual cues to notice changes in depth. If the remaining eye is impaired, the student will qualify for services from a program for students who are visually impaired. If vision remains in one eye, safety glasses with polycarbonate lenses should be worn—whether a prescription is needed or not—in order to increase the safety of the remaining eye. A student with vision in only one eye is at increased risk for an eye accident since he or she may not see an object approaching the sighted eye from the blind side.

When Assessing a Child Who Has Retinoblastoma:

- Be careful that the student moves safely in unfamiliar areas and in areas where there are steps and drop-offs.

RETINOPATHY OF PREMATURITY (ROP) This condition occurs in infants who are premature, because the eyes have not developed as they would have in a full-term baby. The blood vessels supplying blood to the retina become too thick and overgrown. Several factors are suspected of contributing to ROP, including the baby receiving oxygen in an incubator for a long period of time and the baby being exposed to too much light. The malformed blood vessels pull on the thin layers of retina causing scarring and, sometimes, detachment from the back of the eye.

Some premature babies recover from the overgrowth of blood vessels without intervention, and others are helped by a procedure called cryotherapy. In this procedure parts of the retina are frozen from the outside to prevent more growth of blood vessels. Laser treatment may be used for the same purpose. If cryotherapy is unsuccessful or if ROP is discovered too late, it may be possible to reattach the retina surgically. Sometimes the sclera is buckled inward and against the retina again in order to give more support to the retina. These procedures do not totally restore vision but may prevent further vision loss. They often cause retinal scarring, which adds to the visual field loss.

ROP is often associated with high *myopia* and may be associated with *cataracts, glaucoma, nystagmus, strabismus,* and/or *microphthalmia.* It is not uncommon for people with ROP who have some vision as children to lose that vision as young adults due to retinal detachment.

Some children with ROP become totally blind while they are still young, and others are barely affected. ROP is described in stages from 1 to 5, depending on how pervasive the overgrowth of the blood vessels has become. It is also described by the zone in which the blood vessels are growing. Children with stage 1 and 2 ROP will not necessarily become visually impaired, although the risk of *my-*

opia or **strabismus** is high for premature children. In stage 3, the blood vessels grow uncontrollably toward the center of the eye, scar tissue develops on the retina, and the visual fields may be affected. A student whose eyes have reached stage 3 is in danger of retinal detachment, and is a candidate for surgical treatment. In stage 4, the retina is actually pulled away from the back of the eye, further restricting the visual fields, depending on the location of the detachment. An eye at stage 5 has a completely detached retina, and no vision.

Many premature children with ROP also have developmental delays. Frequently there are heart and lung problems due to incomplete formation and development of those organs prior to birth. Brain problems are frequent as well. Incomplete brain and nervous system development is possible in many premature children, and brain bleeds and hydrocephalus are frequent. The result can be a student who is visually impaired and has learning disabilities, cerebral palsy, language delays or impairment, and some degree of cognitive disability.

When Assessing a Child Who Has ROP:

- Magnification and enlargement may be helpful. The closed-circuit television may be useful for some children who have ROP.
- High illumination may be needed.
- Use caution in situations where the student might receive a blow to the head—such as on a playground where balls are being thrown—which might result in retinal detachment.
- Look for sensory integration problems and other signs of developmental delay.

ROD-CONE DYSTROPHY   Rods and cones are the photoreceptors in the back of the eye on the retina. See Chapter 4 for a description of the function of rods and cones. Rod-cone dystrophy is an umbrella term describing eye conditions in which a child is born with either the cones or the rods not working, causing visual impairment.

Eye conditions associated with ***Leber's congenital amaurosis, retinitis pigmentosa*** and ***Usher's syndrome*** fall under the umbrella of rod-cone dystrophy, and there are many less common syndromes which include rod-cone dystrophy. If a person was born with cones not working or cones degenerating, the condition is sometimes referred to as ***cone-rod dystrophy.*** If the rods are deteriorating fastest or the person was born without functional rods, peripheral vision is most affected. If the cones are deteriorating fastest or if the person was born without functional cones, detail (central) vision is most affected. ***Achromotopsia*** is the name given to the eye condition in which cone dystrophy is static, rather than degenerative.

When Assessing a Child Who Has Rod-Cone Dystrophy:

- Find out whether the periphery or central vision is most affected.

If the rods are most affected:

- Detail vision may be intact and assessment tasks requiring reading or close viewing may be minimally affected.
- Care must be taken when the student is moving from one location to another that he or she does not collide with obstacles.
- Vision will be greatly impaired in dimly lit areas.

If the cones are most affected:

- Detail vision will not be dependable.
- It is important to reduce lighting to optimize vision use and to increase the student's comfort.
- Do not use test items requiring color vision.

SCOTOMA   A scotoma is a spot on the retina where light is not being received by any nerves: a blind spot in the visual field. Depending on its location, it will affect peripheral or central vision. Multiple scotomas may affect reading and distance viewing efficiency because parts of the visual target may be missed. A scotoma can be the result of a variety of causes including scarring due to surgery, a degenerative disease such as *retinitis pigmentosa,* or an *infection* affecting the retina.

When Assessing a Child Who Has a Scotoma:

- Determine whether the loss is to central vision or peripheral vision by checking with the eye care specialist.
- If there is a loss of central vision, magnification and enlargement may be helpful. The teacher of students who are visually impaired may be able to determine what size is most beneficial for the specific student.
- Accommodate eccentric viewing. The student may need to use a part of the retina that does not allow him or her to face the target object directly. Introduce materials to the area where viewing seems optimal.
- Adjust lighting. Diffuse lighting will allow the pupil to open wider, which will enlarge the area of the retina receiving light. Dim light or tinted glasses may permit the peripheral vision to function more adequately. If practical, ask the student to adjust the lighting.

SEPTO-OPTIC DYSPLASIA (DEMORSIER SYNDROME)   See **Optic nerve hypoplasia.**

STARGARDT DISEASE   Children with macular degeneration are often diagnosed with Stargardt disease and have a reduction of their central vision. Their peripheral vision is intact. They have difficulty seeing detail and color and see better in dimly lit areas and at night. *Nystagmus* is common in children with Stargardt disease. This is an inherited condition.

When Assessing a Child Who Has Stargardt Disease:

- Use diffuse lighting and tinted glasses to allow the rods in the retina to work. If possible, allow the student to adjust the lighting. The pupil will open wider in dim light and more of the residual central vision may also be used.

- Tactile materials and braille may be needed.
- Allow eccentric viewing. The student may not appear to be looking directly at the target object because he or she is using her peripheral vision.
- Magnification and enlargement may be helpful.
- High-contrast materials may be helpful.

STRABISMUS   Strabismus is a misalignment of the eyes that most often involves an inward eye turn affecting one eye. The misaligned eye often has poorer vision. Strabismus is often, but not always, secondary to other eye conditions. It can be surgically corrected in many cases with varying long-term success. In young children, strabismus may result in *amblyopia.*

When the eye turns outward toward the temple, the condition is called *exotropia.* When the eye turns inward toward the nose, the condition is called *esotropia.* When the eye turns upward, the condition is called *hypertropia. Hypotropia* is the condition of the eye turning downward.

A student with strabismus is only using one eye at a time and, therefore, has no real depth perception.

When Assessing a Child Who Has Strabismus:

- Determine, based on the eye care specialist's report, whether there is any visual impairment present in addition to the monocular viewing. Students with strabismus alone usually do not need the help of a program for students who are visually impaired.
- Watch out for fatigue. Viewing with one eye or switching from eye to eye can be a tiring task for the brain. Students with strabismus may experience frequent headaches.
- Present visual material to the stronger eye.

TOXOCARA   See *Infections.*

TOXOPLASMOSIS   See *Infections.*

USHER SYNDROME This syndrome affects both hearing and vision and is of three types.

Students with type 1 are born with little or no hearing. They develop *retinitis pigmentosa* vision loss at around 5 or 6 years of age and have balance problems.

Children with type 2 lose their hearing in childhood, usually after they are old enough to speak, through a progressive hearing loss. *Retinitis pigmentosa* begins between the ages of 10 and 20 years. Balance is not a problem.

Type 3 is similar to type 2 with a more rapid degeneration of both hearing and vision.

When Assessing a Child Who Has Usher Syndrome:

- See the recommendations for **retinitis pigmentosa.**
- Determine the communication system the student has already developed. Many people with Usher syndrome are fluent signers and use their hands to read American Sign Language (ASL) once they are unable to read with their vision. An ASL interpreter may be helpful during the assessment. Other students with Usher syndrome may use various combinations of writing and speech to communicate.

BIBLIOGRAPHY

Chen, D. (Ed.) (1999). *Essential elements in early intervention.* New York: AFB Press.

Ferrell, K. A. (with A. R. Shaw & S. J. Deitz). (1998). *Project PRISM: A longitudinal study of developmental patterns of children who are visually impaired. Final report* (Grant H023C10188, US Dept. of Education, Field-initiated research, CFDA 84.023). Greeley, CO: University of Northern Colorado. Available at http://vision.unco.edu/Faculty/Ferrell/PRISM/default.html

Fraiberg, S. (1977). *Insights from the blind.* New York: Basic Books.

Hazecamp, J. (1997). *Program guidelines for students who are visually impaired.* Sacramento: California Department of Education.

Holbrook, M. C. (Ed.) (1996). *Children with visual impairments: A parents' guide.* Bethesda, MD: Woodbine House.

Korsten, J. E., Dunn, D. K., Foss, T. V., & Francke, M. K. (1993). *Every move counts.* San Antonio, TX: Therapy Skill Builders.

Lueck, A. H., Chen, D., & Kekelis, L. S. (1997). *Developmental guidelines for infants with visual impairment.* Louisville, KY: American Printing House for the Blind.

Scott, E. P., Jan, J. E., & Freeman, R. D. (1977). *Can't your child see?* Baltimore, MD: University Park Press.

Strickling, C. (1998). *Impact of vision loss on motor development.* Austin: Texas School for the Blind and Visually Impaired.

Warren, D. H. (1984). *Blindness and early childhood development.* New York: American Foundation for the Blind.

Warren, D. H. (1998). *Blindness and children: An individual differences approach.* New York: Cambridge University Press.

Parent Inventory and History Form

PARENT INVENTORY AND HISTORY FORM

Introduction: Please fill in as much of this form as you are able. If you can't remember, leave the item blank or make your best estimate. This information will be extremely helpful in providing the Assessment Team with as complete a picture of your child as possible.

The information contained herein is confidential and may be included in the final assessment report, which is also confidential.

Please attach additional pages as necessary.

Name of person filling out this form _____

Relationship to child _____ Date _____

Current Living Situation

Child's name _____ Date of birth _____

Child's primary address _____

_____

_____

Home telephone _____

With whom does child primarily live? _____

Who has legal custody of child? _____

Noncustodial Parent's Address

Name _____

Address _____

_____

Home telephone _____ Work telephone _____

Child's primary language _____ Other languages spoken _____

Child's ethnicity, race, or culture _____

Reason for referral _____

_____

_____

Desired assessment outcomes _____

_____

_____

Source: J. Richard Russo, California School for the Blind Assessment Program, Fremont, CA, 2002. Reprinted with permission.

Others Living in Home

Name	Age	Relationship	Grade or occupation
_____	____	_____	_____
_____	____	_____	_____
_____	____	_____	_____
_____	____	_____	_____
_____	____	_____	_____
_____	____	_____	_____

How Child Communicates

_____ Verbal (sounds and words)   _____ Communication device

_____ Sign language   _____ Gestures/pointing

_____ Pictures   _____ Written/braille messages

_____ Other (please specify): _____

Vision _____

Hearing _____

Other impairments _____

Other Eligibilities or Agencies Serving Child

_____ Regional Center   _____ Blind Babies Foundation

_____ MEDI-CAL   _____ Developmental Services

_____ SSI   _____ Children's Protective Services

Social or case worker name _____ Telephone _____

Is child: _____ Right-handed _____ Left-handed _____ Switches

School child currently attends _____

Grade _____ Special class or center type _____

Specialists working with child

Name	Specialty	Frequency of service
_____	_____	_____
_____	_____	_____
_____	_____	_____
_____	_____	_____
_____	_____	_____

APPENDIX B (*continued*)

Source: J. Richard Russo, California School for the Blind Assessment Program, Fremont, CA, 2002. Reprinted with permission.

Future Expectations

What do you see as your child's future living situation as an adult? (Please explain)

_____ Independent living: _____

_____ At home with you or a relative: _____

_____ A group home: _____

_____ A sheltered apartment: _____

_____ An institution or other facility: _____

Educational History

School or facility	Location	Level or grade	Dates
_____	_____	_____	_____
_____	_____	_____	_____
_____	_____	_____	_____
_____	_____	_____	_____
_____	_____	_____	_____
_____	_____	_____	_____
_____	_____	_____	_____
_____	_____	_____	_____

What do you see as your child's future educational pursuits as an adult?
(Please explain)

_____ None after current course of study: _____

_____ Apprenticeship or other vocational training: _____

_____ Community college: _____

_____ Four year college: _____

_____ Other (please specify): _____

What do you see as your child's future occupational pursuits as an adult?
(Please explain)

_____ Adult activity program: _____

_____ Sheltered workshop: _____

_____ Competitive part-time employment: _____

_____ Competitive full-time employment: _____

_____ Other (please specify): _____

APPENDIX B (*continued*)

Source: J. Richard Russo, California School for the Blind Assessment Program, Fremont, CA, 2002. Reprinted with permission.

Birth Parents' Health and History

Birth mother's current health: _____

Birth mother's education: _____

Birth mother's occupation: _____

Birth father's current health: _____

Birth father's education: _____

Birth father's occupation: _____

Does anyone related to the child have a history of any of the following (especially include birth parents of child)?

_____ Visual problems _____ Seizures or convulsions

_____ Hearing problems _____ Mental retardation

_____ Speech problems _____ Heart problems

_____ Emotional problems _____ Learning disabilities

_____ Birth defects _____ Other

If yes to any of the above, please describe: _____

_____

Pregnancy and Birth History

Mother's age at child's birth _____ Father's age at child's birth _____

Did mother use drugs (including those prescribed by a physician), alcohol, or tobacco during pregnancy? Yes _____ No _____

If yes, please describe: _____

_____

Mother's health during pregnancy (please explain)

_____ Accidents: _____

_____ Illnesses (any type): _____

_____ Bleeding: _____

_____ Radiation exposure (including X-rays): _____

Length of pregnancy _____ Birth facility _____

Length of labor _____ Type of anesthesia _____

Labor was: Easy _____ Difficult _____ Very difficult _____

APPENDIX B (*continued*)
_____

Source: J. Richard Russo, California School for the Blind Assessment Program, Fremont, CA, 2002. Reprinted with permission.

Position of baby and delivery

_____ Normal   _____ Breech

_____ Forceps used   _____ Caesarean

Complications: _____

_____

Condition of baby at time of birth: _____

_____

Apgar score   1st _____   2nd _____   Cry response _____

Breathing quality _____

Activity level _____ Birth weight _____ Lbs. _____ Ozs.

Other: _____

Describe any special problems, or special treatment after birth: _____

_____

Length of hospital stay after birth _____

_____

Health History and Developmental Milestones

Please describe child's health, medical treatments, and developmental milestones:
(include illnesses, injuries, surgeries, etc.)

Age Range	Medical/health problems	Milestones
0–1 Yrs.		
1–2 Yrs.		
2–3 Yrs.		
3–4 Yrs.		
4–5 Yrs.		
5–7 Yrs.		
7–10 Yrs.		
10–		

Additional information: _____

_____

_____

APPENDIX B (*continued*)

Source: J. Richard Russo, California School for the Blind Assessment Program, Fremont, CA, 2002.
Reprinted with permission.

Current Medical Supervision and Treatment:

Is child currently under medical treatment or supervision (including physical therapy, occupational therapy, or psychotherapy)? Yes _____ No _____

If yes, please describe: _____

Physician or practitioner _____

Conditions being treated for: _____

Medications

Medication	Dosage	Frequency	Condition being treated for
_____	_____	_____	_____
_____	_____	_____	_____
_____	_____	_____	_____
_____	_____	_____	_____
_____	_____	_____	_____

APPENDIX B (*continued*)

Source: J. Richard Russo, California School for the Blind Assessment Program, Fremont, CA, 2002. Reprinted with permission.

 ABBREVIATIONS USED BY OPHTHALMOLOGISTS AND OPTOMETRISTS

A	Assessment (SOAP format); Angle of anomaly	AION	Anterior ischemic optic neuropathy
A	Atropine (followed by percent concentration, e.g., A1% = Atropine 1%)	AK	Astigmatic keratotomy; autokeratometer
		AL	Argon laser
ABD	Abduction	ALT	Argon laser trabeculoplasty; alternate/alternating (strabismus)
ABK	Aphakic bullous keratopathy		
AC	Anterior chamber: graded by Van Herick method on a 0–4+ scale (followed by Q or C if quiet)		
		AMBL	Amblyopia (maybe preceded by NUTR-nutritional, TOX-toxic, CONG-congenital, STRAB-strabismus, HYST-hysterical, MERD-meridional, STIM DEPR-stimulus deprivation, REFR-refractive)
AC/A	Accommodation-convergence ratio		
ACC	Accommodation		
ACE	Angiotensin converting enzyme		
		AMPPE	Acute multifocal placoid pigment epitheliopathy
ACG	Acute angle closure glaucoma		
ACV	Acyclovir (Zovirax)	ANA	Antinuclear antibodies (lab test indicating presence of either SLE or non-specific collagen vascular disease)
ADD	Adduction; also, bifocal power following M or SRx		
Adv	Advanced	ANT	Anterior
Ag	Antigen	AODM	Adult onset diabetes mellitus

Adapted with permission from P. L. Woolf, M. J. Giese, T. R. Stelmack, T. T. McMahon, & M. S. Berman, "Optometric Clinical Abbreviations," *Journal of the American Optometric Association*, 65(7) (July 1994), pp. 480–487. Copyright © 1994, American Optometric Association.

APD	Afferent pupillary defect (Marcus Gunn pupil defect), preceded by R or L	BU	Base-up prism, also BUP, BUΔ
		BUT	Break-up time (of the tear film) (Also TBUT)
AR	Autorefractor	Bx	Biopsy
ARC	Anomalous retinal (cortical) correspondence	c̄	With (cum), often with dash on top
ARMD	Age-related macular degeneration; age-related maculopathy; also AMD, preceded by exudative or atrophic	C&S	Culture & sensitivity
		CA	Carcinoma (Ca)
		CAC	Convergence-accommodation ratio
ARN	Acute retinal necrosis	CACG	Chronic angle closure glaucoma
ASA	Aspirin		
ASTIG	Astigmatism	CAI	Carbonic anhydrase inhibitor
ATR	Against the rule	CAPS	Capsule
AVx	Anterior vitrectomy	CAT(s)	Cataract(s)
A/V	Artery-to-vein ratio	CB	Ciliary body
B	Betoptic; g: betaxolol (followed by % concentration)	cc	Chief complaint; with correction
BACT	Bacteria; bacterial	CCC	Central corneal clouding (grade on a scale of 0–4+)
BAK	Benzalkonium chloride	C/D	Cup-to-disc ratio (grade: horizontal to vertical (e.g., 0.2/0.4)
B.C.	Base curve		
BCC	Basal cell carcinoma		
BD	Base down prism; also BDP, BDr	CE	Cataract extraction
		CELL	Cells (e.g., cells in aqueous or vitreous grade by number seen on scale of 0–4+)
BI	Base-in prism; also BIP, BIr		
BID	Two times a day ("bis in die")		
BIO	Binocular indirect ophthalmoscopy	CF	Count fingers (note: CF 10′ 20/400), also FC; central fixation
BLEPH	Blepharitis	CFF	Critical flicker frequency
BM	Basement membrane	CHRPE	Congenital hypertrophy of the retinal pigment epithelium
BO	Base-out prism; also BOP, BOΔ		
		Cj	Conjunctiva; also Conj
BRAO	Branch retinal artery occlusion	CL	Contact lens (HCL-hard, SCL-soft, EWCL-extended wear, GPCL-gas permeable, RGP more commonly used); also corneal laceration
BRVO	Branch retinal vein occlusion		
BSTT	Basal Schirmer tear test		
BTG	Betagan; g: levobunolol		

CME	Cystoid macular edema	D	Diopter; deep; day
CMV	Cytomegalovirus	D	Diamox (followed by mg amount, e.g., D250, D500, mg amount is subscript)
CN	Cranial nerve (followed by roman numeral indicating CN, e.g., CN I)		
		D & I	Dilate & irrigate lacrimal canaliculi (also called probe and irrigate lacrimal canaliculi P & 1)
CNS	Central nervous system		
CNVM	Choroidal neovascular membrane; also CNM (see SRNVM)		
		D/C	Discontinue (e.g., to D/C a medication); discharge
C/O	Complains of or complaining of		
		D & C	Deep and clear
COAG	Chronic open angle glaucoma (modifiers, e.g., 2° to or with ACG component)	DDT	Dyslexia determination test
		DDx	Differential diagnosis (also DD)
CONG	Congenital	DFE	Dilated fundus exam
Conj	Conjunctiva; also Cj	Dk/L	Oxygen transmissibility of a contact lens
COP	Cicatricial ocular pemphigoid		
CR	Chorioretinal (e.g., CR lesion)	DM	Diabetes mellitus
CRAO	Central retinal artery occlusion	DME	Diabetic macular edema
		DNKA	Did not keep appointment
CRVO	Central retinal vein occlusion	DO	Direct ophthalmoscopy
CSME	Clinically significant macular edema (in reference to diabetic retinopathy)	DPE	Dipivalyl-epinephrine; also dipivefrin HCl (Propine), (followed by % conc., e.g., $DPE_{.1\%}$)
CSR	Central serous retinopathy; also CSC, central serous choroidopathy		
		D/Q	Deep & quiet (anterior chamber)
CT	Cover test (ACT-alternating, UCT-Unilateral); computerized tomography scan	DR	Diabetic retinopathy (see NPDR, PDR, NVE, NVD, IRMA) *(BDR and PPDR are not currently being used. New classification based on ETDRS results)
CV	Color vision		
CVA	Cerebral vascular accident		
CWS	Cotton wool spots	DRS	Diabetic retinopathy study
Cx	Culture	DSL	Dislocated
CYL	Cylinder	DV	Distance vision
Ck	Check	DW	Daily wear
Cl	Clear (also means closed when listed on gonioscopy exam)	Dx	Diagnosis
		DS	Disease, also Dz

E	Esophoria at 6M (infinity)	E(T')	Intermittent esotropioa at near
E'	Esophoria at near	ETDRS	Early treatment diabetic retinopathy study (results currently used for classification of diabetic retinopathy)
E	Epinephrine (followed by % concentration, e.g., $E_{1/2}$, $E_{1/4}$, E_2)		
EMBD	Epithelial basement membrane dystrophy or disease	EUA	Examination under anesthesia (e.g., infant exam)
ECCE	Extracapsular cataract extraction, followed by Right, Left, Bilateral andACIOL or PCIOL	EV	Eccentric viewing
		EW	Extended wear; EWCL = extended wear contact lens; EWSCL = extended wear soft contact lens
ECTR	Ectropion	EXFOL	Exfoliation
EDS	Equivalent dioptric sphere	EXT	External
EEG	Electroencephalogram	FA	Fluorescein angiography; also FANG
EF	Eccentric fixation		
EKC	Epidemic keratoconjunctivitis	FAZ	Foveal avascular zone
ELISA	Enzyme-linked immunosorbent assay	FB	Foreign body
		FBS	Fasting blood sugar
EM	Electron microscopy	FC	Finger counting at 'x' distance (note: FC 10′ 20/400) (see CF)
EMM	Emmetropia		
ENT	Ear, nose, throat	FD	Fuch's dystrophy (cornea)
ENTR	Entropian	FHx	Family history
EOG	Electro-oculogram	FML	Fluoromethalone (0.10% drop or ointment)
EOM	Extraocular muscles; extraocular movement		
EP	Esophoria at far	FMLf FML	Forte g: fluoromethalone alcohol (0.25%)
EP'	Esophoria at near	FMH	Family medical history
EPI	Epikeratophakia	FOHx	Family ocular history
ERG	Electroretinogram	FROM	Full range of motion (motility)
ERM	Epiretinal membrane (see PRF)	FTA-ABS	Fluorescent treponemal antibody absorption (test for syphilis)
ESRD	Endstage renal disease in diabetic consults		
		FTFC	Full to finger count (used with confrontation field testing)
ET	Esotropia at far (6M, infinity)		
ET'	Esotropia at near	F/U	Follow-up
E(T)	Intermittent esotropia at far	FUNCT	Functional

Fx	Fracture	Hx	History; also HX
GA	General anesthesia	HYPH	Hyphemia (blood in AC)
GC	Gonorrhea or gonococcus	HYPP	Hyperphoria at far (e.g., LHYPP, left hyperphoria at far)
GENT	Gentamicin; also G, GNT; GAR and GARA = garamycin		
GLC	Glaucoma	HYPP′	Hyperphoria at near
GONIO	Gonioscopy (List structures anterior to posterior)	HZO	Herpes zoster ophthalmicus
		HZV	Herpes zoster virus (see VZV)
GVF	Goldmann visual field	I&D	Incision and drainage (incise and drain)
gtts Drops	"guttae"; also GTTS		
GSW	Gunshot wound	I&A	Irrigation and aspiration
HA	Headache	IBx	Incisional biopsy
HAB	Habitual (e.g., HAB SRX)	IC	Intracapsular; iridectomy clip
H&P	History and physical	ICCE	Intracapsular cataract extraction
HCL	Hard contact lens; (see RGP)		
HCTZ	Hydrochlorothiazide (may cause retinal hemorrhages)	ICE	Irido-corneal-endothelial syndrome
		ICK	Infectious crystalline keratopathy
HCVD	Hypertensive cardiovascular disease		
		ICLI	Intracorneal lamellar implant
HEM	Hemorrhage; also HEME	ICR	Intrastromal corneal ring
HEME	Hemorrhage (blood); also HEM	IDDM	Insulin dependent diabetes mellitus
Hgb	Hemoglobin as in Hgb electrophoresis	IDU	Idoxuridine (treats herpetic corneal infections)
HHP	Hollenhorst plaque	IF	Inflamase forte 1%
HM	Hand motion (acuity)	Ig	Immunoglobulin
H/O	History of	IK	Interstitial keratitis
HPPM	Hyperplastic persistent pupillary membrane	I/L	Iris & lens
		IMP	Impression (same as assessment)
hr(s)	Hour(s)		
h.s.	Bedtime ("hora somni")	INF	Infection or infected; interferon
HSK	Herpes simplex keratitis		
HSV	Herpes simplex virus	INJ	Injection or injected
HTN	Hypertension	INO	Internuclear ophthalmoplegia, BINO = binocular IO, WEBINO = wall-eyed BINO
HVF	Humphrey visual field (followed by protocol, e.g., 30–2)		
		INT	Intermittent

INQ	Inferonasal quadrant
IO	Inferior oblique muscle; intraocular; indirect ophthalmoscopy
IOH	Intraocular hemorrhage
IOL	Intraocular lens (preceded by PC for posterior chamber, and AC for anterior chamber)
ION	Ischemic optic neuropathy
IOP	Intraocular pressure (tension)
IP	Iris prolapse
IPD	Interpupillary distance (see PD)
IR	Inferior rectus muscle
IRMA	Intraretinal microvascular abnormalities
ITQ	Infratemporal quadrant
IV	Intravenous (injection of infusion)
J	Jaeger near acuity (e.g., J-1, J-5)
JCC	Jackson cross cylinder
JODM	Juvenile onset diabetes mellitus
JRA	Juvenile rheumatoid arthritis
K	Keratometry
K's	Keratometry reading (e.g., K 45.25 × 44.75 @ 180)
KCS	Keratoconjunctivitis sicca
KP	Keratic precipitates
KS	Keratoscopy: graded on 0–4+ scale (e.g., 0 = no distortion, 1+ = irreg. mires, 2+ = markedly irreg. but some values reliable, 3+ = barely distinguishable, 4+ = non-distinguishable mires)
L	Lid, e.g., preceded by R (right) or L (left) and followed by UL

	for upper lid or LL for lower lid, e.g., RUL right upper lid
LE	Lupus erythematosus or left eye
LHON	Leber's hereditary optic neuropathy
LHYPP	Left hyperphoria
LHYPP'	Left hyperhoria at near
LI	Laser interferometry
LK	Lamellar keratoplasty
LOGMAR	Logmar chart (acuity)
LP	Light perception (acuity) mark (+) or (–) in quadrant tested
LP & P	Light perception and projection (acuity)
LPI	Laser peripheral iridotomy
LQ	Lower quadrant
LR	Lateral rectus muscle
LS	Lid scrubs
LTP	Laser trabeculoplasty
LTQ	Lower temporal quadrant
LUL	Left upper lid
LV	Lid vesicles; low vision
LVA	Low vision aids
M	Manifest refraction (also MR)
MAC	Macula; macular
MARG	Margins
MAX	Maximum
MEDS	Medications
MEM	Monocular estimate method (near retinoscopy)
MERD	Meridional (amblyopia)
MEWDS	Multiple evanescent white dot syndrome
MFS	Monofixation syndrome
MGC	Meibomian gland carcinoma

MGD	Meibomian gland dysfunction	NFC	Negative fusional convergence
MGMT	Management	NFL	Nerve fiber layer
MIN	Minimum; minute(s)	NFLD	Nerve fiber layer defect
MM	Malignant melanoma	NG	No growth (e.g., bacterial Cx)
MMC	Malignant melanoma of conjunctiva	NI	No improvement
MML	Malignant melanoma of eyelid	NIDDM	Non-insulin dependent diabetes mellitus
MOT	Motility	NKDA	No known drug allergies
MR	Medial rectus muscle	nl	Normal
MRD	Margin reflex distance, measures of lid position— MRD_1 = distance in positive number of mm from 1st Purkinje reflex to center of upper lid margin while in primary gaze. MRD_2 = distance in positive number in mm from 1st Purkinje reflex to center of lower lid margin while in primary gaze. MRD_3 = MRD while in maximum upgaze. $MRD+MRD_2$ = intrapalpebral fissure width. Difference between R and L MRD_1's = amount of unilateral ptosis.	NLP	No light perception
		NPA	Near point of accommodation
		NPC	Near point of convergence
		NPDR	Non-proliferative diabetic retinopathy (see ETDRS)
		NQ	Nasal quadrant
		NR	No refill
		NRC	Normal retinal (cortical) correspondence
		NS	Nuclear sclerosis (LCOS III classification)
		N/S	No show (patient did not show for appointment)
		NSC	Nuclear sclerotic cataract, most use NS
MVA	Motor vehicle accident	NTG	Normotensive glaucoma (old term low tension glaucoma, LTG); Nitroglycerine
N	Neptazane (followed by mg amount, e.g., N_{50}) (treats glaucoma) or near, near vision		
N/A	Not applicable, also NA	NV	Near vision; neovascular or neovascularization
NAG	Narrow angle glaucoma		
NAP	No apparent pathology	N&V	Nausea and vomiting
N/C	No charge	NVD	Neovascularization at the disc (optic disc)
NCT	Non-contact tonometer		
NEG	Negative	NVE	Neovascularization elsewhere (not at disc)
NEI	National Eye Institute		
NEO	Neovascularization; neosynephrine followed by % concentration, e.g., NEO 10%	NVG	Neovascular glaucoma
		NVI	Neovascularization of iris
		NVK	Neovascular keratitis

NVM	Neovascular membrane
O	Objective (SOAP format)
OAD	Overall diameter (contact lens)
OAG	Open angle glaucoma (preceded by P for primary and C for chronic)
OAIO	Overaction of the inferior oblique
OBS	Organic brain syndrome
OCP	Ocular cicatricial pemphigoid
OVF	Octopus visual field (followed by protocol e.g., G1)
OD	Doctor of optometry; right eye (oculus dexter)
ODM	Ophthalmodynamometry
OFHx	Ocular family history (see FOH$_X$)
OHTN	Ocular hypertension
OHx	Ocular history (also POH, previous ocular history)
OINT	Ointment (see UNG)
OKN	Optokinetic nystagmus
ON	Optic nerve (neuropathy)
ONA	Optic nerve atrophy
ONH	Optic nerve head; optic nerve hypoplasia
OPE	Open-sky phacoemulsification (to break up cataract)
ORTHO-K	Ortho-keratology
OS	Left eye
OU	Both eyes
P	Pachometry (corneal); periphery; plan (SOAP format); proparacaine; pulse
P	Pilocarpine; followed by % concentration e.g., $P_{2\%}$, $P_{3\%}$, $P_{4\%}$, $P_{6\%}$ (see PILO)
PE	Pilocarpine with epinephrine, e.g., P_1E_1 = Pilocarpine 1% with Epinephrine 1%; also P_2E_1, P_3E_1, P_4E_1 (treats glaucoma)
PAM	Potential acuity meter
PAN	Preauricular lymph node (in front of ear, enlarge with viral eye infections)
PAS	Peripheral anterior synechiae
PBK	Pseudophakic bullous keratopathy
PC	Peripheral curve (contact lens); posterior capsulotomy; posterior chamber
PCF	Pharyngoconjunctival fever
PD	Interpupillary distance (see IPD)
PDR	Proliferative diabetic retinopathy (see ETDRS)
PDRP	Prone dark room provocative (test)
PDS	Pigment dispersion syndrome
PE	Physical examination
PEE	Punctate epithelial erosion
PEH	Past eye history; also PEHx
PEK	Punctate epithelial keratitis (keratopathy)
PERF	perforated
PERRLA	Pupils equal round reactive to light and accommodation
PF	Pred Forte (steroid eyedrop brand)
PG	Pred-G (drug)
PHNI	Pinhole no improvement
PHACO	Phacoemulsification (breaking up of a cataract)
PHPV	Persistent hyperplastic primary vitreous

PHx	Past history		PTK	Phototherapeutic keratectomy
PI	Peripheral iridectomy; peripheral iridotomy		PVD	Posterior vitreous detachment
PI	Phospholine iodide (followed by % concen %); also PI$_{.06\%}$, PI$_{.125\%}$, PI$_{.25\%}$ (treats glaucoma)		Px	Physical; prognosis
			PXE	Pseudoxanthoma elasticum
			R	Resident; retinoscopy; remove
PILO	Pilocarpine (see P)		RA	Rheumatoid arthritis
PK	Penetrating keratoplasty (also PKP)		RBC	Red blood cells
			RBON	Retrobulbar optic neuritis
PLT	Preferential looking technique		RD	Retinal detachment
PMH	Past medical history; also PMHx		RE	Regarding; right eye
			REE	Recurrent epithelial erosions
POE	Postoperative endophthalmitis		REFD	Referred
			REL	Release
POHS	Presumed ocular histoplasmosis syndrome (OHS currently used)		RES	Resident
			RF	Respiratory failure
PP	Punctal plug; pressure patch		R.F.	Rheumatoid factor
PPA	Peripapillary atrophy		RG	Ruptured globe
PPLOV	Painless progressive loss of vision		RGP	Rigid gas permeable
			RHYPP	Right hyperphoria at far
PPM	Pseudophakic pupillary membrane		RHYPP′	Right hyperphoria at near
			RI	Relaxation incision
PPVx	Pars plana vitrectomy		RK	Radial keratotomy; refractive keratoplasty
PRF	Pre-retinal fibrosis (see ERM)			
PRK	Photorefractive keratectomy		ROP	Retinopathy of prematurity; (old term RLF)
PRN	As necessary (pro re nata)			
PRP	Pan-retinal photocoagulation		RP	Retinitis pigmentosa; running prolene
PS	Posterior synechiae			
PSC	Posterior subcapsular cataract (grade on 0–4+ scale)		RPE	Retinal pigment epithelium
			RPL	Replace
PSI	Punctate subepithelial infiltrate		RR	Red reflex; rust ring; remove and replace (e.g., RR-IOL)
PST	Photostress test		RD	Retinal detachment (ERD = exudative RD, RRD = rhegmatogenous RD, TRD = tractional RD)
PSS	Purse-string suture (PK or RK)			
PT	Patient; physical therapy; polytrim			
			RS	Reiter's syndrome

RT	Right; return	SPK	Superficial punctate keratitis
RTC	Return to clinic	SQ	Subcutaneous
Rx	(Take) prescription	SR	Subjective refraction; superior rectus muscle (e.g., RSR, LSR); suture removal
S	Subjective (SOAP format)		
s	Without, often with a dash on top		
		SRNV	Subretinal neovascularization (see SRNVM)
SCC	Squamous cell carcinoma		
SCL	Soft contact lens	SRNVM	Subretinal neovascular membrane; also SRNV, subretinal neovascularization; CNM or CNVM, choroidal neovascular membrane
SD	Stromal dystrophy; standard deviation		
SEF	Subepithelial fibrosis		
SEI	Subepithelial infiltrates	SS	Sjogrens syndrome; stainless steel; scleral spur
SEM	Scanning electron microscopy		
SFB	Scleral foreign body	STAT	Immediately (statim)
SGC	Sebaceous gland carcinoma	STD	Standard; sexually transmitted disease
SI	Sector iridectomy		
SIG	Let it be written	STQ	Superotemporal quadrant
SJS	Stevens-Johnson syndrome	STRAB	Strabismus
SL	Serum lysozyme used in diagnosis of sarcoid; Schwalbe's line	SUBJ	Subjective (see SR)
		SUB Q	Subcutaneous
		SUSP	Suspect
SLE	Systemic lupus erythematosus; slit lamp examination (biomicroscopy) (see SLEx)	SUT	Suture
		SX(s)	Symptoms
		SX	Surgery
		T	Topical; temperature; tonometry (e.g., TA-applanation, NCT-non-contact, S-Schiotz, M-Mackay-Marg); tobrex; timolol
SLEx	Slit lamp examination		
SLK	Superior limbic keratoconjunctivitis		
Sn(s)	Signs		
SNQ	Superonasal quadrant	T	Timoptic; followed by % concentration, e.g., $T_{1/2\%}$; tropicamide, e.g., $T_{1\%}$
SO	Superior oblique muscle (RSO, LSO), sympathetic ophthalmia		
		TA	Temporal arteritis
SOAP	Subjective, objective, assessment and plan (SOAP format)	Ta	Tension (IOP) by applanation
		TCN	Tetracycline
S/P	Status post	TD	Tobradex (antibiotic/steroid)
SPH	Sphere or spherical lens	TDx	Tentative diagnosis

Tec	Tectonic (structural)		V	Vasculature; vitreous; vancomycin
TED	Thyroid eye disease		VA	Visual acuity
TEM	Transmission electron microscopy		VAcc	Visual acuity with correction
TF	Trifluridine (viroptic); (see VIR)		VAsc	Visual acuity without correction
TFI	Tear film insufficiency		VC	Viral culture
TFM	Tear film meniscus		VCTS	Vitreal corneal touch syndrome
TFT	Trifluorothymidine (viroptic) (see TF) (see VIR), also thyroid function tests		VD	Venereal disease
			VDE	Viral disciform edema (herpetic)
TIA	Transient ischemic attack		VDRL	Veneral disease research laboratory (agglutination test for syphilis)
TM	Trabecular meshwork			
TOB	Tobramycin (tobrex)			
TQ	Temporal quadrant		VEE	Visual efficiency evaluation
TR	Trauma or traumatic		VEP	Visual evoked potential (also VER-visual evoked response)
TRAB	Trabeculectomy			
TRACH	Trachoma		VF	Visual field
T.S.	Telescope, e.g., 2.5 × T.S.		VID	Visible iris diameter
TSH	Thyroid stimulating hormone		VIR	Viroptic (see TF = trifluridine) (see TFT = trifluorothymidine)
TSP	Thrombospondin			
Tx	Treatment or therapy		VIT	Vitreous
TYP	Transcleral YAG cyclophotocoagulation		VKC	Vernal keratoconjunctivitis
			VKH	Vogt-Koyanagi-Harada syndrome
U	Unplanned, e.g., UECCE			
UA	Urinalysis		VPE	Visual perception evaluation
UBC	Upper bulbar conjunctiva		VS	Vital signs
UCT	Unilateral cover test		VTW	Vitreous-to-wound
UL	Upper lid		VZV	Varicella-zoster virus (herpes zoster)
UNG	Ointment (see OINT)			
UNQ	Upper nasal quadrant		W	Wound; wydase
URI	Upper respiratory tract infection		w/o	Without
			WBC	White blood cells (leukocytes)
UTC	Upper tarsal conjunctiva		WC	Warm compresses
UTI	Urinary tract infection		WC/LS	Warm compresses/lid scrubs
UTQ	Upper temporal quadrant		WD	Wound; also W, Wd; wound dehiscence

W.D.	Working distance
WNL	Within normal limits
WRA	With the rule astigmatism
WTR	With the rule astigmatism (see WRA)
X	Axis; exophoria at far
X′	Exophoria at near
XBx	Excisional biopsy
XH	Expulsive hemorrhage
XO	Exophthalmos
XP	Exophoria at far
XP′	Exophoria at near
XT	Exotropia at far
XT′	Exotropia at near
X(T)	Intermittent exotropia at far
X(T′)	Intermittent exotropia at near

Y	YAG laser
YAG	Yttrium aluminum garnet (laser)
YLI	YAG laser iridectomy
y/o	Year old
YPC	YAG laser posterior capsulotomy
YR(S)	Year(s)

Also:

$\underline{25\ 25}$ Δ	Hertel exopthalmometry (triangle Δ equals base number measurement)
≈	Approximately
=	Equal
Δ	Prism
∴	Therefore

Sample State Eye Report Form for Children with Visual Impairments

California State Department of Education
Form #SE-03 (Rev. 7-81)

To be filled in by
school personnel.

CONFIDENTIAL **Eye Report for Children with Visual Problems** R L B

NAME OF PUPIL _____ SEX _____
(Type or print)   (First)   (Middle)   (Last)

ADDRESS _____ DATE OF BIRTH _____
(No. and street)   (City or town)   (County)   (State)   (Month) (Day) (Year)

GRADE _____ SCHOOL _____ ADDRESS _____

I. HISTORY
    A. Probable age at onset of vision impairment. Right eye (O.D.) _____ Left eye (O.S.) _____

    B. Severe ocular infections, injuries, operations, if any, with age at time of occurrence _____
    _____

    C. Has pupil's ocular condition occurred in any blood relative(s)? _____ If so, what relationship(s)? _____

II. MEASUREMENTS (See back of form for preferred notation for recording visual acuity and table of appropriate equivalents.)
    A. VISUAL ACUITY

	DISTANT VISION			NEAR VISION			PRESCRIPTION		
	Without correction	With best correction*	With low vision aid	Without correction	With best correction*	With low vision aid	Sph.	Cyl.	Axis
Right eye (O.D.)	_____	_____	_____	_____	_____	_____	____	____	____
Left eye (O.S.)	_____	_____	_____	_____	_____	_____	____	____	____
Both eyes (O.U.)	_____	_____	_____	_____	_____	_____	Date _____		

    B. If glasses are to be worn, were safety lenses prescribed in: Plastic _____ Tempered glass _____ *with ordinary lenses

    C. If low vision aid is prescribed, specify type and recommendations for use. _____
    _____

    D. FIELD OF VISION: Is there a limitation? _____ If so, record results of test on chart on back of form.

        What is the widest diameter (in degrees) of remaining visual field? O.D. _____ O.S. _____

    E. Is there impaired color perception? _____ If so, for what color(s)? _____

III. CAUSE OF BLINDNESS OR VISION IMPAIRMENT
    A. Present ocular condition(s) responsible for vision impairment. (If more than one, specify all but <u>underline</u> the one which probably first caused severe vision impairment.)
        O.D. _____
        O.S. _____

    B. Preceding ocular condition, if any, which led to present condition, or the underlined condition, specified in A. O.D. O.S.
        O.D. _____
        O.S. _____

    C. Etiology (underlying cause) of ocular condition primarily responsible for vision impairment. (e.g., specific disease, injury, poisoning, heredity or other prenatal influence.) O.D. O.S.
        O.D. _____
        O.S. _____

    D. If etiology is injury or poisoning, indicate circumstances and kind of object or poison involved. _____

IV. PROGNOSIS AND RECOMMENDATIONS
    A. Is pupil's vision impairment considered to be: Stable _____ Deteriorating _____ Capable of improvement _____ Uncertain _____

    B. What treatment is recommended, if any? _____

    C. When is reexamination recommended? _____

    D. Glasses: Not needed _____ To be worn constantly _____ For close work only _____ Other (specify) _____

    E. Lighting requirements: Average _____ Better than average _____ Less than average _____

    F. Use of eyes: Unlimited _____ Limited, as follows: _____

    G. Physical activity: Unrestricted _____ Restricted, as follows: _____

TO BE FORWARDED BY EXAMINER TO:
    Date of examination _____
    Signature of examiner _____ Degree _____
    Address _____
        Name
    If clinic case: Number _____ of clinic _____

Source: Reprinted with permission from *Program Guidelines for Students Who Are Visually Impaired,* copyright © 1997, California Department of Education, P.O. Box 271, Sacramento, CA 95812-0271.

Preferred Visual Acuity Notations

DISTANT VISION. Use Snellen notation with test distance of 20 feet. (Examples: 20/100, 20/60). For acuities less than 20/200 record distance at which 200 foot letter can be recognized as numerator of fraction and 200 as denominator. (Examples: 10/200, 3/200). If the 200 foot letter is not recognized at 1 foot record abbreviation for best distance vision as follows:

HM	HAND MOVEMENTS (Specify inches or feet)
PLL	PERCEIVES AND LOCALIZES LIGHT IN ONE OR MORE QUADRANTS
LP	PERCEIVES BUT DOES NOT LOCALIZE LIGHT
No LP	NO LIGHT PERCEPTION

NEAR VISION. Use standard A.M.A. notation and specify best distance at which pupil can read. (Example: 14/70 at 5 in.)

TABLE OF APPROXIMATE EQUIVALENT VISUAL ACUITY NOTATIONS

These notations serve only as an indication of the approximate relationship between recordings of distant and near vision and point type sizes. The teacher will find in practice that the pupil's reading performance may vary considerably from the equivalent shown.

Distant Snellen	A.M.A.	Near Jaeger	Metric	%Central Visual Efficiency for Near	Point	Usual Type Text Size
20/20 (ft.)	14/14 (in.)	1	0.37 (M.)	100.0	3	Mail order catalogue
20/30	14/21	2	0.50	95	5	Want ads
20/40	14/28	4	0.75	90	6	Telephone directory
20/50	14/35	6	0.87	50	8	Newspaper text
20/60	14/42	8	1.00	40	9	Adult text books
20/80	14/56	10	1.50	20	12	Children's books 9–12 yrs.
20/100	14/70	11	1.75	15	14	Children's books 8–9 yrs.
20/120	14/84	12	2.00	10	18 ⎫	Large type test
20/200	14/140	17	3.50	2	24 ⎭	
12.5/200	14/224	19	6.00	1.5		
8/200	14/336	20	8.00	1		
5/200	14/560					
3/200	14/900					

FIELD OF VISION. Record results on chart below.

Type of test used: _____   Illumination in ft. candles: _____

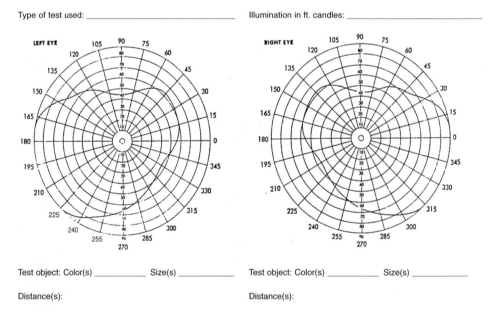

Test object: Color(s) _____ Size(s) _____   Test object: Color(s) _____ Size(s) _____

Distance(s):   Distance(s):

Used with permission from the Northern California Society to Prevent Blindness, 4200 California St., Suite 101, San Francisco, CA 94118.

APPENDIX D (*continued*)

Source: Reprinted with permission from *Program Guidelines for Students Who Are Visually Impaired,* copyright © 1997, California Department of Education, P.O. Box 271, Sacramento, CA 95812-0271.

Educationally Oriented Vision Report
(To be completed by the eye specialist)

Date: Month   Day   Year   Student's name: Last   First   Middle

The following information would be helpful in determining educational programming based on the needs of the student. We would appreciate your completing this form in addition to the ":Eye Report for Children with Visual Problems."

1. What is the cause of the visual impairment?

   _____

   _____

2. Is any special treatment required? If so, what is the general nature of the treatment?

   _____

   _____

3. Is the visual impairment likely to get worse, better, or stay the same?

   _____

   _____

4. What symptoms would indicate a need for reexamination?

   _____

   _____

5. Should any restrictions be placed on the student's activities?

   _____

   _____

6. Should the student wear glasses or contact lenses? If so, under what circumstances?

   _____

   _____

7. If it was not possible to do a visual acuity measure, what is your opinion regarding what the student sees?

   _____

   _____

8. Are the student's focusing ability, tracking, and eye muscle balance adequate? If not, please describe:

   _____

   _____

APPENDIX D *(continued)*

Source: Reprinted with permission from *Program Guidelines for Students Who Are Visually Impaired,* copyright © 1997, California Department of Education, P.O. Box 271, Sacramento, CA 95812-0271.

9. If the student's visual field was not testable, what is your opinion regarding this student's field of vision?

_____

_____

10. Please describe the object size and distances that are optimal for the student.

_____

_____

11. What lighting conditions would be optimal for the student's visual functioning?

_____

_____

12. Do you have any additional specific recommendations concerning this student's use of vision in learning situations?

_____

_____

13. When should this student be examined again?

_____

_____

14. Additional comments and recommendations:

_____

_____

_____

_____

_____

_____

Please return this form to:

APPENDIX D (*continued*)

Source: Reprinted with permission from *Program Guidelines for Students Who Are Visually Impaired,* copyright © 1997, California Department of Education, P.O. Box 271, Sacramento, CA 95812-0271.

CHECKLIST FOR CLASSROOM OBSERVATION OF COMMUNICATIVE BEHAVIOR

CHECKLIST FOR CLASSROOM OBSERVATION
OF COMMUNICATIVE BEHAVIOR

Attention and Behavior

What quality of attention did the student display?

☐ Focused
☐ Distractible
☐ Nonengaged
☐ Self-absorbed
☐ Easily over-stimulated

During what type of tasks was the student's attention and behavior best/worst?

_____

_____

During what type of tasks was the student able to attend for a greater/lesser length of time?

_____

_____

How independent or prompt dependent was the student?

What kind of prompts were given (verbal, physical, environmental)? _____

_____

How frequently were prompts provided? _____

_____

Which were helpful to the student? _____

_____

Which interfered with the student's attention/behavior? _____

_____

What did the student do during free time?

Independent activities? _____

_____

Self-stimulation behaviors/other? _____

_____

What kinds of challenging behaviors, if any, did the student display as a form of unconventional communication?

_____

_____

_____

Source: California School for the Blind Assessment Program, Fremont, CA. Reprinted with permission.

How did the student accept transitions?

Between activities? _____

_____

Between instructors? _____

_____

Notes/examples:

Comprehension of Language in the Classroom

How did student follow directions in the classroom? Write examples of directions given to student. Note:

- Context
- Type of response
- Number of repetitions necessary
- Additional prompts given, what type?
- Speed of response

Direction	Context	Response

What additional cues were available to students with normal vision? _____

_____

What adaptions were used for the student with visual impairment? _____

_____

APPENDIX E (*continued*)

Source: California School for the Blind Assessment Program, Fremont, CA. Reprinted with permission.

How did the student follow a functional activity routine, such as using the bathroom, having a snack, performing a (pre)vocational job?

What prompts were provided?

- ☐ Touch cues
- ☐ Verbal directions
- ☐ Picture cards
- ☐ Written words
- ☐ Signs
- ☐ Tangible symbols
- ☐ Environmental (location, time of day, timers)

What happened when the task was completed? _____

_____

Notes/examples:

Social Interaction and Pragmatics

In what ways and how frequently did the student interact with peers?

In the classroom? _____

On the playground? _____

In other environments? _____

In what ways and how frequently did the student interact with adults?

In a group? _____

_____

One to one? _____

_____

What kind of facilitated opportunities did the student have to scaffold his or her ability to interact with peers?

_____

_____

_____

APPENDIX E (*continued*)

Source: California School for the Blind Assessment Program, Fremont, CA. Reprinted with permission.

Notes/Examples:

Expressive Language

What types of communication did the student display? To the greatest degree possible, record all types of communicative output including:

- ☐ Body language
- ☐ Vocalizations
- ☐ Behaviors
- ☐ Sign language
- ☐ Augmentative/alternative communication
- ☐ Verbalizations
- ☐ Other

Attempt to record the sequence of utterances, to show the pattern of initiations and responses with respect to frequency of initiations and responses:

Student	Peer/teacher	Communicative intent	Context

What is student's most usual form of communication in the classroom? _____

_____

Did student display unconventional communicative behaviors in the form of:

- ☐ Echolalia
- ☐ Incessant questioning
- ☐ Perseverative language and topics of interest
- ☐ Challenging behavior
- ☐ Other

APPENDIX E (*continued*)

Source: California School for the Blind Assessment Program, Fremont, CA. Reprinted with permission.

Resources

The organizations listed in this appendix are primary sources of information and referral and are a good place to start to find answers to any questions about visual impairment, services for people who are visually impaired, and ways to assist your student and his or her family. The *AFB Directory of Services for Blind and Visually Impaired Persons in the United States and Canada*, published by the American Foundation for the Blind and found in many libraries, offers more comprehensive listings of organizations and services and volunteer groups in each state and nationwide. It can also be searched electronically at the AFB Web site, www.afb.org.

American Council of the Blind
1155 15th Street, NW, Suite 1004
Washington, DC 20005
Telephone: (202) 467-5081 or
          (800) 424-8666
Fax: (202) 467-5085
E-mail: info@acb.org
Web site: www.acb.org

A national clearinghouse for information, the council promotes the effective participation of blind people in all aspects of society. It provides information and referral; legal assistance and representation; scholarships; leadership and legislative training; consumer advocate support; assistance in technological research; a speaker referral service; consultative and advisory services to individuals, organizations, and agencies; and assistance with developing programs.

American Foundation for the Blind
11 Penn Plaza, Suite 300
New York, NY 10001
Telephone: (212) 502-7600 or
            (800) 232-5463
            Fax: (212) 502-7777
E-mail: afbinfo@afb.net
Web site: www.afb.org

This national organization provides services to and acts as an information clearinghouse for people who are visually impaired and their families, the public, professionals, schools, organizations, and corporations. It conducts research and mounts program initiatives to promote the inclusion of visually impaired persons, including the National Literacy Center and the National Employment Center; advocates for services and legislation; and maintains the M. C. Migel Memorial Library and the Helen Keller Archives. AFB maintains offices in Atlanta, Chicago, Dallas, San Francisco, and Huntington, West Virginia, and a governmental relations office in Washington, D.C. It produces videos and publishes books, pamphlets, the *Directory of Services for Blind and Visually Impaired Persons in the United States and Canada*, the *Journal of Visual Impairment & Blindness*, and *AccessWorld*. In addition, it provides information about the latest technology available for visually impaired persons through its Technology and Employment Center and operates a toll-free information hotline.

American Printing House for the Blind
1839 Frankfort Avenue
Louisville, KY 40206

Telephone: (502) 895-2405 or
             (800) 223-1839
Fax: (502) 899-2274
E-mail: info@aph.org
Web site: www.aph.org

This national organization receives an annual appropriation from Congress to provide textbooks and educational aids for legally blind students who attend elementary and secondary schools or special educational institutions. It produces a wide variety of books and learning materials in braille and other media and manufactures computer access equipment, software, and special education and reading devices for visually impaired persons. The organization maintains an educational research and development program and a reference catalog database providing information about textbooks and other materials that are produced in accessible media.

**Association for Education and Rehabilitation
of the Blind and Visually Impaired**
1703 North Beauregard Street
Suite 440
Alexandria, VA 22311
Telephone: (703) 671-4500
Fax: (703) 671-6391
E-mail: aer@aerbvi.org
Web site: www.aerbvi.org

AER serves as the membership organization for professionals who work in all phases of education and rehabilitation with visually impaired persons of all ages on the local, regional, national, and international levels. It seeks to develop and promote professional excellence through such support services as continuing education, publications, information dissemination, lobbying and advocacy, and conferences and workshops.

**Center on Disabilities
California State University, Northridge**
18111 Nordhoff Street
Northridge, CA 91330-8340

Telephone: (818) 677-2684 (voice/TTY)
Fax: (818) 677-4932
E-mail: sdr@csun.edu
Web site: www.csun.edu/cod/

The Center on Disabilities is committed to providing outstanding services to students with disabilities, and to making a contribution to the field of disabilities in general and to those who provide services to people with disabilities by the dissemination of information through training programs, conferences, workshops, seminars, and electronic media, and may also conduct applications-oriented research as a means of improving the lives of persons with disabilities and the professional skills of those who work with them.

Closing the Gap
526 Main Street
P.O. Box 68
Henderson, MN 56044
Telephone: (507) 248-3294
Fax: (507) 248-3810
E-mail: info@closingthegap.com
Web site: www.closingthegap.com

Closing the Gap provides a newspaper, annual conference, and web site. The organization provide practical, up-to-date information on assistive technology products, procedures, and best practices.

Council for Exceptional Children
Division on Visual Impairments
1110 North Glebe Road, Suite 300
Arlington, VA 22201-5704
Telephone: (703) 620-3660 or
            (888) CEC-SPED;
            (703) 264-9446 (TTY)
Fax: (703) 264-9494
E-mail: service@cec.sped.org
Web site: www.cec.sped.org
Division on Visual Impairments: www.ed.arizona.edu/dvi

CEC is a professional organization of teachers, school administrators, and others who are concerned with children who require special services. It publishes periodicals, books, and other materials on teaching exceptional children, advocates for appropriate government policies, provides professionals development, and disseminates information on effective instructional strategies. The Division on Visual Impairments focuses on the education of children who are visually impaired and the concerns of professionals who work with them.

Council of Schools for the Blind
c/o Overbrook School for the Blind
6333 Malvern Avenue
Philadelphia, PA 19151
Telephone: (215) 877-0313
Web site: www.COSB1.org

The Council of Schools for the Blind is a consortium of specialized schools in Canada and the United States whose major goal is improving the quality of services to children who are blind and visually impaired. Sponsored activities include the Outreach Forum (www.tsbvi.edu/Outreach) an association of professionals from schools for the blind who are available to provide services to school-aged children, and the Assessment Symposium, an association of professionals from schools for the blind who provide support on issues regarding assessment and psychological/counseling services for school-aged children.

Howe Press
Perkins School for the Blind
175 North Beacon Street
Watertown, MA 02171
Telephone: (617) 924-3400
Fax: (617) 926-2027
E-mail: HowePress@perkins.put.kas.ma.us
Web site: www.perkins.pvt.k12.ma.us/brailler.htm

Howe Press manufactures and sells a variety of products for visually impaired persons, including the Perkins Brailler (manual or electric);

slates; styli; mathematical aids; braille games; braille-vision books for children; heavy- and light-grade braille paper; and Tactile Drawing Kits.

National Association for Parents of Children with Visual Impairments

P.O. Box 317
Watertown, MA 02272-0317
Telephone: (617) 972-7444 or
(800) 562-6265
Fax: (617) 972-7444
Web site: www.napvi.org

This membership association supports state and local parents' groups and conducts advocacy workshops for parents of visually impaired children and youths. In addition, it operates a national clearinghouse for information, education, and referral; fosters communication among federal, state, and local agencies that provide services or funding for services; and promotes public understanding of the needs and rights of visually impaired children and youths.

National Braille Press

88 St. Stephen Street
Boston, MA 02115
Telephone: (617) 266-6160 or
(888) 965-8965
Fax: (617) 437-0456
E-mail: orders@nbp.org
Web site: www.nbp.org

The National Braille Press provides braille printing services for publishers and other organizations, including the Library of Congress; offers transcription of documents related to school or work; and sponsors a children's Braille Book-of the-Month Club.

National Federation of the Blind

1800 Johnson Street

Baltimore, MD 21230
Telephone: (410) 659-9314
Fax: (410) 685-5653
E-mail: nfb@nfb.org
Web site: www.nfb.org

The federation, with affiliates in all states and the District of Columbia, works to improve the social and economic conditions of visually impaired persons. It evaluates programs and provides assistance in establishing new ones, grants scholarships to people who are visually impaired, and conducts a public education program. It also publishes *The Braille Monitor* and *Future Reflections*, a magazine for parents.

**National Library Service for the Blind
and Physically Handicapped**
Library of Congress
1291 Taylor Street, NW
Washington, DC 20542
Telephone: (202) 707-5100 or
          (800) 424-8567;
          (202) 707-0744 (TDD)
Fax: (202) 707-0712
E-mail: nls@loc.gov
Web site: www.loc.gov/nls

The National Library Service for the Blind and Physically Handicapped conducts a national program to distribute free reading materials–classics, current fiction, and general nonfiction–in braille and on recorded disks and cassettes to persons with visual or physical disabilities who cannot utilize ordinary printed materials. Materials are distributed and playback equipment is lent free of charge through a network of regional and subregional libraries and machine-lending agencies. In addition, the service operates a reference information section on all aspects of blindness and other physical disabilities that affect reading. It functions as a bibliographic center on reading materials for people with disabilities and organizations that lend reading materials in special media.

Recording for the Blind and Dyslexic
20 Roszel Road
Princeton, NJ 08540
Telephone: (609) 452-0606 or
              (800) 883-7201
E-mail: custserv@rfbd.org
Web site: www.rfbd.org

Recording for the Blind and Dyslexic lends recorded and electronic educational materials and textbooks at no charge to people who cannot read standard print because of visual, physical, or learning disabilities.

Index